WALES AND THE FRENCH REVOLUTION

General Editors: Mary-Ann Constantine and Dafydd Johnston

WALES AND THE FRENCH REVOLUTION

# *Welsh Responses to the French Revolution: Press and Public Discourse 1789–1802*

MARION LÖFFLER

UNIVERSITY OF WALES PRESS
CARDIFF
2012

*www.uwp.co.uk*

British Library Cataloguing-in-Publication Data
A catalogue record for this book is available from the British Library.

ISBN 978-0-7083-2489-9
e-ISBN 978-0-7083-2490-5



Typeset in Wales by Eira Fenn Gaunt, Cardiff
Printed by CPI Antony Rowe, Chippenham, Wiltshire

Impromptu. On the new Impost on Newspapers.

> Says Billy to Harry
> "These prints make me ill:"
> "A fresh impost lay on them,"
> Says Harry to Bill.
> "By the L– –d we must choak them,
> (Cries PITT to DUNDAS)
> "Or they'll prove me a ROGUE,
> "And your Worship an ASS . . ."

*Chester Chronicle*, 7 July 1797.

Y Cylchgrawn uniawn a'i enwi – drws yw
I drysor goleuni;
Llyfr hoff, hardd, er hyfforddi
Trigolion bro trwy gael bri.

(The upright Magazine to name it – is a gate
to enlightenment treasure;
marvellous, handsome book, for instructing
the inhabitants of a country by acquiring esteem.)

D. Sa[u]nders in *Cylch-grawn Cynmraeg*, no. III (1793), 121.

WALES AND THE FRENCH REVOLUTION

The French Revolution of 1789 was perhaps the defining event of the Romantic period in Europe. It unsettled not only the ordering of society but language and thought itself: its effects were profoundly cultural, and they were long-lasting. The last twenty years have radically altered our understanding of the impact of the Revolution and its aftermath on British culture. In literature, as critical attention has shifted from a handful of major poets to the non-canonical edges, we can now see how the works of women writers, self-educated authors, radical pamphleteers, prophets and loyalist propagandists both shaped and were shaped by the language and ideas of the period. Yet surprising gaps remain, and even recent studies of the 'British' reaction to the Revolution remain poorly informed about responses from the regions. In literary and historical discussions of the so-called 'four nations' of Britain, Wales has been virtually invisible; many researchers working in this period are unaware of the kinds of sources available for comparative study.

The Wales and the French Revolution Series is the product of a four-year project funded by the AHRC and the University of Wales at the Centre for Advanced Welsh and Celtic Studies. It makes available a wide range of Welsh material from the decades spanning the Revolution and the subsequent wars with France. Each volume, edited by an expert in the field, presents a collection of texts (including, where relevant, translations) from a particular genre with a critical essay situating the material in its historical and literary context. A great deal of material is published here for the first time, and all kinds of genres are explored. From ballads and pamphlets to personal letters and prize-winning poems, essays, journals, sermons, songs and satires, the range of texts covered by this series is a stimulating reflection of the political and cultural complexity of the time. We hope these volumes will encourage scholars and students of Welsh history and literature to rediscover this fascinating period, and will offer ample comparative scope for those working further afield.

Mary-Ann Constantine and Dafydd Johnston
General Editors

# *Contents*



## SELECTION OF DOCUMENTS

# *Figures*

# *Preface*

In the introduction to his volume, *The Scottish People and the French Revolution*, Bob Harris wrote of our need 'to return to the evidence before seeking to explain . . . to pay more attention to the contemporary experience of radicals and those who sought to defeat them'. The present series of texts aims to answer this need by providing evidence for some of the experiences of Welsh men and women in the long revolutionary decade of 1789–1802. In Wales, an almost leaderless minority of radicals and rioters, concentrated in the hot spots of rational Dissent in south-west Wales and of industrial unrest in the north-east, faced a well-organized traditional élite who controlled potentially serious developments through paternalism and the press or by using military force and the law courts. This anthology from the serial literature current in Wales between 1789 and 1802 reveals how the press was used to call the 'ancient Britons' to arms and to reinforce the state's authority against rioters and agitators, but also how Welsh radicals attempted to enlighten their compatriots and criticize the state and the Established Church. It does not present a ready history of a revolutionary, a loyalist or a patriotic Wales, but attempts to let the reader interpret the texts here assembled, thus creating his or her own story.

This anthology breaks new ground in several ways. Firstly, it pays attention to the distribution and contents of those provincial papers which have largely been ignored by researchers because they were published close to the Welsh border, well away from London and prominent centres of radicalism. The texts from the newspapers in this selection may help to change the still prevailing perception that the English provincial press functioned as an agency of cut-and-paste from the metropolis. Secondly, this is the first time that a collection of 1790s texts from a radical periodical press in a British language other than English has been published and translated. It is hoped that it will not only highlight the bilingual character of the public discourse in late eighteenth-century Wales, but also bring into focus a country which has remained, in the words of Mary-Ann Constantine, a 'blind spot' in the 'four-nations criticism' of the last decades. Thirdly, this anthology treats of Wales, much as Katrina Navickas recently did in her monograph on *Loyalism and Radicalism in Lancashire 1798–1815*, as a regional entity which was of course influenced by the political and administrative centre in London, but which in response developed its own characteristic discourse and style. Ideas and concepts were not simply transferred from metropolis to province in the 1790s, but entered into a complex process of exchange whose course this volume seeks to chart.

The AHRC grant awarded to the University of Wales Centre for Advanced Welsh and Celtic Studies project on 'Wales and the French Revolution' made this volume possible. It enabled me to work on periodical publications of late eighteenth-century Wales and especially to study the English provincial newspapers close to the Welsh border, which are not easily accessible but eminently relevant to the public discourse in Wales. It also enabled the National Library of Wales, in co-operation with us, to make available to the public digitized versions of the three radical Welsh periodicals in this study. They will be part of the Library's 'Digital Mirror' at *http://www.llgc.org.uk*.

I am indebted to fellow team members Cathryn Charnell-White, Ffion Mair Jones and Heather Williams, as well as to the project leader, Mary-Ann Constantine, for helpful comments and criticism of text and sources. A special debt of thanks is owed to my colleague Elizabeth Edwards for enabling me to gain new insights during long sessions of discussing our respective volumes. The director of our Centre, Dafydd Johnston, gave much-appreciated and generous advice on difficult passages of Welsh poetry and their translation, and my colleague Barry Lewis grappled with the Latin texts in this collection. Nia L. Davies deserves my heart-felt thanks for assisting in the transcription of texts and for her general support.

I would also like to thank the project's Advisory Panel for their support, especially John Barrell (York), Damian Walford Davies (Aberystwyth), Hywel Davies (Aberystwyth), Martin Fitzpatrick (Aberystwyth) and Geraint H. Jenkins (Aberystwyth). They gave generously of their knowledge, in conversation and correspondence. I am indebted to Mark Philp (Oxford) for his enlightening e-mails on new concepts and words in the 1790s and to Niall Ó Ciosáin (Cork) for readily sharing his knowledge of popular print culture in Ireland.

The Centre co-operates closely with the National Library of Wales and I am grateful to the desk staff who located rare copies of periodicals and pamphlets, as well as some uncatalogued manuscripts which I required for this volume. Manon Foster Evans and her team at the Department of Printed Books made available the entire collection of Welsh almanacs held at the National Library of Wales; Branwen Rhys and Scott Waby at Digital Development granted me access to copies of digitized periodicals at an early date.

Further afield I am indebted to Bethan Jenkins, History Faculty Library, Bodleian Libraries, for assisting with translations from *Y Geirgrawn*. The staff at Cheshire County Record Office and Hereford County Record Office were always helpful and efficient and I am grateful for their support. Jon Isherwood of The Digital Landscape Company, *http://www.thedlc.co.uk*, provided expert assistance with creating the maps for this volume.

Our editorial officer, Gwen Gruffudd, and the team at the University of Wales Press, especially Sarah Lewis, Siân Chapman and Dafydd Jones, must be thanked for steering this varied selection of texts through the editorial and printing process so skilfully and patiently.

Diolch i Elsie Mai a Daniel Tryfan am fod yn amyneddgar gyda mam.

April 2012 Marion Löffler

# *Acknowledgements*

Digital Landscapes / Jon Isherwood and Marion Löffler: Figs. 1, 2

The National Library of Wales: Figs. 3, 4

# *Abbreviations*

| | |
|---|---|
| *BBCS* | *Bulletin of the Board of Celtic Studies* |
| *CCAHE* | John T. Koch (ed.), *Celtic Culture: A Historical Encyclopedia* (5 vols., Santa Barbara, 2006) |
| *CIM* | Geraint H. Jenkins, Ffion Mair Jones and David Ceri Jones (eds.), *The Correspondence of Iolo Morganwg* (3 vols., Cardiff, 2007) |
| *DWB* | *Dictionary of Welsh Biography down to 1940* (London, 1959) |
| *HHSC* | R. T. Jenkins and Helen M. Ramage, *A History of the Honourable Society of Cymmrodorion and of the Gwyneddigion and Cymreigyddion Societies (1751–1951)* (London, 1951) |
| *JWBS* | *Journal of the Welsh Bibliographical Society* |
| *LCFR* | Colin Jones, *The Longman Companion to the French Revolution* (London, 1990) |
| *NCLW* | Meic Stephens (ed.), *The New Companion to the Literature of Wales* (Cardiff, 1998) |
| NLW | National Library of Wales |
| *NLWJ* | *National Library of Wales Journal* |
| *ODNB* | *Oxford Dictionary of National Biography* at *http://www.oxforddnb.com* |
| *THSC* | *Transactions of the Honourable Society of Cymmrodorion* |
| *WHR* | *Welsh History Review* |

# *Editorial Principles*

I have striven to keep my selection of texts from the serial literature current in Wales between 1789 and 1802 as authentic as possible. For this reason, and because form was often part of the message, most spelling and especially printing conventions adhered to by Welsh and English writers and publishers at the time of publication have been retained. Glaring errors and misprints, especially those which interfere with comprehension, have been silently corrected.

In order to improve the flow of the text in the introduction, the English translation here precedes the Welsh original, which is given in brackets. In the selection of documents, all texts in a language other than English are followed by an English translation at the conclusion of the item, but short Welsh or Latin passages within an English text are immediately followed by a translation in brackets. Especially in the case of the Welsh poetry, my translation does not aim at and cannot convey the highly stylized and intricate character of the originals, which often used internal rhyme as well as the end rhyme with which modern English readers will be familiar. Biblical passages have not been translated anew, but were given the equivalent English passage from the King James Bible.

To this day, many Welsh poets and authors are best known by their bardic names. Therefore, and to avoid confusion (there is mention of at least four different men named 'John Jones' in this volume), the regular bardic names used by Welsh poets are utilized in this anthology. At the first mention, first name and surname are cited, followed by the bardic name in brackets, e.g. Thomas Evans (Tomos Glyn Cothi). Thereafter, the regular bardic name is used. A list of bardic names at the end of this book assists the reader in identifying who is who. The occasional pseudonyms given in contributions to serials in order to hide a real identity are not explained in this table.

Some of the serials current in Wales during the period under review changed title several times, while others had cumbersome and misleading titles. Therefore the following short titles are used:

| | |
|---|---|
| ***Hereford Journal*** | *The British Chronicle or Pugh's Hereford Journal* (1771–92); *Hereford Journal* (1792–1926) |
| ***Shrewsbury Chronicle*** | *Shrewsbury Chronicle and Shropshire, Montgomeryshire, Denbighshire, Merionethshire, Flintshire, &c. General Advertiser* (1772) |
| ***Salopian Journal*** | *Salopian Journal and Courier of Wales* (1794) |
| ***Chester Chronicle*** | *Chester Chronicle; or Commercial Intelligencer* (1775–92); *Chester Chronicle and Cheshire and North Wales Advertiser* (1792) |
| ***Adams's Weekly Courant*** | *Adams's Weekly Courant* (1732). Also cited as *Chester Courant* |
| ***Cylch-grawn Cynmraeg*** | *Cylch-grawn Cynmraeg; Neu Drysorfa Gwybodaeth* [Welsh Magazine; Or Treasury of Knowledge] (No. I; February 1793); *Cylchgrawn Cynmraeg* [Welsh Magazine] (No. II; May 1793); *Cylchgrawn Cymraeg: Neu Drysorfa Gwybodaeth* (No. III; August 1793); (No. IV; [Autumn] 1793); *Welsh Magazine. Y Cylchgrawn; Neu Drysorfa Gwybodaeth* (No. V; January and February 1794) |
| ***Y Drysorfa Gymmysgedig*** | *The Miscellaneous Repository: Neu, Y Drysorfa Gymmysgedig* (No. I; Summer Quarter 1795); (No. II; Autumn Quarter 1795); (No. III; [Beginning of] 1796) |
| ***Y Geirgrawn*** | *Y Geirgrawn: Neu Drysorfa Gwybodaeth* [The Magazine: Or Treasury of Knowledge] (Nos. I–IX; [monthly] February 1796–October 1796) |

# *Introduction*

> I have another favour to ask of you which I hope you will not deny to fulfil and not only myself but also the two Hereticdogs who lodge with us, who are like myself excited a little with the spirit of whiggism, and to beg of you to grant it unto us, and that is to lend us the two Books called "The Hog's Wash", which shall be kept as secret as they are at present in the study at Lloyd-Jack, you may depend upon it; Now Sir, if they are not yours, (which I think to be the case) we must beg of you to intercede for us, and tell Mr David J. Rees that we shall be very much obliged to him if he will be so liberal as to satiate our desires in this case; please to tell him farther that they shall be kept clean, and if possible be returned without being a bit worse, nobody shall hear that they are with us, nor never see them if it will be required.[1]

This letter was written in 1808 by Timothy Davi[e]s, one of the sons of the powerful Arian preacher, revered schoolmaster and Welsh poet David Davis (Castellhywel), and sent from municipal Swansea into rural Cardiganshire, about forty miles north.[2] For fifteen years the radical metropolitan serial *Hog's Wash* had been kept safe in the study of the Unitarian minister John James, on behalf of a well-known benefactor to the Unitarian cause, David Jenkin Rees.[3] Now it attracted the younger generation, aware of its importance. The two volumes had long been part of a public discourse which rendered texts available to anyone who could afford to buy them, received them through free distribution, or who heard them read in formal and informal meetings.[4] In Wales published and unpublished reading matter was further circulated by informal lending, copied into manuscript, creatively imitated and translated, and performed at traditional cultural and new religious gatherings.[5] Serial literature in late eighteenth-century Wales, a country on the cusp of modernization, fitted into a surviving manuscript culture and helped maintain the bardic networks which were in the process of recasting the medieval eisteddfod as a modern, national institution. It also provided the public platform where Welsh churchmen and Dissenters, loyalists and patriots, populists and radicals debated what concerned them, in poetry and prose, in Welsh or English. Wales's public discourse – unlike that of the other three nations of the British Isles – was bilingual, and thus almost always aided by a knowledge of two languages and some skill in translation.[6] The serials in the present collection reflect this, revealing as they do the topics important to the participants in this discourse, along with their discordant mental maps of Wales. The Wales of the 1790s was a 'cauldron of conflicting ideologies', and it shows in the diversity of voices which speak to us from the printed pages of its serial press.[7]

The characteristics of this discourse must be viewed against the background of Wales in the 1790s; an economically and socially backward part of Great Britain which was overwhelmingly rural, sparsely populated and without a centre.[8] Wales had no equivalent of Dublin or Edinburgh – Cardiff had a population of only 1,870 in 1801 – and most of the Welsh élite resided in London, which remained the capital of Wales until 1955. In 1801 the rapidly developing town of Swansea alone boasted something akin to an urban culture, yet it had a population of just 6,099.[9] In the same year, only the regional centres of Carmarthen, Haverfordwest, Wrexham and Caernarfon possessed more than 3,500 inhabitants, no match for English foci of radicalism, such as Sheffield and Manchester, or even 'Jacobin' Norwich.[10] Town and bourgeoisie – the backbones of the 'public sphere of civil society' in late eighteenth-century England – were essentially lacking here,[11] and even the artisan networks that in England sustained what Terry Eagleton has called a 'counter-public sphere' of corresponding societies, political associations, dissenting churches and the radical press, were as yet underdeveloped.[12] Yet a small group of vociferous Welshmen, radical and loyalist, maintained a public discourse well beyond what may have been expected from a country so lacking in urban centres and roads to connect them.

The historical foundations for this lay in the publication of the Welsh Bible in 1588, the subsequent development of a network of printing houses that published religious literature, and a succession of charity school ventures which taught the poor to read this religious literature in their own language, culminating in the 'circulating schools' of Griffith Jones, Llanddowror, and the Sunday schools of Thomas Charles, Bala.[13] It is estimated that even by the time of Griffith Jones's death in 1761, his circulating schools alone had taught over 200,000 children and adults to read Welsh, thus creating a powerful reading public in a country of only 587,245 in 1801.[14] Eighteen publishing houses within the country catered for this market in religious texts, but they increasingly brought out secular works, too, among them dictionaries, literary anthologies and political and religious pamphlets.[15] From the 1770s till the end of the eighteenth century it is reckoned that the output in political literature alone multiplied sixfold.[16] In addition to the traditional outlets of bookshop and fair – where itinerant hawkers peddled almanacs, ballads and manuals – the increasing popularity of Methodism (as yet within the Established Church) and the development of rational Dissent in some areas of Wales furnished new networks of distribution, especially for religious and political reading matter. By the 1790s England's first colonial backwater boasted a comparatively good infrastructure for the publication, distribution and 'significant reading' of serial literature, which came into its own in the 'unusual political conditions' of that decade.[17]

There is ample evidence that the gentry and the upper classes had been receiving serials from urban and metropolitan England since the beginning of the eighteenth century. In 1738 Robert Pritchard, a sea-captain from Pentraeth, Anglesey, noted that it was 'the pleasure of many a *Welshman*, to Read / the English news of *Chester* or *London*; / searching for a strange new tale, / no matter where from, be it truth, be it a Lie' ('Pleser llawer *Cymro* yw Darllain, / Newyddion Seisnig *Caer* neu *Lundain*; / Chwilio am chwedl rhyfedd newydd, / Ni waeth o ble, bid gwir, bid Celwydd').[18] The correspondence of the influential Morris brothers is rife with references to serials.[19] Richard Morris, a naval officer in London, regularly despatched newspapers to William, a customs officer in Holyhead, Anglesey, and to Lewis who superintended Crown mines in Cardiganshire.[20] The brothers sent each other articles from and corresponded about English periodicals, such as the *Critical Review* and the *Gentleman's Magazine*.[21] The well-off had no shortage of serial literature, as their libraries and diaries show, and within the local squirearchy exchange was brisk.[22] Even for small squires, such as John Johnes of Dolaucothi, Carmarthenshire, newspapers were a normal part of everyday life and their absence was noted with a vexed 'received no paper'.[23] The Griffith family of Garn and Plasnewydd, Denbighshire, were so familiar with the structure of the local weeklies that they mocked up a handwritten 'Gazette Extraordinary' for 6 January 1794, complete with real 'Domestic Occurrences' and 'Advertisements' from the area.[24] The 'Poets Corner' reflected the contents of the local weeklies as well as the mood among the gentry of north-east Wales by featuring several of the themes prominent in the selection of documents in this volume: an anti-French interest in the guillotine, general adulation of Sir Watkin Williams Wynn, fifth baronet, of neighbouring Wynnstay (then MP for Beaumaris and lord lieutenant of Merionethshire), and an affirmation of Welsh loyalty to the Crown:

> A letter from Simkin in Wales to Tony Lumkin in Town:
> My D$^{r}$ Tony Lumkin, you make such a Pother
> Bout Robertspierre, Danton & citizen Barrere
> of such rascals & Blood hounds with you I am sick

That I wish they were gone / they must soon / to old Nick
So write me no more, of their vile Tricks & machine
That conventional Monster, y clep'd Guillotine
& now my D$^{r}$ Tony I have News for y$^{r}$ Ear
Sir Watkin's come down our Hearts for to cheer
Which faith he does bravely to our utmost Desire
God so [will], he'll be like as two Peas to his Sire[25]
In hospitallity great of his wine not afraid
of this we had proff at the late Masquerade
He's loyal, he's social, By the Leek he's the thing
On 12th Night he gave it to honour the King
& believe me its true ev'ry Cambrian did join
To God bless his Majesty in bumbers of wine
So do you my D$^{r}$ Tony in y$^{r}$ neat jolly frettin[g]
Drink a Health to Sir Wat. & long flourish the Leek.[26]

Lower down the social ranks, the adventurous Englishwoman Elizabeth Baker provides evidence of how serials reached less affluent circles of society. In the late 1780s, she copied poetry and prose from over twenty different publications received in the neighbourhood of Dolgellau, north-west Wales: from the *Morning Post* and the *London Gazette* to the *Middlesex Magazine* and the *Anti-Jacobin*.[27] She did not buy these, but was lent them by her neighbour, Rice Jones of Rhiwlas, whose regular parcels she obviously enjoyed.[28] When ship-carpenter William Luke enquired if he might borrow the serials, she refused to loan them on, but agreed to 'read to him which the man said was preferable to reading it himself ingenuously confessing he could not have understood many paragraphs, that he asked me to explain'.[29] Early subscription libraries, book clubs, inns and coffee houses provided similar reading services.[30] Despite the fact that the hiring out of newspapers was made illegal in 1789 under a penalty of £5 (a measure reinforced in 1797, together with a further rise in stamp duty), traders could stock a 'subscription reading room' with newspapers and periodicals, as was done in Swansea by Mrs Oakey and her daughter, who kept a 'Circulating Library and Reading Room'.[31] Shrewd newspaper editors, like Thomas Wood of the *Shrewsbury Chronicle*, gave detailed advice on how to avoid such penalties by pooling resources to buy a paper or by hiring the relevant room at the inn instead of the reading material.[32] Welsh inns such as the Black Lion in Aberystwyth followed the trend by including in their advertisements references to a well-stocked 'coffee-room'.[33] During the turbulent 1790s literate Welshmen of modest means took every opportunity to transcribe from serials while they had access to them. North-Walian loyalist poets and authors, such as Walter Davies (Gwallter Mechain) and David Thomas (Dafydd Ddu Eryri), copied from publications like the *Ladies Magazine*, the *Salopian Journal* and *Fox's Journal*.[34] The correspondence of the radical Glamorgan stonemason, antiquary, poet and literary forger, Edward Williams (Iolo Morganwg), shows that he had Coleridge's short-lived *Watchman* sent to him, as well as ordering the *Argus*, the *Cambridge Intelligencer* and *Pig's Meat*.[35] The contents of *Pig's Meat* and *Hog's Wash*, but also of more loyalist serials, such as the *Hereford Journal*, made their way into the commonplace books of radical Unitarians and poets, such as the Carmarthenshire weaver Thomas Evans (Tomos Glyn Cothi).[36] From there, the texts journeyed on into the writings of lesser figures, such as John Davies (Siôn Dafydd y Crydd), deep in rural Cardiganshire.[37] The radical Welsh-language periodicals, much of whose contents were free adaptations of material from English publications like the *Chester Chronicle*, the *Cambridge Intelligencer, Pig's Meat* and *Hog's Wash* were copied into the same manuscripts. In 1790s Wales, almanacs, newspapers and periodicals were more than ephemeral reading matter. They were treasured because they brought new literatures and ideas to those who could read and they gave a voice to those who dared to make their opinions public.[38] As in more 'revolutionary' Ireland, some of these serials took on a life far beyond the limits of initial print-run and private reading.[39] The impact of the two volumes of *Hog's Wash* mentioned earlier was certainly profound and long-lasting. In what follows I shall be discussing the groups of serials which inhabited overlapping geographical and social sections of the public discourse in Wales: the long-established Welsh almanacs, the flourishing English provincial papers published close to the Welsh border and the nascent Welsh periodical press.

## *Almanacs: the oldest native serials*

Annual almanacs were, according to R.W. Jones, 'the periodical, the newspaper and the diary' of the common people of Wales in the eighteenth century.[40] They were certainly the only long-lived indigenous serials appearing between 1680, when the first Welsh almanac was published by Thomas Jones of Corwen, and the Napoleonic Wars.[41] As is apparent from their very titles, Jones and his successors followed the English model, but Welsh almanacs, in addition, included Welsh carols, ballads and classical strict-metre poetry.[42] They furthered the production of native literature by celebrating members of the gentry who still patronized Welsh poets, by organizing small bardic meetings, and, from 1789, by advertising and printing the results of the eisteddfodau organized by the London Gwyneddigion society.[43] In the 1790s at least four almanac-printers, operating from Carmarthen,

Brecon, Shrewsbury and, apparently, Dublin, supplied the whole country (Fig. 1), reaching a larger audience than any other non-religious publication in eighteenth-century Wales and pulling the country together by indicating Welsh fairs and routes of communication as well as through reproducing poetry well beyond their regional base.[44] The Welsh pocketbook almanac was a continuous presence in many a household. It was consulted for the advice it contained, utilized as a diary, and kept for the literary treasures in it.[45]

In the 1790s collators of almanacs, like John Harris and Mathew William, reflected the political Zeitgeist by commenting on political and religious matters in editorials and astrological texts, by translating authors like Benjamin Franklin and by including old and new poetry and prose which they judged to be relevant for their audience. The prevailing tenor of the literary and political material featured in the almanacs was loyalist, but this loyalism was punctured by praise for Dissenting academies, the condemnation of wayward Anglican priests, and satires on unfair taxes.[46] All of this was interspersed with references to the age-old differences between the English and the Welsh and overlaid with a steady stream of poetry in praise of the Welsh language.[47]

Like other collators, Mathew William (a land-surveyor near Llandeilo, Carmarthenshire) traditionally ended the predictions for the year in his *Britanus Merlinus Liberatus* with English- or Welsh-language verse. In the 1790s he used this convention to admonish landholders to share 'some of their wealth with the weak and the lowly' ('beth o'ch golud, i'r gweiniaid ac i'r gwael'),[48] and to remind the common people of their duty to obey a Jesus, 'who bought the *rights of man*' with his blood [DOCUMENT 1.1], thus imbuing superficially simple astrological texts with political meaning.

In another example, the attempted landing of French troops at Fishguard in 1797 prompted William to take an unambiguously patriotic, British stance and give the new vocabulary of the 1790s a loyalist meaning [DOCUMENT 1.2]. At the same time, the editorial became a celebration of Welshness. Instead of the usual 'Reader', William addressed 'The Welsh' ('Y Cymru'), whom he thanked for defending their country from the godless French rabble, but whom he also asked to accept new taxes in good faith, because they were necessary for the defence of 'our Liberty, our Possessions, our Laws, and our Lives' ('ein Rhydd-did, ein Meddiannau, ein Cyfreithiau, a'n Bywydau'). It was more customary though for political sentiments to be expressed in the form of poetry. One of several poems in which politics, war and religion were closely intertwined was Edward Jones's 'New Song on the Tone called God Save the King' ('Can newydd ar y Dôn a elwir, Duw Gadwo'r Brenin'), which appeared in John Harries's *Vox Stellarum et*

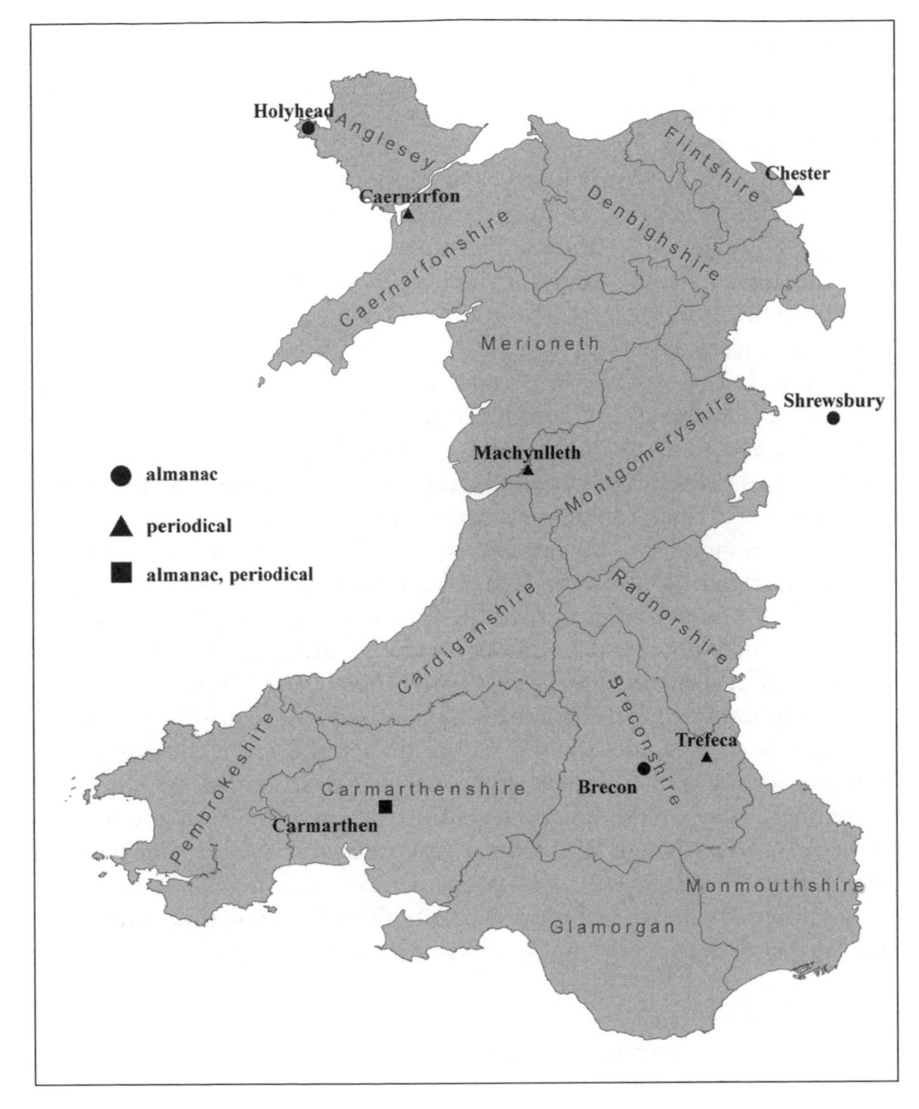


Figure 1. Welsh almanacs and periodicals published in the 1790s

*Planetarum* for 1795 [DOCUMENT 1.3].[49] Like Mathew William, Jones distinguished between England ('Lloegr') and the 'good Welshman' ('Cymro glân'), yet united them in their struggle against the villainous French. Reminders of the heroism of admirals Hood and Howe, recently celebrated in an Anglo-Welsh poetry competition [DOCUMENT 5.5], and of unnamed dukes and soldiers, bound the reader ever tighter into the common British effort.

The poem with which Dafydd Risiart, Llandybïe, defended himself against accusations of disloyalty in 1796 was more ambiguous and illustrates the religious aspects of the reception of the French Revolution in Wales. A verbal attack by a Catholic acquaintance moved this Welsh Dissenter from Carmarthenshire, who was rumoured to sympathize with the French Revolution, to depict Thomas Paine as an instrument of God whose deeds should therefore be judged by God alone. The poet proclaims his loyalty to England, but reprimands 'All the earthly princes' ('Holl dywysogion daear') who have been drinking their fill of the alluring cup of the Roman whore and condemns the 'bloody *Capet* family' ('[t]eulu'r *Capets* gwaedlyd') outright. Cautiously, but in the same vein as more well-known Welsh radicals, such as Morgan John Rhys and Tomos Glyn Cothi, he focuses on God as the only judge and on man's 'eldest Brother' ('hynaf Frawd') Jesus Christ as the only compass point [DOCUMENT 1.4]. More light-hearted and pursuing a more political track was a poem from the same area in Harris's almanac for 1798. It responded to the tax William Pitt had raised on dogs in 1796.[50] In 'The Dream of John of the Hill, Llandeilo-Fawr, and his Dog Cupid' ('Breuddwyd Sion o'r Bryn, Llandilo-Fawr, a'i Gi Ciwpit') the author, who wisely does not reveal his identity, indulges in a seditious hallucination which ends in a call to arms against 'Billy Pitt' [DOCUMENT 1.5].

The responses which the Welsh almanacs were able to provide, however, were restricted by genre. Only a few of the usual forty-eight pages were available for political comment, and proofs were signed off in August or September, to be advertised and distributed during the last three months of the year. Thus, though Welsh almanacs certainly conveyed some political education to a wide audience of all layers of society and therefore contributed to the public discourse in response to the French Revolution, they were not capable of conveying topical news or in-depth analysis.

### *Provincial English newspapers in Wales*

The main conduits of news and public opinion from without and within Wales were the English provincial newspapers published close to the Welsh border. Until 1804, when the Swansea *Cambrian* was founded,[51] no newspaper was published in Wales itself, a situation which contrasted sharply with the remainder of the British Isles. In the 1790s, London alone counted at least fourteen daily papers; up to seventy provincial papers circulated in England; and Scotland supported between ten and fifteen newspapers during the same period.[52] A Welsh newspaper had been seen as a desideratum as early as 1691, when Thomas Jones advertised in his almanac a monthly 'Summary of all the news Published in England' ('Gynhilliad or hôll newŷddion a Gyhoedder yn Lloeger'), of which, however, no known copy has survived.[53] Until the advent of a Welsh newspaper, the English periodical press integrated Wales into England, for in its absence Welsh readers of all political and religious persuasions had long turned to English serials, from the *Gentleman's Magazine* and *Woodfall's Diary* to *Pig's Meat* and the *Kentish Gazette*.[54] In the 1790s, radicals like David Jones (Welsh Freeholder) attempted to utilize the border newspapers in order to voice criticism and only turned to the form of the pamphlet when their contribution had been refused by the editor.[55] In December 1792 Thomas Pennant, a stalwart of loyalism in Flintshire, requested of John Reeves that the establishment of Welsh loyalist associations 'after the example of some of the *English* counties, cities and towns' be advertised in the London papers.[56] The 'inhabitants of the hundred of Bromfield' resolved that their declaration of loyalty be inserted in 'The Star, the General Evening Post, and in the two Chester papers' [DOCUMENT 5.3]. The Dissenting ministers who met on 13 February 1793, desperate to allay the suspicions against them, decided that their resolutions 'be inserted in the English Chronicle, the Bristol and Hereford Papers' [DOCUMENT 2.5].

The provincial English weeklies published just across Offa's Dyke were an integral part of the Welsh public discourse. They served as the main channel through which news, fashions and opinions reached the country, they imported foreign and state news into Wales by copying the official gazettes, and they communicated royal commands, ministerial announcements and changes in the law to the Welsh population. By relaying what established serials of differing political outlooks wrote about America, religious Dissent, Joseph Priestley or John Wesley, and by choosing whether to reprint Burke or Paine on their 'page four', they relayed the battle lines of warring ideologies into the heart of rural Wales. Some emphasized the power of law and state by printing detailed court reports of the treason trials, and repository-tract inspired texts, such as 'Reasons for not Rioting'.[57] Others undermined authority by reproducing satirical political vocabularies,[58] or by criticizing loyalist rituals, such as the burning of the effigy of Thomas Paine [DOCUMENT 5.2].

First and foremost however they gave an enduring public platform to voices *from* Wales. As all Welsh-language periodicals published before 1815 were short-lived and the main function of the Welsh almanacs lay elsewhere, the only constant agencies of public opinion for Wales were the *Hereford Journal* (Hereford), the *Shrewsbury Chronicle* and the *Salopian Journal* (Shrewsbury), and the *Chester Chronicle* and *Adams's Weekly Courant* (Chester). All of the above were more than partly geared towards Wales, a comparatively

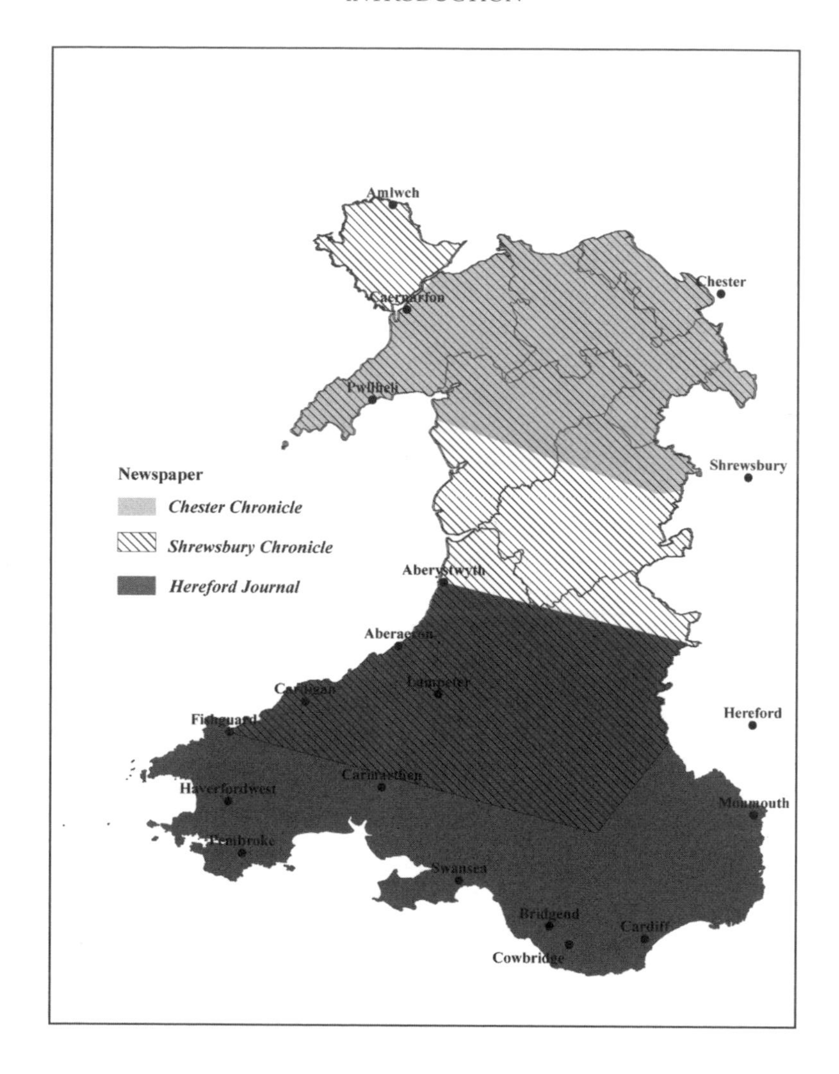


Figure 2. Spheres of influence of the *Hereford Journal*, *Shrewsbury Chronicle* and *Chester Chronicle* in Wales

'underexploited market' in an otherwise crowded scene (Fig. 2).[59] The *Hereford Journal*, described as the provincial paper with the 'greatest unrivalled area of distribution' in England, relied heavily on Welsh readers and advertisers.[60] Eighteen out of its twenty-three agents were in Wales: from Hay-on-Wye and Monmouth hard by the English border to the far western reaches of Pembrokeshire and along the coast to Aberystwyth.[61] 'Caractacus' voiced the opinion of many in the southern part of Wales when he called the *Hereford Journal* their 'only Silurian paper'.[62] Between 1791 and 1802 the paper was printed and edited by D. Walker, a shadowy figure about whom not much is known, except that he took a loyalist stance and that the paper flourished under his editorship.[63] Some fifty miles north, the *Salopian Journal* had also been founded with loyalism and the Welsh market in mind. The consortium which set up what it named the *Salopian Journal and Courier of Wales* in 1794 immediately hired a Welshman, John Jones, to carry the paper to Welshpool and beyond, granting him a loan to buy a horse for his rounds.[64] The paper's *impressum* listed agents in Wrexham, Welshpool, Dolgellau and Machynlleth and keenly rejected the 'unfounded Insinuations *of* Disaffection *and* Jacobinical Principles' raised against it [DOCUMENT 4.1]. Yet it struggled to survive during the first few years of its existence, averaging sales of only about 680 copies a week.[65] The reason for this was the pre-eminence of the *Shrewsbury Chronicle*, founded in 1772, whose title page announced that it was circulated 'thro' Shropshire, Montgomeryshire, Merionethshire, &c., also thro' Part of Cheshire, Staffordshire, Worcestershire, Denbighshire, Radnorshire, Cardiganshire, Flintshire, Carnarvonshire and Anglesea'.[66] Welsh local news reached it from coastal villages like Aberaeron and developing ports like Amlwch, and a 'regular correspondent' wrote in from Aberystwyth, right in the centre of Wales. Poems and reports signed 'north Wales' and 'Montgomeryshire' were ubiquitous.[67] The printer and editor of the *Shrewsbury Chronicle*, Thomas Wood, was well known to Welsh writers. He employed the poet Evan Thomas (Ieuan Fardd Ddu) to supervise and correct Welsh-language material, and the loyalist Gwallter Mechain even mentioned meeting fellow-poets in Wood's 'printing loft'.[68] This explains why another 'native of North Wales . . . knowing that your Paper very extensively circulates among my friends', addressed his celebratory *englyn* 'On the Enlargement and Improvement of the Shrewsbury Chronicle' just to 'Tomos'.[69] The editor permitted the public exchange of letters discussing contentious matters, such as rational Dissent, in the first years of the 1790s,[70] but following a wider change in public opinion, took a sharp turn towards loyalism in autumn 1792.[71] Consequently, he was able to increase the size of the paper at the end of 1793 (which, in its turn, led to increased sales). Until his death in 1801 (when his widow Mary assumed editorship), his annual message to readers illustrates its continuing resonance 'particularly in the Principality' and perhaps demonstrates the degree of popular politicization there [DOCUMENT 3.5].[72] Counting in multiple readers of each copy, Wood claimed to reach 20,000 people.[73] The loyalism of the *Shrewsbury Chronicle* – arguably the most widely read newspaper in Wales – had a paternalist timbre. It celebrated every event in the life of Sir Watkin Williams Wynn of Wynnstay, fifth baronet, his regiment, the Antient British Fencibles, and even his exotic plants [DOCUMENTS 3.3, 3.4, 3.17].[74] In its keenness to play down reports which might damage the image of Wales as a well-ordered, yet picturesque, mountain fastness, it did not shy from admonishing its main rival, the *Chester Chronicle*, for over-reporting incidences of rioting [DOCUMENT 3.10].

The *Chester Chronicle and Cheshire and North Wales Advertiser* – with (self-proclaimed) weekly sales of 1,700 copies an equally successful provincial paper – was politically very different.[75] William Cowdroy, who edited the paper for the owner John Fletcher, took a radical stance all through the 1790s, even after he was threatened with being shot as a 'rueful Jacobin' in the streets of the town [DOCUMENT 5.6].[76] While the *Chester Chronicle* did not receive letters from as many locations in Wales as the *Shrewsbury Chronicle*, it nevertheless maintained agents in Pwllheli and Caernarfon on the north-west coast and was copied into manuscript as far away as rural south Cardiganshire.[77] According to Bob Harris, the *Chester Chronicle* was circulating into Scotland, which means that Scottish readers may thus well have encountered radical Welsh-language poetry during the 1790s.[78]

### *Welsh poetry in the English provincial papers*

The *Chester Chronicle* was the only newspaper in this group which gave *radical* Welsh voices a sounding-board between 1789 and 1802, and it did so mainly in the form of poetry. Iolo Morganwg, who – in the privacy of his manuscripts – obsessively imagined publishing his seditious compositions, yet who contributed curiously little to the Welsh serial literature of the time, published here a version of his pacifist 'Ode on Converting a Sword into a Pruning Hook' [DOCUMENT 5.4].[79] John Jones (Jac Glan-y-gors), arguably the most influential Welsh radical and pamphleteer of the time and enmeshed in radical circles in London, contributed squibs and longer poems anonymously and under his own name, in English, in Welsh and bilingually. His bilingual hymn on the occasion of the public fast-day announced for 26 February 1796 and his new 'Welsh litany' used established religious forms as vehicles for topical political and anti-war satire [DOCUMENTS 5.11, 5.14].[80] A very different poem written for the St David's day dinner of a London Welsh society eulogized the Whig politician Charles Howard, eleventh duke of Norfolk, whom Glan-y-gors claimed for Wales by virtue of the duke's self-proclaimed descent from the family of rebellious Owain Glyndŵr [DOCUMENT 5.12]. The Welsh elegy which Glan-y-gors wrote for his friend and fellow-London Welshman David Samwell (Dafydd Ddu Feddyg), surgeon to Captain Cook on his last journey, assumed political meaning (like several other texts in this anthology) through its

English paratext [DOCUMENT 5.16].[81] In these English newspapers an English frame which may encompass title, introduction and footnotes supported, explained or politicized Welsh and Anglo-Welsh poetry. In the Welsh radical periodicals, such paratexts in either Welsh or English were used to politicize religious texts [DOCUMENTS 7.7, 8.6], contextualize translations [DOCUMENT 9.5], explain new concepts like 'democracy', 'Jacobin' or 'Royalist' [DOCUMENTS 7.5, 7.9, 9.2] and highlight the editor's political standpoint [DOCUMENT 9.6].[82]

The *Chester Chronicle* continued to publish politically daring material in the Welsh language well into the late 1790s, but as the effects of the war at home intensified and legal strictures became more pressing, the editor was forced to compromise by refusing to print problematic texts, and by giving loyalist sentiments and voices a platform [DOCUMENTS 5.15, 5.17].[83] Dafydd Ddu Eryri, revered as poet *and* loyalist, contributed religious poetry in Welsh and English as well as such translations from Welsh poetry as fitted the mood of the time.[84] He had probably also taken part in the competition organized by Welsh-language poets bent on writing an *English* poem in celebration of Lord Howe's victory against the Spanish forces [DOCUMENT 5.5]. Both the competition and the report are intriguing as rare instances in which the Welsh language was not deemed appropriate as a medium for the deeply felt loyalism these Welsh poets wished to convey to the public. The true homes of loyalist poetry from Wales, however, were *Adams's Weekly Courant,* the *Salopian Journal* and, most importantly, the *Shrewsbury Chronicle* [DOCUMENTS 3.6, 3.18]. *Adams's Weekly Courant*, the older of the two Chester papers, printed a very able Latin epigram by Paul Panton, junior (Monensis) of Plas Gwyn on Anglesey – who was to become high sheriff in 1807 – which claimed England as the real home of 'true liberty' [DOCUMENT 6.4]. Among the poems by Dafydd Ddu Eryri was an English ode to the Druidical Society of Anglesey – a charitable club for the leading men of the island – in which he expressed the wish for a 'freedom' which was 'obedient to the laws', thus echoing his eisteddfod prize-winning Welsh ode on 'Rhyddid' (Liberty), which ended in a paean to George III [DOCUMENT 6.1].[85]

The 'resident poet' at the *Shrewsbury Chronicle* was Thomas Jones (Rhaiadr) from Clocaenog near Ruthin, who had initiated the new eisteddfodau held in north Wales and sponsored by the London Gwyneddigion society, and was a friend of Dafydd Ddu Eryri.[86] Rhaiadr contributed detailed reports on the Gwyneddigion eisteddfodau,[87] celebrated Watkin Williams Wynn in poetry and prose [DOCUMENT 3.3], and supplied Welsh and English poems which revealed his conviction that the Welsh had been loyal since time immemorial [DOCUMENT 3.16].[88] At times, he shared page and poetical subject with other loyalist poets, testimony to their strong social networks. In 1795 Dafydd Ddu Eryri and Rhaiadr contributed a series of *englynion* on the subject 'Heddwch' (Peace) [DOCUMENT 3.9] which may well have been the result of a friendly poetic competition. Another staunch loyalist who lived nearby, Gwallter Mechain, the author of a prize-winning essay (deceptively entitled 'Rhyddid', like Dafydd Ddu Eryri's ode), had already co-rhymed with Rhaiadr in 1790. In a bilingual exercise in Welsh sublime, they wrote a short poem each – Rhaiadr in English, Gwallter Mechain in Welsh – on 'Elizabeth Parry [who] undertook . . . to walk from one end to the other of that tremendous natural arch at Pystyll (the Waterfall of) Rhaiadr'. They had apparently observed the feat together.[89] The loyalist poets in the north were able and eager to advertise their connections in these newspapers, much more so than their radical counterparts, the majority of whom lived in the south. Manuscript sources and later anthologies confirm that radical poets such as Tomos Glyn Cothi, David Davis, Castellhywel, and Edward Evan, Aberdare, also co-operated in, for instance, creating adaptations of radical English poetry.[90] However, far fewer of their efforts were published before the advent of less dangerous times [DOCUMENT 8.3]. Thus, perhaps, not Iolo Morganwg only, but half a dozen radical Welsh poets and writers are among the 'lost generation' of the 1790s.[91]

*Loyalism proclaimed*

As the 'mist of suspicion that permeated the monarchies of Europe' settled on Britain,[92] the ascription of loyalism to the Welsh people and its public display by the Welsh themselves (whether real or pretend) grew to be a major theme in all these newspapers. It was played out through news and reports from Wales (especially those connected with the winter of Reevesian hysteria, 1792–3, and the attempted landing of the French at Fishguard in 1797) and through a politicized picturesque and sublime which enveloped the landscape, language and history of Wales.[93] Occasionally, however, this concerted attempt at depicting Wales as a paternalist haven of loyalism broke down, notably so in the hunger years of 1795–6 and of 1801, when the papers could but print reports of rioting from all over Wales, angry or pleading letters by frightened magistrates, and Judge Hardinge's public speeches at sentencing the perpetrators of crimes connected with these disturbances. It is striking, however, that insurrection – from riot through to sentencing – was either framed in terms of class conflict or understood to be the exception to 'normal' Welsh behaviour.

*The Reevesian winter of hysteria (1792–3)*

Hywel M. Davies has charted the swift spread of the Association for the Preservation of Liberty and Property against Republicans and Levellers in Wales and the astonishing number of letters sent to its founder John Reeves by local Welsh Associations.[94] Publishing versions of these letters served to reinforce the atmosphere of informal suppression of radical and oppositional voices back home in Wales, but these proclamations of loyalty also shed light on regional variations in the country. One of the first letters to be published in the *Hereford Journal* came from Talgarth, Breconshire, where an Association had been formed as early as 10 December 1792. It displayed not only the customary declarations of loyalty, but an acute sense of belonging to the larger political unit:

> though we inhabit a small division of the kingdom, as compared to the whole, yet as the whole is composed of several parts, it seems to us, that if each part was to declare itself, it would effectually tend to silence those who are eagerly busied in endeavouring to destroy the whole [DOCUMENT 2.4].

Public pressure was exerted on the inhabitants of the parish. They were urged to sign a book 'now opened and signed by us' (the committee members) and the newly formed Association threatened 'to reduce to obedience of the laws, those who may manifest their defiance or contempt of them'.[95] A relatively short letter published in the same newspaper on 27 February 1793 was very different. It reported a meeting of forty 'Protestant Dissenting Ministers, of the three Denominations, in the Counties of Cardigan, Carmarthen, and Pembroke', who had assembled to assure their 'Loyalty and Adherence to the Constitution under the Revolution in 1688, consisting of King, Lords and Commons' [DOCUMENT 2.5], but who also took the opportunity to remind the Government of their 'exclusion from the common rights of citizens'. The meeting had been called by the influential Baptist minister William Williams, who had personally written to ministers in south and west Wales, inviting them to attend (see endnote 11 to the 'Selection of Documents'). He addressed the assembly and was, most probably, the author of the published texts. The meeting and the publications which arose from it were more indicative of the atmosphere of persecution prevalent among Dissenting communities in south-west Wales than of a genuine loyalism, as a letter dated 25 February 1793 reveals. Zecharias Thomas, Baptist minister at Aberdyar, had been invited to attend the meeting or send a letter expressing his loyalty, but did neither, because he deemed that its purpose was the appeasement of political pressure only.[96] The extent of the Dissenters' paranoia was highlighted by the fact that, for maximum impact, a bilingual version of the resolutions was published, together with a Welsh ballad.[97]

Further north, the *Shrewsbury Chronicle* willingly published a letter by its regular correspondent from Aberystwyth, which confirmed the town as a true centre of loyalism in mid Wales. It reported on the 'respectable Meeting' to form an Association there, which was combined with a 'general illumination' and a jolly bonfire on which 'Tom Paine's libel entitled "The Rights of Man" was burnt' [DOCUMENT 3.2].[98] Even the *Chester Chronicle* could not but report that 'meetings have been held, and associations formed, at Holywell, Warrington, Whitchurch, Congleton, and other places in the neighbourhood, for the purpose of evincing an attachment to the laws and constitution of the country. All of these meetings were no less numerous than respectable.'[99] At Wrexham a meeting whose list of committee members reads like a *Who's Who* of old and new money in the area, like the earlier letter from Talgarth expressed an acute awareness of the links between the 'sowers of sedition' in Wales and the 'present state of anarchy and wretchedness' in France [DOCUMENT 5.3].[100] The burnings and hangings of Thomas Paine's effigy reported in the *Chester Chronicle* and in *Adams's Weekly Courant* during the same weeks were likely also to be connected to these public displays of loyalty [DOCUMENTS 5.2, 6.2, 6.3]. The respectable burghers of Welsh towns, in many of which – established around Anglo-Norman castles and deliberately settled with Englishmen – a system of apartheid had been operated until the Acts of Union in 1536/1543,[101] were keen to manifest ownership of their civic spaces through loyalist ritual and to advertise this fact clearly.

*The Fishguard affair (1797)*

The increasing militarization of society throughout the mid-1790s prepared the ground for a second media event which united the newspapers (and, apparently, the 'ancient Britons') in defence of both their country and the kingdom. With hindsight, the attempted landing of a French force at Fishguard, Pembrokeshire, on 24 February 1797 was a more pathetic than tragic affair, but at the time, it induced private panic and public bravery.[102] Whilst it was not front page news in any of the newspapers in this collection, all faithfully reported on page two the royal gazettes and the official letters sent by Lord Milford (lord lieutenant for Pembrokeshire), by Lord Cawdor (commander of the Cardigan militia) and by Lieutenant Hearn (forty-third regiment stationed at Carmarthen), describing in detail how the local squirearchy rallied the populace [DOCUMENTS 2.11, 4.3].[103] The reports attempted to keep a balance between accentuating the seriousness of the situation and an unshaken belief that the country was never in danger, though several accounts confirmed the rumour-induced private panic which prevailed in some quarters. Jane Johnes, wife of the famous Thomas Johnes of Hafod, for instance, not only wrote to her brother for help, but prepared to die in defence of her estate:

> I have this moment heard that the sails of the French are off Aberystwith & Aberairon. If you are able let me beg you to come over & bring with you what Arms you can powder & shot. They will not sell any at Aberystwith . . . I feel oddly in this business but I will defend the house as long as I can. Trust to God for the rest & if I fall hope to be happy hereafter.[104]

An 'active witness of all the circumstances' reported from the retinue of Lord Cawdor that 'There was much alarm on their first landing, which was naturally distressing, to several families', but swiftly assured the public that 'THE WELSH WERE NEVER CONQUERED, and I verily believe not a man would have disgraced his Ancestors' [DOCUMENT 2.12]. Like his report, most of the narratives published on the theme of the attempted invasion seared vivid images of Welsh loyalty in action into the British consciousness.[105] A month before the landing, all 'Brother Britons' had been reminded of their duties in the *Salopian Journal*, where 'An Ancient Briton' had felt obliged to publicly appease misgivings about the recent Supplementary Militia Act.[106] He called on 'every part of society' to serve 'in the way best suited to its condition and situation' [DOCUMENT 4.2]. When the need arose, according to Lord Cawdor's account, 'The spirit of loyalty which [had] pervaded all ranks of people throughout this country [was] infinitely beyond what I can express' [DOCUMENT 4.3]. The 'active witness of all the circumstances' confirmed that, though the French claimed to have been invited, such letters could not have been 'written by Welshmen, who detest every thing disloyal, or that has a tincture of French in it' [DOCUMENT 2.12]. *Adams's Weekly Courant* gushed how 'the brave descendants of the Ancient Britons exerted themselves' [DOCUMENT 6.5] and even the *Chester Chronicle*, though it criticized the official gazettes (as well as scorning this poor attempt by the French), reported that it had been pleased to observe:

> the zeal with which the natives of Wales poured down from their mountains to resist this inroad. It appears that above 3000 countrymen and miners assembled, armed with forks, scythes, and other ready weapons, besides the militia and volunteers of Pembroke and Cardigan [DOCUMENT 5.13].

However, the *Chester Chronicle* was not the only paper to highlight that the only difficulty in connection with the military operation 'was to restrain the impetuosity of the mountaineers, who fell upon the French without order, indeed, but with irresistible fury' [DOCUMENTS 5.13, 6.5]. Despite their proven loyalty, the Welsh were still the hot-headed, mountain-dwelling 'natives' of Britain.

For one particular group, the Methodists in Wales, a sect deeply (and unjustly) suspected of seditious activities by the authorities and equally loathed by rational Dissenters,[107] Fishguard and its aftermath proved to be a golden opportunity for regaining public ground. The *Shrewsbury Chronicle* readily obliged, by printing the anecdote of a Methodist minister and his congregation who rushed to the defence of their country, mid-service; by reporting a 'thanksgiving meeting' held in conjunction with the quarterly Methodist Association meeting of June 1797, attended by 'about fourteen thousand . . . conscious of the excellent government they lived under' and offering 'fervent prayers for its long continuance'; and by advertising an 'Anniversary Day of Thanksgiving' to be held on Goodwick Sands in February 1798 [DOCUMENT 3.12]. None of the provincial papers published close to the border with Wales participated in the general witch-hunt against (Welsh) Methodists instigated by other serials.[108] For rational Dissenters in south-west Wales, however, the aftermath of the landing confirmed their wariness of state and Established Church. In the days following the event, five Dissenters were arrested, of whom two, the Baptist preacher Thomas John and the Presbyterian Samuel Griffiths, were brought to trial for high treason in September 1797. The evidence against them, however, was so slim that the case was dismissed. The writer of the letter recounting the court proceedings made sure he used the occasion to highlight, once more, that the collapse of the trial confirmed Welsh loyalty in all quarters [DOCUMENT 4.4].[109] The Fishguard affair was rounded off with a letter from loyalist Caernarfon, sent by 'A Friend to his Country' to the Duke of Portland and published in *Adams's Weekly Courant*. Inevitably invoking the 'ancestors' of the Welsh and their 'spirit of unchangeable constancy, loyalty, and the love of honourable danger in a generous cause', the writer called for England's help in defending Welsh coasts in the form of an even stronger military presence in Caernarfonshire and on Anglesey [DOCUMENT 6.6].

*Welsh history and landscape*

Fishguard and its aftermath inspired those who placed Welsh history, the landscape and the Welsh language in the service of the 'united kingdom'. The anniversary of the landing (in conjunction with the ever more alarming news from rebellious Ireland) led to public reflection on the heroism of the Welsh from time immemorial in reiteration of the need for unity. Following a petition from Carmarthenshire against new taxes in January 1798,

'A Welsh Freeholder' called the 'Inhabitants of the Principality of Wales' to arms in the *Shrewsbury Chronicle*.[110] His graphic and detailed description of the terror of a French occupation, 'when Great Britain is but too likely to be dyed throughout, and deluged, with the blood of all her natives' [DOCUMENT 3.13] culminated in an appeal to their dual identity as ancient and modern Britons.[111] Fortified with capital letters and italics, all parts of the kingdom must now stand by England, for:

> *Dissentions* gave *Britain* to the aspiring *Romans*, *Dissentions* gave *Britain* to the cruel *Saxons* – *Dissentions* gave Britain to the overwhelming *Normans*! – *To-day*, SIRS! awake – accord – arise! Otherwise *Dissentions* will TOMORROW give *Great Britain* to the *aspiring*, *cruel*, *overwhelming* Rebels and Banditti of FRANCE! [DOCUMENT 3.13]

The French threat surpassed all previous historic enemies to the 'sons of Albion'. Two months later, the *Chester Chronicle* published an even longer monologue by the 'Ghost of Llewellyn', in which Shakespeare's *Hamlet*, Welsh history, the Welsh landscape and loyalism were woven into a tapestry of common effort in defence against Ireland [DOCUMENT 5.15]. As if on stage, Llywelyn ap Gruffudd, the last native Prince of Wales (who was murdered by the soldiers of Edward I), admonished the Welsh from the peak of Carnedd Llywelyn, the mountain in the Snowdonia range named after him. Reminding the audience that 'the national jealousies and antipathies' of his own 'barbarous period' were history and that Welshmen were now 'governed by the same wholesome laws' as Englishmen, he warned that a failure to arm would leave the unprotected coasts of Wales exposed to the 'united force of France and Ireland'. In this layer-cake of meaning, two of the quotations from *Hamlet* were patriotized by replacing references to the protagonist's father with 'England' and the 'dear country'. The English prose was inlaid with Welsh verse invoking Arthur as a unifying British figure, thus uniting both literary cultures, while again conflating the two meanings of 'British' as a label of ancient ethnicity and an expression of modern political adherence.

The Welsh landscape, ancient history, and the Welsh language itself had long been inscribed with loyalist meaning. None of the newspapers along the Welsh border perceived Wales as a political unit. 'Wales', unlike 'Scotland', 'Ireland' or 'America' only rarely appeared as a headline. News, letters and poetry were signed from Welsh counties, villages and towns or, at best, from 'north Wales' or 'south Wales'. Nevertheless, Wales *was* imagined: as a picturesque landscape of disparate mountains, rivers and valleys peopled by natives endowed with an exotic language and literary culture, significantly all taking part in the modern British project. Translations from Welsh medieval poetry served this purpose,[112] as did 'banal' texts, like advertisements for the sea-bathing resorts of Tenby, Aberystwyth and Abergele.[113] Factual accounts from a paternalist society were shot through with these themes. The coming of age celebrations for Sir Watkin Williams Wynn, fifth baronet – an event which undoubtedly pulled together a large area of north-east Wales (and the English border country) in the first year of the war – combined pastoral images of happy tenants and colliers sitting down at open-air tables laden with meat and ale with visual representations of historic Wales (such as a druid and a view of a mansion) and of the loyalist ritual of 'illuminating' towns and villages.[114] A Welsh-language poem (written by Rhaiadr) was declaimed *in situ*, and in the evening 'all the neighbouring hills appeared to join their plaudits, by noble bonfires smiling at each other' [DOCUMENTS 3.3, 3.4]. A well-ordered, contented part of the kingdom indeed. Visiting English poets, such as Anna Seward, who interpreted 'Llangollen vale' as 'another Eden',[115] and William Lisle Bowles, who praised the 'steps of Culture' that elevated the summer residence of Thomas Grove, 'Coombe Ellen',[116] deepened this public image of a country in which the different social orders and nature coexisted in harmony.[117]

Much of the poetry published in the newspapers during this long decade, often by otherwise unknown Welsh poets or anonymously, evoked the theme of a landscape reflective of loyal steadfastness. A 'Montgomeryshire Farmer' poet may have lived 'On a lone Mountain's rugged side' . . . close to 'where old MATHRAVAL' (the Welsh royal seat of medieval Powys) once stood, but this did not prevent him from reading the *Shrewsbury Chronicle* and clinging firmly to 'Country, Church and King!' [DOCUMENT 3.8]. Bala Lake (Llyn Tegid, the largest lake in Wales) remained undisturbed by 'eastern storms' and easily accommodated 'the greatest rains', yet would rise with 'sudden rage', like the natives, if its peace was disturbed [DOCUMENT 3.11]. The mountains of Snowdonia along the coast played a special role in this political landscape, since coastal defence was justifiably important to the Welsh, and the kingdom at large. The jagged rock of Penmaen-mawr near Conwy, became a 'monarch' with a 'Druid face' towering above and withstanding the 'madd'ning malice' and 'fretful falsehood' foaming at it base.[118] The 'genius' of Snowdon ruled sublime and unmoved over the 'feeble rage of fierce conflicts'.[119] A symbol of Welsh resistance against the English in the past, it was now a compass-point used by the Right Honourable Lord Viscount Bulkeley, lord lieutenant of Caernarfonshire, to rally his compatriots to the defence of Great Britain:

> If, in days of yore, our valiant ancestors, the Antient Britons, poured in irresistable torrents from their mountains and fastnesses, against those whom they considered their invaders or oppressors, how much more ought we of this day to plant the flag of union on the top of old Snowdon, and rally round it in defence of all the endearments of society and friendship; in defence of all the comforts of domestic life; in defence of our government, our King and our country; and particularly in defence of our holy religion, which not only supports us in this world, but gives us the assurance of a future and endless state of happiness.[120]

Further west, the very shores of the Menai straits, which separated mainland Wales from Anglesey and the Irish Sea, became symbolic of the historically deep dichotomy of the peace of bard and druid at one with nature and the military prowess necessary to shield their 'Freedom' to enjoy their 'philosophic blaze' [DOCUMENT 6.1]. Bard and druid, however, had also aided ancient British warriors in defending their isle and its freedom. The 'War Song' from William Tasker's historical tragedy *Arviragus* was specifically addressed to the *Shrewsbury Chronicle* and thus to the Welsh.[121] 'Llewellin', here not a Welsh prince but a 'British bard', urged the Britons to 'Sling the javelins – hurl the darts, / Infix them in the Roman hearts'.[122] The rather comic song Rhaiadr penned for St David's Day 1799 equally recounted Welsh bravery from Julius Caesar until their deliverance by Henry Tudor on Bosworth Field in 1485 [DOCUMENT 3.16]. The master of interlacing landscape and history in the quest for a politically vague 'freedom' (often in the *Chester Chronicle*) was the 'Anglo-British' poet Richard Llwyd, whose footnotes swelled to ever greater complexity as his poetic career unfolded so that his message must have been difficult for any but his most learned contemporaries to interpret, and today reveals its meaning only reluctantly.[123]

The narrative of a warlike nation which had always repulsed invaders was only rarely interrupted by native texts of a more pacific character in the newspapers, most of which found their home in the *Chester Chronicle*. Among them were the anti-war satires and poems by Jac Glan-y-gors and Iolo Morganwg (who here signed as Edward Williams) [DOCUMENTS 5.4, 5.11, 5.14], and a sequence of poetry and prose from north and mid Wales which highlighted the war-induced plight of its inhabitants during the hungry summer of 1795. On 21 August 1795 an untitled poem from Denbigh and a letter by 'Juvenis' from Welshpool appeared side by side. The poem focused on the 'humble poor' now starving along the coast of north Wales, counter-posing the cliché of the 'happy isle' with the stark reality of 'A mother gathering chaff for bread, / To feed her hungry child' [DOCUMENT 5.7], while 'Juvenis' engaged in a more abstract religious condemnation of this war as based on principles 'which Christ abhorred, as utterly repugnant to the mild and gracious designs of his gospel' [DOCUMENT 5.8]. A month later an anonymous correspondent from 'North Wales' declared himself 'the enemy of the present war' because it was pursued by government officials who did not consider the suffering of the 'emaciated soldier' and the 'weather-beaten sailor' or of the 'unfortunate females' whose husbands were no more [DOCUMENT 5.8]. Such contributions, however, were rare in the other newspapers, and never as daring. Dafydd Ddu Eryri and Rhaiadr may have chosen peace as a subject for their common effort published in the *Shrewsbury Chronicle* in April 1795 [DOCUMENT 3.9], but their invocation was free of the radical overtones Jac Glan-y-gors, Iolo Morganwg and the anonymous contributors to the *Chester Chronicle* brought to the subject.

*The Welsh language*

The majority of the texts which imbued the landscape and history of Wales with loyalist or patriotic meaning were in English, but a politically emasculated Welsh language was an intrinsic part of the patriotic project pursued by the English newspapers which carried contributions in it. Published radical literature in Welsh was largely confined to pamphlets, sermons and the short-lived Welsh-language periodical press of the 1790s (see below).[124] The public message of the papers was that the majority of the inhabitants of the Principality of Wales may speak an 'other' language, but that this did not weaken their loyalty to the Crown, as Irish Catholicism, radicalism and rebellion evidently did. There is no evidence that the Welsh-language texts inserted in these weeklies excited suspicion or evoked a negative public response from English-language readers. The fact that all the newspapers in this collection carried advertisements for Welsh-language publications throughout the period and that a loyalist weekly like the *Shrewsbury Chronicle* included Welsh-language poems and squibs, sometimes just to fill a column, indicates that Welsh was an accepted feature of life in the extended border country along Offa's Dyke.[125] A proud report of the exemplary conduct of the Carmarthen militia in Ireland stressed that 'not a man born on this side the Severn appertains to the regiment, and but few of the privates speak English' [DOCUMENT 3.15]. Ireland was a threat and a hostile power, where Welsh soldiers fought, whose refugees Wales embraced with open arms and where even Sir Watkin Williams Wynn might be slandered [DOCUMENTS 3.14, 5.15, 5.18]. Wales, on the other hand, was an integral part of the kingdom where a '*learned* Blacksmith' and a 'very *classical* Taylor' could hotly discuss the etymology of the word 'Democrate' using their knowledge of Welsh, and with its assistance conclude that it meant nothing else than 'may the devil take me' [DOCUMENT 3.7].

The regular bulletins dispatched by members of the London Gwyneddigion and Cymreigyddion societies about their revived cultural festival, the eisteddfod, were imbued with the same spirit. London Welsh circles may have counted radicals in their ranks who circulated hand-written seditious bills during at least one eisteddfod and wrote seditious poetry,[126] but what was made public about their societies does not bear out Gwyn Alf Williams's assertion that they were 'an instrument of Jacobinism'.[127] The eisteddfod accounts focused on the peaceful history of this hallowed institution, which had enjoyed royal and noble patronage since its inception in the Middle Ages [DOCUMENT 2.1].[128] The subject for competition at the St Asaph eisteddfod of May 1790 may have been 'Liberty', but conservative entries triumphed and the silver medal for the best prose essay featured 'the head of Cambria, with some emblems of liberty, and on the reverse, a lion defending Britannia (who resembles a child grasping venomous serpents) against foreign enemies' [DOCUMENTS 5.1, 5.17].[129] The brand new cultural institution of the Gorsedd, on the other hand, which the defiant Iolo Morganwg devised as the liberal answer by the brotherhood of southern bards and which soon attracted the unwanted attention of the state authorities,[130] was only advertised once, in the *Salopian Journal* on 7 March 1798. It did not fit the hegemonic narrative of a loyalism backed up with centuries of Welsh song and military prowess.

### *Rebellion disowned*

Neither of course did the public disturbances and riots over food shortages and military service which unsettled some areas of Wales from 1789 all through to 1802 and which, at times, turned industrializing towns and parishes, such as Wrexham and Merthyr Tydfil, into zones of military occupation. The short notes and long reports of riots and the letters written by magistrates took care not to damage the image of loyal *Cambria*. They did, however, introduce an element of class war into this well-settled society, which pitched the town-dwelling middle class and gentry against the revolting rabble and the more dangerous organized force of the miners.[131] The major disturbances reported in the papers came from those districts where grain was collected for export and where a large body of the working classes was already present. At times, restoring order seems to have been difficult. Diary entries by local notables like Hester Piozzi reveal a private millenarian panic which the shorter bulletins in the newspapers were, perhaps, attempting to mask:

> Last of Oct$^{r}$. 1794. We have strange Weather here, Thunder, Lightening Hail & heat over Night – Snow upon all the Mountains early next Morn$^{g}$. The

> People are alarmed too, & agitated with these Reports of Treason Rebellion Impiety all around so – our Regiment of Militia – the Denbighshire Corps – have it in Charge to guard the French Prisoners at Porchester, and write us word hither that those Sparks make it their Business to curse the Holy Trinity every Night before they sleep – & cut the Neck of our King's Head on every Coyn they can get, to shew their Desire of Decapitation: such things with a putrid Fever to boot, make it a Dangerous Office to have Care of them – both their Principles & their Putrescence are contagious. Add to all this, that the parts of Tom Payne's Book most easy to comprehend, have been all translated into Welch, and are supposed to do no small Mischief among the low People hereabouts.[132]

In north-east Wales, the rioting which was to continue, on and off, for more than a decade, began in the summer of 1789, when it was reported that colliers, seemingly in concerted action, repeatedly seized grain and threatened government officials. These were declared to be 'all the natural effects of a body of people without order' [DOCUMENT 3.1]. When the thirty-fourth regiment moved into Wrexham (from Manchester) and restored order, the colliers moved on to Ruabon, in order to continue their concerted action there.[133] Disturbances rumbled on in the area for months, explained by the prevalence of a 'leveling spirit among the class',[134] so that by the end of August four companies were ordered to stay at Wrexham during the Assizes.[135] In March 1795 the *Hereford Journal* reported on a succession of corn-riots from St Clears and Carmarthen in the south to Aberystwyth in mid Wales and Conwy and Bangor Ferry in the far north [DOCUMENTS 2.7, 2.8].[136] The strategies adopted to quell the disturbances varied, though the preferred method was to call in the military. The Somerset Fencible Cavalry put paid to the rioting in the north, while the respectable townsfolk of Aberystwyth went at it themselves to defend their rights and their property against the lead-miners from the surrounding hills:

> . . . Mr. Lloyd, an active Magistrate, again desired them to disperse, but without effect; and, in attempting to secure one of the ringleaders, he was violently assaulted, which brought on a general engagement between the rioters and the worthy Magistrate and his friends, in which many on both sides were severely wounded. The former having received a warmer reception than they expected, chose to retreat, but not without threatening to return in more considerable numbers [DOCUMENT 2.7].

At this point, the burghers called in the Carmarthenshire Yeomanry, whose conduct occasioned high praise from the Aberystwyth correspondent. In order to avoid a repetition of such bloody clashes in the streets of Aberystwyth, traditionally paternalistic measures were then taken, and broadcast by the gentlemen of the county of Cardiganshire [DOCUMENT 2.10]. The organized character of the 'mobs' of hundreds of 'miners and colliers' as a rule attracted the fearful attention of observers like the Denbighshire magistrate whose letter was published in *Adams's Weekly Courant* [DOCUMENT 6.3], but the account of the rather disciplined action taken by three hundred colliers from the Forest of Dean in south-east Wales carried a rare element of admiration [DOCUMENT 2.9]. Again, the *Chester Chronicle* provided a lone antidote to those reports that whipped up hostility against this 'swinish multitude' by printing the letters sent by an unnamed 'Flintshire Magistrate' to Prime Minister Pitt in early 1796. The Magistrate suggested that, instead of meting out violence to a starving people, an effective way of restoring '*general peace and harmony*' would be doubling the wages of the working poor or fixing the price of basic provisions [DOCUMENT 5.10].

The published accounts of the trials against the perpetrators of these crimes, as a rule, provided an opportunity of recouping some of the ground lost to the power of the common people and to publicize the state's authority.[137] The *Hereford Journal* was particularly fortunate that the senior judge for the counties of Brecon, Glamorganshire and Radnorshire was George Hardinge, a man who revelled in expressing his thoughts on those he condemned to prison, transportation and death. In April 1800 it printed a long report from one of the few trials for sedition which came to court in Wales during these years.[138] Hardinge used his lengthy speech to the defendant John Griffith to praise the scarcity of sedition cases involving the Welsh language and to admire the loyalty shown by Glamorgan men through their 'zeal against incendiaries' like him [DOCUMENT 2.15]. Relatively lenient sentences were also meted out to William Phillip and John David, who had prevented the transporting of barley meal from Llangattock to Merthyr Tydfil in April 1800. Hardinge, in his address to the prisoners justified this with the fact that it was 'only the second instance of this kind that I have attended here' [DOCUMENT 2.16]. He did, however, warn that 'The horrors in France began with outrages like these' and that future punishments must take this into consideration. Following an autumn and winter of discontent in the valleys of south Wales, he decided, therefore, 'to make an example of three ironworkers' involved in the Merthyr Tydfil riots of autumn 1800.[139] On this occasion, his speeches from the two days of trial were not reproduced in the newspapers, though they were translated into the Welsh language and circulated as pamphlets.[140] A short account of the execution of two of the men he had sentenced to death, published in the *Shrewsbury Chronicle*, backfired. Instead of demonstrating the power of the state, it gave the first martyrs of nineteenth-century Merthyr Tydfil an enduring presence:

> Aaron Williams, during the course of his prayers, before they were turned off, observed "that they were going to suffer for hundreds," Samuel Hill replied, "yes, for thousands, but I never knew so happy a day as this in the course of my life" [DOCUMENT 3.21].

Be that as it may, the provincial English newspapers published close to the border with and geared towards Wales, and which controlled a large share of its public discourse, mainly served British loyalism, and that largely in the English language. Their evidence, however, is not indicative of a structured loyalist movement in Wales, but of the local and regional responses to the crises of the decade and the desire to assert the loyalty of the *cultural* Welsh nation as part of the *political* British nation in the making.[141] Welsh-language loyalist poetry was allocated pride of place in some newspapers, notably in the *Shrewsbury Chronicle*, while radical poetry in the Welsh language, though present, only appeared sporadically. Neither can be interpreted as a coherent response to French Revolutionary ideas or the Franco-British war on a par with the rebellion pursued by the United Irishmen and the campaigns enacted by radical circles in London, Sheffield and Manchester, or even the efforts of the weavers of Lancashire.

### *Welsh radical periodicals: Enlightenment, cultural nationalism and radicalism*

It would have been interesting to read the reaction of the radical Welsh press to the execution of the first working class leaders of Merthyr Tydfil in 1801. Alas, by then the three progressive Welsh periodicals produced by a small band of writers between London, Wales and North America had long disappeared. Their impermanence is unfortunate, but does not surprise. All three were amateur efforts, written and edited by men who earned an often meagre living by other means and some of whom seem to have been almost entirely self-educated. They carried no advertisements and therefore had to maintain themselves on sales alone, which was a well-nigh impossible undertaking in 1790s Wales. Even in the major centres of radicalism in England, radical serials tended to be transitory and Scotland only succeeded in producing two radical newspapers in the English language.[142] While the United Irishmen produced four newspapers in the 1790s, among them the influential *Northern Star*, their attempt in 1795 to publish a periodical in the Irish language, *Bolg an tSolair: or, Gaelic Magazine*, only ran to one number.[143]

It is remarkable that in Wales – a country more similar to the Scottish Highlands than the urbanized Lowlands; or the impoverished rural west of Ireland than the more developed eastern half dominated by Belfast and Dublin – altogether seventeen numbers of radical serial literature in the indigenous Welsh language appeared. There were even plans for further serial publications. In his editorial to the last issue of *Cylch-grawn Cynmraeg*, Morgan John Rhys canvassed the public on behalf of *Y Cofiadur Cymraeg* or the *Welsh Remembrancer*, which was to appear fortnightly [DOCUMENT 7.12].[144] As early as 1780, Iolo Morganwg had been collecting material for 'a sixpenny Quarterly' which he intended to call *Dywennydd Morganwg* (The Happiness of Glamorgan),[145] and in 1796 he wrote of his intention to bring out a quarterly entitled *Y Bardd Teulu* (The Family Poet).[146] The fact that launching a general serial publication in the English language was not a consideration for Welsh radicals reveals the unique linguistic and cultural standing of Wales's print culture among the four nations of the British Isles.

The first periodical in the Welsh language had been established by Lewis Morris, customs officer at Holyhead, Anglesey, as early as 1735. His *Tlysau yr Hen Oesoedd* (Gems of the Past Ages) aimed at gathering texts and making them available to the Welsh-speaking nation, while its preface 'To the English Reader' and its English explanations – aimed at gathering in the Anglicized gentry – set a precedent for the later coexistence of Welsh and English in serial publications.[147] The second Welsh-language periodical, edited by the Unitarian Josiah Rees of Gelli-gron near Swansea, was also connected with the Morris brothers. The London-based Richard Morris influenced the undertaking in a way that became paradigmatic for the development of the periodical press and, perhaps, the working of the Enlightenment in Wales during the last quarter of the eighteenth century. Initially, this *Trysorfa Gwybodaeth, neu Eurgrawn Cymraeg* (Treasury of Knowledge, or Welsh Magazine) was to be a Welsh *Magazin* but Richard Morris took offence at this:

> Magazin: an abominable word to be introduced in a new work in the language: ought by no means to be admitted. Several compounds may be expressive to this purpose; but I think Eurgrawn as proper as any.[148]

His suggestion *Eurgrawn* was not only accepted but recurred as a periodical title until the end of the nineteenth century.[149] England may have provided the cultural concept of the periodical, but onto this rootstock, Welsh intellectuals in London and Wales grafted not only the Welsh language, but also Welsh cultural mores and religious requirements. In this process, Welsh

Enlightenment efforts and cultural patriotism went hand in hand.[150] The Carmarthen printer John Ross had ambitious plans for the *Eurgrawn*. He advertised distributors in every town in Wales as well as in London, Bristol and Shrewsbury and announced that he planned to employ three or four salesmen to tour the counties of south Wales.[151] If this fortnightly publication had survived, it would have been a truly national venture, but its fate was that of most periodicals in Wales until the 1810s: it failed after only fifteen numbers, the publisher noting that he had already incurred a loss of £100 and regretting that he could not afford to continue.[152]

This first progressive Welsh-language periodical did not find a successor until 1793. Until then Welsh enthusiasm for French Revolutionary ideas had expressed itself within the framework of the London Welsh Gwyneddigion and Cymreigyddion societies whose cultural nationalism saw in the overthrow of the old order an opportunity for their historic nation to take its rightful place in the world.[153] It had manifested itself through the anti-slavery efforts of men like Morgan John Rhys and found an outlet in his attempts to bring the Bible to the poor benighted French whom the Revolution had released from the Babylonian bondage of Catholicism.[154] The execution of Louis XVI on 21 January 1793 and the declaration of war between France and Britain on 1 February 1793, however, had severely tempered the initial enthusiasm of many for the principles of the French Revolution. The former ushered in the Reign of Terror in France, while the latter rang in the era of government informers, oppressive legislation and treason trials in Great Britain. Yet the production of radical literature in the metropolis continued. Indeed, 1793 saw the appearance of the radical serials *Hog's Wash* and *Pig's Meat*, both of which exerted an enormous influence on the 'loose-textured but potent organic intelligentsia' who dared challenge the loyalist hegemony of public discourse in Wales.[155] Just as Richard Morris and Josiah Rees had Cymricized the concept of the progressive periodical in the 1770s, the Welsh radicals of the 1790s remodelled English radical efforts by means of translation, adaptation and creative imitation.

Inspired by the English radical press and by each other, three radical periodicals in the Welsh language appeared between 1793 and 1796. Along with the political pamphlets and sermons published by radical Welshmen and the Gorsedd meetings for the bardic fraternity invented and staged by Iolo Morganwg, they constituted the most important manifestation of a radical Welsh reaction to the ideas of the French Revolution. In 1793 the Baptist minister Morgan John Rhys inaugurated the quarterly *Cylch-grawn Cynmraeg neu Drysorfa Gwybodaeth* (The Welsh Magazine or Treasury of Knowledge), sold at fourpence. It was followed, in the spring of 1795, by *The Miscellaneous Repository neu, Y Drysorfa Gymmysgedig* (The Miscellaneous

Repository or, The Mixed Treasury) edited by Tomos Glyn Cothi, the first Unitarian minister in Wales, which sold for sixpence. In February 1796 the Independent minister David Davies, Holywell, brought out the first number of the monthly, *Y Geirgrawn: neu Drysorfa Gwybodaeth* (The Magazine: or Treasury of Knowledge), sold at fourpence (Fig. 3). All three editors were Dissenters who originally hailed from south Wales and whose radicalism would bring them into conflict with the state. Morgan John Rhys (1760–1804), born in Glamorganshire and enrolled at the Bristol Academy in 1786–7, partly 'to learn the English tongue so as to preach in it',[156] had already translated English sermons and anti-slavery tracts into the Welsh language.[157] In 1791 he had extended his evangelical mission to France, where, in his own words, he 'preach[ed] the law of liberty' ('yn pregethu cyfraith rhyddid'),[158] and where his religious and political beliefs were further radicalized.[159] On his return he founded branches of the Society of the Friends of the People and organized the establishment of Welsh-language Sunday schools in south Wales before founding his *Cylch-grawn Cynmraeg* and publishing a collection of hymns.[160] His emigration to America in August 1794, while grounded in his ideology, was, according to oral tradition, triggered by the threat of imminent arrest in Carmarthen.[161]

The weaver Tomos Glyn Cothi (1764–1833) received very little formal education and spent most of his life in the tiny hamlet of Gwernogle in Carmarthenshire or travelling around the fairs of Glamorganshire to sell his ware. Yet he corresponded with William Frend and received books from Theophilus Lindsey, whose support also enabled him to build the first Unitarian chapel in Wales in 1796, though he had preached Unitarianism from a consecrated part of his paternal home since 1786.[162] By 1794, when he set up his intensely religious but highly radical periodical, he had published the first Unitarian sermons in Welsh and translated Joseph Priestley's *An Appeal to the Serious and Candid Professors of Christianity*, thus earning himself the byname 'little Priestley' ('Priestley bach').[163] In 1801 he was sentenced to two years in prison, to be pilloried twice, and bound over to keep the peace for seven years for allegedly singing a seditious song at what appeared to be a local bid-ale.[164] While this particular charge may have been trumped up, the contents of his surviving manuscript 'Y Gell Gymysg' (The Mixed Repository) and of his serial publication were clearly seditious. The punishment did not put an end to his Unitarian convictions – he published a volume of hymns in 1811 and became the Unitarian minister of Hen Dŷ Cwrdd chapel in Aberdare in the same year – but it diminished his radical political voice.[165]

The least is known about David Davies (d. 1807), the editor of the Chester-published *Geirgrawn*, who also hailed from Carmarthenshire and trained at the Dissenting academy, then at Swansea, in 1786.[166] From 1790 he ministered at Holywell church in north Wales, from where he also edited his periodical. There is evidence that Davies's congregation in Holywell had been unhappy with his radical leanings for some time before he left in 1800. Nothing was heard of him until 1802, when he moved to minister in Welshpool. He spent the last four years of his life as the respected minister of Stoneway church in Bridgnorth.[167]

Significantly, all three periodicals appeared mainly in areas marked by moderate urbanization and a strong incidence of either religious radicalism or populist rioting. Morgan John Rhys may have published the first two numbers of his *Cylch-grawn Cynmraeg* at the Methodist settlement of Trefeca, where he had sought refuge on his return from France, but he was not suffered for long. The commune's minutes display anxieties about this radical and his publications, and the leader of the 'family', Moses Evans, prayed almost daily for the removal of this dangerous man.[168] His wish was granted and the remaining three numbers of *Cylch-grawn Cynmraeg* were printed by John Ross at Carmarthen.[169] 'Rebellious Carmarthen town', the economic centre of the fertile Towy lowlands situated on the main postal road from London to St David's, was not only the 'Emporium of south-east Wales',[170] but the most important centre of Welsh publishing in the eighteenth century, the location of a Dissenting academy and situated in an area where rational Dissent had flourished for nearly a century.[171] It is where one would expect the emergence of a radical Welsh serial. Unsurprisingly, Tomos Glyn Cothi's *Drysorfa Gymmysgedig* was also printed by John Ross at Carmarthen. It publicly connected itself with its predecessor by advertising that it was 'similar to the Cylchgrawn which was published recently' ('cyffelyb i'r Cylchgrawn a argraphwyd yn ddiweddar').[172] David Davies's *Geirgrawn* came from the riot-prone north-east, an industrializing region so shaken by disturbances that even the Methodists came under strong suspicion of preaching sermons based on Paine's *Rights of Man* here in the mid-1790s.[173] Edited in Holywell, an important centre of Welsh print-culture, it was brought out by the short-lived publishing house of J. Minshull in nearby Chester, a town which had been the urban focus for its Welsh hinterland since Roman times.[174]

The three editors aimed at all parts of Welsh-speaking Wales as well as their compatriots in London, but the scale of their undertaking may be measured by David Davies's sales pitch that 'Hundreds can reach and read books of a value as reasonable as *Four pence*, every month, who do not have the money to buy nor the leisure to read more substantial books' ('Gall cantoedd gyrraedd a darllain llyfrau o werth môr rhesymmol, a *Phedair ceiniog*, bob mis, nad oes ganthynt nag arian i brynu na hamdden i ddarllain

Y

# GEIRGRAWN;

NEU

DRYSORFA GWYBODAETH.

AM FAI, 1796.

GAN

D. DAVIES.

GWELL GWYBODAETH NAG AUR.

RHIF. IV.

PLYG. I.

CYNNWYSIAD.



CAERLLEON:

ARGRAPHWYD AC AR WERTH GAN W. MINSHULL:

AR WERTH HEFYD GAN E. CARNES, TREFFYNNON; W. EDWARDS, CROESOSWALLT; E. EDWARDS, RUTHIN; T. RODEN, DINBYCH; J. ROSS, AC J. DANIEL, CAERFYRDDIN; A. TYE. WREXHAM; A CHAN BAWB LLYFRWERTHWYR TRWY GYMRU :....A CHAN D. PRICE, RHIF. 25, WALBROOK, A D. A P. DAVIES, RHIF. 5, TOOLEY-STREET, GERLLAW PONT, LLUNDAIN.

*(GWERTH PEDAIR CEINIOG.)*

Figure 3. Title page of *Y Geirgrawn*

llyfrau mwy') [DOCUMENT 5.9]. Religious publications, Welsh almanacs and the flood of cheap, mostly loyalist Welsh ballads probably reached many more Welsh readers than these rather high-brow and relatively expensive periodicals. The information on distribution and readership of the journals, gleaned from manuscripts, inscriptions in printed items, and the pages of the periodicals themselves, speaks mainly of difficulties. *Cylch-grawn Cynmraeg* announced in its *impressum* that it was sold in Carmarthen, Machynlleth, Amlwch, Caernarfon, Aberystwyth, Merthyr Tydfil, Cardiff and Cardigan, as well as in Bristol and London, and Morgan John Rhys wrote of sending twelve copies to a Welsh bookseller in London with whom he was acquainted.[175] In another letter, he complained about 'the blundering printer' who had sent too many copies to north Wales 'till he had none left for London & even some places in south Wales'. Fifty of these were to be sent off to London.[176] The print run of his serial, therefore, must have been in the lower hundreds. Distribution was difficult, too. In the third number of his *Cylch-grawn Cynmraeg*, Rhys noted that 'Only two things prevent the *Magazine* from taking its place through Wales generally; these are, the difficulty of distributing it and of collecting the money for it' ('Nid oes ond dau beth yn attal y *Cylchgrawn* rhag cymmeryd lle yn gyffredinol trwy Gymru; hynny yw, yr anhawsdra o'u dosbarthu a chasglu'r arian am danynt') [DOCUMENT 7.6]. He hoped that the situation could be remedied by finding patriotic Welshmen to distribute the serial throughout Wales, but on 2 April 1794 he had to inform William Owen Pughe in London that 'for want of time to pay proper attention, and sufficient encouragement I am oblig'd to give up the Welsh magazine'.[177] The last number of *Cylch-grawn Cynmraeg* clarifies that the reason for its failure was lack of finance and distribution, but hope for a successor bi-weekly was sustained [DOCUMENT 7.12]. Thomas Evans's *Drysorfa Gymmysgedig*, with its strong focus on the politico-religious message of Unitarianism, was even less likely to succeed financially. It does not surprise that it only lasted three numbers. A note on the last page of its last number indicates that a fourth was anticipated, but it never appeared.[178] *Y Geirgrawn*, the most professionally conducted of the three serials, listed individual agents in Holywell, Oswestry, Caernarfon, Carmarthen and London as well as stressing that the journal was sold by every bookseller in Wales,[179] but it disappeared as suddenly as *Y Drysorfa Gymmysgedig* amid rumours of the editor's harassment by government officials. Davies himself had used the editorial notes on the inside cover of his serial to defend his publication against accusations of spreading 'riot and rebellion' ('terfysg a gwrthryfel') and Thomas Roberts, Llwynrhudol, the author of the radical pamphlet *Cwyn yn erbyn Gorthrymder* (A Complaint against Oppression), also indicated that *Y Geirgrawn* ceased because Davies had been threatened by the state authorities.[180] Several contributions in the last number were 'to be continued', among them the eulogy on America which closes this anthology [DOCUMENT 9.9].

Yet, there is evidence that *Y Cylch-grawn Cynmraeg* was read by young Dissenters in mid Wales, who regarded studying it as part of their education.[181] In the same area, the cobbler John Davies not only copied poetry out of *Y Cylch-grawn Cynmraeg* and *Y Geirgrawn*, but noted the further distribution of the former in his diary: 'Lent my cylchgrawn to Thos. Davies', who returned it after a month.[182] Letters of leading London Welsh figures provide evidence that *Y Cylch-grawn Cynmraeg* reached them, too, although the judgement of Owen Jones (Owain Myfyr), who financed most of the London Welsh efforts on behalf of the Welsh language and its culture, was that it was 'too narrow and partisan' ('rhy gyfyng a phleidiol') in its contents. He would have preferred something along the lines of the *Eurgrawn* of 1770.[183] The inscription of his nephew, the gifted scribe and amateur artist Hugh Maurice,[184] in his bound volume of *Y Geirgrawn* shows that leading Welsh radical Jac Glan-y-gors took care to distribute this serial among the London Welsh:

> Y Geirgrawn hon a gefais gan John Jones Glan y Gors ef oedd yn ei gwerthu dros y Goruchwiliwr David Davies yma yn Llundain ac yn fynych yn gwneud cyfleusdra iddo. A'r Goruchwiliwr a dalodd adref yn helaeth iddo drwy gymryd llawer faint o Ogan y gwyr a fuant mor rhyfygus a cheisio pigo y Seren tan Gwmwl.[185]

> (I got this Geirgrawn from John Jones Glan y Gors who was selling it on behalf of the Editor David Davies here in London and would often do him favours. And the Editor paid him back handsomely by publishing much of the Lampooning of the men who dared to try and prick the Seren tan Gwmwl [Star under a Cloud].)

An address on behalf of *Y Geirgrawn* to a meeting of the Gwyneddigion society confirms Jac Glan-y-gors's role as a connecting link between the editor and the London Welsh [DOCUMENT 9.7]. The news provided in the periodicals clearly also underwent 'significant reading' and evoked public responses. The report of the defection of the Republican General Charles François Dumourier, for instance, first reported in *Y Cylch-grawn Cynmraeg*, was later satirically interpreted in an 'Epitaph to the Traitor Dumourier' composed by David Davis, Castellhywel [DOCUMENT 7.10].[186] The newsflash from the Continent contained in the fourth number of *Y Geirgrawn* provided the translator of the 'Marseillaise' with material for his radical introduction to the song [DOCUMENTS 9.4, 9.5]. The

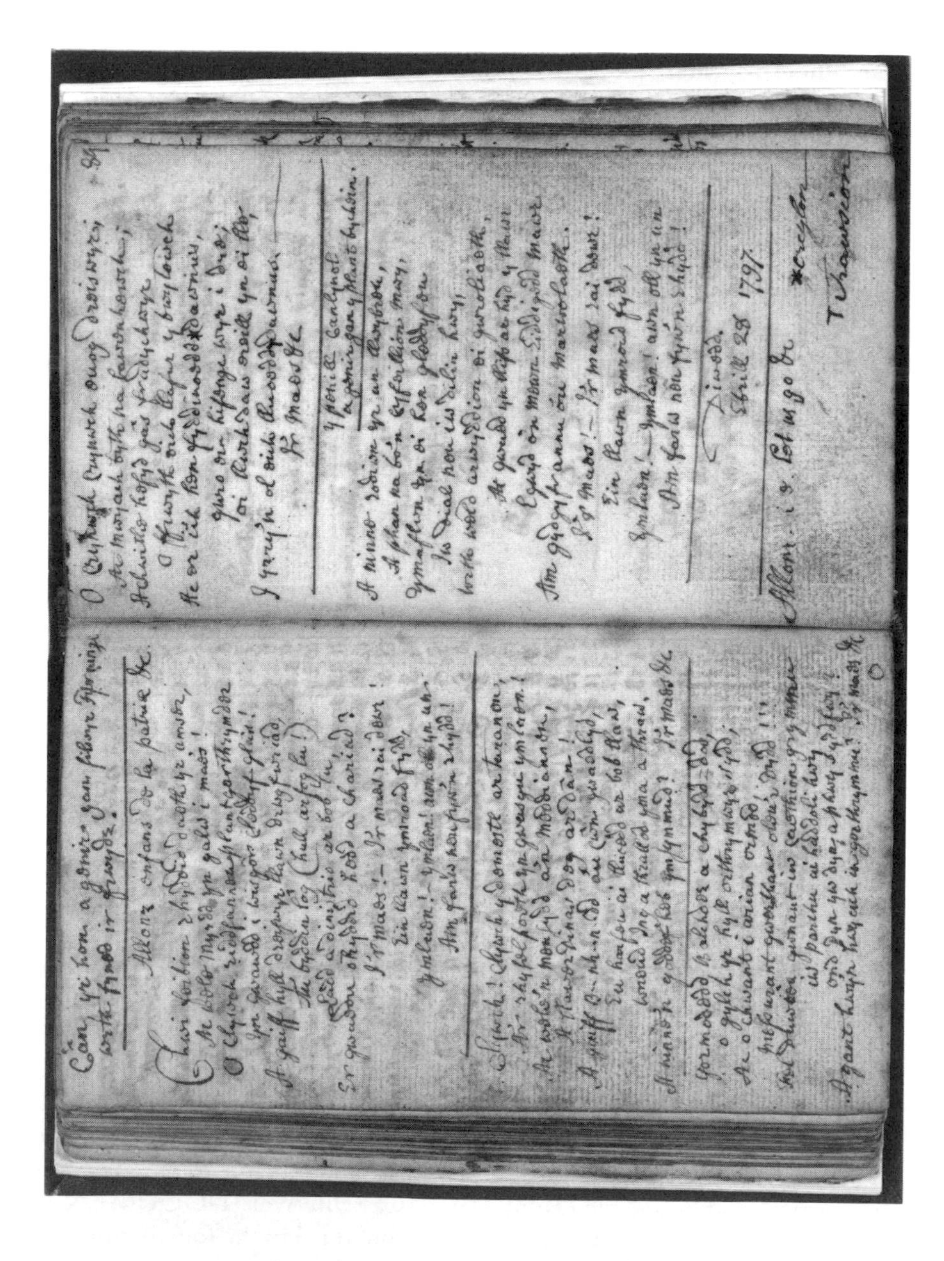

Figure 4. A copy of 'Cân Rhyddid', the Welsh 'Marseillaise', in the diary of John Davies, Llanfihangel Ystrad, Cardiganshire

resulting 'Cân Rhyddid' (The Song of Liberty) itself was not only copied into various manuscripts (Fig. 4), but was added to and became part of a Welsh 'treason trial'.[187]

It is striking, however, that less material than from English serial publications appears to have been copied from these Welsh periodicals into manuscript. They may have been more readily available than the English papers, which is also illustrated by the fact that various copies survive in bound volumes of miscellanea of the period. They may have been considered too dangerous to display and therefore remained hidden, like the *Hog's Wash* in David Jenkin Rees's study. Alas, they may just have been too high-brow, too radical and too expensive to make a decisive impact.[188]

### *A Welsh Enlightenment*

However short-lived, these three Welsh periodicals were brave attempts to revolutionize the public discourse in Wales by giving monolingual Welshmen public media in their own language, thereby achieving the double aim of enlightening them and doing so in their native tongue. All three editors were political and religious radicals, yet their publications pursued a wider Enlightenment project which encompassed the whole nation. Morgan John Rhys wished to place 'before the Welshman the various opinions which he hears being discussed, so that he may know something about them' ('o flaen y Cymro, yr amrywiol farnau y mae'n clywed dadleu yn eu cylch, fel y gallo wybod rhyw beth am danynt') [DOCUMENT 7.6], while David Davies announced that his *Geirgrawn* would be open to everybody 'to express their thoughts on religious and political matters, as long as they convey them in a spirit of tenderness and love' ('i fynegi eu meddyliau am bethau crefyddol a dinasaidd, ond iddynt eu hamlygu mewn yspryd addfwynder a chariad') [DOCUMENT 5.9]. What enabled this broad platform was a Welsh cultural nationalism that transcended political and religious divisions. Enlightening the nation was as important for the Welsh intelligentsia as it was for the radical organizations of the other three nations of the British archipelago.[189] In Wales, however, the medium was the indigenous language, Welsh. Teaching its appreciation, developing its potential as a modern medium of communication, and presenting its literary treasures and historic feats were essential components of the Welsh Enlightenment.

Issue three of *Cylch-grawn Cynmraeg*, for instance, opened with an 'Enlightenment' sequence of poetry and prose by contributors from a wide political and religious spectrum. A Welsh poem by the Baptist Dafydd Sa[u]nders greeted the journal as a 'gate to enlightenment treasure' ('drws yw / I drysor goleuni') (see p. v above), while the editor himself promised 'to enlighten the country in things natural as well as spiritual' ('goleuo'r wlad mewn pethau naturiol yn gystal ac ysbrydol') [DOCUMENT 7.6].[190] His editorial was followed by a letter whose style and contents suggest that this may be the contribution the radical Iolo Morganwg had long promised him.[191] Using the pseudonym 'Bruttwn Bach' (Little Briton), Iolo addressed Wales in its entirety, but chiefly called on the educated classes to rally to the task of enabling the 'nation of the Welsh' ('cenedl y Cymry') – which had 'no less reason, ability and readiness to receive education than other Nations' ('Nid . . . yn gronyn llai eu synwyr, eu medr, a'u parodrwydd i dderbyn addysg nag ydoedd Cenhedloedd eraill') – to achieve its full potential [DOCUMENT 7.6]. Hard on his heels, his conservative arch-enemy, Dafydd Ddu Eryri, also called on learned Welshmen to share their knowledge, comparing their forsaking the Welsh language to the immoral act of disowning one's mother:

> mae'n resyn eich bod yn diystyru eich Iaith gynhenid, Iaith yr hon a roddes i chwi faeth a sugn, Iaith y Wlad, ymha un yr agorasoch gyntaf eich amrantau i weled goleu dydd. Pa leshâd yw i chwi fod yn gydnabyddus mewn gwledydd pellenig ac yn ddieithr gartref. O chwychwi, feibion anffyddlon *Cambria*, gwridwch a chywilyddiwch am y gwall [DOCUMENT 7.6].
>
> (It is a pity that you scorn your native Language, the Language of her who nourished and suckled you, the Language of the Country in which you first opened your eyelashes to see the light of day. Of what advantage to you is it to be acquainted with far-flung countries and foreign at home. Oh, you unfaithful sons of *Cambria*, blush and be ashamed of this negligence.)

Dafydd Ddu Eryri ended this series with a second poem in praise of the Welsh language.[192] The only long prose text in the Welsh language found in the provincial papers which catered to the Welsh reading public, the advertisement for David Davies's *Geirgrawn*, also pitched itself as a means of helping the 'monolingual Welsh' ('Cymry uniaith') compete with their English neighbours by 'dispersing the fog of ignorance which envelopes Wales' ('i chwalu ymaith y gaddug anwybodaeth sy'n gorchuddio Cymru') [DOCUMENT 5.9]. Davies's opening address in the periodical itself was in a similar vein, yet here the cultural nationalism was more openly leavened with English-inspired radicalism:

> Ereill ag sy'n ymhonni o'u dysg a'u gwybodaeth, gan faint eu hynfydrwydd, a'u balchedd, rhodres, a choegni, ydynt yn eich diystyru chwi, ac yn eich tybied

> ddim yn amgen, na chwaith yn deilwyng o well enw, na *lliaws mochaidd*, wedi eu trefnu gan ragluniaeth i ddim amgenach na thrin a thrafod y baw. Gresynol yw meddwl, eich bod yn cael eich esgeuluso gan rai, a'ch dirmygu gan ereill; ac nad oes moddion cymmwys yn cael eu harfer gan y gwybedyddion, medrus yn eich iaith eich hunain, tu ag at eich dwyn i adnabod mae dynion ac nid ysgrubliaid ydych, ac i fod breintiau dynol yn perthyn i chwi.[193]

> (Others, who boast of their learning and their knowledge, because their foolishness and their pride, pomp and vanity are so great, they disregard you, and consider you nothing more, nor deserving of a better name than the *swinish multitude*, ordained by providence for nothing other than to handle the dung. It is deplorable that you are neglected by some and despised by others; and that no suitable methods are employed by the learned men, skilled in your own language, towards bringing you to recognize that you are men and not beasts, and that human rights belong to you.)

In the last number of his *Cylch-grawn Cynmraeg* Morgan John Rhys struck a similar chord in linking a denial of free enquiry in the press with ignorance and despotism:

> Dylai'r argraph-wasg gael ei chynnal yn rhydd ac yn agored, i ymresymmu a dadleu ar bob pwngc o ddifinyddiaeth a llywodraeth . . . Un o'r pechodau mwyaf atgas yn y byd yw gwrthwynebu ymofyniad rhydd am y gwirionedd. Y mae'n profi'n ddiamheuol, achos drwg, os na oddef ddywedyd ac ymresymmu'n deg yn ei erbyn; y canghenau sy'n tarddu'n naturiol oddiar y gwreiddyn hwn yw pob math o draws-lywodraeth; a pha le bynnag y byddo hyn i'w weled, y mae anfoesoldeb yn cynhyddu; canys nid y *drwg*, eithr y *da*, y mae gormeswyr yn wastad yn ei wrthwynebu.[194]

> (The press should be conducted free and openly, to reason and argue on any subject of theology and government . . . It is one of the most odious sins in the world to stand in the way of free enquiry after the truth. A cause which does not suffer speaking and fair reasoning against it is indisputably proven as bad; the branches which naturally come from this root are all manners of despotism; and wherever it is to be observed, immorality increases; because it is not the *bad*, but the *good*, which oppressors always stand against.)

As happened among other 'small, submerged peoples',[195] all three periodicals endeavoured to develop Welsh into a suitable medium for communicating the new concepts and branches of learning and to make the literary treasures and history of the Welsh language better known to its speakers. Morgan John Rhys showed public support for the linguistic reforms of William Owen Pughe which, he privately hoped, would 'restore the Welsh language to its primitive purity as well as to improve the minds of our countrymen'.[196] He opened the first number of *Cylch-grawn Cynmraeg* with eleven points of advice on how to 'learn to Read correctly' ('i ddysgu Darllain yn gywir') and an introduction, in the new orthography, to Owen Pughe's reformed Welsh spelling.[197] Alas, the Welsh public proved unready for this new system, which looked curiously like a Welsh version of Thomas Spence's equalizing English orthography of the 1780s and was almost contemporaneous with the first attempts by Noah Webster to 'nationalize' American English.[198] Even in April 1793 Rhys had to inform his friend 'that there is but little encouragement to the proposed amendment in the language'.[199] The traditional orthography, used in Welsh publications since 1588, was thus upheld, but editors and contributors alike strove to expand the Welsh lexicon by creating new terms. The English equivalent or explanation of a new word was mostly added in brackets or in explanatory footnotes. This new vocabulary, much of it inspired by the French Revolution, thus entered Welsh via the English language. It centred on politics, coining Welsh expressions for concepts such as 'feudal law', 'high treason', 'republicans', 'democrats' and 'national convention' [DOCUMENTS 7.1, 7.9],[200] but also encompassed the natural sciences. Both *Cylch-grawn Cynmraeg* and *Y Geirgrawn* ran series of articles on what was then known as 'natural philosophy' ('anianyddiaeth'),[201] and Welsh readers were familiarized with expressions for concepts such as the 'solar system' ('crynodeb') and the 'universe' ('bydyssawd').[202] Printing influential Renaissance texts, such as a Welsh version of John Davies's Latin preface to his *Dictionarium Duplex* of 1632, reminded readers of past literary achievements, while assisting them in improving the rhetoric and style of their Welsh.[203] Poems from the classical canon of Welsh literature may have served a similar purpose, but, together with descriptions of Welsh historical traditions and antiquities, they also presented contemporary Welshmen with a vision of a glorious past in which native princes governed justly and patronized the arts.[204]

### *America*

Prehistoric Britain and medieval Wales may have furnished a glorious past, but for many Welshmen, the future lay in the religious and civil liberty offered by America. The idealization of America was a constant presence in these serials, either as theme or as background. Here, almanacs and provincial papers had already prepared the ground. In 1789, for instance, the *Hereford Journal* had printed a series of letters 'from a Gentleman in America to his friend in south Wales' which described the riches of the country and the success of the Moravians there.[205] Welsh radicals followed suit by broadcasting how religious and civil liberty had been secured in America by separating church and state [DOCUMENTS 7.8, 9.3],[206] by describing the economic success of a country which had so far steered clear of involvement in the European wars [DOCUMENT 7.9], and by printing letters from America [DOCUMENT 9.1] which confirmed this success story.[207] Translations from the work of Benjamin Franklin and appreciative American addresses to Joseph Priestley received pride of place.[208] All contributions on the theme of America stressed the contrast between the old world – which was ravaged by wars and where Dissenters were oppressed by an alliance of church and state – and America, where liberty and humanity had made their home [DOCUMENT 9.9].

Wales's past and America's present blended in the sixteenth-century story of Welsh Prince Madog's discovery of America in the 1170s and the possible survival of Welsh descendents in central north America, which excited the imagination of Welsh radicals towards the end of the eighteenth century.[209] The *Hereford Journal* had publicized an assertion of this fact in 1789 [DOCUMENT 2.2], advertised John Williams's 1791 volume, *An Inquiry into the Truth of the Tradition Concerning the Discovery of America by Prince Madog ap Owen Gwynedd*, and printed extracts from it, all of which fanned Welsh 'Madoc fever'.[210] A 'Madogeion' society was established in London and both Iolo Morganwg and John Evans prepared to sail for America, but only Evans set out in autumn 1792. While he failed to find the fabled Welsh Indians, he was successful in mapping 2,000 miles of the river Missouri and attained a position of authority among the Mandan Indians before returning to St Louis in 1797, where he died in 1799.[211] Back home in Wales, as well as in Welsh American circles, his journey excited high hopes and was eagerly reported in *Cylch-grawn Cynmraeg* and later in *Y Geirgrawn* [DOCUMENTS 7.4, 9.1].[212] Like Iolo Morganwg's 'ancient' brotherhood of democratic druids and William Owen Pughe's efforts to take the Welsh language itself back to its most primitive and therefore purest form, the search for 'Welsh Indians' distilled a desire to reinstate a naturally democratic society of ancient Britons *à la* Rousseau, before the advent of the double yoke of Roman church and Saxon state. Prince Madog's fictional speech on leaving the war-torn shores of the British Isles, a key text of Welsh Romanticism which was probably authored by Morgan John Rhys himself, was the perfect vehicle for expressing this coded message of disaffection with the present British state [DOCUMENT 7.3].[213] Within three years, Morgan John Rhys had put his rhetoric into practice by founding 'Cambria', a Welsh colony in the Allegheny Mountains whose capital he named Beulah, after Isaiah 62: 4.[214] There the Welsh, so he hoped, might settle together, enjoying liberty and religious toleration. The classical poetic exhortation by Dafydd Saunders to 'say farewell' ('ffarwèlo') and travel 'to dear *Washington*' ('at *Washington* anwyl'), which appeared at the end of the last issue of *Y Geirgrawn* [DOCUMENT 9.9], may well have been inspired by Rhys's description of his travels there in an earlier issue of the periodical [DOCUMENT 9.1].

*Politics and religion*

In 1793, however, Morgan John Rhys had not yet given up hope of reforming and educating his compatriots at home. With the first number of *Cylch-grawn Cynmraeg* he began a series perhaps inspired by Montesquieu, which aimed at giving 'the history, (each in its turn) of the system of the governments of the world', ('roddi hanes, (yn ei dro) am drefn llywodraethau'r byd'), beginning with 'the government of England' ('[l]lywodraeth Lloegr') [DOCUMENT 7.1].[215] Like other lengthy contributions to the periodicals, the series aimed at educating rather than radicalizing, although it contained some criticism of war and an exhortation for a fairer system of voting. Gwallter Mechain's prize-winning essay, tantalizingly advertised in the *Chester Chronicle* as the 'first attempt in the Welsh tongue' on the subject of 'liberty',[216] and serialized in *Y Geirgrawn*, may have employed tropes current in progressive writing at the end of the eighteenth century, but it was essentially a unionist text. Having explained how the Saxons imposed their 'iron yoke' ('iau haiarnaidd') on the Britons, for which they were punished with their own, Norman, yoke,[217] he outlined how the Welsh regained their liberty through Henry VIII's Acts of Union (1536/1542), which abolished Wales as an entity and prohibited the official use of the Welsh language, but gave Welshmen equal rights with the English as subjects of the English Crown. In a Welsh take on the Whig interpretation of history, he rejoiced:

> Yn awr, disglaer belydr Rhyddid a dywynodd ar ardaloedd *Cymru,* cafodd ei thrigolion fwynhau yr un hynawsaidd gyfreithiau a'i gelynion gynt.[218]
>
> (And then the splendid ray of Liberty shone on the regions of *Wales*, whose inhabitants were allowed to enjoy the same genial laws as their former foes.)

Only *Y Geirgrawn* dared explore the political background to the French Revolution and the Revolutionary Wars in a radical political series correspondent with the strongly republican 'Brief Sketch of the French Revolution, and of the Motives which Led to the War between the Confederate Powers and the French; Extracted from the Most Popular Authors', which had only just appeared in the neighbouring *Chester Chronicle*, signed 'W. X.'.[219] The historical account justified the 'memorable revolution' ('wiwgof gyfnewidiad') as necessary by giving graphic descriptions of the cruelty of 'feudal tyranny' before celebrating the overthrow of the *ancien régime*:

> Pan gafodd yr arglwyddaidd lywodraeth ag oedd wedi gormesu pobl Ffrainc dros oesoedd ei diddymmu, hwy a ddechreuasant y gwaith, o lunio trefn-lywodraeth newydd i ddiogelu ei breintiau fal dinasyddion a deiliaid gwlad rhydd.[220]

> (When the despotism, which had oppressed the French people for ages, was destroyed, they began the work of forming a Constitution, to secure their rights as citizens and subjects of a free nation.)[221]

The unfavourable reaction of the remainder of the European *ancien régime* to the ideals of this free nation, which led to the present wars, was outlined in further instalments in the *Chester Chronicle*. In *Y Geirgrawn*, these were missing. The editor had received accusations of 'spreading riot and rebellion' ('lledu terfysg a gwrthryfel') and may have had to adopt a more cautious approach for the remaining issues of his journal.[222]

In the face of accusations and threats, the editors pursued a range of tactics to convey their political message: by granting publication of texts or censoring them, by contributing material themselves, and by commenting on that which appeared. Long footnotes and even longer rejoinders refuted the unacceptable content of conservative contributions [DOCUMENT 9.6]. The negative account given of 'Cyflwr Crefydd yn America' (The State of Religion in America), for instance, was followed by an editorial vindication which was nearly twice as long as the original article.[223] David Davies used the cover of his periodical for a monthly castigation of politically suspect practices and writings. In his first address 'To our Correspondents' ('At ein Gohebwyr'), he censured the London preacher who, in a religious service, had:

> *dywe'yd wrth ei wrandawyr fod* Tom Paine *wedi gwneuthur mwy o ddrwg yn y byd na deugain o gythreuliaid; a son am ei zeal i offrymmu gwaith y gwr (*enwog!*) hwnnw, ag oedd wedi cael ei fenthyg i'r Tân.*[224]

> *(told his listeners that* Tom Paine *had done more evil in the world than forty demons; and who had spoken of his zeal to sacrifice the work of this (*famous!*) man, which he had been lent, to the Fire.)*

The editors' Enlightenment values may have led them to allow the voicing of selected establishment views, but certain subjects were unacceptable to their religious and political radicalism. No material in support of war appeared whatsoever, for instance. In fact, all three periodicals carried a strongly anti-war message. A graphic account of a battle bemoaned the fate of the common man, 'who possesses the natural right to enjoy liberty' ('yr hwn sydd yn meddu hawl naturiol i fwynhau rhyddid'), who is barbarized and then killed on the bloody battlefield.[225] Radical anti-fast-day prayers and hymns called on God to punish bloodthirsty despots [DOCUMENTS 8.2, 8.3, 8.4] and poems in praise of peace condemned the insanity of the current bloodshed [DOCUMENT 9.9].[226]

*News as politics*

The news sections of the periodicals also contained strong condemnations of the present wars as 'the refuse of antichrist' ('Gweddill anghrist') [DOCUMENT 7.5], and often ended in invocations to the Lord to 'hasten the time when the swords will be turned into ploughshares and the spears into pruning-hooks, and the nations will cease to counsel war anymore' ('brysuro'r amser, i'r cleddyfau i gael eu troi yn sychau a'r gwaew ffyn yn bladuriau, a'r cenhedloedd i beidio dysgu rhyfel mwyach') [DOCUMENTS 9.4, 7.5].[227]

Featured in all three periodicals under headings such as 'Arwyddion yr Amserau' (Signs of the Times), 'Myfyrdodau ar yr Amserau' (Meditations on the Times), 'Newyddion Pellenig a Chartrefol' (Foreign and Home News), 'Yr Amserau' (The Times) or in the form of letters, the news provided another opportunity of imparting radical political education. Short notes on trials for libel embedded in these news sections [DOCUMENT 7.9] as well as translations of treason trial pamphlets sided with the accused and thus gave English radicals, such as Jeremiah Joyce, an additional stage in a different language.[228] The report on the execution of Marie Antoinette in *Cylch-grawn Cynmraeg* [DOCUMENT 7.11] differed markedly from the accounts in the loyalist papers, such as the *Shrewsbury Chronicle*, 1 November 1793, which labelled it a 'murder' [DOCUMENT 2.6]. Reporting the news in 'Arwyddion yr Amserau' enabled Morgan John Rhys to criticize the British electoral system more openly than he had dared in the educational series on government, and to advocate 'dear liberty' ('cu ryddid') [DOCUMENT 7.5]. In his news reports, he recommended the Society of the Friends of the People, 'which every man who loves his country should support' ('a ddylai pob dyn sy'n caru ei wlad ei chynnorthwyo').[229] The news that Catherine the Great, empress of Russia, had held a day of thanksgiving for the successful conquest of Poland was an opportunity to ask his readers two pertinent questions:

> A ydyw'r Hollalluog ddim yn gofyn cyfiawnder oddiwrth ymerawdwyr a brenhinoedd yn gystal a'r cyffredin bobl? Ac a ydyw'n llai o bechod ynddynt hwy i ladd dynion a lladratta nag eraill?[230]
>
> (Does the Almighty not ask justice of emperors and kings as well as of the common people? Is it less sinful for them to kill people and to steal than for others?)

It was only in his 'Myfyrdodau ar yr Amserau' (Meditations on the Times) in the final number of *Cylch-grawn Cynmraeg* that Morgan John Rhys debated the importance of liberty, past and present, for common man and state alike. Here he felt free to proceed from the biblical account of Moses's liberation to the anti-slavery ideas of Montesquieu and the destruction of 'that cruel dungeon, the *Bastille*' ('y carchar creulon hwnnw, y *Bastile*').[231] However, following radical English writing of the time, his 'Arwyddion yr Amserau' (Signs of the Times) also had an eschatological explanation for the French Revolution as 'God's retributive justice for the Capet's bloody persecution of the Protestants and for their vicious abuse of power'.[232] His compatriots were not exempt from the coming wrath of God. He warned that they must:

> deffroi i gyfiawnder, ac ystyried yn ddwys, pa un a ydyw'r barn yn hongian uwch eu pen hwythau ai peidio; nid beio a melldithio'r *Ffrangcod*, ond ymgadw rhag bod yn euog o'u pechodau, a diwygio'n bucheddau yw'r ffordd i ymgadw rhag y gospedigaeth. Mae'n sicr na all y deyrnas hon ddim dihangyd rhag barn Duw, os na edifarha a diwygio ar frys . . . [DOCUMENT 7.9]
>
> (wake up to justice, and consider earnestly whether or not the judgement hangs over their heads; not to blame and curse the *French*, but to refrain from being guilty of their sins, and to reform our lives is the way to avoid the punishment. It is certain that this kingdom cannot escape God's judgement if it does not repent and reform in haste . . .)

*Religion as politics*

According to Gwyn A. Williams the language of the popular movement in Britain was 'steeped in the Bible'.[233] In Wales, a country in which Baptists and Quakers as well as Methodists and Unitarians competed with the Established Church for the hearts and minds of the common people, the close connection between religion and politics was even more pronounced than in England. Religious education was part of the Welsh Enlightenment project and all editors professed to advocate a broad church. Morgan John Rhys promised to refrain from promoting one denomination at the expense of another in this wilderness of religious voices [DOCUMENT 7.6], and in a touching meditation on religion Tomos Glyn Cothi invited representatives of all denominations to join him in prayer and to 'have supper together with good will towards one another, like a virtuous society' ('swpperu ynghyd gyd ag ewyllys da y naill at y llall, fel cymdeithas rinweddol') [DOCUMENT 8.1]. This tolerance meant that the most vociferous Churchmen, Dafydd Ddu Eryri, Peter Bailey Williams (Peris) and Edward Charles (Siamas Wynedd), were invited to contribute.[234] But like the news, their views became the foil to the radical and dissenting voices which dominated the discourse here. The '*Cywydd* to the Trinity' ('Cywydd i'r Drindod') by 'I. E.' was placed directly opposite 'The Song of Liberty' ('Cân Rhyddid') [DOCUMENT 9.5],[235] and the anti-Methodist rants of Siamas Wynedd were only tolerated in one contribution before receiving a public refutation.[236] Peris may have been allowed to publicly defend the Established Church in a two-part contribution,[237] but he was countered by a letter,[238] and by a dialogue between 'A Christian Bishop and a Disciple Called Serious Inquiry' ('Ymddiddan rhwng Esgob Crist'nogol a Disgybl a Elwir Dyfal-Geisio'), which strongly denied establishment the authority of God:

> Rhaid i bawb gyfaddef, fod yn angenrheidiol i'r cyfryw a gymmerant y gwaith mewn llaw o sefydlu crefydd, i dderbyn awdurdod oddiwrth Dduw i wneuthur hynny; ond ni roddodd Duw y cyfryw awdurdod yn ei air, na thrwy neb moddion eraill; nac i'r Pab, na 'chwaith i Mahomet; nac i neb rhyw dreiswyr eraill; am hynny, rhyfyg, i'r graddau mwyaf, yw i neb, pa bynnag, i honni fod ganddynt y cyfryw awdurdod.[239]
>
> (Everyone must admit that it is necessary for those who take the work of establishing a faith in hand to receive authorization from God to do so; but God did not give such authority in his word, nor through any other means; not to the Pope, nor to Mohamed; nor to any other tyrants; therefore, it is presumptuous in the highest degree for anybody to claim to have such authority.)

In the political climate of the 1790s, in which 'to attack the established church was to attack the established regime in the state',[240] this was a radical political message.

The main religious principles advocated in all three periodicals were the promotion of Dissenting Protestantism, a return to the equality and simplicity of the early church, and a refutation of any connection between religion and state power, especially its use in the conduct of war. 'Establishment' was an obstruction and a danger to true Christianity. Religious contributions thus embraced a history and philosophy of Christianity which highlighted the biographies of martyrs and leaders of Protestant Christianity – from

Servetus and Thomas de Laune to Andrew Dudith, George Whitefield and Joseph Priestley – and featured translations of their writings.[241] 'Question and Answer' pieces explained 'Why I Dissent from the Established Church' ('Pa ham yr Ydwyf yn Ymneillduo oddi wrth yr Eglwys Sefydledig'),[242] and *Y Drysorfa Gymmysgedig*, the most radically religious of the three periodicals, featured two series explaining the advantages of Unitarianism to those still shackled by the Trinity, in which Luther and Calvin were cited in defence of the doctrine of the *One* God.[243]

Historical essays outlined the 'degeneration' ('dirywiaeth') of the Christian faith from its pure beginnings.[244] In the British Isles, this was exemplified by the introduction of regular tithes by King Offa of Mercia, which, in the series on 'Hanes Degymau' (A History of Tithes), conveniently also served the anti-English cause.[245] Tomos Glyn Cothi's sermon on the 'true nature of the church of Christ' ('gwir nattur eglwys Crist') stressed the 'general equality' ('gogyfuwchdra cyffredinol') prevalent in the early church, which was now lost, and attacked any 'CHURCH ESTABLISHED by LAW' ('EGLWYS SEFYDLEDIG trwy y GYFRAITH') as 'unchristian' ('anghristaidd') and therefore dangerously weak [DOCUMENT 8.6]. He concluded that 'there cannot be any kind of alliance between *his church* and the kingdoms of this world' ('ni's gall fod un math o gyngrair rhwng *ei eglwys ef* a theyrnasoedd y byd hwn'). His subversive prayers and hymns on the occasion of the official fast-days directly opposed the British government which was using the Christian faith to aid such an unchristian, secular purpose [DOCUMENTS 8.2, 8.3, 8.4].[246] In these texts Tomos Glyn Cothi called on God himself to throw down the bloodthirsty despots, free the slaves and ensure justice for all to enjoy the fruits of their labour and the rights of man [DOCUMENT 8.3].

The sustained attack on religious misgovernment was often openly connected with a critique of despotic governments. The superficially anti-Catholic poem which 'Philorectum' contributed to *Cylch-grawn Cynmraeg* made the link via a long note beginning with the remark that 'the poetry may be applied to *political* as well as *religious* tyranny' ('Gellir cymmwyso'r farddoniaeth at draws-lywodraeth *ddinasaidd* yn ogystal âg *eglwysaidd*'), because 'Political and religious liberty always go together; and stand or fall with each other' ('mae rhyddid dinasaidd ac eglwysaidd yn wastad yn cyd-fyned; ac yn sefyll, neu syrthio gyd â'u gilydd') [DOCUMENT 7.7]. St Paul's Epistle to the Romans 13: 1–7 and St Peter 2: 13–18, which church representatives regularly utilized to confirm that the authority of government derived from God,[247] were put to very different use by the editors of these periodicals. Morgan John Rhys continued his biblical citation on the divine origin of authority with an exhortation for the common vote, reminding his readers that submitting oneself to ordinances of man for the Lord's sake did 'not in the least abolish every man's right, as a member of society, to have a *voice* in the choice of officers of state' ('nad yw hyn mewn un mesur yn dinystrio'r hawl sydd gan bob dyn, fal aelod o'r gymdeithas, i fod a *llais*, yn newisiad y swyddwyr gwladol') [DOCUMENT 7.1]. David Davies's criticism of Peris's contribution to the *Seren tan Gwmmwl* debate inscribed Paul's words with the even stronger radical message that it was 'utterly impossible for us to honour a wanton, prodigal, drunken, oppressive, despotic and bloody man' ('hollol amhosibl i ni anrhydeddu dyn anllad afradlon, meddw, trahaus, gormesol a gwaedlyd') [DOCUMENT 9.6]. The power of the true Christian church lay in all its members, not in elevated officials or external attributes of power, just as the true authority of the state was with its voters. By separating church and state and promoting religious toleration America had set the world an example which Britain would do well to follow [DOCUMENT 7.8].

*External influence: English radical publications*

Most of the news, ideas and concepts of the French Revolution reached Wales filtered through the English response and the English language, and many of the items in the Welsh radical periodicals originated with English source material or were inspired by contemporary English pieces and genres. Yet even the basic information that a piece was a translation was often missing and the only pointer to translation activity may be a footnote in which the 'translator' ('cyfieithydd') explained a choice of word or phrase.[248] The names of author and translator were often withheld, hidden or disguised. At times, the original author may be guessed from initials, such as 'J. P.', which in this case appeared without comment at the conclusion of a text on the nature of true ordination.[249] Other texts were published using occasional pseudonyms, such as 'Philorectum', 'Carwr Rheswm' (A Lover of Reason), 'Carwr Trefn' (A Lover of Order), 'G' or 'Bŵ' (Boo), which remain enigmatic. In the oppressive climate of the mid-1790s this disappearing act of author and translator was an effective protective strategy, but it has made determining the provenance and authorship of many texts difficult and led later researchers to overestimate the cultural independence and originality of Welsh authors in the 1790s.

Only cautious estimates of the ratio of translated to original material may thus be attempted. Hywel M. Davies has calculated that over 40% of the contents of *Cylch-grawn Cynmraeg* were 'a direct translation or a précis from an English or American source'.[250] In my opinion, at least 30% of the contributions to *Y Drysorfa Gymmysgedig* and *Y Geirgrawn* were rendered from English sources in England and North America. The Welsh radicals, loyalists and patriots who contributed to the serial literature in Wales employed a variety of strategies and techniques, from close translation to paraphrasing and free adaptation,[251] but all had adopted a 'domesticating' approach which attempted to write Welsh texts that would appear natural to their intended audience, not pieces that seemed foreign.[252] This approach has added to the impression of originality which many of the Welsh texts of the period convey and makes the identification of unmarked translations in the three serials problematic.

Many translations, however, such as treason trial reports, excerpts from the accounts of Baptist missionaries in India, chapters from books extolling the advantages of life in America, and translation from famous Protestants like William Frend, were relatively simple renditions of published English texts in Welsh, which concentrated on relaying the information contained in the source text and were sometimes even marked as a 'translation' ('cyfieithiad').[253] The more political and literary pieces tended to be free adaptations, combinations of adaptation and original writing, or texts which were inspired by, rather than translated from, English sources. Morgan John Rhys, for instance, used his wide background reading in Baptist history (perhaps acquired during his time at the Bristol academy) for several series in his *Cylch-grawn Cynmraeg*. His articles on government [DOCUMENT 7.1], according to Hywel M. Davies, resembled the preface to the fifth edition of fellow-Baptist Robert Robinson's *Plan of Lectures*.[254] In the same way, he utilized *An Enquiry into the Obligations of Christians* for his series on the history of the Christian religion in terms of its progress.[255] The influential *Signs of the Times: or the Overthrow of the Papal Tyranny in France, the Prelude of Destruction to Popery and Despotism, but of Peace to Mankind* by James Bicheno was recast by him as part of his series on 'Arwyddion yr Amserau' (The Signs of the Times), interspersed with appeals to his Welsh brethren, even before the first review of the original text appeared.[256]

Tomos Glyn Cothi used a variety of translation techniques while he was editing and writing his *Drysorfa Gymmysgedig*. The writings of his heroes and teachers, such as Benjamin Franklin and William Frend, were translated closely and furnished with references to the original author.[257] Uncovering the provenance of other pieces allows us to follow the creative process which led him from close translation to adaptation and original writing. His first 'Prayer to be used by those people who live under a cruel and tyrannical government, on a day of fast' ('Gweddi i'w harfer gan y bobl a fyddo yn byw dan lywodraeth greulon drahaus, ar ddydd ympryd') [DOCUMENT 8.2] was a close translation of a prayer published in *Politics for the People* in 1794.[258] This was followed by a radical hymn, which was more freely rendered from the same source, and to which he had added at least three new stanzas [DOCUMENT 8.3].[259] The sequence closed with 'Another Prayer to be used by the friends of mankind at the end of worship' ('Gweddi arall i'w harfer gan gyfeillion dynolryw ar ddiwedd addoliad') [DOCUMENT 8.4], which may well be an original composition. Tomos Glyn Cothi also translated another satirical 'Hymn for the Fast Day to be Sung by the Privileged Orders of Europe', which followed the source text of his hymn in *Politics for the People*,[260] as 'Hymn iw chanu gan Orthrymwyr Dynion, ar eu dyddiau ympryd' (A Hymn to be sung by the Oppressors of Men on their fast-days).[261] It was surely intended for a later issue of *Y Drysorfa Gymmysgedig*, but even in the manuscript, the dangerous English source has disappeared.

*Y Geirgrawn* also featured texts which elude simple interpretation. Its radical series on the causes of the French Revolution (see pp. 40–1 above) appeared almost concurrently with the *Chester Chronicle*'s 'Brief Sketch of the French Revolution'. Both versions are so similar and read so fluently that they may well have been composed by the same author and simultaneously.[262] In its fourth number, *Y Geirgrawn* printed the first Welsh version of the 'Marseillaise', entitled 'Cân Rhyddid', i.e. 'The Song of Liberty' [DOCUMENT 9.5], sent it by a 'Gwilym' whose identity still puzzles researchers. 'Gwilym' paraphrased the first three stanzas of the English adaptation of four of the original seven stanzas of the 'Marseillaise', which had appeared in several radical publications, most famously in *Pig's Meat*.[263] The English translator, perhaps Robert Thom[p]son, had 'domesticated' the song with key references to British circumstances, which were reproduced in the Welsh translation. The Welsh allusion to the tyrants who '*Measure, Sell, the light of day!!!*' ('*Mesurant, Gwerthant oleu'r dydd!!!*') was thus not, as E. Gwynn Matthews has surmised, 'original and striking', but closely followed the English translator, who had responded to Thomas Paine's attack on the window tax in the second part of *Rights of Man*.[264] Following stanza three, 'The Song of Liberty' departed from the English version in that it continued with a translation of stanza four of the original, which directly threatened the oppressors, and concluded with stanza five of the original. A detailed treatment of this Welsh translation of the 'Marseillaise' will be published elsewhere,[265] but it deserves our attention that the Welsh translator took his song as far as was possible in the direction of abstract values. The 'children of the fatherland' ('enfants de la patrie'), for instance, who rallied to the banner in the original, became 'sons of France' in the English version, but in Welsh were transformed into 'sons of Liberty' ('[m]eibion Rhyddid'). In the chorus, Welsh citizens were not called to let impure blood water their furrows or march to victory or death, but, adopting the central motto of the French Revolution, they were encouraged to 'go as one, / to die or to live *free*!' ('awn oll yn un, / Am farw, neu fyw'n *rhydd*!'). 'Cân Rhyddid' was one of only two pieces in these periodicals of which parts may have been translated directly from the French original. The other was the 'Hynod Weledigaeth Gŵr Bonheddig o Ffraingc' (The Strange Vision of a Gentleman from France) published in the fourth number of *Cylch-grawn Cynmraeg*, an adaptation of chapter fifteen of the English version of *Les Ruines, ou Méditation sur les Révolutions des Empires* by Constantin François Chassebeuf de Volney. Its opening lines, Gwyn A. Williams has argued, 'are remarkably reminiscent of the original Volney' and may well have come directly from the French.[266]

A close look at the contents of the radical serials in this collection, however, leads us to conclude that the ideas and concepts of the French Revolution largely reached Wales via England and the Welsh language via English. The enormous increase in translation activity and subsequent expansion of the Welsh vocabulary which the 1790s witnessed may, therefore, be counted among the cultural influences the French Revolution exerted on Wales. The rather timid contributor 'Eiddil' (Feeble) pleaded for patience in the last number of *Y Geirgrawn* with the remark that 'though the translator is *old* and *grey-headed* as regards his days, he is only *young* in the art of translation' ('er fod y cyfieithydd yn *hen* ac yn *benllwyd* o ran dyddiau, nid ydyw ond *ieuangc* yn y gelfyddyd o gyfieithu').[267] Not only experienced translators and radicals, then, but novices to the art also participated in this awakening.

### *Internal difference: discussing* Seren tan Gwmmwl

Of course, the French Revolution also inspired original poetry and prose writing in the Welsh language, which is reflected in this collection and elsewhere.[268] Among the prose contributions to the radical periodicals, the frank exchange of opinions on the most influential radical Welsh pamphlet of the time, *Seren tan Gwmmwl* (A Star under a Cloud), stands out. Running from numbers one to eight of *Y Geirgrawn*, this first sustained public political discussion conducted in the Welsh language amounted to twenty-two pages, which made it half as long as the text discussed, and involved seven of the most prolific Welsh writers of the decade. It proves that it was possible for the Welsh intelligentsia to publicly discourse on such an incendiary text in a style they clearly enjoyed writing and which probably made reading politics enjoyable for their readers too. In the absence of an urban focus and indigenous university, *Y Geirgrawn* became a forum of national discussion for participants who rarely met. The discussion was opened by Siamas Wynedd, here using the occasional pseudonym 'Antagonist', who centred his attack on *Seren*'s core message that 'Before there were kings there was no war; which may be taken to mean that if there were no kings, the world would be in peace, unity and love' ('Cyn bod brenhinoedd nid oedd rhyfel; wrth hynny gellir meddwl, ped fae heb frenhinoedd, y byddai'r byd mewn heddwch, undeb a chariad') [DOCUMENT 9.2].[269] He determined the direction of the discussion by – characteristically for (Welsh) political discussion of the decade – attacking the author's interpretations of key biblical texts, such as 1 Samuel, but also by his use of pertinent symbols of revolution, power and Welsh culture, such as the Bastille, the Crown and the poet Dafydd ap Gwilym. 'Antagonist' also set the tone for much of the debate by belittling the linguistic prowess and learning of his political opponent. 'Tudur', who wrote from the 'Fountain of Truth' ('Ffynnon y Gwirionedd') in defence of the pamphlet, reinterpreted the religious point made by 'Antagonist' and attacked his style, but also transferred the argument from the biblical past to the political present by comparing Versailles and the British royal court in a rather threatening manner:

> Drych dychrynnedig i Reolwyr Brydain yw *Ffraingc.* LLYS VERSAILLES, ychydig o flynyddoedd a aeth heibio, oedd mor wych o wag ogoniant ac ydyw LLYS ST. IAGO yn bresennol. Mae gorthrymder a hen arferion Llysoedd yn myn'd allan o arfer, ac y mae balchder yn sicr o gael ei gwymp [DOCUMENT 9.3].
>
> (*France* is a terrible example for the Rulers of Britain. THE COURT OF VERSAILLES was as full of vain splendour a few years ago as the COURT OF ST. JAMES is at present. The oppression and old customs of Courts are going out of use, and pride is sure to have its fall.)

This was followed by a review of the defence of *Seren tan Gwmmwl* by 'A Lover of Fair Play' ('Hoffwr Chwarae Teg'), who satirically sided with the:

> gwerinos, a ydynt a'r bendro arnynt, mor chwannog i duchan a chwyno bod yn galed arnynt, pan y maent yn gweled pawb o'u cylch yn byw yn ddiormes – ddieisau – ddigonol, ac mewn hufen byd.[270]
>
> (rabble who are giddily looking around, so eager to grumble and complain that it is hard for them when they see everybody around them living without oppression – contented – satisfied, and in the best of worlds.)

Peris, who contributed the next instalment, did not hide behind an occasional pseudonym in his serious and blunt attack on the Welsh 'followers of *Tom*

*Paine*' ('canlynwyr *Tom Paine*'), whom he accused of rejecting any kind of faith and piety [DOCUMENT 9.6]. He, too, went over the first chapter of 1 Samuel, which had been cited in *Seren tan Gwmmwl*, but for good measure he also presented the establishment interpretation of St Peter that commanded obedience to worldly authority (see p. 45 above). For this, however, he was severely censored in an extended footnote by the editor, who updated St Peter to mean that when a worldly ruler turned:

> yn drahaus, yn anfad, yn orthrymmwr, ac yn sychedig am waed . . . ein dyledswydd ninnau sy'n newid; ac y mae yn awr gymmaint o rwymau arnom i ffieiddio'r dyn, ag oedd o'r blaen arnom i'w anrhydeddu ef [DOCUMENT 9.6].
>
> (oppressive, wicked, a despot, and bloodthirsty . . . then our duty changes too; and we are now as much bound to despise the man as we had been to honour him before.)

This refutation of Peris's defence of kings, tithes and state authority was reinforced by 'Carwr Rheswm' (A Lover of Reason).[271] Interestingly, he rejected Peris's claim that *Seren tan Gwmmwl* was a translation, since the 'flow of the language in the book was nothing like a *translation*' ('rhediad ymadroddion y llyfr ddim yn debyg i *gyfieithad*').[272] Most importantly, however, 'Carwr Rheswm' described some of Thomas Paine's experiences in France as in the *vita* of a saint and compared him to St Peter, letting his readers choose whom to respect:

> Nid af i ymhelaethu; gadawaf i'r darllenydd amyneddgar farnu pa un oedd bura i'w broffes, a'i *Pedr* yr apostol yr hwn oedd yn tyngu, ac yn rhegu celwydd, a'i *Thomas Paine*, yr hwn oedd yn foddlon i ddioddef marwolaeth o blaid RHYDDID A CHYFIAWNDER DYN?[273]
>
> (I shall not enlarge; I shall let the patient reader judge whose convictions were purer, those of the Apostle *Peter*, who swore and cursed a lie, or *Thomas Paine* who was willing to suffer death for LIBERTY AND THE JUSTICE OF MAN?)

This was closely followed by 'C. S.' who, citing every tyrant of the Old Testament from Ahab to Herod, returned to the defence of Nimrod by 'Antagonist' and advised this 'opponent to the truth' ('gwrthwynebwr gwirionedd') to hold his counsel in future.[274] The discussion was closed by the author of *Seren tan Gwmmwl*, Jac Glan-y-gors, who summed up the main accusations levelled against him, scorned the preoccupation of some of his opponents with style and took the opportunity to advertize his second radical pamphlet *Toriad y Dydd* (The Break of Day), which was published in 1797. He concluded the series with the declaration that he would rather:

> gael yr anrhydedd o *farw* yn ddyn RHYDD, na chael yr anglod o *fyw* yn ddistaw, yn gaethwas tan rwymau gorthrymder, mewn gwlad lle mae cwyno yn amyneddgar am Ryddid a chyfiawnder yn cael ei gyfrif yn drosedd [DOCUMENT 9.8].
>
> (have the honour of *dying* a FREE man, than to have the ignominy of *living* quietly, as a slave under the shackles of oppression, in a country where calling patiently for Liberty and justice is counted a crime.)

## *Conclusion*

Passionate as Jac Glan-y-gors's final remarks may have been, by October 1796 and issue nine of *Y Geirgrawn*, the Welsh attempt to create a radical periodical press was over. The 'struggle for the control of discourse'[275] in Wales had been unevenly pitched and those few Welsh radicals who still dared to make their opinions public utilized the pages of the *Chester Chronicle*, published pamphlets or assembled on the hillsides of Glamorgan, where Iolo Morganwg had relocated his gorseddau. The cultural nationalism which united the Welsh intelligentsia was stripped of any radical message, though it persisted in attempting to 'bring Wales to the attention of history' by collating and publishing the collections of Welsh antiquities and literary material which formed the corner-stone of Welsh history writing until the last quarter of the nineteenth century: the *Cambrian Repository* and the *Myvyrian Archaiology of Wales*.[276] The disgruntled, yet largely leaderless, Welsh 'rabble' continued to riot, while its more discerning representatives 'voted with their feet' and left for America.[277] The first decade of the nineteenth century belonged to Welsh-language periodicals founded by Methodists, loyalists, patriots and eisteddfod enthusiasts, not to radical Wales.

Between 1789 and 1802 Wales shared in the public discourse of its larger neighbour, England. The same legal constraints on what might be published and circulated (and at what price) operated in England and Wales, thus setting the basic framework for the possible.[278] The leading cultural societies of Wales had been located in London for decades and thus the London Welsh intelligentsia was heavily exposed to English cultural forms, which they grafted on to their native culture back home. In Wales itself, radicals and loyalists also looked towards English centres of ideology and their representatives for guidance. Undeniably, the Welsh response to the French

Revolution was heavily mediated through England and the English language. The main difference between Wales and the remainder of the British Isles was that the public discourse in Wales was bilingual. Most of those whose writings are included in the following selection were bilingual, many wrote in both languages and translated from one into the other, either adapting English ideas to the Welsh context or making what they considered key texts of Welsh culture available to the wider world.

Judging from the Welsh voices encountered in the almanacs and the provincial English newspapers along the border, the main public responses from Wales were a loyalism which emphasized the special contribution of the Welsh in their history and language to the British war effort and strove to ascribe populist unrest over food shortages, military recruitment and enclosures to class, not Welsh ethnicity. As in other parts of Britain, Welsh radicals failed to inject these popular protests with political aims, but they succeeded in maintaining three radical periodicals over three years in the mid-1790s.[279] Thus they created a stage for a new and surprisingly strongly worded national Welsh discourse on political and religious questions of importance, which rehearsed Welsh public communication within a national framework, created a new Welsh political terminology and developed a novel style of Welsh prose writing. Despite the backlash which postponed the founding of another reform-minded serial in the Welsh language until 1814, these achievements were not easily undone.

## *Notes*

1 NLW MS 4367E, Timothy Davis to Revd John James, Lloyd Jack, near Lampeter, 24 February 1808. The two volumes of this periodical were originally published by Daniel Isaac Eaton as *Hog's Wash; or, a Salmagundy for Swine* in 1793 (London, 1793) and republished in 1794–5 under the title *Politics for the People; or a Salmagundy for Swine*.

2 David Davis (Dafis Castellhywel; 1745–1827) played an active part in the religious and poetic controversies in south-west Wales in the 1790s. Timothy Davi[e]s (1779–1860), his second son, was a Unitarian minister at Llwynrhydowen, Coventry and Evesham. *DWB* s.n. Timothy Davies; David Davis ('Dafis Castellhywel'; 1745–1827).

3 David Jenkin Rees (*c.*1760–1817) is one of the forgotten pioneers of Unitarianism in Wales. A substantial farmer at Lloyd Jack near Lampeter, he outgrew the Arianism of David Davis, played a major part in the financing of the early Unitarian chapel at neighbouring Llwyn-y-groes and was among the founder members of the Unitarian Society of South Wales in 1802. See T. Oswald Williams, *Undodiaeth a Rhyddid Meddwl* (Llandysul, 1962), pp. 239–41.

[4] Paul Magnuson, *Reading Public Romanticism* (Princeton, New Jersey, 1998), pp. ix, 13.

[5] See, for instance, the forthcoming volume in this series by Cathryn Charnell-White, *Welsh Poetry of the French Revolution 1789–1805*, much of whose texts come from manuscript sources.

[6] The importance of translation is discussed in detail by Marion Löffler and Heather Williams in the forthcoming volume in this series, *Translating the French Revolution in Wales 1789–1815*. For a discussion of the neglect of Wales in the writing of 'four nations criticism', see Mary-Ann Constantine, 'Beauty Spot, Blind Spot: Romantic Wales', *Literature Compass*, 5, no. 3 (2008), 577–90.

[7] Gwyn A. Williams, *When was Wales?* (Harmondsworth, 1985), p. 152.

[8] Geraint H. Jenkins, *The Foundations of Modern Wales 1642–1780* (Cardiff, 1987), pp. 285–9.

[9] Harold Carter, *The Towns of Wales* (Cardiff, 1965), pp. 39, 41, 53, 57; Louise Miskell, *Intelligent Town: An Urban History of Swansea, 1780–1855* (Cardiff, 2006), p. 18.

[10] Philip Jenkins, 'Wales', in Peter Clark (ed.), *The Cambridge Urban History of Britain. Volume II: 1540–1840* (Cambridge, 2000), p. 141; Carter, *The Towns of Wales*, pp. 56, 58–60, 124; Jenkins, *The Foundations of Modern Wales*, pp. 286–9; John Williams, *Digest of Welsh Historical Statistics* (2 vols., Aberystwyth, 1985), I, pp. 62–7; C. B. Jewson, *The Jacobin City: A Portrait of Norwich in its Reaction to the French Revolution 1788–1802* (Glasgow and London, 1975); Gwyn A. Williams, *Artisans and Sans-Culottes: Popular Movements in France and Britain during the French Revolution* (2nd edn., London, 1989), pp. 64–5.

[11] Jürgen Habermas, *The Structural Transformation of the Public Sphere: An Inquiry into a Category of Bourgeois Society* (London, 1989), pp. 22–3, 30, 110–11.

[12] Terry Eagleton, *The Function of Criticism: From The Spectator to Post-Structuralism* (London, 1984), p. 36.

[13] John Ballinger, *The Bible in Wales* (London, 1906); Eryn M. White, 'Popular Schooling and the Welsh Language 1650–1800', in Geraint H. Jenkins (ed.), *The Welsh Language before the Industrial Revolution* (Cardiff, 1997), pp. 317–42.

[14] White, 'Popular Schooling and the Welsh Language', p. 331. This number of inhabitants is according to the first census for Wales, taken in 1801. See Williams, *Digest of Welsh Historical Statistics*, I, p. 7. See also R. J. W. Evans, 'Was there a Welsh Enlightenment?', in R. R. Davies and Geraint H. Jenkins (eds.), *From Medieval to Modern Wales: Historical Essays in Honour of Kenneth O. Morgan and Ralph A. Griffiths* (Cardiff, 2004), pp. 142–59.

[15] Thomas Parry, *A History of Welsh Literature*, trans. H. Idris Bell (Oxford, 1962), pp. 260–3; Jenkins, *The Foundations of Modern Wales*, pp. 204–11; Eiluned Rees, *The Welsh Book-Trade before 1820* (Aberystwyth, 1988), pp. xxix–lxix, cii; David Williams, *A History of Modern Wales* (2nd edn., Cardiff, 1977), pp. 233–42, 288–9. Short-lived printing ventures have not been included. Printing houses in Chester, Shrewsbury and Hereford also published Welsh and Anglo-Welsh literature.

[16] Gwyn A. Williams, 'The Beginnings of Radicalism', in Trevor Herbert and Gareth Elwyn Jones (eds.), *The Remaking of Wales in the Eighteenth Century* (Cardiff, 1988), p. 112; *idem*, *Artisans and Sans-Culottes,* p. xl.

[17] On Wales as England's first internal colony, see Michael Hechter, *Internal Colonialism: The Celtic Fringe in British National Development, 1536–1966* (London, 1975), pp. 53–69. For 'significant reading', see Magnuson, *Reading Public Romanticism*, p. 21.

[18] Robert Prichard, 'Rhyfedd-fyrr Olygiad yn Nrych y Drindod', in David Jones, *Blodeu-gerdd Cymry* (Y Mwythig, 1759), p. 425. I am grateful to E. Wyn James for this reference.

[19] Richard, Lewis and William Morris from Anglesey were central to the eighteenth-century Welsh cultural renaissance and the Welsh Enlightenment. See Gerald Morgan, 'The Morris Brothers', in Branwen Jarvis (ed.), *A Guide to Welsh Literature, c.1700–1800* (Cardiff, 2000), pp. 64–80; *HHSC*, pp. 16–45. On the Enlightenment in Wales, see Martin Fitzpatrick, 'Enlightenment', in Iain McCalman (ed.), *An Oxford Companion to the Romantic Age: British Culture, 1776–1832* (Oxford, 1999), pp. 302–3.

[20] John H. Davies (ed.), *The Letters of Lewis, Richard, William and John Morris, of Anglesey (Morrisiaid Mon) 1728–1765* (Aberystwyth, 1909), pp. 4, 36, 420; Hugh Owen (ed.), *Additional Letters of the Morrises of Anglesey (1735–1786)* (2 vols., London, 1947, 1949), II, p. 773.

[21] Davies (ed.), *The Letters of Lewis, Richard, William and John Morris*, pp. 150, 191–2, 530, 534, 538; Owen (ed.), *Additional Letters of the Morrises of Anglesey*, II, p. 735.

[22] Eiluned Rees, 'An Introductory Survey of 18th Century Welsh Libraries', *JWBS*, X, no. 4 (1971), 236; Katharine C. Balderston (ed.), *Thraliana: The Diary of Mrs. Hester Lynch Thrale (Later Mrs Piozzi) 1776–1809* (2nd edn., 2 vols., Oxford, 1951), *passim*; B. G. Charles, 'Letters of Hester Lynch Piozzi', *NLWJ*, II, no. 2 (1941), 54.

[23] NLW Dolaucothi Collection, 8748, *Vox Stellarum: or, A Loyal Almanack . . . 1793*, containing entries by John Johnes, Dolaucothi, 21 February 1793. John Johnes was the brother-in-law of the better-known Thomas Johnes of Hafod.

[24] NLW Garn Estate Records, FL 1/1/9. I am grateful to Mary Chadwick for drawing my attention to this file. See also T. A. Glenn, *The Family of Griffith of Garn and Plasnewydd in the County of Denbigh* (London, 1934).

[25] The highly revered Watkin Williams Wynn, fourth baronet, had only died in 1789.

[26] The amusing, politically charged *Letters from Simkin the Second, to his Dear Brother in Wales, for the Year 1790; Giving a Full and Circumstantial Account of All the Most Material Points in the Trial of W. H., in the three last Sessions of the last Parliament* (London, 1791), on which this poem is modelled, appeared as pamphlets and in many newspapers until the middle of the 1790s.

[27] NLW Elizabeth Baker Papers, esp. 467, 485, 514.

[28] NLW Peniarth 416A, 'Mrs. Baker's Journal', 24 December 1779 to 4 January 1780. Rice Jones (or Rhys Jones) was a well-known poet, and editor of an

important early anthology of Welsh poetry, *Gorchestion Beirdd Cymru* (Amwythig, 1773). See *DWB*; *NCLW*.

29 NLW Peniarth 416A, 'Mrs. Baker's Journal', 7 January 1780. For the life of this interesting woman, see Ben Bowen Thomas, *The Old Order: Based on the Diary of Elizabeth Baker (Dolgelley 1778–1786)* (Cardiff, 1945); Simone Clark, 'Visions of Community: Elizabeth Baker and late 18th Century Merioneth', in Michael Roberts and *eadem* (eds.), *Women and Gender in Early Modern Wales* (Cardiff, 2000), pp. 334–58.

30 Rees, 'An Introductory Survey of 18th Century Welsh Libraries', 252–6.

31 *Hereford Journal*, 29 July 1789; Eiluned Rees and G. Walters, 'Swansea Libraries in the Nineteenth Century', *JWBS*, X, no. 1 (1966), 43.

32 *Shrewsbury Chronicle*, 31 July 1789; ibid., 21 June 1797; ibid., 28 June 1797. For the practice of hiring out newspapers in rural England in the 1790s, see A. Aspinall, 'The Circulation of Newspapers in the Early Nineteenth Century', *The Review of English Studies*, XXII, no. 85 (1946), 37, 42.

33 *Shrewsbury Chronicle*, 26 August 1791.

34 NLW MS 1674B, f. 124; NLW MS 1785B, ff. 18, 40.

35 *CIM*, I, pp. 789, 801–2, 811.

36 NLW MS 6238A, 'Y Gell Gymysg', *passim*; NLW 4363B, f. 16. The latter reference to a poem translated from *Hog's Wash* is signed from Aberdare, where Tomos Glyn Cothi became minister of the Unitarian chapel in 1811.

37 NLW MS 12350A, 'Diary, &c., of John Davies, Ystrad', *passim*.

38 The unpublished radical material extant in manuscript illustrates that much more was produced than was published. This material was circulated by being read out aloud and copied.

39 Kevin Whelan, *The Tree of Liberty: Radicalism, Catholicism and the Construction of Irish Identity 1760–1830* (Cork, 1996), p. 72.

40 R.W. Jones, *Bywyd Cymdeithasol Cymru yn y Ddeunawfed Ganrif* (Llundain, 1931), p. 123.

41 Geraint H. Jenkins, *Thomas Jones yr Almanaciwr 1648–1713* (Caerdydd, 1980), pp. 40–71.

42 Bernard Capp, *Astrology and the Popular Press: English Almanacs 1500–1800* (London, 1979), pp. 59, 228.

43 *Tymmorol, ac wybrennol Newyddion, Neu Almanac Newydd, Am . . . 1790 . . . Ymmha un y cynhwysir amrywiol Bethau; ynghyd a BARDDONIAETH EISTEDDFOD CORWEN, a gynhaliwyd yn y Flwyddyn 1789. O Gasgliad a Myfyriad Cain Jones, Glyn Ceiriog* (Mwythig, 1789), 2. Cain Jones advertised every eisteddfod thereafter until his almanac ceased in 1795.

44 Parry, *A History of Welsh Literature*, p. 265. The 'Dublin' pirate almanac was, most probably, published in Holyhead, Anglesey.

45 The archives of people as different in time, location and status as Edmund Jones, 'the old prophet', squire John Johnes of Dolaucothi, and Unitarian minister Tomos Glyn Cothi, as well as local libraries contain almanacs which were used as diaries, to note down sermons and to copy other texts. I am grateful to Adam Coward for his advice on Edmund Jones.

46 See Sion Dafydd, 'Cywydd i Ddau Offeiriad am feddwi' (A *Cywydd* to Two Priests for being drunk), in *Tymmhorol, ac wybrennol newyddion, neu almanac newydd . . . Cain Jones* (Mwythig, 1787), 13–16; Mathew William, *Britanus Merlinus Liberatus* (Caerfyrddin, 1780), 6; William Walters, 'Ychydig Hanes . . . am y Braw a'r Trallod a fu ar Drigolion Twyn-yr-Odyn, o achos tri o Drigolion a aethant i lettya i Arwydd y Seren, ym Mhentref Merthyr-Tydfil, yn Sir Forganwg. – Rhai Gwragedd SYNHWYROL a ddychmygent, mai Tri o'r Pressgang oeddynt; eraill a honnent, mai Tri o'r Frensh oeddynt . . .' (A Short Account . . . of the Fright and the Distress suffered by the Inhabitants of Twyn-yr-Odyn, on account of three Men who stayed at the Sign of the Star, in the Village of Merthyr Tydfil, in Glamorganshire. – Some SENSIBLE Women imagined that they were Three from the Press-gang; others maintained that they were Three Frenchmen), in *Vox Stellarum et Planetarum . . . gan John Harris* (Carmarthen, 1795), 12–13.

47 See, e.g., the anti-English poem by the sixteenth-century poet Sion Mowddwy in *Britanus Merlinus Liberatus . . . gan Mathew William* (Carmarthen, 1793), 38–9.

48 *Britanus Merlinus Liberatus . . . gan Mathew William* (Aberhonddu, 1796), 32.

49 John Harris's mainly Welsh-language almanac always contained an English-language advertisement for his school, which was kept at Kidwelly until 1797, when it removed to Carmarthen. He taught 'astronomy, geography, mathematics, navigation and surveying'.

50 Ingrid H. Tague, 'Eighteenth-Century English Debates on a Dog Tax', *The Historical Journal*, 51, no. 4 (2008), 901–20.

51 Aled Jones, 'The Newspaper Press in Wales, 1804–1945', in Philip Henry Jones and Eiluned Rees (eds.), *A Nation and its Books: A History of the Book in Wales* (Aberystwyth, 1998), pp. 209–19.

52 Hannah Barker, *Newspapers, Politics, and Public Opinion in Late Eighteenth-Century England* (Oxford, 1998), pp. 110–12; *eadem*, 'England 1760–1815', in *eadem* and Simon Burrows (eds.), *Press, Politics and the Public Sphere in Europe and North America* (Cambridge, 2002), p. 103; Douglas Simes, 'Ireland 1760–1820', in ibid., pp. 113–39; Whelan, *The Tree of Liberty*, p. 62; Bob Harris, *The Scottish People and the French Revolution* (London, 2008), pp. 16, 71.

53 'Annog', *Newyddion Mawr oddiwrth y Sêr, neu Almanac . . . O wneuthuriad Thomas Jones* (London, 1691), 4.

54 Welsh contributions to English journals and newspapers, especially the *Gentleman's Magazine*, the *Critical Review* and the *European Review*, are too numerous to cite here. They focused on Welsh antiquities, history and literature, and featured topics such as the Welsh eisteddfod and the rumoured existence of a Welsh-language 'native' tribe in America.

55 *A Letter to the Right Reverend Samuel, Lord Bishop of St. David's, on the Charge He lately delivered to the Clergy of his Diocese. Second Edition. With a Preface. By a Welsh Freeholder* (London – Carmarthen, 1791), p. 9. The newspaper in question was most probably the *Gloucester Journal*.

56 Hywel M. Davies, 'Loyalism in Wales, 1792–1793', *WHR*, 20, no. 4 (2001), 700.

[57] 'Reasons for not Rioting', *Salopian Journal*, 1 July 1795. This is in the vein of Hannah More's poem 'The Riot; or Half a loaf is better than no bread', which was published in August of the same year.

[58] 'Phrases', *Chester Chronicle*, 12 February 1796.

[59] Barker, *Newspapers, Politics, and Public Opinion*, p. 124. Robert Raike's *Gloucester Journal*, and the *Worcester Journal*, as well as the Bristol papers, had a smaller share in the Welsh market and cannot therefore be considered in this study.

[60] Barker, *Newspapers, Politics, and Public Opinion*, p. 122.

[61] *Hereford Journal*, 2 December 1779; ibid., 5 August 1789; ibid., 2 January 1793.

[62] Ibid., 17 December 1794. 'Caractacus' (correct Caratacōs), king of the Catuvellauni and the Trinovantes, was a key figure in the fight of the British tribes against the Roman invasion, *c.* AD 43–51. Having lost south-east England to Roman forces, he escaped west and continued his resistance from present-day Wales and northern England. See *CCAHE*, I, p. 343.

[63] F. C. Morgan, 'Herefordshire Printers and Booksellers', *Transactions of the Woolhope Naturalists' Fieldclub* (1941), 114–16, 124.

[64] Barker, *Newspapers, Politics, and Public Opinion*, p. 119.

[65] *Salopian Journal*, 29 January 1794. Barker estimates that for a weekly to succeed, sales of about 1,000 copies a week had to be achieved in the 1790s. See Barker, *Newspapers, Politics, and Public Opinion*, pp. 104, 114.

[66] *Shrewsbury Chronicle*, 27 April 1792.

[67] Ibid., 26 August 1791; ibid., 10 February 1792; ibid., 28 December 1792; ibid., 6 May 1796; ibid., 15 February 1799.

[68] James Ifano Jones, *A History of Printing and Printers in Wales to 1810, and of Successive and Related Printers to 1923: Also, A History of Printing and Printers in Monmouthshire to 1923* (Cardiff, 1925), p. 113.

[69] *Shrewsbury Chronicle*, 7 February 1794. An *englyn* is a Welsh four-line poem. For the popularity of the paper see also DOCUMENT 3.8.

[70] *Shrewsbury Chronicle*, July–December 1791, *passim*.

[71] The events which led to this change in opinion are ably summed up in Harris, *The Scottish People and the French Revolution*, p. 51.

[72] *Shrewsbury Chronicle*, 1 January 1796; ibid., 6 January 1797; ibid., 29 December 1797; ibid., 10 April 1801. Cf. Whelan, *The Tree of Liberty*, p. 66.

[73] *Shrewsbury Chronicle*, 26 December 1794.

[74] Ibid., 4 April 1794; ibid., 3 April 1795; ibid., 21 August 1795; ibid., 11 August 1797; ibid., 26 October 1798.

[75] *Chester Chronicle*, 2 January 1789; ibid., 28 December 1792. For sales of other English provincial papers during this period, see Barker, *Newspapers, Politics, and Public Opinion*, p. 114.

[76] *Chester Chronicle*, 21 November 1794. Information on the Cowdroy family is to be found in D. Nuttall, 'A History of Printing in Chester', *Journal of the Chester Archaeological Society*, 54 (1967), 64–7, 74; Katrina Navickas, *Loyalism and Radicalism in Lancashire, 1798–1815* (Oxford, 2009), pp. 145–51.

[77] NLW MS 1235A.

[78] Harris, *The Scottish People and the French Revolution*, p. 49.

[79] This was based on Isaiah 2: 4. Iolo's only other contributions to *Welsh* serials during the 1790s were two poems in John Harris's *Vox Stellarum et Planetarum*, some short poems in the *Salopian Journal* and the *Shrewsbury Chronicle*, and one poem in *Cylch-grawn Cynmraeg*, none of them overtly political. On Iolo Morganwg's contributions to the public discourse in London, see Mary-Ann Constantine and Elizabeth Edwards, 'Bard of Liberty: Iolo Morganwg, Wales and Radical Song', in John Kirk, Andrew Noble and Michael Brown (eds.), *Political Poetry and Song in the Age of Revolution. Volume 1: United Islands? The Languages of Resistance* (London, forthcoming).

[80] Jac Glan-y-gors is, possibly, the most influential satirist Wales has ever had. By far the best source for his life and letters is still, Middleton Pennant Jones, 'John Jones of Glan-y-Gors', *THSC* (1911), 60–94. See also J. B. Edwards, 'John Jones (Jac Glan-y-Gors): Tom Paine's Denbighshire Henchman?', *Denbighshire Historical Society Transactions*, 51 (2002), 95–112; Marion Löffler, 'Cerddi Newydd gan John Jones, "Jac Glan-y-Gors"', *Llên Cymru*, 33 (2010), 143–50; *HHSC*, pp. 108–9. Iolo Morganwg also used this religious form in his pretend translation 'from the ancient British' entitled 'John Bull's Litany', alas only in the privacy of his manuscript, NLW MS 21401E.

[81] For David Samwell, see *HHSC*, pp. 106–7; William Ll. Davies, 'David Samwell (1751–1798): Surgeon of the "Discovery", London-Welshman, and Poet', *THSC* (1928), 70–133; Martin Fitzpatrick, 'The "Cultivated Understanding" and Chaotic Genius of David Samwell', in Geraint H. Jenkins (ed.), *A Rattleskull Genius: The Many Faces of Iolo Morganwg* (Cardiff, 2005), pp. 343–402; *idem*, Nicholas Thomas and Jennifer Newell (eds.), *The Death of Captain Cook and Other Writings by David Samwell* (Cardiff, 2006).

[82] Magnuson, *Reading Public Romanticism*, pp. 5–6.

[83] The editor's weekly messages to contributors on page three of the paper bear witness to his increasing caution.

[84] *Chester Chronicle*, 22 July 1791; ibid., 21 October 1791; ibid., 25 January 1799; ibid., 24 January 1800. David Thomas (Dafydd Ddu Eryri; 1759–1822), a weaver in early life and a schoolmaster in various locations in Snowdonia for most of the remainder, was, perhaps, the most influential poet and teacher of the rules of Welsh poetry of his time. A corresponding member of the London Gwyneddigion society, he was among those organizing the eisteddfodau of the 1790s, as well as winning prizes there for his poetry. He was an ardent loyalist and the animosity between him and Iolo Morganwg has become proverbial. *DWB*; *NCLW*. Cathryn A. Charnell-White, *Barbarism and Bardism: North Wales versus South Wales in the Bardic Vision of Iolo Morganwg* (Aberystwyth, 2004), p. 20.

[85] See M. F. Jolliffe, 'The Druidical Society of Anglesey, 1772–1844', *THSC* (1941), 189–99. For remarks on Dafydd Ddu Eryri's Welsh ode on 'Rhyddid' (Liberty), see Marion Löffler, 'Serial Literature and Radical Poetry in Wales at the End of the Eighteenth Century', in John Kirk, Michael Brown and Andrew Noble

(eds.), *Political Poetry and Song in the Age of Revolution. Volume 2: The Cultures of Radicalism in Britain and Ireland* (London, forthcoming).

[86] Thomas Jones was an excise collector stationed at Llanrhaeadr-ym-Mochnant near Corwen in north-east Wales until 1795, when he was moved to Bristol. See *HHSC*, pp. 125–6. Contrary to perceived opinion (G. J. Williams, 'Eisteddfodau'r Gwyneddigion', *Y Llenor*, XIV (1935), 13–17), his move to Bristol did not prevent him from continuing to publish in the *Shrewsbury Chronicle*.

[87] *Shrewsbury Chronicle*, 31 May 1793; ibid., 10 July 1795.

[88] Ibid., 25 June 1790; 10 December 1790; 23 January 1795; 26 February 1796.

[89] Ibid., 10 December 1790. Gwallter Mechain (1761–1849), a graduate of Oxford and Cambridge, which he attended with the financial help of the London Welshman Owen Jones (Owain Myfyr), was the curate of Meifod in Montgomeryshire and an acclaimed Welsh poet and author. He participated in eisteddfodau from 1789 until 1849. His tract, *Rhyddid: Traethawd a Ennillodd Ariandlws y Gwyneddigion* (London, 1791), was reprinted in instalments in the radical Welsh periodical *Y Geirgrawn* in 1796. See also Geraint H. Jenkins, 'An Uneasy Relationship: Gwallter Mechain and Iolo Morganwg', *Montgomeryshire Collections*, 97 (2009), 73–99.

[90] Löffler, 'Serial Literature and Radical Poetry'.

[91] Marion Löffler and Elizabeth Edwards, 'Iolo Morganwg and the "Lost Generation"' (unpublished paper delivered at the 'Wales and the French Revolution' one-day forum, Aberystwyth, September 2011). See also Kenneth R. Johnston, 'Whose History? My Place or Yours? Republican Assumptions and Romantic Traditions', in Damian Walford Davies (ed.), *Romanticism, History, Historicism: Essays on an Orthodoxy* (London, 2009), pp. 90–2.

[92] John Barrell, *The Spirit of Despotism: Invasions of Privacy in the 1790s* (Oxford, 2006), p. 2.

[93] See Lynda Pratt, 'Southey in Wales: Inscriptions, Monuments and Romantic Posterity', in Damian Walford Davies and *eadem* (eds.), *Wales and the Romantic Imagination* (Cardiff, 2007), pp. 90–1.

[94] Davies, 'Loyalism in Wales', 688–716.

[95] For letters in the same vein, see *Hereford Journal*, 2 January 1793 (Laugharne, Brecon, Hay-on-Wye); ibid., 9 January 1793 (Aberystwyth, Haverfordwest); ibid., 16 January 1793 (Abergavenny); ibid., 23 January 1793 (Llandovery, Radnor, Pembroke).

[96] Davies, 'Loyalism in Wales', 709. For the text of this (Welsh) letter, see R. T. Jenkins, 'Political Propaganda in West Wales in 1793', *BBCS*, VI, part III (1932), 276.

[97] See David Davies, *The Influence of the French Revolution on Welsh Life and Literature* (Carmarthen, 1926), pp. 116–18. Text and translation of the ballad, 'Y Brenin a'r Llywodraeth, neu, y Refoliwsion yn 1688 wedi Gwneuthur Ail Refoliwsion yn Afreidiol i'r Brutaniaid' (The King and the Government, or, the Revolution in 1688 having Made a Second Revolution Unnecessary for the Britons) (Caerfyrddin, 1793), are reproduced and discussed in a volume in this series by Ffion M. Jones, *Welsh Ballads of the French Revolution 1793–1815* (Cardiff, 2012), pp. 82–91.

[98] A note in *Berrow's Worcester Journal*, 23 January 1793, confirms that the meeting held at Llandovery to found an Association, reported in the *Hereford Journal*, 23 January 1793, had also been combined with a burning of Thomas Paine in image. See Frank O'Gorman, 'The Paine Burnings of 1792–1793', *Past & Present*, 193 (2006), 132. See also Sharon Howard, 'Riotous Community: Crowds, Politics and Society in Wales, *c.*1700–1840', *WHR*, 20, no. 4 (2001), 675–6.

[99] *Chester Chronicle*, 28 December 1792; ibid., 22 February 1793 (Hope, Caernarfon, Wrexham).

[100] See also Davies, 'Loyalism in Wales', 698–701.

[101] This system of apartheid with regard to castle boroughs is evidenced by charters and petitions throughout the Middle Ages. See Marion Löffler, *Englisch und Kymrisch in Wales: Geschichte der Sprachsituation und Sprachpolitik* (Hamburg, 1997), pp. 189–96.

[102] For recent treatments of the Fishguard landing, see Roland Quinault, 'The French Invasion of Pembrokeshire in 1797: A Bicentennial Assessment', *WHR*, 19, no. 4 (1999), 618–42; Hywel M. Davies, 'Terror, Treason and Tourism: the French in Pembrokeshire 1797', in Mary-Ann Constantine and Dafydd Johnston (eds.), *'Footsteps of Liberty and Revolt': Essays on Wales and the French Revolution* (Cardiff, forthcoming).

[103] See also *Hereford Journal*, 1 February 1797; ibid., 8 March 1797; ibid., 15 March 1797; ibid., 29 March 1797; *Shrewsbury Chronicle*, 3 March 1797; ibid., 10 March 1797.

[104] NLW Dolaucothi Correspondence V7/77, Jane Johnes, Hafod, to her 'dear Brother', Dolaucothi, n.d. ['Thursday morning']. The diary entry of the addressee, however, only reads: 'Friday 24 February 1797: 2. past three. Report says that the french have landed at Milford.' He dutifully rode up to Hafod, but was back home at nine o'clock on Saturday evening, having dined at Lampeter on the way home! See NLW Dolaucothi Collection, 8552, 24 February 1797 to 25 February 1797.

[105] *St. David's Day, or, the Honest Welchman* (London, 1800), a 'ballad farce, in two acts' by Thomas Dibdin with an overture and music by Thomas Atwod (using Welsh airs supplied by Edward Jones, Harpist to the King), is much in the same vein as these newspaper reports and may have been inspired by them. *NCLW*, s.n. Edward Jones (Bardd y Brenin; 1752–1824), s.v. *St. David's Day, or the Honest Welshman*.

[106] On disturbances connected with the Supplementary Militia Act, see *Chester Chronicle*, 17 April 1795.

[107] For the extent of animosity and the war of pamphlets which ensued, see Damian Walford Davies, '"Sweet Sylvan Routes" and Grave Methodists: Wales in De Quincey's Confessions of an English Opium-Eater', in *idem* and Pratt, *Wales and the Romantic Imagination*, pp. 217–21; Davies, 'Loyalism in Wales', 705–7; Alfred Neobald Palmer, 'John Wilkinson and the Old Bersham Iron Works', *THSC* (1899), 46.

[108] The *Salopian Journal*, September–October 1800, *passim*, and the *Chester Chronicle*, 23 January 1801, printed excerpts from *A Tour round North Wales Performed during*

*the Summer of 1798* by William Bingley (London, 1800), but they avoided those passages which connected the Methodists with 'Jacobinism'.

[109] The imprisonment and trial of the two Dissenters lead to the publication of a Welsh 'treason trial' pamphlet written by the radical Baptist minister William Richards (Lynn), *Cwyn y Cystuddiedig. A Griddfannau y Carcharorion Dieuog* (Caerfyrddin, 1798). The advertised translation of this pamphlet into English was never published. Text and translation will be included in a forthcoming volume in this series by Marion Löffler, *Political Pamphlets and Sermons from Wales 1790–1805*.

[110] This is unlikely to be the David Jones who published his radical pamphlets as 'Welsh Freeholder', for he published the text first as 'William de Common Church' in *The Oracle*, 29 January 1798. See endnote 21 to the 'Selection of Documents'.

[111] For a spotlight on dual identity in appellations of the Welsh in the 1790s, see Davies, 'Loyalism in Wales', 687.

[112] *Shrewsbury Chronicle*, 15 April 1791; *Chester Chronicle*, 17 August 1790; ibid., 30 December 1796; ibid., 5 May 1797. Such translations will be explored by Dafydd Johnston, 'Translations of Medieval Welsh Poetry in the Age of the French Revolution', in Constantine and *idem*, *'Footsteps of Liberty and Revolt'*.

[113] *Hereford Journal*, 24 June 1789; ibid., 14 May 1794; *Shrewsbury Chronicle*, 31 July 1795; *Salopian Journal*, 11 June 1800.

[114] General illumination as an expression of loyalty or patriotism was a well-known aspect of life in Georgian Britain. For examples from elsewhere, see Navickas, *Loyalism and Radicalism in Lancashire*, pp. 54–5; Padhraig Higgins, 'Bonfires, Illuminations, and Joy: Celebratory Street Politics and Uses of "the Nation" during the Volunteer Movement', *Éire-Ireland*, 42, nos. 3 and 4 (2007), 173–206. The symbolism of 'rustic bliss' is discussed by John Barrell, 'Cottage Politics', in *idem*, *The Spirit of Despotism*, pp. 210–46. Sir Watkin Williams Wynn, fifth baronet (1772–1840) became MP for Beaumaris in 1792 and sat for Denbighshire from 1796 until his death in 1840. See *DWB*.

[115] *Chester Chronicle*, 20 May 1796; ibid., 10 June 1796.

[116] *Hereford Journal*, 20 February 1799. See also 'The Genius of Havod', *Shrewsbury Chronicle*, 21 August 1795.

[117] The interpretation of Welsh nature in Anglo-Welsh poetry of the period is explored in a forthcoming volume in this series by Elizabeth Edwards, *English-Language Poetry from Wales 1790–1806*.

[118] *Shrewsbury Chronicle*, 2 March 1800. This poem, here signed 'Holyhead, G. D. H.' is one of the *Holyhead Sonnets* (London, 1801) published by the comic actor George Davies Harley (d. 1811) and discussed in Edwards, *English-Language Poetry from Wales*. 'The Return' from the same collection was published in the *Salopian Journal*, 1 October 1800, and 'On Seeing a Poor Welsh Girl Pass my Window in a Storm' by 'G. D. H.' appeared in *Adams's Weekly Courant*, 1 April 1800. I am grateful to Elizabeth Edwards for pointing out the identity of 'G. D. H.'.

[119] *Chester Chronicle*, 2 June 1797.

[120] Ibid., 8 June 1798.

[121] Arviragus was a British leader current during the reign of Domitian (AD 81–96), who is only attested in one line by the poet Juvenal (*Satire IV*: 126–7). His legend was elaborated by Geoffrey of Monmouth in his *Historia Regum Britanniæ*, where he was conflated with Caratacōs (son of Cunobelinus). See endnote 62 above.

[122] *Shrewsbury Chronicle*, 30 September 1796.

[123] See *Chester Chronicle*, 16 July 1790; ibid., 13 August 1790; ibid., 29 October 1790; ibid., 7 January 1791; ibid., 3 June 1791; ibid., 2 March 1792; ibid., 30 December 1796; ibid., 21 March 1800; *Adams's Weekly Courant*, 1 April 1800; *Salopian Journal*, 2 April 1800. Poems by Richard Llwyd are discussed in Edwards, *English-Language Poetry from Wales*.

[124] The few exceptions to this were the poetry of Jac Glan-y-gors and the advertisement for the radical Welsh journal, *Y Geirgrawn*, in the *Chester Chronicle* [DOCUMENT 5.9].

[125] *Hereford Journal*, 6 November 1793; ibid., 31 August 1796; ibid., 8 May 1799; *Chester Chronicle*, 1 September 1797; *Shrewsbury Chronicle*, 30 May 1789; ibid., 23 August 1793; ibid., 14 March 1794; ibid., 5 December 1794; ibid., 5 August 1796; ibid., 11 December 1801.

[126] NLW MS 13221, ff. 339–43; NLW BL 76.

[127] Williams, 'The Beginnings of Radicalism', pp. 115, 129.

[128] *Adams's Weekly Courant*, 10 November 1789; ibid., 28 June 1791; *Chester Chronicle*, 11 June 1790; ibid., 16 December 1791; ibid., 25 May 1798; *Shrewsbury Chronicle*, 16 October 1789; ibid., 7 March 1791; ibid., 15 June 1792; ibid., 31 May 1793; ibid., 27 June 1794; ibid., 10 July 1795. This is only a selection of advertisements and reports.

[129] Later eisteddfodau, with the exception of the 1792 eisteddfod, rarely boasted even vaguely radical themes on which to compete. See *CIM*, I, p. 525; Charnell-White, *Welsh Poetry of the French Revolution*.

[130] On the gestation and later history of this national institution, see Thomas Shankland, 'Hanes Dechreuad "Gorsedd Beirdd Ynys Prydain"', *Y Llenor*, III (1924), 94–102; Geraint and Zonia Bowen, *Hanes Gorsedd y Beirdd* (Llandybïe, 1991); Cathryn A. Charnell-White, *Bardic Circles: National, Regional and Personal Identity in the Bardic Vision of Iolo Morganwg* (Cardiff, 2007); Marion Löffler, *The Literary and Historical Legacy of Iolo Morganwg, 1826–1926* (Cardiff, 2007), pp. 41–77.

[131] *Chester Chronicle*, 11 March 1796; *Shrewsbury Chronicle*, 15 February 1793.

[132] Balderston (ed.), *Thraliana: The Diary of Mrs. Hester Lynch Thrale*, II, pp. 897–8. No Welsh-language adaptation of Tom Paine's work had as yet been published, but Jac Glan-y-gors, whose adaptation, *Seren tan Gwmmwl* (A Star under a Cloud), appeared in 1795, may well have been working on it. Text and translation of *Seren tan Gwmmwl* will appear in a forthcoming volume in this series by Löffler, *Political Pamphlets and Sermons from Wales*.

[133] For accounts of rioting in Wrexham and the military presence there, see Davies, 'Loyalism in Wales', 698; David J. V. Jones, *Before Rebecca: Popular Protests in Wales 1793–1835* (London, 1973), *passim*. However, the level of organization was

not on a par with, for instance, the 'rolling strikes' and pan-regional co-operation observed in more established industrial areas of Britain. See, for instance, Navickas, *Loyalism and Radicalism in Lancashire*, pp. 180–5.

134 *Shrewsbury Chronicle*, 28 August 1789.

135 Ibid., 4 September 1789; ibid., 3 May 1793; ibid., 27 February 1795; ibid., 5 June 1795; ibid., 28 August 1795; ibid., 24 October 1800; ibid., 14 November 1800.

136 See also Howard, 'Riotous Community', 673–5.

137 On the power of the trial as a public stage, see Nancy E. Johnson, 'Fashioning the Legal Subject: Narratives from the London Treason Trials of 1794', *Eighteenth-Century Fiction*, 21, no. 3 (2009), 413–43.

138 Tomos Glyn Cothi was also tried by George Hardinge. See Geraint H. Jenkins, '"A Very Horrid Affair": Sedition and Unitarianism in the Age of Revolutions', in Davies and *idem* (eds.), *From Medieval to Modern Wales*, pp. 175–96. Notes on his harsh speech on this occasion are to be found in NLW MS 2137D, f. 8.

139 For a full account of the Merthyr riots, see Jones, *Before Rebecca*, pp. 206–13; Howard, 'Riotous Community', 673–5.

140 *Araith yr Unad Hardinge, Dydd Llun y 6ed o Ebrill, 1801, yn Llys yr Uchel Eisteddfod (Great Sessions) a Ddaliwyd dros Sir Forganwg* (Caerfyrddin, 1802); *Annerch yr Unad Hardinge, i'r Rhai a Euogfarnwyd ger ei Fron Ef, yn Sesiwn Fawr Caerdydd, ar yr Wythfed o Ebrill, 1801* (Caerfyrddin, 1802). The English text of the latter speech is reprinted in Jones, *Before Rebecca*, pp. 215–20.

141 This follows the assumptions of Linda Colley, *Britons: Forging the Nation 1707–1837* (New Haven, 1992).

142 H. T. Dickinson, *British Radicalism and the French Revolution 1789–1815* (Oxford, 1985), pp. 19–20; William Christie, 'Newspapers', in McCalman (ed.), *An Oxford Companion to the Romantic Age*, pp. 622–3; Harris, *The Scottish People and the French Revolution*, pp. 5, 64–5.

143 Mary Helen Thuente, *The Harp Re-strung: The United Irishmen and the Rise of Irish Literary Nationalism* (Syracuse, 1994), pp. 9, 94–5.

144 See also Morgan John Rhys to William Owen [Pughe], n.d. [February 1794], in G. J. Williams (ed.), 'Original Documents: 4. Letters of Morgan John Rhys to William Owen [-Pughe]', *NLWJ*, II, nos. 3 and 4 (1942), 136.

145 G. J. Williams, *Iolo Morganwg – Y Gyfrol Gyntaf* (Caerdydd, 1956), pp. 387–91; See also Jenkins, 'An Uneasy Relationship: Gwallter Mechain and Iolo Morganwg', 134.

146 *CIM*, I, p. 811, Iolo Morganwg to Gwallter Mechain, 10 May 1796.

147 John James Evans, 'Y Cylchgronau Cymraeg Cynharaf', *Yr Ymofynnydd*, XLII, no. 12 (1942), 162–4; Owen (ed.), *Additional Letters of the Morrises of Anglesey*, I, p. 10, Lewis Morris to (?) William Vaughan (draft), Caergybi [1730], note on reverse side of folio. See also Catherine McKenna, 'Aspects of Tradition Formation in Eighteenth-Century Wales', in Joseph Falaky Nagy (ed.), *Memory and the Modern in Celtic Literature: CSANA Yearbook 5* (Dublin, 2006), pp. 37–60.

148 D. Rhys Phillips, 'The "Eurgrawn Cymraeg" of 1770', *JWBS*, V, no. 1 (1937), 54; Owen (ed.), *Additional Letters of the Morrises of Anglesey*, II, p. 767, Richard Morris to Hugh Hughes, 17 April 1770.

[149] Owen (ed.), *Additional Letters of the Morrises of Anglesey*, II, p. 768, Richard Morris to Evan Evans, 23 June 1770.

[150] Colin Kidd, 'Wales, the Enlightenment and the New British History', *WHR*, 25, no. 2 (2010), 209–30, demonstrates that cultural nationalism is not necessarily restricted to Romanticism.

[151] Evans, 'Y Cylchgronau Cymraeg Cynharaf', 179.

[152] Phillips, 'The "Eurgrawn Cymraeg" of 1770', 55–6.

[153] William Davies Leathart, *The Origin and Progress of the Gwyneddigion Society of London Instituted M.DCC.LXX* (London, 1831), pp. 20–39; *HHSC*, pp. 125–32.

[154] See Mary-Ann Constantine, '"This Boiling and Unsettled State": The Welsh in Paris 1789–1798', in *eadem* and Johnston, *'Footsteps of Liberty and Revolt'*.

[155] Williams, 'The Beginnings of Radicalism', p. 123.

[156] Hywel M. Davies, '"Transatlantic Brethren": A Study of English, Welsh and American Baptists with Particular Reference to Morgan John Rhys (1760–1804) and his Friends' (unpublished University of Wales PhD thesis, 1984), pp. 246–71. See also John T. Griffith, *Rev. Morgan John Rhys: The Welsh Baptist Hero of Civil and Religious Liberty of the Eighteenth Century* (Carmarthen, 1910).

[157] Davies, '"Transatlantic Brethren"', pp. 256, 465.

[158] See John James Evans, *Dylanwad y Chwyldro Ffrengig ar Lenyddiaeth Cymru* (Lerpwl, 1928), p. 74.

[159] Davies, '"Transatlantic Brethren"', pp. 367–71; Constantine, '"This Boiling and Unsettled State"'.

[160] Morgan John Rhys, *Pigion o Hymnau a Salmau* (Caerfyrddin, 1794); Davies, '"Transatlantic Brethren"', pp. 489–90; Williams, *Undodiaeth a Rhyddid Meddwl*, pp. 197–8.

[161] Griffith, *Rev. Morgan John Rhys*, pp. 22–3; Davies, *The Influence of the French Revolution on Welsh Life and Literature*, pp. 23–46; Davies '"Transatlantic Brethren"', pp. 478, 507. See also E. Wyn James, '"Seren Wib Olau": Gweledigaeth a Chenhadaeth Morgan John Rhys (1760–1804)', *Trafodion Cymdeithas Hanes y Bedyddwyr* (2007), 5–37.

[162] Geraint Dyfnallt Owen, *Thomas Evans (Tomos Glyn Cothi): Trem ar ei Fywyd* (n.p., 1963), *passim*; Williams, *Undodiaeth a Rhyddid Meddwl*, p. 236.

[163] John James Evans, *Cymry Enwog y Ddeunawfed Ganrif* (Aberystwyth, 1937), pp. 168–72.

[164] *Hereford Journal*, 26 August 1801; Jenkins, '"A Very Horrid Affair"', pp. 175–96.

[165] Thomas Evans, *Cyfansoddiad o Hymnau* (Caerfyrddin, 1811); D. Jacob Dafis (ed.), *Crefydd a Gweriniaeth yn Hanes Hen Dŷ Cwrdd Aberdâr* (Llandysul, 1951), pp. 25–30.

[166] Evans, *Cymry Enwog y Ddeunawfed Ganrif*, pp. 182–4; *DWB*.

[167] Evans, *Cymry Enwog y Ddeunawfed Ganrif*, p. 184; E. Gwynn Matthews, 'Holywell and the Marseillaise', *Flintshire Historical Society Journal*, 38 (2010), 121–2.

[168] See J. Dyfnallt Owen, 'Morgan John Rhys yn ei Gysylltiad a Threfecca', *Cylchgrawn Hanes y Methodistiaid*, VII, no. 1 (1922), 14–20.

[169] Although the printer Titus Evans, Machynlleth, appears in the imprint of the fourth number, the work was not printed by him. See Jones, *A History of Printing*

*and Printers in Wales and Monmouthshire*, pp. 136–7. It is worth noting that Titus Evans was also considering emigration to America at that time.

170 Carter, *The Towns of Wales*, pp. 53, 55–6.

171 Jenkins, *The Foundations of Modern Wales*, pp. 181–3, 192, 195; Williams, *Undodiaeth a Rhyddid Meddwl*, pp. 96–194, 282–95. For the link between Dissent and radical thought in Scotland, see Harris, *The Scottish People and the French Revolution*, p. 86.

172 T. Evans, *Datganiad Ffydd, a Gafodd ei Thraethu yn Gyhoeddus gerbron Gweinidogion ac Eraill, Gerllaw y Gwarnogau, yn Sir Gaerfyrddin, Medi 11, 1794* (Caerfyrddin, 1795), p. ii.

173 Palmer, 'John Wilkinson and the Old Bersham Iron Works', 46. See also W. Lloyd Davies, 'The Riot at Denbigh in 1795', *BBCS*, IV, part I (1927), 61–73; Williams, *Artisans and Sans-Culottes*, p. 75.

174 Nuttall, 'A History of Printing in Chester', 69; Carter, *The Towns of Wales*, pp. 36, 56, 58–9. The nodal point within Wales in this region would later increasingly be Wrexham.

175 *Cylch-grawn Cynmraeg*, no. II (1793), 57.

176 Williams (ed.), 'Original Documents: 4. Letters of Morgan John Rhys to William Owen [-Pughe]', 134, 136.

177 Ibid., 136; NLW MS 13221.

178 The note said, 'Yr ydys yn bwriadu Cynhwysiad y pedwar Rhifyn yn y nesaf' (It is planned to give the Contents of the four Numbers in the next). *Y Drysorfa Gymmysgedig*, no. III (1796), 146.

179 *Y Geirgrawn*, no. I (1796), title page.

180 'At ein Gohebwyr a'r Cyffredin', ibid., nos. III and V (1796), cover; R. T. Jenkins, *Hanes Cymru yn y Bedwaredd Ganrif ar Bymtheg: Y Gyfrol Gyntaf (1789–1843)* (Caerdydd, 1933), pp. 25–7. The pamphlet and its translation are published in Löffler, *Political Pamphlets and Sermons from Wales*.

181 T. Phillips, 'Y Parch. Morgan John Rhys a'i Ddydd-Lyfr', *Seren Cymru*, 17 Mai 1867.

182 NLW MS 12350A, ff. 2, 8, 88–9.

183 W. Ll. Davies (ed.), 'Original Documents: 3. Some Letters of Owen Jones, "Owen Myvyr"', *NLWJ*, II, no. 2 (1941), 64.

184 E. D. Jones, 'Hugh Maurice (?1775–1825), a Forgotten Scribe', *NLWJ*, I, no. 4 (1940), 230–2.

185 Inscription in the miscellaneous volume NLW YX2 GEI.

186 *Cylch-grawn Cynmraeg*, no. II (1793), 119.

187 Marion Löffler, 'The Marseillaise in Wales', in Constantine and Johnston, *'Footsteps of Liberty and Revolt'*.

188 In comparison, *Pig's Meat* sold at one penny and the *Hog's Wash or Politics for the People* sold at twopence.

189 Whelan, *The Tree of Liberty*, p. 65; Harris, *The Scottish People and the French Revolution*, pp. 25–32; Dickinson, *British Radicalism and the French Revolution*, pp. 18–20.

190 Dafydd Saunders contributed various poems to *Cylch-grawn Cynmraeg* and *Y Geirgrawn*. See also DOCUMENT 9.9. D. Stansfield, 'Agweddau ar Fywyd

a Gwaith Dafydd Saunders', *Trafodion Cymdeithas Hanes y Bedyddwyr* (2008), 35–51.

[191] Williams (ed.), 'Original Documents: 4. Letters of Morgan John Rhys to William Owen [-Pughe]', 132, 134.

[192] Other poems in praise of the new publishing ventures and the Welsh language appeared in *Y Drysorfa Gymmysgedig*, no. I (1795), 42; *Y Geirgrawn*, no. I (1796), 2; ibid., no. II (1796), 64. See also Löffler, 'Serial Literature and Radical Poetry in Wales'.

[193] 'Annerchiad y Goruwchwilwyr at eu Cywleidiadon Un-iaith; Yn dangos NATTUR ag AMCAN y GEIRGRAWN', *Y Geirgrawn*, no. I (1796), 3.

[194] 'Myfyrdodau ar yr Amserau', *Cylch-grawn Cynmraeg*, no. V (1794), 242.

[195] Williams, *Artisans and Sans-Culottes*, p. xix.

[196] Williams (ed.), 'Original Documents: 4. Letters of Morgan John Rhys to William Owen [-Pughe]', 132.

[197] 'Ychydig o Gyfarwyddiadau Byrrion i Ddysgu Darllain yn gywir' and 'At Oruçwylwyr y Cylç-grawn Cynmraeg', *Cylch-grawn Cynmraeg*, no. I (1793), 2–4. For aspects of William Owen Pughe's linguistic efforts and life, see Glenda Carr, *William Owen Pughe* (Caerdydd, 1983); *eadem*, 'William Owen Pughe and the London Societies', in Jarvis, *A Guide to Welsh Literature* c.*1700–1800*, pp. 168–86; *eadem*, 'An Uneasy Relationship: Iolo Morganwg and William Owen Pughe', in Jenkins, *A Rattleskull Genius*, pp. 443–60.

[198] Jon Mee, 'Language', in McCalman (ed.), *An Oxford Companion to the Romantic Age*, pp. 374–5; David Simpson, *The Politics of American English, 1776–1850* (New York, 1962), pp. 53–6, 60–3. See also Williams, *Artisans and Sans-Culottes*, pp. xix–xxiii.

[199] Williams (ed.), 'Original Documents: 4. Letters of Morgan John Rhys to William Owen [-Pughe]', 134.

[200] *Y Geirgrawn*, no. II (1796), 40.

[201] 'Barddas, neu Gylch Gwybodaeth', *Cylch-grawn Cynmraeg*, nos. II–IV (1793–4), 60–1, 130–1, 203–5; H. Parry, 'Anianyddiaeth', *Y Geirgrawn*, no. VII (1796), 209–13, 271–3; *idem*, 'Corfforyddiaeth', ibid., no. IX (1796), 271–4.

[202] 'Athronaeth Grist'nogol', *Y Geirgrawn*, no. II (1796), 37; 'Anianyddiaeth', ibid., no. VII (1796), 210.

[203] 'Cyfeithad o Ragymadrodd y Dr. John Davies o flaen ei Eirlyfr Cymraeg a Lladin, i'r Gymraeg, er Dywenydd i'r Cymry', ibid., nos. III–IX (1796), 80–5, 101–3, 133–5, 231–3, 262–3.

[204] 'Ar Lŷs Ifor Hael, o Faes Haleg yn Swydd Fonwy; o waith y Parchedig Evan Evans (neu Evan Brydydd hîr) o Lan Rheidiol, yn Swydd Garedigion', *Cylch-grawn Cynmraeg*, no. II (1793), 98; 'Hynafiaeth, neu Hanes am Gantre'r Gwaelod', ibid., no. IV (1793), 226–8; 'Pum Brenhinllwyth Cymru', 'Eisteddfod Caerfyrddin', *Y Geirgrawn*, no. VIII (1796), 252; 'Hynafiaethau yn Enlli a Lleyn', ibid., no. IX (1796), 277–81.

[205] *Hereford Journal*, 7 January 1789; ibid., 21 January 1789; ibid., 4 March 1789; ibid., 22 April 1789.

[206] 'Cyflwr Crefydd yn America', *Y Geirgrawn*, no. IV (1796), 106–12; 'Annerch y Gymdeithas Dammaniaidd yn America i Dr. Priestley ar ei Dychweliad i'r wlad honno', *Y Drysorfa Gymmysgedig*, no. I (1795), 19–22.

[207] See also 'Llythyr o Ogleddol Barthau o America', *Y Drysorfa Gymmysgedig*, no. II (1795), 92–6; 'Talfyrriad o Lythyr oddiwrth Wr Ieuangc yn America', *Y Geirgrawn*, no. V (1796), 146–52; 'Llythyr o Gaerefrog Newydd (*New York*)', ibid., 152–4; 'Llythyr o America', ibid., no. VI (1796), 179–83.

[208] 'Llythyr y Dr. Franklin', *Cylch-grawn Cynmraeg*, no. II (1793), 87; 'Sylwadau ynghylch Indiaid yr America Ogleddol gan Dr. B. Franklin', ibid., no. V (1794), 262–3; 'Y Bibell, gan Dr Franklin', *Y Drysorfa Gymmysgedig*, no. II (1795), 49.

[209] Gwyn A. Williams, *Madoc: The Making of a Myth* (Oxford, 1987); Caroline Franklin, 'The Welsh American Dream: Iolo Morganwg, Robert Southey and the Madog Legend', in Gerard Carruthers and Alan Rawes (eds.), *English Romanticism and the Celtic World* (Cambridge, 2003), pp. 69–84; Helen Braithwaite, 'From the See of St Davids to St Paul's Churchyard: Joseph Johnson's Cross-Border Connections', in Davies and Pratt, *Wales and the Romantic Imagination*, pp. 53–5.

[210] *Hereford Journal*, 9 March 1791; ibid., 4 May 1791; ibid., 25 May 1791; Gwyn A. Williams, 'John Evans's Mission to the Madogwys, 1792–1799', *BBCS*, XXVII, part IV (1978), 570, 574–5. For the literary expression of this 'Madoc fever' among the London Welsh, see also W. Ll. Davies, 'David Samwell's Poem – "The Padouca Hunt"', *NLWJ*, II, nos. 3 and 4 (1942), 142–52.

[211] Williams, 'John Evans's Mission to the Madogwys', 569–601.

[212] See also 'Llythyr John Evans', *Cylch-grawn Cynmraeg*, no. II (1793), 114–16.

[213] See also Davies, '"Transatlantic Brethren"'; Williams, 'John Evans's Mission to the Madogwys', 573–4.

[214] Gwyn A. Williams, 'Morgan John Rhys and his Beulah', *WHR*, 3, no. 4 (1967), 441–72; *idem*, *The Search for Beulah Land: The Welsh and the Atlantic Revolution* (New York, 1980).

[215] Anne M. Cohler, Basia Caroline Miller, Harold Samuel Stone (eds.), *Montesquieu, The Spirit of the Laws* (Cambridge, 1989).

[216] *Chester Chronicle*, 24 December 1790.

[217] 'Amrywiol Ddamweiniau y'Nghodiad a Gostyngiad Rhyddid Wladwriaethol o'r Cynfyd hyd ei Sefydliad ym Mrydain (a Dynnwyd allan o Draethawd Gwallter Mechain)', *Y Geirgrawn*, nos. III–IX (1796), 78–80, 103–6, 141–4, 175–9, 198–202, 229–31, 265–8. The original essay was *Rhyddid: Traethawd a Ennillodd Ariandlws y Gwyneddigion* (London, 1791).

[218] 'Amrywiol Ddamweiniau y'Nghodiad a Gostyngiad Rhyddid Wladwriaethol o'r Cynfyd hyd ei Sefydliad ym Mrydain (a Dynnwyd allan o Draethawd Gwallter Mechain)', *Y Geirgrawn*, no. IX (1796), 268.

[219] *Chester Chronicle*, 13 November 1795; ibid., 11 December 1795; ibid., 8 January 1796; ibid., 15 January 1796; ibid., 29 January 1796; 'Crynodeb o'r Achosion o'r Cyfnewidiad yn Ffrainc', *Y Geirgrawn*, nos. I–III (1796), 23–5, 40–3, 87–90.

[220] *Y Geirgrawn*, no. III (1796), 87.

[221] *Chester Chronicle*, 25 December 1795.

[222] 'At ein Gohebwyr, a'r Cyffredin', *Y Geirgrawn*, nos. III and V (1796), cover.

[223] 'Cyflwr Crefydd yn America', ibid., no. IV (1796), 106–8, 108–12.

[224] Ibid., no. I (1796), cover.

[225] 'Brwydr yn Cael ei Darlunio', *Cylch-grawn Cynmraeg*, no. V (1794), 266–7.

[226] See also 'Ar Heddwch', *Y Drysorfa Gymmysgedig*, no. II (1795), 89; Dafydd Sa[u]nders, 'Ochenaid am Heddwch', *Y Geirgrawn*, no. IX (1796), 288.

[227] Isaiah 2: 4 inspires peace movements to this day.

[228] 'Hanes Daliad y Parchedig Mr. Jeremiah Joyce am Ymddygiad Bradwriaethol', *Y Drysorfa Gymmysgedig*, nos. I–II (1795), 30–8, 65–73. See Johnson, 'Fashioning the Legal Subject', 413–43.

[229] 'Newyddion', *Cylch-grawn Cynmraeg*, no. V (1794), 288.

[230] 'Newyddion', ibid., no. IV (1793), 237.

[231] 'Myfyrdodau ar yr Amserau', ibid., no. V (1794), 243.

[232] Hywel M. Davies, 'Morgan John Rhys and James Bicheno: Anti-Christ and the French Revolution in England and Wales', *BBCS*, XXIX, part I (1980), 114.

[233] Williams, *Artisans and Sans-Culottes*, pp. xxiv, 12–13. See also Robert Hole, *Pulpits, Politics and Public Order in England, 1760–1832* (Cambridge, 1989), pp. 120–6.

[234] Peris, 'Amddiffyniad y Grefydd Sefydledig', *Cylch-grawn Cynmraeg*, no. IV (1793), 208–10; ibid., no. V (1794), 245–8. For Peter Bailey Williams (Peris), see *DWB*; *NCLW*.

[235] 'Cywydd i'r Drindod', *Y Geirgrawn*, no. IV (1796), 126.

[236] 'At Ein Gohebwyr', ibid., no. VII (1796), cover.

[237] Peris, 'Crefydd Sefydledig yn cael ei Hamddiffyn', *Cylch-grawn Cynmraeg*, no. IV (1793), 208–12; *idem*, 'Amddiffyniad y Grefydd Sefydledig', ibid., no. V (1794), 245–8.

[238] Philopax, 'Ateb i Amddiffynwr y Grefydd Sefydledig', ibid., no. V (1794), 258–60.

[239] 'Ymddiddan rhwng Esgob Crist'nogol a Disgybl a Elwir Dyfal-Geisio', ibid., 250.

[240] Hole, *Pulpits, Politics and Public Order in England*, pp. 125–6.

[241] 'Rhan o Lythyr oddi wrth yr Enwog Andrew Dudith at y Parchedig Beza', *Cylch-grawn Cynmraeg*, no. I (1793), 26–9; 'Bywgraffiad Servetus', ibid., no. II (1793), 94–5; 'Ymadroddion Detholedig a Dynnwyd allan o Bregethau'r Diweddar Barch. G. Whitefield', *Y Geirgrawn*, no. IV (1796), 123–4; 'Hanes Dioddefiadau Mr. Thomas de Laune, Awdwr y Traethawd Rhagorol a Elwir "Dadl dros yr Anghydffurfwyr"', ibid., no. VII (1796), 203–8; J. P., 'Meddyliau ar Urddiad', *Y Drysorfa Gymmysgedig*, no. I (1795), 8–11; 'Annerch y Gymdeithas Dammaniaidd yn America i Dr. Priestley ar ei Ddychweliad i'r Wlad Honno', ibid., 19–22.

[242] 'Gofyniad – Pa ham yr Ydwyf yn Ymneillduo oddi wrth yr Eglwys Sefydledig', *Y Drysorfa Gymmysgedig*, no. I (1795), 13.

[243] 'Annerch Prysur at Ddrindodiaid a Chalfiniaid Annysgedig gan Undodwr Cristianogol', ibid., nos. I–II (1795), 23–30, 64–9; 'Annerch at Aelodau Eglwys Loegr, ac at Ddrindodiaid Protestanaidd yn Gyffredin Oll i'r Diben i'w Hannog Hwynt

i Droi oddi wrth yr Addoliad Gau o Dri Bersonau i'r Addoliad o'r Un Gwir Dduw yn Saesonaeg gan W. Frend', ibid., no. III (1796), 127–35. See also 'Dr. Courayer ar Berson Christ', *Cylch-grawn Cynmraeg*, no. IV (1793), 205–8.

[244] 'Hanes Crefydd o ran ei Dirywaeth', *Cylch-grawn Cynmraeg*, no. I (1793), 16–21.

[245] 'Hanes Degymau', ibid., no. III (1793), 153–4.

[246] See also 'Hymn Berthynol ar Ddydd Ympryd', *Y Drysorfa Gymmysgedig*, no. III (1795), 106; 'Ffurf o Weddi', ibid., 107.

[247] Hole, *Pulpits, Politics and Public Order in England*, pp. 12–13.

[248] 'Pregeth ar 1 Tim. II. 6', *Y Drysorfa Gymmysgedig*, no. II (1795), 61.

[249] 'Meddyliau ar Urddiad', ibid., no. I (1795), 11.

[250] Davies, '"Transatlantic Brethren"', p. 329.

[251] Eugene Nida, 'Principles of Correspondence', in Lawrence Venuti (ed.), *The Translation Studies Reader* (2nd edn., New York, 2004), pp. 156–7.

[252] Friedrich Schleiermacher, 'On the Different Methods of Translating (1813)', in Douglas Robinson (ed.), *Western Translation Theory from Herodotus to Nietzsche* (Manchester, 1997), pp. 233–4.

[253] 'Hanes Daliad y Parchedig Mr. Jeremiah Joyce am Ymddygiad Bradwriaethol', *Y Drysorfa Gymmysgedig*, nos. I–II (1795), 30–8, 65–73; 'Troedigaeth Parbootee', *Y Geirgrawn*, no. VI (1796), 170; 'Ychydig o Ddesgrifiad KENTUCKY, y Dalaith newydd yn AMERICA', *Cylch-grawn Cynmraeg*, no. III (1793), 164–6; 'Annerch at Aelodau Eglwys Loegr, ac at Ddrindodiaid Protestanaidd yn Gyffredin Oll i'r Diben i'w Hannog Hwynt i Droi oddi wrth yr Addoliad Gau o Dri Bersonau i'r Addoliad o'r Un Gwir Dduw yn Saesonaeg gan W. Frend', *Y Drysorfa Gymmysgedig*, no. III (1795), 127–35. This was to be continued in the fourth number which did not appear.

[254] Davies, '"Transatlantic Brethren"', p. 243; Robert Robinson, *A Plan of Lectures on Nonconformist Principles for the Instruction of Catechumens* (London, 1778). Robinson was also a friend of William Richards, Lynn, another Welsh Baptist and radical author who was in touch with Morgan John Rhys.

[255] Davies, '"Transatlantic Brethren"', pp. 375, 411; William Carey, *An Enquiry into the Obligations of Christians, to Use Means for the Conversion of the Heathens* (Leicester, 1792); 'Hanes Crefydd o Ran ei Llwyddiant', *Cylch-grawn Cynmraeg*, nos. I–III (1793), 8–15, 70–1, 161–3.

[256] Davies, 'Morgan John Rhys and James Bicheno', 112; 'Arwyddion yr Amserau', *Cylch-grawn Cynmraeg*, no. III (1793), 170–8.

[257] 'Y Bibell, gan Dr. Franklin', *Y Drysorfa Gymmysgedig*, no. II (1795), 49–51; 'Annerch at Aelodau Eglwys Loegr, ac at Ddrindodiaid Protestanaidd yn Gyffredin Oll i'r Diben i'w Hannog Hwynt i Droi oddi wrth yr Addoliad Gau o Dri Bersonau i'r Addoliad o'r Un Gwir Dduw yn Saesonaeg gan W. Frend', ibid., no. III (1795), 127–35.

[258] 'A Prayer for the People who Live under Despotic Governments', *Politics for the People*, II, no. V (1794), 4–6.

[259] 'An Hymn for the Fast Day, to be Sung by the Friends of Mankind', ibid., II, no. IV (1794), 3–5.

[260] 'A Hymn for the Fast Day to be Sung by the Privileged Orders of Europe', ibid., 5–7.

[261] NLW MS 12365D, f. 526.

[262] *Chester Chronicle*, 13 November 1795; ibid., 11 December 1795; ibid., 8 January 1796; ibid., 15 January 1796; ibid., 29 January 1796; 'Crynodeb o'r Achosion o'r Cyfnewidiad yn Ffrainc', *Y Geirgrawn*, nos. I–III (1796), 23–5, 40–3, 87–90.

[263] 'The Marseilles March', *Pig's Meat*, I (1793), 67–8; 'The Marseilles March', in *A Tribute to Liberty. Or, A New Collection of Patriotic Songs* (London, 1793), pp. 59–60; 'The Marseilles March', in *An Asylum for Fugitive Pieces* (London, 1793), pp. 25–6.

[264] Matthews, 'Holywell and the Marseillaise', 118; Mark Philp (ed.), *Thomas Paine: Rights of Man, Common Sense, and Other Political Writings* (Oxford, 1995), pp. 303, 311.

[265] Löffler, 'The Marseillaise in Wales'.

[266] 'Hynod Weledigaeth Gwr Bonheddig o Ffraingc', *Cylch-grawn Cynmraeg*, no. IV (1793), 221–3; Gwyn A. Williams, 'Morgan John Rhys and Volney's *Ruins of Empires*', *BBCS*, XX, part I (1962), 64; *idem*, *Artisans and Sans-Culottes*, pp. xxvii–xxviii.

[267] 'Hanes a Gafwyd yn Llyfr-gell Brenhin Ffraingc', *Y Geirgrawn*, no. IX (1796), 275.

[268] See Löffler, 'Serial Literature and Radical Poetry in Wales'.

[269] John Jones Glan-y-Gors, *Seren Tan Gwmmwl. Toriad y Dydd* (Liverpool, 1923), p. 4. The pamphlet and its translation are published in Löffler, *Political Pamphlets and Sermons from Wales.*

[270] 'Golwg ar y Gwrthwynebiad i'r Seren Tan Gwmmwl', *Y Geirgrawn*, no. III (1796), 78.

[271] 'Golwg ar Ymddyffiniad *Peris* o Frenhinoedd, Esgobion, &c.', ibid., no. VIII (1796), 236–9.

[272] Ibid., 237.

[273] Ibid., 239.

[274] 'Cyhoeddwr', ibid., 242.

[275] Williams, *Artisans and Sans-Culottes*, p. xvi.

[276] G. J. Williams, 'Hanes Cyhoeddi'r "Myvyrian Archaiology"', *JWBS*, X, no. 1 (1966), 2–12; Andrew Davies, '"Redirecting the Attention of History": Antiquarian and Historical Fictions of Wales from the Romantic Period', in Davies and Pratt, *Wales and the Romantic Imagination*, pp. 104–21; Löffler, *The Literary and Historical Legacy of Iolo Morganwg*, p. 1; Mary-Ann Constantine, 'Welsh Literary History and the Making of "The Myvyrian Archaiology of Wales"', in Dirk Van Hulle and Joep Leerssen (eds.), *Editing the Nation's Memory: Textual Scholarship and Nation-Building in Nineteenth-Century Europe* (Amsterdam, 2008), pp. 109–28; Geraint H. Jenkins, 'Clio and Wales: Welsh Remembrancers and Historical Writing, 1751–2001', *THSC* (2002), 119–36.

[277] Williams, 'Morgan John Rhys and his Beulah', 444.

[278] Magnuson, *Reading Public Romanticism*, p. 3.

[279] Williams, *Artisans and Sans-Culottes*, pp. 101–2.

# *Selection of Documents*

## *1 Welsh almanacs*

*Annual almanacs in the Welsh language had been published since 1680. Most of their contents followed the model of the English almanac, but they also provided some political comment and, uniquely, showcased Welsh poetry.* Britanus Merlinus Liberatus *was collated and published by the land surveyor Mathew William in Carmarthen from 1777 until 1795 and Brecon from 1796 until 1814.* Vox Stellarum et Planetarum *was published by John Harris, who kept a technical school at Kidwelly and (from 1797) at Carmarthen, where his almanac was also published.*

### *1.1 An astrological prediction*

*Britanus Merlinus Liberatus . . . am y Flwyddyn . . . 1795 . . . O Gynnulliad Mathew William, Mesurwr Tir. Caerfyrddin* (*Britanus Merlinus Liberatus* . . . for the Year . . . 1795 . . . Collected by Mathew William, Land-Surveyor. Carmarthen), 31.

Am Gwarter Hydref

Cwarter Hydref sy'n dechrau ar ddyfod Sol, Titan neu Apollo i arwydd y Fantol, yr hyn sy'n digwydd yn y flwyddyn hon ar y trydydd dydd ar hugain o fis Medi, am 32 wedi dau o'r bore, ar y cyfryw amser mae 24 gradd o'r Llew yn ascennu yn y terfyngylch ac un gradd ar ddeg o'r Tarw yn dyrchafu ynghanol y ffurfafen, Sadwrn yn y Gefeilliaid, Iau yn yr Afr, Mawrth a Gwener yn y Forwyn, &c.

Wrth yr amrywiol dremiadau sy'n digwydd yn y Cwarter hwn, ni welwn fod rhyw derfysgiadau yn magu braidd ym mhob ran o'r ddaear, ac fel tonnau'r môr yn ymchwyddo o flaen 'stormydd neu fath o *hurricans* ac sy'n arferol o fod mewn gwledydd tramôr. Nid yw'r addurn yma'n dangos fod y byd yn gwella fawr oddi wrth eu hanlladrwydd a'u pechod fucheddau; yma y gwelir mae nid y dynion doethaf yw'r dynion mwyaf eu parch a'u derbyniad; yma y gwelwn fod llawer yn byw yn abal ac yn uchel eu cymeriad o herwydd nad 'ynt byth yn talu dyledion: nid yw ddim yn rhyfedd fod rhai yn ymgyfoethogi pan maent yn cadw eiddo eraill yn eu dwylo. Digwydd na chair clywed rhyw newyddion lled anymunol yn y Cwarter hwn neu ddechreu'r llall; yr hyn am dyg i derfynu fy marnedigaeth yn y geiriau canlynol:

Mawr iawn yw pechod dynion er cael rhybuddion rhad,
Mawr iawn sydd o gynhorion rai glewion yn ein gwlad;
Mawr iawn y fu rhyfeloedd ar foroedd ac ar dir,
Sef, ffrwythau o annifeirwch chwi welwch hyn yn wir.

Good will no public grievance can devise;
Real religion *wills* – no strain'd supplies,
All christians, were sincere, pursue one plan,
*Peace* – taught by *One*, who bought the *rights of man*.

(*On the Autumn Quarter*

The autumn quarter begins with the Sun, Titan or Apollo coming into the sign of Libra, which happens this year on the twenty-third day of the month of September, 32 minutes after two in the morning, at which time 24 degrees of Leo is ascending at the horizon and the eleventh degree of Taurus is advancing in the middle of the firmament, Saturn is in Gemini, Jupiter in Capricorn, Mars and Venus in Virgo, &c.

By the various aspects which happen in this Quarter, we see that some disturbances are brewing in almost every part of the world, and like the waves of the sea are swelling before storms or the kind of *hurricanes* that usually occur in overseas countries. This illustration does not show that the world is improving from its debauchery and its sinful life; here one sees that the wisest men are not the most respected and revered; we see here that many live in opulence and high status because they never pay their debts: it is not strange that some grow rich when they keep the property of others in their hands. It so happens that rather unpleasant news will not be heard in this Quarter or the beginning of the next, which leads me to end my judgement with the following words:

Very great are the sins of men though they have had gracious warnings,
very great is the number of valiant leaders in our country;

very great were the wars on oceans and on land,
which are the fruits of impenitence, indeed, you see it.

Good will no public grievance can devise;
Real religion *wills* – no strain'd supplies,
All christians, were sincere, pursue one plan,
*Peace* – taught by *One*, who bought the *rights of man*.)

## *1.2 A loyalist address in the wake of the Fishguard landing*

*Britanus Merlinus Liberatus . . . am y Flwyddyn . . . 1798 . . . Gan Mathew Williams, Land Surveyor . . . ABERHONDDU (Britanus Merlinus Liberatus* . . . for the Year . . . 1798 . . . Collected by Mathew William, Land-Surveyor . . . Brecon), 2.

At y CYMRU

Fy Nghydwladwyr,

ER pan gefais ddiwetha' y pleser i'ch annerch, fe welwyd yn ofynnol, oblegid angenrheidiau'r wlad, ddodi Tal chwanegol ar yr Almanac; er mor anhyfryd y gall hyn fod i ni y Cyfansoddwyr, ac i chwithau fy Narllenyddion, etto pan ystyrioch y gellwch, am ychydig yn rhagor na ffyrlling yn yr wythnos trwy gymmorth y llyfrau hyn, gael allan dyddiau'r mis neu'r wythnos, Newid y lleuad, y ffeiriau yng Nghymru, Cyfnewid y tywydd, a llawer o bethau neillduol eraill, ag sydd ddefnyddiol i'r Bonheddig yn gystal ag i'r Ffermwr a'r Masnachwr, pan gofioch mai trwy nerth y Trethi y sy yn ein gwasgu (er trymmed ydynt) ynghyd a chalondid ac ymddygiad ein Lluoedd ar For a Thir, y rhai a gynnorthwyasoch chwi fy Nghydwladwyr mor rhagorol a gwrol-wych ar achos diweddar pan ryfygodd y Gelynion dirio yn eich Gwlad, pan gofioch meddaf, mai trwy y rhai'n (dan Ragluniaeth) yr amddiffynwyd ni rhag gormes didrugaredd Ciwed o Ffrangcod diffaith a'u Cefnogwyr, y rhai a sathrasant sanctaidd Ordinhadau Duw a pharchedig Osodiadau dyn dan draed, y rhai y gellir dilyn gwaedlyd ol eu traed trwy Anghyfannedd-dra, Tlodi, a Newin (p'le bynnag y gadawodd yr Hollalluog i'r fflangell gwympo) ac yn olaf, pan edrychoch ar eich cyflwr eich hunain, yr hwn wrth ei gydmaru ag eiddo'r lleill o Ewrop, neu f'allai'r byd, sydd gyflwr o berffaith happusrwydd: mi wn yn dda, na welir un Cymro yn grwgnach nac yn achwyn ar yr achos hwn, ond yn y gwrthwyneb, yr wyf yn llwyr gredu y cynnorthwywch allan o'ch cariad at eich gwlad, tuag at sicrhau ein diogelwch, a thrwy wneuthur felly, y bwriwch eich hatling er cynnal yr achos clodfawr hwnnw o amddiffyn ein Rhydd-did, ein Meddiannau, ein Cyfreithiau, a'n Bywydau.

(To the WELSH

My Compatriots,

SINCE I last had the pleasure of addressing you, it was seen to be necessary, because of the hardships of the country, to raise the price of the Almanac; however unpleasant this might be for us the Composers, and for you my Readers, when you consider that you can, for not much more than a farthing a week through the help of these books, find out the days of the month or of the week, the Changes of the moon, the fairs in Wales, Changes in the weather, and many other particular things, which are useful to the Noble as well as for the Farmer and the Merchant, when you remember that through the power of the Taxes which press on us (heavy as they are) together with the bravery and the feats of our Forces on Sea and Land, the ones which you my Compatriots so outstandingly and gallantly supported on the recent occasion when the Enemies dared land in your Country, when you remember, I say, that through these (under Providence) we were protected from the merciless oppression of a Rabble of vile French and their Supporters, those who had trampled God's sacred Ordinations and the revered Constitutions of man under foot, those whose bloody footprints we can follow through Desolation, Poverty, and Famine (wherever the Almighty let the scourge fall) and lastly, when you look at your own state, which compared with the state of others in Europe, or perhaps the world, is a state of perfect happiness; I know well, not one Welshman will be seen grumbling or complaining in this case, but on the contrary, I fully believe that you will assist out of love for your country, towards securing our safety, and by doing so, you will throw in your mite in order to sustain this praiseworthy cause of defending our Liberty, our Possessions, our Laws, and our Lives.)

### *1.3 A patriotic song*

*Vox Stellarum et Planetarum . . . Am y Flwyddyn . . . 1795 . . . gan John Harris, Dysgawdwr Rhifyddiaeth yng Nghydwely* (*Vox Stellarum et Planetarum* . . . For the Year . . . 1795 . . . by John Harris, Teacher of Arithmetic in Kidwelly), 10–11.

*Can newydd ar y Dôn a elwir,* DUW GADWO'N BRENIN.

1 Cydnesed plant dynion, groesaw pob Cristion,
Gwrandawed yn gyson ar gân,
Mae'r Ffrangcod mor ffyrnig, a'u meddwl mileinig,
Yn myn'd fel yn gyrnig eu grân:
Sef, 'mostwng i *Gustin,*[1] a mwrddro eu brenin,
Trwy ei roi e'n y *gulotine* gâs,
Digio pob pen-iaith cyfarwydd â'r gyfraith,
Wrth fyned â'u mawr-waith i maes.
Mae'r Ffrangcod dû, 'sgeler, am lwgi hen Loegr,
A'n rhoi ni mewn caethdŷ dan gûr;
Ond Duw mawr, ein Brenin, yr hwn all ymddiffyn,
A gostwng pob gwerin yn wir.

2 Mae llawer llong dacclus a'i hwyliau mor hwylus,
Yn disgwyl ei grymmus *ffleet* gre',
Gan *Hood* a *Howe*[2] dirion, ar wyneb yr eigion,
A'u *canons* yn llawn yn eu lle:
Os digwydd rhyw *fattel*, neu rwyfo am ryfel,
Mae pawb yn y gafael â'u gwaith,
Ni safwn yn gefnog, go-lân yn galonog,
Ar gefn y tonog môr maith:
Nid gwiw i ni geisio, na galw am gilio,
Ni fynnwn ei mentro ar y môr;
Mae llaw all ein safio, os yw e'n 'wyllysio,
Cyn caffon' hwy farno ar ein *Sôr*.

3 Pwy ŵyr pwy ymgeledd oedd ar y pum troedfedd
O gyrph oedd yn gorwedd yn garn;
Ond Duw oedd yn gwybod pa faint oedd eu pechod,
Pan doent hwy i ymgyfarfod âr farn:
A'r Duc mawr ei uchder o du Brenin Lloegr,[3]
A safodd yn gryfder fel gwr;
Tair gwaith lladd ei geffyl, a'i glwyfo fe'n gynnil,
Ond safai fe'n syfil yn siwr;
A llawer glân Gymro, iaith union oedd yno,
Yn barod i'w bwyo i'r bedd,
Heb feddwl y boreu wrth gychwyn ei siwrneu,
Ddim lladd nad o'r goreu eu gwedd.

4 Er enbaid y milwyr, 'doedd yno fawr gysur,
Wrth weled y frwydr mor friw;
Rhai oedd yn glwyfus, a nifer yn nafus,
O'r gwir mwyaf grymmus yn y *griw*.
Wrth hyn gallwn feddwl bod llawer o drwbl,
Pob un ar ei sawdl mor syth,
Yn *lodo* eu *gwnau* yn hwyr ac yn fore,
I blannu plwm belau yn eu plith.
'Doedd yno fawr hidio 'mo'r gwyr yn och'neidio,
Ar ol iddynt gwympo dan draed,
Ond yn swrth yn eu sathru, 'doedd neb yno'n gwenu,
A'n gwyr oedd yn gwanu trwy'r gwaed.

5 Un fil a saith can mlwydd, mae pawb yn gyfarwydd,
Yw oedran ein Harglwydd yn hwn,
A naw maith o ddegau, mae hynny'n hir ddyddiau,
A phedair rhyw foreu ddaw'n bwn:
Ond Duw gadwo'n Brenin, yn ddiffael i 'mddiffyn,
Rhag dyfod un gelyn i'n gwlad;
A digon o filwyr i gadw'r ffordd gywir,
Rhag dyfod un frwydr o frad.
Bid hir i'r gwaedoliaeth i *riwlo* yn helaeth,
Na weled neb sur-waith na sen,
Ffwrdd ddrwg-feddyliau, yn hwyr ac yn for[au],
A'r Mawredd fo'n maddau, Amen.

Edward Jones, Mwynwr, ai cânt.[4]

(*A new Song on the Tone called,* GOD SAVE OUR KING.

1 Come closer, children of men, welcome to every Christian,
listen closely to a song,
the French are so ferocious, with their barbarous intent,
going as if they had horns:
namely submitting to Custine,[1] and murdering their king,
by putting him in the odious guillotine,
angering every ruler who is familiar with the law,
in carrying out their great work.
The black, wicked French want to starve old England,
and throw us in prison to languish;

but the great God, our King, he can defend,
and, indeed, subdue every people.

2 Many a tidy ship with sails well trimmed,
is waiting for their mighty fleet,
under fair *Hood* and *Howe*,[2] on the face of the ocean,
and their cannons are fully in place:
if there happens some battle, or voyaging to war,
all set to work,
we shall stand firm, all of good heart,
on the face of the vast ocean waves:
it is not befitting to call for retreating,
we will take our chance on the sea;
there is a hand which can save us, if it is his will,
before they can judge our *George*.

3 Who knows what succour had the five feet
of bodies which lay there in a heap;
only God knew the magnitude of their sins,
when they came to meet with the judgement:
and the great tall Duke on the side of the King of England,[3]
who stood in his manly strength;
three times was his horse slain and he was slightly wounded,
but he stood graciously indeed;
and many a pure, honest-tongued Welshman was there,
ready to be struck down to the grave,
without thinking in the morning while setting out on his journey,
of killing, but in the best of spirits.

4 Though perilous the soldiers, there was not much comfort,
in seeing the battle so harsh;
some were wounded, a number maimed,
of the strongest men in the band.
By this we may imagine that there was much trouble,
every one so straight on their heels,
*loading* their *guns* all day long,
to plant leaden balls in their midst.
Not much notice was taken of the men who were groaning,
after they fell underfoot,
but trampling them helpless, none there was smiling,
and our men were stabbing through the blood.

5 One thousand seven hundred years, as all know well,
is the age of our Lord in this,
and nine long decades, these are long days,
and four years some morning comes in total:
but the Lord keep our King, without fail to defend,
against the coming of one enemy to our country;
and enough soldiers to keep the right way,
lest there should come any battle by treason.
Let the bloodline rule long and wide,
and not face resentment or censure,
away, bad thoughts, evening and morn,
and may the Almighty forgive us, Amen.

Edward Jones, the Miner, sang this.)[4]

### *1.4 A poem on Thomas Paine as the instrument of God's vengeance*

*Vox Stellarum et Planetarum . . . Am y Flwyddyn . . . 1796 . . . gan John Harris, Dysgawdwr Rhifyddiaeth yng Nghydweli* (*Vox Stellarum et Planetarum* . . . For the Year . . . 1796 . . . by John Harris, Teacher of Arithmetic in Kidwelly), 8–10.

*Bydded hyspys i'r Darllenydd i Awdwr y Gân ganlynol gael ei gyffroi gan un ag oedd yn selog iawn ymhlaid Pabyddiaeth, ac a roddodd Enllib ar yr Awdwr ar Gam, trwy ddywedyd ei fod yn groes i Lywodraeth a Chyfreithiau'r Deyrnas, ar ba Achosion y gwnaeth ei Ymddiffyniad fel y canlyn.*

MINNAU A ATTEBAF FY RHAN, MINNAU A DDYWEDAF FY MEDDWL. *Job* xxxii. 17.

1 Cydwybod sy'n fy nghymmell, ond doniau sydd yn wan,
I roddi i chwi atteb mewn undeb yn y man;
O Dduw rho i mi'th gymmorth i'm cynnal ar fy nhaith,
Rho yspryd hen *Elias* o'm mynwes at y gwaith.

2 Os Pab sy'n maddeu pechod, a rhoddi cymmod glân,
A chuddio'n hanwireddau a'n beiau fawr a mân;
Os yw'n ein cadw'n hollol rhag dialeddol wŷn,
Pa raid oedd Crist i farw i gadw enaid dyn?

3 Ni chei di ganddo, heb arian, o'i anian gadair aur,
Na chusan bawd na phardwn, ond dwnsiwn gyd â'r gair;
A'th farnu i eigion purdan, yn ol ei anian syth,
O'i gadair grin sigledig, yn felldigedig fyth.

4 Mae'n cadw'r bobl dlodion mewn modd anraslon, clyw,
Mewn dygn anwybodaeth o'u hiechydwriaeth wiw;
Carcharu, lladd, a'u llosgi, a'u sathru dan ei draed,
Rhag profi 'mo'r gwirionedd a rhinwedd pardwn rhad.

5 Ac am ei waith yn harddu bedd Iesu'n Harglwydd ni,
I dwyllo'r bobl dlodion, anraslon, greulon, gri;
Ac am ei lamp annedwydd hi ddiffydd ddiwedd dydd,
Heb olew gras i'w chynnal, un feddal, byw ni fydd.

6 Nid yn ninas Rufain bu Crist ar bren y groes
Yn diodde' dros bechodau ddoluriau angeu loes;
Dioddefodd yn Judea, ar ben Calfaria fryn,
Ac yno mae'r bedd sanctaidd, pwy ŵyr pa wedd pryd hyn?

7 Y bara a'r gwin cysegrant, hwy dd'wedant yno'n syn,
*Gwir gnawd a gwaed ein Harglwydd* yw'r pethau sanctaidd hyn;
A mil o gamsyniadau, heb ammau, fwy na rhi',
Sy' 'mysg yr holl Babyddion anraslon greulon gri.

8 Os *Paine* a ga'dd ei alw yn hoyw ar ei hynt,
I dorri'r iau haiarnaidd fel *Jehu*[5] giaidd gynt;
I dorri *Ahab*[6] enbyd a'i deulu gwaedlyd wawr,
Am ladd prophwydi'r Arglwydd penllywydd nef a llawr:

9 Caiff *Paine* ei alw i gyfri' pan ddelo ei waith i ben,
'Nol cwpla'r hyn a dd'wedodd, arfaethodd Brenin nen;
Ac oni bydd ei galon yn union ger bron Duw,
Caiff fel Senac'rib[7] gwympo trwy ddwylaw rhai o'i ryw.

10 Gwaith nid rhai tirion daear, broffeswr claiar, clyw,
Gaiff ddial gwaed y seintiau fu'n diodde' tros eu Duw;
Ond ef trwy ragderfyniad sy'n trefnu yn ddiwad,
Cynddrwg rhai a hwythau ryw brydiau wneud eu brad.

11 Rhyfelwyr ydyw'r seintiau, ond deall di'n ddiwad,
Nad yw eu hymdrechiadau yn erbyn cig a gwaed,
Ond yn erbyn tywysogaethau, ac awdurdodau, a gwg,
Gelynion eu heneidiau'r llew a'i ruadau drwg.

12 Ti roddaist arnaf w'radwydd, annedwydd oedd dy naws,
Fy mod i'n erbyn *Lloegr* yn traethu doethder traws;
Er cymmaint yw dy gabledd, a'th naws anweddaidd wŷn,
Dymunaf iddi ffyniant a llwyddiant ymhob llun.

13 Boed llwyddiant gyd â'i lluoedd, ar foroedd ac ar dir,
Mor belled elo'i baner o blaid cyfiawnder pur;
Yn farn bo'r holl Babyddiaeth ddrwg effaith giaidd gas,
Gwir lewod tywysog Silo f'o mwy yn cario'r maes.

14 Y Pab efe yw'r bwystfil, anghenfil drwg ei wawr,
A hitheu eglwys *Rufain*, a'i llid, yw'r buttain fawr,
Sy'n feddw ar waed y seintiau, yn eiste' ar ddyfroedd maith,
Arswydus fydd ei diwedd wrth gyrraedd pen ei thaith.

15 Holl dywysogion daear, mewn gerwin alar gri,
Fu'n yfed yn ddigonol o'i chwppan hudol hi;
Cânt yfed cwppan arall, digofaint diwall Duw,
Mewn llyn o dân trag'wyddol, ynghwmp'ni diafol ryw.

16 Rho heibio'th sel bartiol o blaid y Pab a'i hil,
Fe laddodd Brotestaniaid, heb arbed, lawer mil;
A theulu'r *Capets* gwaedlyd,[8] ymysg y *Ffrangcod* syn,
Fu'n lladd y rhai'n yn lluoedd mewn garw fodd cyn hyn.

17 Mae gwae a gwaed y rhei'ny yn gwaeddi cuwch a'r nef,
Cynhyrfodd brenin Alpha, Jehofa ydyw ef;
Fe gododd lu ciwdawdol i'w ddialeddol lid,
I ddial gwaed y seintiau fu'n dioddef o bryd i bryd.

18 Colofnau cryfion anghrist, sy'n athrist grynu 'nawr,
Y buttain Fabilonaidd yn swrth a syrth i'r llawr;
Caiff rhai fu'n rhwym gan Satan yn fuan dd'od yn rhydd,
I ryddid gogoneddus plant Duw ar ddiwedd dydd.

19 Cair gweled plant y deyrnas uwch cyrraedd byd a chnawd,
Yn dyrfa ogoneddus ynghwmp'ni ei hynaf Frawd,
Dyrchafant gân o foliant, yn bendant iddo ef,
Am eu gwaredu o rwymau byd, cnawd, ac uffern gref.

20 Duw cadw Siors ein brenin, iawn ryddin yn ei ryw,
Tro'i galon at ddoethineb, duwioldeb meibion Duw;
'Nol 'mado â'i goron yma, Duw dwg ef, gyd â'i dŷ,
I mewn i'r noddfa nefol, drag'wyddol freiniol fry.

DAFYDD RISIART, *Waun-lwyd, Llandybie.*[9]

(*Let it be known to the Reader that the Author of the following Song was upset by one who was very zealously in favour of Popery, and who libelled the Author wrongly, by saying that he was against the Government and the Laws of the Kingdom, on which Points he made his Defence as follows.*

I WILL ANSWER ALSO WITH MY PART. I ALSO WILL SHEW MINE OPINION. *Job* xxxii. 17

1 Conscience urges me, though the talents are weak,
to give you an answer in concord straightaway;
Oh! God give me your help to support me on my journey,
put the spirit of old *Elijah* from my breast to the work.

2 If it is the Pope who forgives sins, and grants pure atonement,
and hides our untruths and our sins, great and small;
if he keeps us completely from the pains of retribution,
why did Christ have to die to save the soul of man?

3 You will not get from him, without money, from his worldly golden chair,
either kissing of hand or pardon, but dungeon at a word;
and he'll condemn you to the depth of purgatory, according to his proud nature,
from his withered shaky chair, forever cursed.

4 He keeps the poor people in a graceless state, listen,
in grievous ignorance of their worthy salvation;
imprisons, murders and burns them, and tramples them under his feet,
lest they should experience the truth and the virtue of a gracious pardon.

5 And for his work adorning the grave of Jesus our Lord
to deceive the poor people, gracelessly, cruelly, rudely;
his miserable lamp, it will go out at the end of the day
without the oil of grace to nourish it, the feeble one, it will not live.

6 It was not in the city of Rome that Christ was on the cross
suffering for sins the pains of death's agony;
he suffered in Judaea, on top of Calvary hill,
and the holy grave is there, who knows how it looks now?

7 The consecrated bread and the wine, they announce it there with surprise,
*the true flesh and blood of our Lord* are these holy things;
and a thousand false beliefs, without doubt, more than can be counted,
are current among all the graceless, cruel, Papists.

8 If it was *Paine* who was called vigorously on his way
to break the iron yoke as brutal *Jehu*[5] did before;
to cut down dangerous *Ahab*[6] and his blood-stained family
for killing the Lord's prophets, the architect of heaven and earth:

9 *Paine* will be called to account when his work is at an end,
when he has finished what he said, which the King of heaven has preordained;
and if his heart is not righteous before God,
like Senac'rib[7] he will fall through the hands of his own kind.

10 For it is not the meek of the world, hark lukewarm Christian,
who will avenge the blood of the saints who suffered for their God;
but he arranges inexorably through preordination
ones as bad as themselves to betray them sometimes.

11 The saints are warriors, but understand, for sure,
that their efforts are not against flesh and blood,
but against principalities, and authorities and wrath,
the enemies of their souls are the lion and his awful roarings.

12 You put calumny on me, wretched was your disposition,
that I expressed wicked views against *England*;
despite your copious blasphemy and your indecent, raging nature,
I wish her prosperity and success in every form.

13 May her forces, on oceans and on land, be successful,
as long as her banner flies for pure justice;
may all Popery be judged, its cruel and horrid mischief,
the true lions of the prince of Shiloh may carry the day.

14 The Pope, he is the monster, the brute with ugly mien
and the angry church of *Rome* is the great whore,
who is drunk on the blood of the saints, sitting on great depths,
her end will be dreadful when she reaches the end of her journey.

15 All the earthly princes in raw harsh grief
have been drinking their fill of her alluring cup;
they'll get to drink another cup, God's abundant wrath,
in a lake of eternal fire, in devilish company.

16 Let go of your partisan zeal for the Pope and his ilk,
it was he who unsparingly killed thousands of Protestants;
and the bloody *Capet* family,[8] amid the stupefied *French*,
had been killing hosts of them savagely before that.

17 The blood and grief of those cry up as high as heaven,
the King of Alpha was disturbed, Jehovah is his name;
he raised a republican force for his avenging rage
to avenge the blood of the saints who suffered from time to time.

18 It is the strong pillars of Antichrist which are sorrowfully
quaking now,
the Babylonian whore is helplessly falling down;
some who were bound by Satan will soon be freed
to the glorious liberty of God's children at the end of the day.

19 The children of the kingdom will be seen above the reach of world and flesh,
a glorious throng in the company of their eldest Brother,
they will raise a song of praise emphatically to him
for freeing them from the ties of the world, the flesh and of strong hell.

20 God keep George our king, the true heart of his line,
and turn his heart to wisdom, the godliness of God's sons;
after parting with his crown here, God take him, with his house,
into the eternal, blessed sanctum, on high.

DAFYDD RISIART, *Waun-lwyd, Llandybie.*)[9]

*1.5 William Pitt's tax on dogs*

*Vox Stellarum et Planetarum . . . Am y Flwyddyn . . . 1798 . . . gan John Harris, Dysgawdwr Rhifyddiaeth yng Nghaerfyrddin* (*Vox Stellarum et Planetarum . . .* For the Year . . . 1798 . . . by John Harris, Teacher of Arithmetic in Carmarthen), 30.

Breuddwyd Sion o'r Bryn, Llandilo-Fawr, a'i Gi Ciwpit.

Pan ddaeth son gyntaf am y dreth annaturiol ar y cwn, mi a freuddwydiais fy mod yn cymmeryd fy nghi i'w grogi; ac yntef yn honni ei ffyddlondeb yn fy ngwasaneth fel y canlyn:

Mi'th wasanaethais di'n onest bob whit,
A chedwais yn gynnes oedd gennyt;
Ffittach nâ chrogi *Ciwpit*,
Ystyn bait i *Bily Pit*.

Rho gennad roi galwad ynghyd,
Faith awen, fytheiad yr holl-fyd;
Ar ei ol e' a Dent hefyd,
Yn ddifrad holl gŵn y byd.

(The Dream of John of the Hill, Llandeilo-Fawr, and his Dog Cupid.

When first there was talk of the unnatural tax on the dogs, I dreamt that I took my dog to be hanged, and he proclaimed his loyalty in my service as follows:

> I served you honestly every instant,
> And I kept warm what was yours;
> More befitting than strangling *Cupid*
> Is extending a bait to *Billy Pitt*.
>
> Great muse, call together
> All the hounds of the world;
> After him and Dent, too
> Faithfully all dogs of this world.)

## 2 *The* Hereford Journal

*Founded as the* British Chronicle, or Pugh's Hereford Journal *in 1770 and known as the* Hereford Journal *from 1793, this weekly, which appeared on Thursdays, served as the main newspaper for south and west Wales. Its editors, Revd J. Duncumb (1789–91) and D. Walker (1791–1802), took a temperately loyalist stance which allowed the reprinting of moderately controversial religious material. The newspaper did not feature much poetry or material in the Welsh language, but its news coverage of events in or concerning Wales was, perhaps, the most detailed of all the provincial papers published along Offa's Dyke.*

### 2.1 *An account of the history of the eisteddfod*

*Hereford Journal*, 22 April 1789.

*WELSH POETRY.*

The national poetry has at all times been a favourite subject of cultivation among the Welsh; the professors of that science have ever been held in great esteem, and their works considered as the first literary treasure of the country.

A Congress of Bards, called *Eisteddfod*, a singular and curious institution, has, from the earliest times, been frequently held in various parts of the principality, in order to afford those who had confidence in their abilities, an opportunity of displaying their skill, in a generous competition with their brethren.

Upon those occasions, the Prince himself appointed judges by commission to decide upon their various merits, and to assign the laurel to the most worthy.

CAERWYS, in Flintshire, was long famous for these meetings, and the *Mostyn* family used to bestow a SILVER HARP upon the Bard who came off victorious in the poetical contest.

In the reign of Queen ELIZABETH an *Eisteddfod* was held at that town by royal authority, which is the last in which we hear of the silver harp having been given to the successful candidate.

Since that period, the custom itself, though deprived of that honourable excitement, which in other times stimulated the bards to the exertion of their talents, has by no means ceased; among this order of men, a generous emulation alone, has served to keep it alive, even to our own days! – A wish to encourage and preserve an institution so ancient and so laudable in itself, has induced the *Gwyneddigion Society of London*, to offer a *Silver Harp* to the bard whose composition, upon a given subject, shall entitle him to that distinction, at an *Eisteddfod* appointed to be held in Merionethshire the ensuing Summer.

This intelligence, which we give our readers from good authority, must be highly pleasing to every lover of the Welsh muse, and we will add, reflects great credit upon the gentlemen composing the *Gwyneddigion Society*, who have in so liberal a manner manifested their regard for the poetry of their country.

## *2.2 The Welsh discovery of America*

*Hereford Journal*, 26 August 1789.

DISCOVERY OF AMERICA.

Many nations contend with COLUMBUS the honour of having first discovered America – amongst these the WELSH seem to have the best pretensions. Madoc ap Owain Gwynedd, a Prince of North Wales, is said to have landed, with a number of his countrymen, upon that continent, long before it was discovered by Columbus. Such authentic intelligence has of late been received of the descendants of the emigrators, who are reported to inhabit the banks of the Mississippi, that a Welsh gentleman, now in London, is actually engaged in an expedition to the New World, in order to fully ascertain the truth of this ancient tradition. This undertaking, if prosecuted, will be much to the benefit of science, and the gratification of antiquarian curiosity.

## *2.3 A petition from Carmarthen town for abolishing the slave trade*

*Hereford Journal*, 14 March 1792.

Among the many excellent petitions presented to the House of Commons for the abolition of the Slave-trade, the following, presented last week by the Hon. Mr. Rice, Member for the county of Carmarthen, seems to deserve particular notice:

"To the Hon. the Commons of Great Britain in Parliament assembled.

"The humble Petition of the Gentlemen, Clergy, Freeholders, and other

Inhabitants of the Town, Parish, and Neighbourhood of the ancient Borough of Llanelly, in the county of Carmarthen,

"Sheweth, That, warmly impressed by those feelings which have so nobly animated the most splendid talents and highest characters in this kingdom, we, your Petitioners, cannot avoid expressing to this Honourable House our abhorrence of the oppressions exercised, by this among other nations of Europe, towards our defenceless brethren of Africa.

"The history of those oppressions is too fully recorded in the evidence already before the House to render it necessary for us here to enumerate them, nor would we offend the House by a repetition of facts at which humanity must shudder.

"In the full enjoyment of all the blessings derived to us from the most excellent of human Governments, under the Administration of a patriot King and an upright and popular Minister, we are led by a comparative view of our own happiness to sympathize more earnestly in the miseries of others; and, in common, with our disinterested fellow-subjects, we wholly reprobate those principles which would continue to allow legal sanction to a traffic of iniquity and murder.

"We trust the time is arrived, when the Commons of Great Britain will not allow the narrow reasonings of interested policy to prevail against the dictates of immutable justice; when Britons, ever forward to defend their own liberties, will become the first to promote the freedom of Africa.

"We therefore humbly pray this Honourable House to adopt such measures for the immediate abolition of the Slave Trade, as in the wisdom of the House that seem meet."

## *2.4 A declaration of loyalty from Talgarth, Breconshire*

*Hereford Journal*, 26 December 1792.

TALGARTH, DEC. 10, 1792.

At a meeting of Several Inhabitants of this parish, held this day.

It was resolved, That it appears to this Meeting, that at a time when, in defiance of the King's late Proclamation, doctrines are held, even in this part of the kingdom, so distant from the seat of Government, which aim at its destruction, it becomes the Inhabitants of this parish, which as well as those of greater opulence participates the benefit of our excellent Constitution, to declare their sentiments of attachment to it.

Resolved, That the Inhabitants of this parish be requested to meet on Friday the 14th instant, at the Lion Inn, Talgarth, at the hour of four in the afternoon.

At a numerous Meeting of the Inhabitants of this parish, held at the Lion Inn, in consequence of the above advertisement,

HENRY ALLEN, Esq. in the Chair,

The Chairman having read the advertisement, and explained the motives for calling the Meeting, it was resolved unanimously,

That it appears that it is proper and expedient in the present state of our country, to declare and publish our respect for the Government of it; because though we inhabit a small division of the kingdom, as compared to the whole, yet as the whole is composed of several parts, it seems to us, that if each part was to declare itself, it would effectually tend to silence those who are eagerly busied in endeavouring to destroy the whole. We therefore DECLARE our steady loyalty to our present Sovereign, and our attachment to our Government in its present form; which we conceive to be the best adapted to secure happiness and real liberty in those who live under it. While we know that our persons and our property, of whatever rank the first, or whatever rate the last, are equally protected by our Laws – while they encourage industry and protect its profits – while they assure us that the earnings of the honest labourer cannot be withheld from him – that his cottage is as fully under their protection as the palace of our princes – while they afford to the weak and poor among us a guard against any injury that may be offered by the strong or the rich, we cannot but declare our submission and attachment to them – while we know that by industry and abilities our fellow subjects, born in poverty and obscurity, may acquire wealth and honourable distinction, we feel, that under our present form of Government, there is as much equality amongst its subjects, as men who respect peace, order, and real liberty, can wish for.

Expressing our attachment to our excellent form of Government, yet as no human institution can be perfect, we are aware that errors and abuses may creep into it, but, we conceive it best to leave the manner and the time of correcting such as may require it, to those whom we have delegated to legislate for us. If we have sometimes felt our taxes heavy, we have satisfied ourselves in the conviction that they were necessary to the Support of that Government which supports us in the free enjoyment of life, property, and substantial liberty. Wishing these blessings to be continued to us, to support the Magistrates in suppressing any tumults or riots in their beginning; and to reduce to obedience of the laws, those who may manifest their defiance or contempt of them; and to endeavour to our utmost, by our example and persuasion, to convince those who may be misled by the enemies to our happy Constitution, of the solid benefits it secures to them by our present happy form of Government.

Resolved unanimously, That a book be now opened and signed by us, and afterwards left at the house of John Price, Esq. For the signature of all other Inhabitants of the parish, who approve of this Declaration and Resolution, and wish to associate with us, for the purpose of preventing seditious conspiracies and doctrines, for the preservation of peace and property within our parish; and for the purpose of uniting ourselves with other bodies determined to act in support of our excellent Constitution.

Resolved, That a Committee be formed of the Chairman and eight Inhabitants, to meet and act as occasion may require, in pursuance of the above Declaration and Resolution, that the Committee consist of

The CHAIRMAN, Samuel Hughes, Esq., John Price, Esq., Rev. John Morgan, Mr. Evan Roberts, Mr. Thomas Prosser, Mr. Thomas Bevan, Mr. Roger Powell, Mr. Evan Prosser.

Resolved, that this Declaration and Resolution, signed by the Chairman, be published in the *Hereford Journal*; and in any other manner the Committee may think most adviseable.

Resolved, that the thanks of this Meeting be given to Samuel Hughes, Esq. (confined by illness) for his loyal, patriotic, and spirited sentiments, communicated by letter to this Meeting.

The Chairman having left the Chair, Samuel Hughes the younger, Esq., moved, seconded, and unanimously resolved, that the thanks of this Meeting be given to the Chairman, for his upright and impartial conduct as Chairman of this Meeting.

The Chairman having returned the Chair. Resolved, That the thanks of this Meeting be given to Mr. Evan Roberts, for the offer of his Printing Press for the service of this Association. The Meeting was then adjourned.

### *2.5 A declaration of loyalty from Dissenting ministers of three counties in west Wales*

*Hereford Journal*, 27 February 1793.

*SALUTATION TAVERN, NEWCASTLE,*[10]

FEB. 13, 1793.

At a General Meeting of PROTESTANT DISSENTING MINISTERS, of the three Denominations, in the Counties of Cardigan, Carmarthen, and Pembroke,

The Rev. W. WILLIAMS,[11] in the Chair,

RESOLVED,

That at this crisis it is proper and necessary for us, as a body, without reservation, to express our Loyalty and Adherence to the Constitution under the Revolution in 1688, consisting of King, Lords and Commons.

That we shall embrace every opportunity to impress on the minds of those connected with us, Loyalty to the King and Reverence for the Laws; and to discountenance every Tumult or Sedition, should such evils spring up within the circle of our influence.

That under the influence of the precepts of Religion, and those impressions it leaves on our minds, as motives of action, having no secular interest or honours to decoy us; deaf to every illiberal and uncandid reflection, from every description of men, and unshaken by an exclusion from the common rights of citizens, we shall chearfully persevere in our obedience to government, and our zealous attachment to an excellent Constitution, which has been improving for ages, and from its very principles has power, without violence or tumult, to correct every remaining imperfection.

RESOLVED,

That the above Resolutions be signed by the Chairman, and inserted in the English Chronicle, the Bristol and Hereford Papers.

WILLIAM WILLIAMS, Chairman.

## *2.6 The execution of Marie Antoinette*

*Hereford Journal*, 30 October 1793.

*EXECUTION* OF THE *QUEEN OF FRANCE.*
PARIS, OCTOBER 16.

The melancholy and unparalleled sufferings of this unfortunate Princess, have at last come to a crisis. The Decree of the Convention, ordering that "the Trial of Marie Antoinette, late Queen of France, should come on within eight days," was implicitly obeyed by the Revolutionary Tribunal. The trial took place yesterday.

The following is an abstract of the Act of Accusation, or Indictment:

Marie Antoinette stands charged,

1st, With having dilapidated and lavished the finances of the Nation, in concert with the execrable Calonne, by causing to be transmitted to the Emperor several millions, which still serve to carry on the war against France.

2dly, With having, in imitation of Brunehaud, and De Medecis, who also called themselves Queens of France, conspired against the Liberty of the French Nation.

3dly, With having fought to starve the People in 1789.

4thly, With having excited the Murders of October 5 and 6.

5thly, With having, in concert with Bailly and La Fayette, caused the Patriots to be butchered in the Champ de Mars.

6thly, With having prevailed on the Swiss to fire on the People on the 10th of August.

7thly, With having, like another Agrippina, forgotten that she was a Mother, in order to commit incest with her Son.

Marie Antoinette heard the reading of the Act of Accusation, without seeming to be in the least moved. Here the Interrogatories began; and the mock forms of Justice being gone through, the Tribunal declared the Widow Capet –

*Guilty of having been accessory to, and having co-operated in, different manoeuvres against the Liberty of France; of having entertained a correspondence with the Enemies of the Republic, – of having participated in a Plot tending to kindle Civil War in the interior of the Republic, by arming Citizens against each other.*

When the sentence was read to the Queen, she cast down her eyes, and did not again lift them up. "Have you nothing to reply upon the determination of the law?" said the President to her. "Nothing," she replied. "And you, officious defenders?" – "Our mission is fulfilled with respect to the widow Capet", said they.

Sentence of Death was then passed upon her, and this day she was guillotined, at half past eleven o'clock in the forenoon.

## *2.7 Rioting in west and north Wales*

*Hereford Journal*, 4 March 1795.

On Saturday last, being market-day at Carmarthen, a mob collected together, and were guilty of some excesses. They went into the Corn-market, from whence they forcibly carried away the Winchester-measure belonging to the Corporation, bore it in triumph to a neighbouring iron-forge, where they beat it to pieces with hammers, and threw the fragments into the river. They afterwards returned to the market, and insisted on being supplied with corn, butter, and other articles of life, at reduced prices; which was complied with through fear; but under that impulse the owners exerted themselves to remove as much of their property as possible from the market, to places of greater security. In the evening, the principal inhabitants were convened, to consider of the most effectual means to check any similar attempts in future, when it was agreed to set on foot a subscription, with which to purchase barley for the use of the necessitous poor, to be retailed at 3s. 6d. per Winchester bushel, which is 6d. below the market-price; and afterwards to have recourse to military aid, should this humane step fail of the desired effect. – Measures were also adopted to frustrate the threatened attempt of the mob to enter the storehouses in the night, and seize the grain by force, notwithstanding the dealers (much to their credit) had all day offered to sell it at prime cost; but the depredators seemed to be actuated, not so much by necessity, as by a desire for plunder. – The prompt and efficacious steps which had been taken, however, deterred the mob from assembling in the evening; and the peace and tranquility of the borough have not again been interrupted.

The miners and colliers who had assembled in a riotous manner in the neighbourhood of Conway and Bangor Ferry, Caernarvonshire, where they had stopped several vessels bound for Liverpool, with corn – immediately dispersed on the arrival of the Somersetshire Fencible Cavalry, under the command of Lieutenant Colonel Strode, who reached the place of their destination on Saturday, after a very fatiguing march from Shrewsbury. The troops still remain quartered at Bangor, Llanrwst, and Conway, and the neighbouring gentlemen have entered into a liberal subscription, to enable the poor to purchase corn at a reduced price.

We are happy in being also enabled to state that the disturbances among the Miners at Aberystwith, mentioned in last week's paper, fortunately subsided without any material mischief. We have been favoured with the following particulars by a Gentleman of the town:

"On Monday last, a number of men, to the amount of about eighty, came to this place, principally from the neighbourhood of Rhos-fair, and in a riotous manner assembled, demanding that the corn purchased by the merchants from the country farmers, for the purpose of exporting eastways, should be prevented from leaving the port; and notwithstanding the remonstrances of the Magistrates, a disposition to riot was evidently shewn; upon which it was thought necessary to read the Riot Act, and explain to the deluded people the consequences, should they persist in such conduct. – Soon after, they retired; but in the evening they re-assembled in the same manner, when Mr. Lloyd, an active Magistrate, again desired them to disperse, but without effect; and, in attempting to secure one of the ringleaders, he was violently assaulted, which brought on a general engagement between the rioters and the worthy Magistrate and his friends, in which many on both sides were severely wounded. The former having received a warmer reception than they expected, chose to retreat, but not without threatening to return in more considerable numbers. – In consequence, an express was immediately sent off to Lord Dynevor,[12] requesting his assistance with the Carmarthenshire Yeomanry Cavalry; and notwithstanding his Lordship was at a considerable distance from his place of residence where the express was dispatched after him to the great surprize of the inhabitants, the troop, with their noble Commander at their head, arrived at this place, twenty-four hours sooner than they were expected. – Every thing remains quiet at present; and it is but justice to add, that upon this occasion the inhabitants, to the number of one hundred and forty, came forward and enrolled themselves as conservators of the peace.

Lord Dynevor shewed the greatest attention to the troop during the march; examined their beds, to see that they were properly aired – insisted on the volunteers messing at the same table with himself – and defrayed the whole of the expence (which was little short of 100.) out of his own private purse. On their return to Llandilo-fawr, his Lordship gave his thanks to the troop on the parade, for their alacrity and good conduct in the discharge of their duty; and too much praise cannot be ascribed to his Lordship, for his polite and generous behaviour on this occasion.

## *2.8 Rioting at St Clears, Pembrokeshire*

*Hereford Journal*, 25 March 1795.

### *INTELLIGENCE FROM SOUTH-WALES, MARCH 23.*

The snow which recently fell, was so extremely deep on Tuesday last, that the surveyor of the highways between Narberth and St. Clear's, was under the necessity of employing a great number of persons to clear it away from the turnpike-road, that a passage might be made for the waggons and carts employed in conveying the baggage of two companies of the Carmarthenshire Militia, from Haverfordwest to Aberystwith, where they have been ordered, to relieve the troop of Horse stationed at that place. The carriages got to New Inn; but, owing to the immense depth of the snow in that quarter, it was found impracticable to proceed further, and they have since been brought back to Carmarthen. Part of the Militia, after a most fatiguing march, arrived at Lampeter, in Cardiganshire, a few days since; but the Officers were obliged to travel on foot, it being impossible for horses to pass.

The snow was drifted in many places on the Milford road, upwards of ten feet deep, so that the mail-coach could not run for several days; but it now goes as usual.

On Friday last, a mob assembled at St. Clear's, nine miles from Carmarthen, to prevent Mr. Waters, a merchant at that place, from loading a vessel with wheat, intended to be sent coastwise. Mr. Waters's servant knocked down one man with a cornshovel, who lay senseless for some time; but on the factor's engaging to desist from carrying the wheat on board the vessel, the mob were prevailed on to disperse, without doing any further mischief.

It is much to be wished that Government would interfere, and hinder wheat from being transported coastwise, this being the chief occasion of the violent measures so repeatedly adopted of late by the populace in various sea-ports in South Wales. The dread of a scarcity of bread-corn, between the present period and the next harvest, universally prevails. – The uncommon severity of the weather has retarded the sowing of Lent-crops, so that the usual supply of oats and barley, of which the poor generally make their bread, will be necessarily diminished. – This has considerably increased the fears of the public mind. – Every prudent measure, therefore, ought unquestionably to be adopted, to keep the corn at home, and to guard against the apprehended deficiency; of which Government will, doubtless, take due care, and remove even the shadow of an excuse for the intervention of rash and lawless mobs – whose conduct has of late become very alarming.

Mr. William Price, apothecary, has been elected, and sworn into the office of Mayor of the Corporation of Carmarthen, in the room of Mr. John Morgan, mercer, deceased. Mr. Price has already exerted himself in a very laudable manner (worthy of general imitation), in putting a stop to forestalling the markets – a practice which has been carried to such an enormous length of late, in that borough, that the hucksters were posted on the roads, at the different entrances into town, to buy up and engross the provisions brought on market-days; by which means the price of the necessaries of life, when retailed again, were enhanced to such a degree, as to be placed almost beyond the reach of the poor!

## *2.9 A report of an organized protest in the Forest of Dean*

*Hereford Journal*, 13 May 1795.

On Saturday last, a body of Colliers, from the Forest of Dean, nearly 300 in number, marched into Monmouth; and, after waiting on the Mayor, informed him it was their intention to regulate the prices of provisions in the market. – They accordingly went to the butter-market, where they sold the whole stock of that article at 8d. per lb. – They also took possession of a cheese-standing, where they disposed of that commodity at 4d. per lb. – Their unexpected appearance in town created a temporary alarm, but as no personal violence was offered to any one, the fears of the inhabitants soon subsided; and after remaining about two hours, they returned home, without disturbance or molestation.

## *2.10 Paternalistic action for the relief of the poor in Cardiganshire*

*Hereford Journal*, 20 May 1795.

*CARDIGANSHIRE.*

At a meeting of the Gentlemen of this County, convened by the High Sheriff, and held at the Talbot Inn, in the town of Aberystwith, on Friday, the 8th day of May, 1795, for taking into consideration the State of the Country, in respect of Corn and Grain, and for adopting such measures as will be most proper and adviseable for supplying the industrious Poor with Corn, at a reduced price,

THOMAS BONSALL, ESQ., SHERIFF,
IN THE CHAIR;

Resolved – That it is the opinion of this Meeting, that there is the appearance of a Scarcity of Corn, in this part of the country, for the consumption of the Inhabitants.

Resolved – That to this effect a Subscription be immediately entered into.

Resolved – That Thomas Bonsall, Esq., Thomas Powell, Esq., John Williams, Esq., Richard Lloyd, Clark, William Richardes, and William Cobb Gilbertson, Esqrs., with such other Gentlemen, being Subscribers, as may attend, be appointed a Committee for carrying the object of this Meeting into execution; that they have a power to adjourn as often as shall or may be necessary; and that any three or more of them be, and are authorized to carry these Resolutions into execution.

Resolved – That the Chairman be requested to send Copies of these Resolutions to such Noblemen and Gentlemen as he may think proper.

Subscribers' Names and Sums Subscribed

| | |
|---|---|
| Thomas Bonsall, Esq., Sheriff | L.100 |
| Thomas Powell, Esq. of Nanteos | 200 |
| John Williams, Esq. of Castlehill | 100 |

| | |
|---|---|
| Richard Lloyd, Clerk | 100 |
| William Richardes, Esq. of Penglais | 100 |
| Thomas Bonsall, for John Smith, Esq. | 100 |
| Wm. Gilberston, Esq. of Dol-y-Clettwr | 50 |
| Charles Jones, Esq. | 20 |

Resolved – That the thanks of this Meeting be given to the Sheriff, for his readiness in calling the same, and his conduct in the Chair.

Resolved – That this meeting be adjourned to the 22nd day of this instant, to be held at the Talbot Inn, in the town of Aberystwith, in the said county.

THOMAS BONSALL

## *2.11 An account of the French landing at Fishguard*

*Hereford Journal*, 1 March 1797.

In addition to the pleasing intelligence contained in the Extraordinary Gazettes, we are enabled to lay the following particulars before our Readers, collected from information obtained through various sources:

*Extract of a Letter from Lieutenant Hearn, of the 43rd regiment, to Lieutenant Colonel Wood, commanding in the Hereford District, dated Carmarthen, Feb. 26.*

"Sir – I have the honour to inform you, that 1400 of the French, who landed near Fishguard, have surrendered themselves prisoners. – The Officers of the 77th regiment, who were sent here to receive the men raised in the county by Act of Parliament, united with me, in volunteering our services on the first alarm; and we mustered, with the Gentlemen of the country, upwards of a hundred, well mounted and armed; but were much disappointed, at meeting an express to inform us, of their having surrendered themselves prisoners, as we hoped to have assisted in welcoming them to this country. – The people have shewn great spirit and loyalty on the occasion."

The French landed their men close under the church of Llanwrda, which is situated on the Bay of Abermeline, on the north west coast of Pembrokeshire, about half way betwixt Fishguard and the Strumble Head, twenty miles from Haverfordwest, and fifteen north of St. David's.

On Thursday morning about two o'clock, an order arrived at Pembroke from the Lord Lieutenant, to summon the Pembroke Fencibles, a part of the Cardigan Militia, that were there guarding the French Prison, and Lord Cawdor's Troop of Yeomen Cavalry. The order was obeyed with the greatest promptitude and chearfulness, and between six and eight, the whole were on their march, though the distance between the residence of home of the Cavalry from each other was 16 or 17 miles. About four or five in the evening they arrived at Fishguard, having marched from Pembroke, about twenty-six or twenty-eight miles, and across Pembroke Ferry, which unavoidably occasioned much delay.

The country people, with a spirit of loyalty and gallantry becoming the legitimate descendants of Ancient Britons, flocked to meet the enemies of their country, armed with pitchforks, scythes, bludgeons, or whatever weapons they could in their hurry pick up. Men, women and children, were all seen hastening to the place where the enemy had landed, and this body, together with the few military and sailors, about 300 of the former, and 200 of the latter, formed near 3000 persons, whose numbers were hourly increasing. When the Frenchmen saw this, at about two o'clock on Thursday they surrendered.

Three Frenchmen were killed – five were seen attempting to carry off a Calf. – They were attacked by the same number of Welshmen, who killed two – the other three made off.

Lord Cawdor, upon this occasion, headed the Yeomanry Cavalry, who acted with great spirit; the greatest difficulty which his Lordship felt, was that of restraining the impetuosity of the Welshmen, who were not willing to allow the invaders to capitulate. Two Welshmen only, we believe, lost their lives.

## *2.12 A letter about the French landing at Fishguard*

*Hereford Journal*, 15 March 1797.

The following letter, written by a person who was an active witness of all the circumstances attending the late Invasion of Wales, contains some interesting particulars, the authenticity of which may be relied upon:

*Fishguard, March* 10.

"You have already heard, through the medium of official details, and private communications, of the recent visit of the French to this coast – I shall, therefore, respecting this subject, confine myself to the relation of a few circumstances which I have not observed in any of the public accounts.

"The French squadron came to another close under the rocks, near Llanwrda Church, about two miles and a half from this place. The colours they carried, and the dispositions they made for landing troops, clearly evinced they were enemies. The report soon reached Fishguard and though our Fencibles were dispersed at many miles distance from each other, we mustered our corps in a few hours, and remained in a state of readiness until next afternoon, when Lord Cawdor joined us, at the head of his own troop of cavalry, a small detachment of the Cardigan Militia, and the Pembroke Fencibles – making in all about 500 under the name of soldiers, but the country people who accompanied us, armed with fowling-pieces, swords, &c. &c. were immense.

"We marched that evening towards the ground occupied by the French; but night coming on, we returned back to Fishguard. This was a fortunate circumstance: for it now seems that they watched our motions, and, had they not been deterred from attacking us, under the idea that we were provided with field-pieces, they might easily have surrounded us, and taken our little force prisoners. That night, however, they proposed to surrender, and were given till ten o'clock next morning to consider of the terms. At an early hour we were drawn up facing their ground, in the most advantageous manner; every countryman that could muster any kind of weapon, was put on the line, and the honest farmers on horseback formed in the rear: the Frenchmen, 1200 in number, then came down to Goodwick Sand, near Fishguard, and delivered up their arms, except a few officers, and about twenty-five sick, who remained at Tre-Howell, a farmhouse near the place where they landed, and have since been conveyed to Fishguard.

"The French soldiers were in general well equipped, and upwards of 600 of them were chosen troops, selected from different regiments, and some, we were told, were even taken from the Sea-service. Their cloathing, was understood to be that which was worn by the emigrants sent from England upon the unfortunate Quiberon expedition. The last division of the prisoners, on Tuesday last, marched from Haverfordwest for Hubberstone, where they are to be embarked, and sent, under a strong convoy, for Portsmouth or Plymouth.

"They had ammunition sufficient for 10000 troops; a great number of barrels of ball cartridges were dashed to pieces against the rocks in their landing, which was a place very unfavourable for such a purpose, on account of its steepness. It is said that they have shewn letters of invitation to this place – but that I can scarce credit – I know they were never written by Welshmen, who detest every thing disloyal, or that has a tincture of French in it.

"They did much damage to the farm houses, by plunder and destruction of furniture. Two Cambrians really made five of them give up their loaded pieces. Some few of the French were shot, and two of our countrymen, who were too adventurous in pursuing a small party, were killed. – One countryman, it is said, imprudently rushing into a body of Frenchmen, attempted to seize one of them, when he received a shot, which his companion observing, immediately retaliated by cleaving the Frenchman's skull in two with a straitened scythe fixed to a pole.

"There was much alarm on their first landing, which was naturally distressing, to several families – but our spirits were soon elevated; resolution swelled every heart, and a determination to stand the event of a stubborn contest was not only resolved upon, but almost desired. – We have by tradition heard that THE WELSH WERE NEVER CONQUERED, and I verily believe not a man would have disgraced his Ancestors."

### *2.13 A letter explaining the meaning of 'Jacobin' and 'Jacobinism'*

*Hereford Journal*, 6 February 1799.

*To the PRINTER of the HEREFORD JOURNAL.*

Sir,

As the words *Jacobin* and *Jacobinism* are naturalizing themselves very fast among us, and have already made their way into the public prints and parliamentary debates, I persuade myself, that it will be a gratification to several of your Readers, to have the meaning of them explained, as far as it can be ascertained.

*Jacobinism*, then, signifies, in general, the principles held by the members of a certain club at Paris, which, from their meeting in a Convent of Jacobin Friars, was called Jacobin. It was founded in the famous year 1789, by some gentlemen of the province of Britanny, and originally called the Breton Club, but, on the rapid and copious accession of members from all parts of the then kingdom, it very soon took its present denomination.

Their first and fundamental principle was, that death is an eternal sleep; or, that there is no future state of account; and this motto was put upon the gates of their burying-places, during the domination of Robespierre, who was a great leader in this Society, and owed all his influence and power to it.

This pregnant principle draws after it several most important consequences – not only is all *Religion* at once annihilated, but there must be a *new morality*. A man who does not believe in a future state of account, is a very different being from one who does; and he has frequently an opposite rule of action. He will think that he may, and will, do any thing that may serve his present purposes, if he can but evade, or has power enough to controul, the laws of his country.

Another avowed principle of the Jacobin Club was, that all Monarchy, whether limited or not, was *tyranny*; and, indeed, that every other form of civil government which was not built upon the *Rights of Man*, as they had laid them down, was *oppression*; and that it was the most sacred duty of every people to rise up, in a mass, and overthrow them. The consequence of which is, that all property acquired under, and all persons protected by such oppressive systems of polity, are fair objects of plunder and attack.

Upon *these principles* has the French Republic been raised, and by them has its conduct, ever since, been invariably governed; in opposition to the established Religions, the established Morality, and established Governments, of Europe.

If, therefore, the word *Jacobinism* is to be adopted into our language, (as I think it ought to be into every language under heaven) it must be understood to signify a very complex idea, combined of *Atheism*, *Immorality*, *Anarchy*, and *Rapine*. I have little doubt but that, if Dr. Johnson were now alive to insert it in a new edition of his Dictionary, he would give it the same explanation.

Your constant Reader,
*Hay, Jan.* 30, 1799 A. B.

*2.14 A letter defending the public fast-day in support of the war*

*Hereford Journal*, 27 February 1799.

*To the EDITOR of the HEREFORD JOURNAL.*

Sir,
As the day on which your next Paper will appear, is by our religious and gracious Sovereign appointed for a solemn fast, in order to humble ourselves before Almighty God, and to implore his blessing upon his Majesty's Arms; I could wish to make it the vehicle of the following Reflections, if they should appear to you as important and suitable to the occasion, as they do to me.

If, according to the system of Epicurus, which the French Jacobins have adopted, there be no Divine Power which concerns itself with and interferes in human affairs, and Death, which is the necessary effect of animal dissolution, be an *eternal sleep* – all prayers, indeed every religious rite, is *an absurdity*. The French Republic, then, acts consistently with its principles. It calls upon no God; proclaims no Fast. Its manifest aim is, by all the means of compulsion, by all the arts of seduction, to congregate such large and irresistible masses of the human species, as may be sufficient, under the delusive pretext of giving them liberty, to massacre, plunder, or subjugate the remainder. And, hitherto, its attempts have proved most *awfully successful*. Europe seems to be appalled and panic struck; nor is there, upon the atheistic system, any well-founded expectation of putting a stop to the democratic torrent, which has well nigh overwhelmed the western side of it.

But it is not so with us, we profess, and have every reason to believe that the eternal spirit infinite in all perfection, who at the first created this world, continues to preserve and govern it by his immediate presence and powers. Upon this ground it is, that we lift up our eyes and hands to Heaven for help in time of need. All, who believe in the Christian Revelation, are, moreover, expressly assured, that this divine Government of the universe is conducted upon religious and moral principles and that unless we repent we shall [illegible] perish upon this ground unless we sanctify our fast and cast our tolerance for the purpose of national humiliation and national repentance.

There never was a time when the help of men appeared more vain. What man can do, has *been done*. Nay, our Naval Glory has been carried to a pitch, which we could scarcely have conceived, and which our posterity will hardly credit. And yet we are entering upon the seventh year of this very eventful and very expensive war, with not much better prospect of its termination than at its very commencement. Awful, indeed, is our situation! Yet are we not to despair, but to seek for succour where alone it is to be found. No successes on our part, however brilliant, will produce a Peace, until it shall please the eternal Spirit, who stilleth the raging of the sea, to assuage this madness of the people. The winds and storms in the moral, as well as in the physical world, do but fulfil his word. And, therefore, the discord and dissentions, which at present desolate the earth, shall, when the purposes of his providence are answered, and not before, subside into a general tranquility. Hither, then, our attention should be chiefly directed – to propitiate the universal Lord, in whose rule and governance are the wills and affections of sinful men, by the fervour of our prayers and the sincerity of our penitence. It may be the last time that we are permitted to assemble together, *as a national Church*. A furious and menacing spirit of innovation is gone forth, and gathers both strength and insolence from success. The ancient Governments of Europe are crumbling to pieces about us; and it is only by the favour, and under the *special protection*, of the *Almighty*, that our own can stand.

Your constant Reader,

A. B.

February 23, 1799.

## 2.15 *A report from a Cardiff trial for sedition*

*Hereford Journal*, 16 April 1800.

At Cardiff Assizes the calendar contained an unusual number of commitments, though only one prisoner was capitally convicted, viz. Martha Watkins, for robbing Benjamin Price, of Merthyr Tydvil. The trial of John Griffith for Sedition – an offence hardly known in that part of the Country – excited the indignation of a crowded Court. The circumstances of the case were, briefly: the Prisoner, after bestowing much praise on the conduct of Bonaparte, uttered words, in Welsh, of a very disrespectful nature to his Majesty. The witnesses, who belonged to the Neath Volunteer Corps, felt it their duty as loyal servants, to give information of what had happened; on which he was committed. On his way to gaol, either with a view to intimidate the Officer of Justice, or to give a specimen of his prophetic Enthusiasm, as a disciple of Brothers, he endeavoured to make him believe that their journey would be marked with singular incidents as the tremendous harbingers of divine vengeance – lightening, and thunder, and rain! The Constable stated, that it did actually rain, and he was not without apprehension as to the rest.

The prisoner being called upon for his defence, said, that he was afflicted with madness and that he did not know right from wrong; but the witnesses for the prosecution, who had known him from the time they were boys, never discovered the least symptoms of mental derangement. He then attempted to prove, by the Gaoler, that he was restless, and noisy and foolish; but the Jury being of opinion that his ravings were the offspring of a crafty, seditious spirit, and not the effusions of a mind deprived of reason, found him *guilty*.

Mr Hardinge[13] then addressed the convict thus: – "You are convicted of seditious words – they are coarse and stupid, as well as impudent features of disaffection to a king, who reigns in the hearts of a generous, enlightened, and free people; – who is at once an example of public spirit and of domestic virtue. Nothing has been a more powerful barrier against the levelling principles imported from the Continent than his worth, and the love that is borne to it. The inhabitants of this country are jealous of the honour which is due to his political office and personal goodness. Your principles are disarmed of their sting, and your malice against the Government is made innocent by the zeal against incendiaries like you, which animates this part of the land. It is the worst part of your offence in that view that you have represented (by a daring and seditious lie) thousands to be of your principles when I am convinced there is not one in the circle of a hundred miles around you in this or the neighbouring counties. Your defiance to the Magistrate and your attempt to seduce the volunteers to whom you addressed yourself – (Charbonniers enrolled in defence of a King they revere and of a Government whose blessing they see) – do not prove a disordered judgment, but a very depraved as well as turbulent spirit. These very men were your prosecutors – I give you joy of Bonaparte *your* hero – such an *abjective Moutard* as no king has ever appeared who was the most absolute in the worst of times – a tyrant without restraint, and without appeal, on the liberty, the conscience, the lives, properties and character, the feelings and the common sense of millions who wear his chains. It happens, however, that he, in spite of the shifting politics and religions has never censured and thus found it even politic to commend the King, whom you have aspersed and vilified. I approve of the Magistrate who committed you, for his defiance of any ridicule which your insignificance and folly should excite. We must endeavour, as you call yourself at the bar a lunatic, to put a kind of straight waistcoat over you and save your neighbours from the disgusting society of such an intellect. You are a madman it is true, half a madman distinguishing enough to devise, as well as to excite, mischief, though destitute of a capacity for the duties of the good subject and a good man."

He was then sentenced to two months imprisonment and to find sureties for future good behaviour.

## *2.16 A report from a Merthyr Tydfil trial for rioting*

*Hereford Journal*, 30 April 1800.

At Brecon Assizes, William Phillip and John David were tried and found guilty with being actively concerned with others in riotously obstructing the free passage of barley-meal, from Llangattock to Merthyr Tydvil. Judge Hardinge, in passing sentence, addressed himself to the prisoners nearly as follows:

"I can say nothing so well as my brother Moysey said, upon this topic on addressing himself to those who fund the bill against you. He observed that you must have acted as if the owners of the property, as a rule in the market, were to answer for the visitation of God, in the difficulties we at present encounter; that you were ungrateful to Parliament who were exerting themselves to give you all the relief they could; that you were ungenerous to your neighbours, who were endeavouring to assist you; and that you were cruel to your fellow sufferers, in their claim to the benevolence of the rich. It is a dangerous and savage principle of conduct, that, in times of general scarcity, those who feel it less than others are to be robbed and plundered by those who feel it more. It leads to that system of rapine which, in the awful and recent experience of the day, has been the iniquity and scourge of all around us. The horrors in France began with outrages like these, and with a rapid stride, advancing in their career, they adopted and cherished the possessional claims of equal property – equal rank – equal power; till these tyrannies upon genius and virtue – those checks to honourable enterprize, ended as they naturally should, in rejecting all government – in abjuring all religion, making *their* liberty the licence of plunder, and *their* Property the right of the arm that should reach it by force. If your doctrine, William Phillip, should prevail – that because it is hard for the Dowlais company to buy grain, and carry it away from your markets, a mob of two hundred men are to detain it by force – we had better at once abandon the legitimate offices of Government, and make every man his own Legislator – give up the advantages of an impartial trust and let every man be his own Judge at the impulse of his own will, directed by the interest of his own appetite. – If this offence had been at all prevalent in the county of Brecon, we should have necessarily made your punishment heavier, but it is only the second instance of this kind that I have attended here. – I wish it had been the first. There is, however, a general spirit in this county, of a different, of an opposite kind – that public spirit which bears with patience and the best of all courage those calamities that are inseparable from the God of Moses and of *Seasons* too. The peace and good order of the community have in general been maintained *here*, in times of severe and pinching distress, a period of all others, in which they are the most endangered and should be the most firmly supported. Without a punctilious regard for legal property, the merest of those who are impatient for support because they suffer and are disorderly because they are impatient, will be destroyed and baffled by themselves. – Grain, like water, finds its level in the market of its produce; if the cultivators are discouraged by tumults or threats, the mass of the supply for the poor must be diminished, as the farmer is not expected, or likely, to nourish them at the peril of his life. It is the interest, therefore, as well as the duty of the lower classes, to facilitate the circulation of this produce and the rights of the purse to its acquisition. Our punishment will make no distinction between you, William Phillip, and your associate, though you are distinguished in the shades of guilt, arising from the degree of activity compared: but I wish to make every man who hears me know, that if he enters in such conspiracy, he will not be less punished because he was misled, or had less personal mischief in the share of the fact. It is in mercy, therefore, and as a warning against offenders in these dangerous combinations, that we look at no such grains and scruples of difference in the two culprits before us. Judges, however, should at all these transactions look out with a merciful eye at every ground for lenity which may be reconciled with public interest. You were both of you induced, by reasoning alone, to give up this property; and the actual mischief that resulted was little more than delay to the owners, though it was a bad example as far as it went. I disapprove the offer made, of converting this monopoly (as *you* called it) into the market, by those who had care of it. If it was all sincere, it was an implicit confession in that a complaint was just: if it was fear alone that prompted the offer, it encouraged these men to enforce upon the market all separate property; if necessity compelled the fear it would have been a wiser panic to have surrendered, than it was to barter, the goods in question. – The Court, endeavouring to adjust the balance of clemency and of example (which is mercy of another kind) order both of you to be imprisoned six calendar months, and to find sureties to keep the peace for one year."

## 3 *The* Shrewsbury Chronicle

*The* Shrewsbury Chronicle and Shropshire, Montgomeryshire, Denbighshire, Merionethshire, Flintshire, &c. General Advertiser, *founded in 1772 and published on Fridays, was the most widely read provincial weekly in Wales during the 1790s. Evidence from the newspaper itself suggests that this was due to the literary talent and business acumen of the editor Thomas Wood (1789–†1802) and his wife Mary. The newspaper's success grew with its loyalism, which stressed the advantages of a paternalistic, traditional society. The editor was well known to Welsh poets and regularly published Welsh-language material, mostly loyalist poetry, sometimes work in progress. The paper also carried much news and advertisements from and concerning Wales.*

### *3.1 A report and letter on rioting*

*Shrewsbury Chronicle*, 31 July 1789.

A correspondent at Wrexham says, that, in consequence of the rumour of supplying France with flour, the heavy rains, and the assiduity of speculating cornfactors, the price of grain took the following sudden rise, at last Wrexham market: Wheat 10s 4d, Muncorn 9s 6d, Blend-corn 7s 6d, Barley 6s 8d, Oats 3s 8d. The small appearance, and its high price, so exasperated the colliers, miners, &c. in that neighbourhood, who depend on a supply from thence, that they collected at night in large bodies, went down to Bangor, unloaded two boats which were bound for Chester, burnt the vessels, and sent their lading which consisted of grain and flour, (in impressed carts) to Wrexham, and also seized a waggon load of barley that was going through the town, and lodged them in there for the next market-day.

On account of the above disturbances, assistance from the army was found requisite; and on Tuesday morning last at three o'clock, an express arrived here from the War-Office, with an order for his Majesty's 34th regiment to go from hence to Wrexham, who with all possible expedition, marched accordingly the same morning, under the command of their Major, the Right Hon. the Earl of Burford.

*Extract of a Letter from Wrexham, dated Thursday Morning, July 30th.*

"The corn that had been seized and conveyed to this town, by the colliers, was exposed to sale on Monday last, when a tumultuous mob so over-awed the market that Wheat sold at 8s 6d, Muncorn 5s 6d, and Barley at 4s 6d per measure, while a party of about 200 colliers ranged along side the River Dee to seize any grain that might be going to Chester; at night they dispersed in small parties to their respective homes. One corn-factor imprudently appeared, but, when chased by the mob, he luckily lodged himself in a crop of beans, in the Star Garden; the master of one of the Inns was obliged to swear before the Justices and mob, that he had no concealed grain; and one farmer who had sold his muncorn at 10s 3d, lost by the difference of price about 23l, all the natural effects of a body of people without order – Much praise is due to Sir Foster Cunliffe, Bart., William Lloyd, Esq., the Rev. Mr. Newcome, and the Rev. Mr. Strong, for their activity, as neighbouring Justices, who personally appeared to settle the wild party differences, and have since issued hand-bills, earnestly requesting the farmers to send in a supply of corn for this day's market. – The town has been quiet since the arrival of the 34th regiment, who paraded last night at twelve o'clock: but the colliers seized at Ruabon, 5 miles off, seven cart loads of grain, which is expected here to-day."

### *3.2 A letter reporting loyalist ritual in the town of Aberystwyth*

*Shrewsbury Chronicle*, 28 December 1792.

*Extract of a letter from Aberystwith, Dec. 22*, 1792.

"Yesterday a very numerous and respectable Meeting of the Gentlemen, Burgesses, and Inhabitants, of this Town and Neighbourhood, assembled at eleven o'Clock in the Forenoon, for the purpose of expressing their Loyalty to the King and Attachment to the Constitution of Great Britain; when an unanimous Declaration of their Affectionate Allegiance to his Majesty, and unalterable Attachment to the Constitution, with their Resolution to maintain it, took place, and passed amidst the Acclamations of several hundred persons present, with not a single dissenting voice; after which a handsome Dinner was sat down to at the Black Lion-Inn, and many loyal Toasts and Songs were given, a general illumination took place, a bonfire was made in the Market-place, in which Tom Paine's libel entitled "The Rights of Man" was burnt, and the evening was spent with every demonstration of joy and tranquillity."

### *3.3 Celebrating the coming of age of Sir Watkin Williams Wynn*

*Shrewsbury Chronicle*, 1 November 1793.

Saturday last being the day on which Sir Watkin Williams Wynn, Bart. came of age, there were great rejoicings at the different towns and villages in the neighbourhood of Wynnstay, Llangedwin, &c.

At Wynnstay the morning was ushered in with ringing of bells in all the churches of the surrounding neighbourhood; three long tables in the great room were covered with 100 dishes of the best viands the country could produce, and where 500 people were entertained in the most plentiful manner; besides an innumerable crowd who were made joyous at an immense bonfire in front of the hospitable mansion, and drank repeated libations of strong beer, brewed at the time the Baronet was born. It was judiciously directed that the oxen, instead of being roasted in the usual way, should be cut up and distributed among the poor families in the neighbourhood.

The village of Ruabon was illuminated, and the meanest inhabitant, who could purchase a farthing candle, stuck it in his window, in honour of the worthy Baronet.

There was scarce a gentleman in the whole circle of the Wrexham neighbourhood that did not attend at the Eagles, to celebrate the day, which was passed with the utmost harmony and festivity; in the evening several hogsheads of beer were distributed among the populace, and the town was illuminated in the most brilliant manner.

At Oswestry, an Ox and plenty of strong beer was given to the populace, and at night there was a general illumination; in which was exhibited in Brook-street, Sir Watkin's Arms in miniature, suspended to a stock of carnations in full blow, truly beautiful.

At Bala, a table was laid under a tent on the green, 70 yards long, at which upwards of three hundred persons dined at once, and the board was well supplied, not only with provisions, but also with new visitors, during the whole afternoon; and the evening was closed with the greatest mirth and harmony. Upwards of 200 loads of Peat were consumed in the bonfire at this place.

At Llangedwin true hospitality was displayed; and, in honour of the day, a Cân, suitable to the occasion, written by the *Bard of Rhaiadr*, was sung with great applause, and, after three times three, encored. – The Bard, in a letter to his friend, says,

Such were the joys of this propitious day,
That e'en poor cripples threw their crutches by;

Each nymph and swain extravagantly gay,
And Cedwyn's feeble grey-beards leap'd for joy:
E'en suckling babes tho' in their mother's arms
Their aid afforded as a chearing ray,
A lustre added to fair Cedwyn's charms,
And strain'd their little throats to hail the day!
Great Watkin's name did to the skies ascend,
Re-echo'd by each Cymrodorian friend.

At Much-Wenlock, a sheep was roasted in the street, and sixteen entertainments were given at the inns and other houses; at each of which a barrel of ale was given, on the above joyful occasion.

Mr. Stephen Senston, of Stanwardine, also roasted a sheep, and gave a barrel of ale to the poor; as did like-wise Mr. Jones, of the Mill-Green.

### *3.4 Further celebrations of the coming of age of Sir Watkin Williams Wynn*

*Shrewsbury Chronicle*, 8 November 1793.

In addition to the Rejoicings in Sir Watkin Williams Wynn's coming of age, (mentioned in our last,) we insert the following, from undoubted authorities.

At Oswestry, the morning was usher'd in with ringing of bells, and at noon Sir Watkin's tenants and friends were entertained with a well covered table, and plenty of strong beer; in the evening the town was most brilliantly illuminated, by which the inhabitants vied in testifying their joy. – Among the many curious devices exhibited, the three most attractive were at the house of R. Lloyd, Esq., viz. A Representation of WALLIA, bearing on her Shield the ARMS of the FAMILY OF WYNNSTAY. – A DRUID. – A PERSPECTIVE VIEW OF WYNNSTAY. On Monday the Gentlemen of the Corporation gave an Ox, which was distributed among the poor; after which the gentlemen of the town and neighbourhood dined together at the Bowling Green, and the evening was concluded with a ball and supper, given by Mr. Lloyd, to a very numerous and brilliant assemblage of Ladies and Gentlemen.

At Trefyclawdd, the Colliers were entertained with plenty of good beef and stingo![14] They behaved with decorum, and parted giving grateful thanks to their worthy benefactor. We are happy to say, the day was spent without the least disturbance, or accident: Though

Myriads of forms from SUBTA TERRA sprung,
With heart and voice to join the joyous throng.[15]

Sir Watkin's tenants within the Manor of Cufeuliog, above three hundred in number, assembled at Machynlleth, where they were by the express desire of the worthy Baronet, regaled with plenty of Beef and good Cwrw; and in the evening a general illumination followed, to crown which, all the neighbouring hills appeared to join their plaudits, by noble bonfires smiling at each other.

At Efel, Llwydiarth, every tenant in the neighbourhood was elevated agreeable to the joy of the welcome day; they were tenants, whose hearts acted with a degree of affection becoming grateful people to an honourable Landlord; the cellars were drained dry by the particular order of the worthy juvenile Bart. and an Ox, whose leathern sides were almost bursting with fat, endured the igneous flame, was distributed among the indigent. – The rich regaled themselves, at their own expence, and shewed that liberality which blazed in their hearts.

At Llanfair, the morning was usher'd in with ringing of bells, firing of guns, &c. and an excellent dinner was given at the Three-Tuns Inn, of which near three hundred gentlemen and tenants partook, and the evening was spent with the utmost conviviality; a large bonfire was made on an adjacent hill, several hogsheads of brown nappy were given to the populace, and every house in town was genteelly illuminated. And on Monday the tenants, &c. met again in town, and had an Ox roasted, which was very judiciously given amongst the poor, with a penny Loaf to each plebeian who attended; and the evening concluded with true festive joy.

### *3.5 The editor confirms his loyalist stance*

*Shrewsbury Chronicle*, 27 December 1793.

*ADDRESS TO THE PUBLIC.*

THE PRINTER begs Leave to embrace the present Season to return his most grateful Thanks to his numerous Friends and Patrons for the great Countenance and Support he has experienced during a Period of Twenty-one Years, since this Paper was first published; and is happy to find, that the Loyalty it weekly displays, gives such universal Satisfaction to the Public in general, (a few individuals excepted). – With respect to his future Conduct, as EDITOR of THIS CHRONICLE, he is determined to pursue that

System of LOYALTY to his KING – of real ATTACHMENT to the CONSTITUTION of this Country, as by Law established – and strict OBEDIENCE to the LAWS OF THIS COUNTRY, which he has hitherto done; and that while he has the Honor of conducting THE SHREWSBURY CHRONICLE, he will never suffer it to be either the Vehicle of FACTION, or the Dupe of SERVILITY; but will labour to preserve a just INDEPENDENCE, without "PARTY BIAS, or PRIVATE VIEWS." His BIAS and VIEWS have hitherto been, and ever shall be, OPEN to the World, and his Determination is to do every thing in his Power to support the true LIBERTY of the SUBJECT, free from the detested Spirit of DEMOCRACY, or the false Principles of the pretended "RIGHTS OF MAN." – These are the Principles, and these alone, on which he solicits the future Countenance and Support of TRUE BRITONS. And as in this, as in his other Engagements he acts from CONSCIENCE, and in the CAUSE of GOD and TRUTH, he is persuaded that the generality of the Inhabitants of the Loyal Town of Shrewsbury, and of the Public at large, (particularly Shropshire and North Wales,) will continue to support him, while he continues a Friend to the British Constitution.

The very extensive Circulation this Print is honoured with having for some Time past occasioned a great influx of long Advertisements, the Printer is preparing to enlarge the Size of his Paper, so as to admit of an additional Column to each Page, which will enable him to give a large Portion of News weekly, which he laments he has lately been deprived of doing. This Enlargement and Improvement will take place as soon as his New extra large Press is received from London; he is sorry it will not be here in Time to begin the New Year with but as soon after as possible.

### *3.6 Loyalist celebrations*

*Shrewsbury Chronicle*, 16 May 1794.

*For the* Shrewsbury Chronicle.

MR PRINTER,

No two places in the Principality could have shewn greater Loyalty on the reception of the late joyful News from the Continent,[16] through the channel of your truly useful Paper of the 2nd instant, than what was displayed at Llanfyllin and Llanrhaiadr, on Saturday 3rd. The bells of each place rang for three days, and at the latter, whilst a large company (uncovered) were drinking *Success to the British Arms*, the under-written Lines, composed on the occasion by a local youth just turned thirteen, were sung by the company to the tune of *God Save the King*.

> *Duw*, dyro i *Siôr*, nerth fo siwr,
> I orchfygu'n glîr ar Dîr a Dŵr,
>     Bôb cynnwr' câs;
> Rhag i'r Gelynnion blinion blaid,
> Fyn'd trwy'r Bŷd llîd heb raid
>     Boed llydan râs.
> Ciciwn draw'r Caccwn drwg
> O blith y Saint er maint yw'r mwg,
> Rhown Blwm drwy eu cîg am gynyg cŵg
>     A'u cilwg certh;
> Cŷd rown weddiau ar liniau 'i lawr,
> Gyda'n *Brenin*, ai Fyddin fawr,
> *Duw*, cadw'r *Eglwys* wiwlys wawr,
>     Yn awr mewn nerth.
>
> (*God*, give *George* strength, for sure,
> to overcome clearly, on Land and Water,
> every malicious disturbance;
> lest the horrible faction of the Enemies
> go through the World in a needless rage,
> let there be comprehensive grace.
> We'll kick away the nasty Hornets
> from amongst the Saints, however much the smoke,
> we'll put Lead through their flesh for offering wrath
> and their terrible scowl.
> We'll all offer prayers with knees on the floor,
> with our *King* and his great Army,
> *God*, keep the worthy heroic *Church*,
> now in strength.)
>
> Llanrhaiad'r ym Mochnant,     May 7, 1794.

### *3.7 A blacksmith and a tailor examine 'democrate'*

*Shrewsbury Chronicle*, 5 December 1794.

In a conversation a few days ago in a Pot-House in North-Wales, a *learned* Blacksmith, (with no little fire) said, he could not approve of the word *Democrate*, which he understood was Latin for *Dimcamrogri*; on this a very *classical* Taylor got up, declaring he felt himself much more hurt than if he had pricked his finger with a needle, at the word *Democrate* being *contur'd* in so bungling a manner; he was perfectly sure that none of *Vulcan*'s family were ever reckoned *Scholards* nor *Politicians* – as for the word *Democrate*, he would venture to say it was originally French. Here *Vulcan* could contain himself no longer, but swore that if *Snip* could not immediately give a Translation of the word, he would *darken his day lights* in two minutes! *Shred*, however, being expert at the *Sheers*, in order to save a drubing, *cut one out* in half the time, and said that *Demo* was French for *Diawl* (devil) and *Crate* was *amkipio* (snatch me).[17] This *beautiful* Translation so satisfied his antagonist, that he paid him the highest encomiums as a Scholar, and spent the evening with him in the greatest harmony.

### *3.8 A loyalist poem*

*Shrewsbury Chronicle*, 2 January 1795.

*For the* Shrewsbury Chronicle

Mr WOOD,
For the satisfaction and pleasure I have received, during several years' perusal of the *Shrewsbury Chronicle*, (if a *Montgomeryshire's Farmer's* Language is worthy your notice) I have sent you, for insertion

*A CHRISTMAS-BOX:*

WHEN Merit fires the lofty Bard,
In verse he shews his warm regard;
In glowing numbers, fondly sings
The fame of Heroes, Statesmen, Kings:
Well – let them act the learned part,
I sing th'effusions of my heart.

Ordain'd by fate, blest fate! t' abide
On a lone Mountain's rugged side;
Pinch'd by this season of the year;
No neighb'ring friends my ev'nings cheer;
Sol scarce affords one feeble ray
To solace each short, gloomy day;
Yet happiness e'en here I find,
And am to other pleasure blind,
Till, WOOD, thy Chronicle arrives,
And weekly every thought revives:
In it I view thee firmly cling
Close to thy Country, Church and King!
For making thus their cause thy own,
In such Repute thy Paper's grown,
'Tis read by all the Neighbourhood
Around where old MATHRAVAL[18] stood!
Go on, blest Champion, in the cause
Of Britons, and their happy laws;
Still in thy loyal duty stand, that Peace may bless fair Cambria's land;
Ne'er Faction, thro' the Vale below
Shall cause brave Britons' blood to flow;
No – led by thee, we'll ever sing
God bless our Laws, our Church, and King!

*Sir Trefaldwyn, Dec.* 26, 1794 E– –n D– – – –s.

*3.9 Two Welsh loyalist poems on peace*

*Shrewsbury Chronicle*, 24 April 1795.

*For the* Shrewsbury Chronicle.

*LINES,*
Adapted to the present Supplications of every well-wisher
to his King and Country.

PRYSURED, deled y dŷdd – i'r *Heddwch*
Gyrhaeddyd pob Gwledydd;
Ac yna pob Trigiannydd
Heddychlon, foddlon a fydd.

Aed arfau i bant, – o derfydd – Fygwth
Cenfigen aflonydd;
Hir Gleddyf ar y Gloywddydd
Rhyded ef, tra rhedo dŷdd!
Dafydd Ddû, o Eryri.[19]

Rhyded, mae'n angenrheidiol – medd Dynion
A doniau prophwydol;
Ac hefyd bydd Bŷd marwol,
Oni wneir ei weinio'n ôl.

Duw, 'nêl, i'r Rhyfel ar hyn' – o gystydd
Gael gwastad iawn derfyn;
Nag ymgais er dyfais dŷn,
I'n golwg, fyth un Gelyn!

O Dâd y Nêf! dôd ini – (er cymmaint
Yw'n camwedd a'n bryntni,)
Iawn nerth, a phraw Aberth ffri
I'n troi unwaith o'n Trueni!
RHAIADR

(May the day soon come for the *Peace*
to reach every Country;
and then every Inhabitant
will be peaceful and contented.

Let the arms go away, it ends the Threat of
restless Jealousy;
the long Sword on the Bright day,
may it rust, while the day lasts!
Dafydd Ddu of Eryri.[19]

May it rust, it is necessary say Men
with prophetic talents;
and also the World will be a deadly place,
unless it is sheathed back.

May God bring the War after this affliction
to a just and lasting end;
and let no Enemy
by man's device ever come into our sight!

Oh God in Heaven give us (however great
our misdemeanour and our vileness)
the true strength and proof of a free Sacrifice
to turn us once from our Wretchedness.
RHAIADR.)

*Llanfair Caer Einion,*
*Ebrill* 14, 1795.

### *3.10 The Act for Raising Men for the Navy*

*Shrewsbury Chronicle*, 1 May 1795.

We are happy to hear that at the Petty Sessions held at Bala and Corwen in Merionethshire, on the 24th and 25th ultimo, to put in execution the Act for Raising Men for the Navy, the Directions of the Act (after an explanation of its true meaning by the Magistrates) were peaceably and cheerfully observed by the Parish Officers, without any obstruction whatsoever. Several respectable Gentlemen of the County attended the Sessions each day to countenance and support due obedience to the laws, had any resistance been attempted; but the populace were perfectly peaceable and satisfied with the measure, which had been before misrepresented by seditious and ill-designing people. – The account given in the Chester Chronicle of Friday the 17th ult. (and thence copied into other papers) of the proceedings of the populace at the Petty Sessions at Bala on the 11th, (we are authorized to say) was erroneous, and very much exaggerated.

### *3.11 A poem on Bala lake*

*Shrewsbury Chronicle*, 28 October 1796.

*For the* Shrewsbury Chronicle
LINES,
*on BALA POOL, in Merionethshire*

WHERE eastern storms disturb the peaceful skies,
In Merioneth the fam'd Plenlyn lies:[20]
Here a vast lake, which deepest vales surround,
His wat'ry globe rolls on the yielding ground,
Encreas'd with constant springs that gently run
From the rough hills, with pleasing murmurs down.
This wond'rous property the waters boast,
The greatest rains are in its channels lost;
Nor raise the flood; but when loud tempests roar,
The rising waves with sudden rage boil o'er,
And conq'ring billows scorn th'unequal shore.

### *3.12 The Methodist response to the Fishguard landing*

*Shrewsbury Chronicle*, 24 March 1797.

Country news . . . The Rev. Mr. Jones of Llangan, was preaching to a crowded congregation in the town of Carmarthen, at the moment when the first intelligence of an invasion arrived. With the greatest presence of mind, he exhorted his audience for the love of God to be firm, to avoid turning their backs on the enemy, assuring them, on these terms, of Divine Protection – finally, *he offered to accompany them in person*! – Words cannot express the effect produced on the minds of his hearers – the proposition was accepted, and after possessing themselves of whatever arms lay in reach, they augmented the great body, actuated by the same spirit of British loyalty.

*Shrewsbury Chronicle*, 9 June 1797.

We hear from Fishguard, in Pembrokeshire, that on Tuesday and Wednesday, the 23rd and 24th ult., the people called Methodists held their quarterly association there, within two miles of the place where the French landed, and where some of their friends had been principal sufferers. The Rev.

Mr. Jones, rector of Llangan, Mr. Grey, and Mr. Lloyd preached on the Strand, but it was impossible for all the multitude to hear as there were deemed to be present about fourteen thousand. It appeared to be a meeting of thanksgiving for their happy deliverance from the designs of the enemy. – All appeared conscious of the excellent government they lived under, and offered fervent prayers for its long continuance.

*Shrewsbury Chronicle*, 5 January 1798.

We hear from Fishguard in Pembrokeshire that at a late meeting of the Welsh Calvinistic Methodists held in that town, it was agreed – that an Anniversary day of Thanksgiving be kept on Goodick Sands, on the 24th of Feb. 1798; to commemorate the gracious deliverance they experienced from the bloody intentions of the French invaders, (who surrendered their arms on that very spot,) and to implore the peculiar blessing of God on our King and Country.

### *3.13 An appeal for Welsh unity against the French*

*Shrewsbury Chronicle*, 2 February 1798.

TO THE INHABITANTS OF THE PRINCIPALITY OF WALES[21]

FRIENDS AND COUNTRYMEN

In the present state of affairs, I beg leave to lay before you the following reflections, written in consequence of the late opposition which government have experienced, and the menaces held out against this country by the Gallic Foe.

I therefore ask, is this a time, when our lives and fortunes lie at stake – when our all is on the utmost brink of destruction – when Great Britain is but too likely to be dyed throughout, and deluged, with the blood of all her natives – the sons of Albion totally extirpated – our parents and children all massacred – our mothers, wives, daughters, and sisters, all brutally ravished, by French ruffians, influenced by no principle, but diabolical enmity to the whole British race: is this a time, when all our palaces, all our towns and temples, are sentenced, by a nation of Rebellious Fiends, to blaze in a general conflagration, from one end to the other of our disasterous island, which is decreed to be one grand scene of devastation; – is this a time (let me repeatedly ask) for Dissentions about Places and Patronage; or, to contest, tooth and nail, whether *Pitt* or a *Fox* shall reign over the British Treasury?

There is at hand a more deadly struggle between *In's* and *Out's*! Whenever the *French* come in, each *Briton* must vanish, either to the dreary coast of Canada, or to the coast from whence there is no return!

The insidious and perfidious Gauls would villainously persuade us, that their intention is to give Liberty to *us*, who are *free-born Britons*! The Liberty they will bestow on *us*, will be the Freedom of all our *Souls* from all our *Bodies*. And thus (*divide et impera*) they aim to render the People disaffected to their Prince, while *they* resolve to overcome, over-run, and overwhelm the whole nation; and to exterminate Britannia's sons to the last man.

But how have they treated their ancient friends, the Venetians? They plundered the *Republic* first; then bartered it to one of the most despotic Potentates in Europe. Are they not plundering the *good and wise* Dutch continually? Are they not, even now, about to plunder the free Cantons of Switzerland? Their perfidy can only be equalled by their insolence and effrontery. Did they not enter the dominions of the *Tuscan* Prince, then perfectly at peace with France, to annoy English Merchants in a neutral port, contrary to the known Law of Nations? Did they not agree that, as a basis of Peace, *Mantua* should be the *Emperor's*? Did they not agree, that the integrity of the German Empire should be the basis of a General Peace on the Continent? Have they not, without assigning the least pretence, suddenly surprised the Elector of Metz and violently seized his Capital? Are they not now amusing the King of Prussia, for his Flemish dominions, with hopes of *Hanover*, whilst they intend to command the *Maritime* Regions from the *Euxine* to the *Baltic*; and propose to give *Silesia*, with *Bavaria*, to the Emperor? Are they not aiming to controul the Commerce of the World? Are we to expect Liberty, or even Peace, from those Rebellious Miscreants, who set all Laws, human and divine, at defiance? Are we to resign our conquests while they retain theirs? We may as well resign our arms, whilst they retain theirs.

It may be urged, that our Country will be aggrieved. But the French are those who aggrieve *us*; and are determined to aggrieve us more and more, even to the utmost. Ought we not to suffer a great burden, even through the newly enacted Tax (which I cannot allow to be unconstitutional, and seems preferable to an immense heap of Mortgages); ought we not to suffer this, rather than not prevent most dreadful destruction: and obviate the tremendous danger at this instant impending over all our heads? – It is ours to employ a good *part* of our property, or else we must lose *all*. *Dissentions* gave *Britain* to the aspiring *Romans*, *Dissentions* gave *Britain* to the cruel *Saxons* – *Dissentions* gave Britain to the overwhelming *Normans*! – *To-day*, SIRS! awake – accord – arise! Otherwise *Dissentions* will TOMORROW give *Great Britain* to the *aspiring*, *cruel*, *overwhelming* Rebels and Banditti of FRANCE!

Lo! the Gauls rush, like some resistless flood –
Our *Gold* they covet – covet more our *Blood*!
Let ALBION's heroes now combine, as one;
Or, *part* deserting *part*, we're all undone![22]

A WELSH FREEHOLDER

## *3.14 A report of Irish refugees landing in Pembrokeshire*

*Shrewsbury Chronicle*, 15 June 1798.

Haverfordwest. This town is now filled with the unfortunate Irish Gentry who have escaped from the murderous bands of the rebels.[23]

It is quite distressing to witness so many objects of pity. We have here a Lady of Fortune who escaped the flames of her own house with nine children and two servants. Her husband the villains had most barbarously murdered. She had travelled several miles across the country with her young, who had barely cloaths to cover them.

On Friday and the following days several vessels came in crowded with fugitives, among whom were several officers and Clergymen. – The officers had been separated from their regiments by the insurgents, and endeavouring to make for Dublin by sea, were driven into Milford. The number of Irish are not less than from 1000 to 1500 persons. The inhabitants are raising contributions for their relief, and are using every means to provide them with lodging and other comforts.

## *3.15 The Carmarthenshire militia*

*Shrewsbury Chronicle*, 23 August 1798.

The Caermarthen regular and supplementary militia, are on their march to be quartered at Market Harborough, Leicester & Loughborough. A part of them volunteered their services in Ireland, during the late rebellion, and such as were in Dublin were decorated by the citizens of that place, with medals and orange ribbons, which they now retain: Their gallantry and orderly good conduct tended greatly to allay the disloyal spirit manifested in Ireland, and they have deservedly acquired the thanks and the grateful remembrance of all its well-disposed inhabitants. It is remarkable that not a man born on this side the Severn appertains to the regiment, and but few of the privates speak English.

### *3.16 A St David's Day poem*

*Shrewsbury Chronicle*, 1 March 1799.

*For the Printer of the* Shrewsbury Chronicle.

Mr. WOOD
As the following Song may not have been known by all the Ancient Britons, your giving it room in your paper, for the amusement of such as are unacquainted with it will oblige your's

*Bristol, Feb.* 29, 1799.

RHAIADR.

'St. DAVID'S DAY'

PALE Winter with thy icy face,
Now bid us all farewell,
A man like MARCH has taken place,
One month with us to dwell,
He's brother to fair April's shower,
And ushers to meet May;
For in his hat he wears a leek,
All on St. David's Day!

When Julius Caesar with his force,
Did first invade this land,
The Welshmen bold on foot and horse
Did this proud foe withstand;
A tribute of them he did crave,
Which they refus'd to pay,
For which they always wear a leek,
All on St. David's Day!

Then afterwards the Saxons came,
Whom Essex did obtain,
And with an army were prepar'd,
This kingdom for to gain;

Each town and city went to rack,
  Whilst Saxons bore the sway,
At length the Welshmen drove them back,
  All on St. David's Day.

The next to them the Danes came in,
  That proud usurping foe,
At Winchester they did begin
  This land to overthrow,
Until at length great Alfred came,
  Who drove them quite away,
And conquer'd all the Danish crew,
  All on St. David's Day.

When Crook'd-back Richard wore the crown,
  As Regent of our land,
No policy could pull him down,
  Nor his proud force withstand;
'Till Henry Richmond entered Wales,
  Whom Welshmen did obey,
And conquer'd him in Bosworth Field,
  All on St. David's Day.

The Welshmen they were always true,
  And had a full intent
To give their King and Prince their due,
  And love each precedent;
And to maintain their ancient fame,
  That never will decay,
Love's blessing light all on each name,
  Who keeps St. David's Day.

### *3.17 The Ancient British Fencibles*

*Shrewsbury Chronicle*, 11 April 1800.

*Ancient British Fencibles* – On the 2nd instant this gallant regiment marched from Wrexham to Wynnstay, for the purpose of being disbanded and depositing their standards. They were received upon their arrival, by the Wrexham Yeomanry and Ruabon Light Infantry, who offered their services to keep the ground upon this occasion. The regiment being drawn up opposite the house of the Colonel, Sir Watkin Williams Wynn, he thanked them in the strongest terms for the loyalty, courage and discipline, which they had so constantly displayed during a period of six years service, and expressed to them his warmest wishes for their future welfare and prosperity. As soon as the standards had been deposited, and the men had dismounted, the whole corps to the number of near 400, sat down to a hot dinner which had been provided for them in the Great Room; after dinner the men resolved on shewing a parting proof of their attachment to their Commander, and in spite of his intreaties, placed him in a chair and carried him round the lines; they then returned to Wrexham, and upon Thursday morning received their discharge.

### *3.18 A Welsh poem on the attempted assassination of the king*

*Shrewsbury Chronicle*, 11 July 1800.

*For the* Shrewsbury Chronicle

DAU BENNILL

Am y rhagorol waredigaeth a gafodd ein grasusaf Frenin George o ddwylaw, y Llofrudd,[24] ar y mesyr a elwir "*God Save the King*".

ERGLYW DI, Arglwydd Dâd,
Cadw'n glŷd Brydain ein gwlâd,
  Rhag brâd a briw:
Rhag gelynion sythion sŷth,
Rhag pob dirgel lofrydd fŷth,
  Oen doeth ein Duw.
Cadw'n Brenin Rhyddyn yr hêdd,
Rhag Bradwyr gau a phryd eu gwêdd,
Cadw SIOR yn bor i'r bedd,
  A'th wêdd heb wâd;
Cadw'n hynys weddus w[a]wr,
Bydd iddi'n fûr bob munud awr,
Rhag unrhyw ddichell fachell fawr,
  Yn awr fy Nhâd.
Diolchwn yn awr bawb i'r Ner,
Am gadw'n siŵr o dan y sêr,
Ein Brenin SIOR;

Rhag y llofrydd annedwydd nôd
'Fynnai ddifa'n glîr fraich ein clôd,
Rhag bod yn bor.
Gogoniant moliant mawr,
I Ben-llywydd Nêf a llawr,
Am gadw SIOR yn bor bob awr,
Yn awr mewn nerth:
Nertha yn glai fŷth ein [glûr],
Yn Frenin dewr i'w freiniol dûr,
Duw cadwo'n bêr SIOR Frenin pûr,
Rhag cur rhai certh.

EDWARD REES, Ci'gwny,
Llangerrig, a'i cant.

(TWO VERSES
On the excellent salvation our gracious King George had from the hands of the Murderer,[24] on the measure called "*God Save the King*".

HEAR US, Lord Father,
keep Britain, our country, safe
from treason and harm:
from proud haughty enemies,
from every secret murderer,
wise lamb of our God.
Keep our King, the Heart of peace,
from false Traitors and their countenance,
maintain GEORGE, as lord, to the grave,
and your image without denial;
keep our fair seemly island,
be for her a bulwark at all times,
from any great crafty guile,
now my Father.
Let us all now thank the Lord,
for keeping safe under the stars,
our King GEORGE;
from the murderer of evil intent
who would wholly destroy the arm of our praise,
to be leader no more.
Glory, great praise,

to the Ruler of Heaven and earth,
for keeping GEORGE as sovereign always.
Now in power:
strengthen fast forever our hero,
to be a brave King to his royal steel,
God keep our sweet pure King GEORGE,
from the blow of the violators.

EDWARD REES, Ci'gwny,
Llangerrig, sang this.)

### *3.19 The Cardiff Volunteer Cavalry*

*Shrewsbury Chronicle*, 24 October 1800.

We feel considerable pleasure in informing our readers that the Cardiff Volunteer Cavalry have received the thanks of his Royal Highness the Duke of York, for their promptitude and exertion in quelling the riots at Merthyr Tydfil; and it will be but justice to add, that during the whole of a very severe night, they kept a constant guard, and patrolled the streets and vicinity of that populous town; which greatly tended to restore peace, and prevent a rescue of the prisoners then in custody. There are 23 delinquents now in Cardiff gaol, 20 out on bail, and nearly 100 absconded.

### *3.20 Rioting in Chirk*

*Shrewsbury Chronicle*, 14 November 1800.

Last week a party of colliers and other workmen, to the number of 100, armed with bludgeons, assembled in a riotous manner in the neighbourhood of Chirk, and by menaces extorted meat, and money at every house in their rout. Information was received on Saturday last by the commander of the Oswestry Yeomanry Cavalry (Captain Warrington in the absence of Major Ormsby) that they had again assembled on that morning, when the core were immediately ordered out, and came up with the rioters at a place called Henlle, near St Martin's, in the act of extorting money, &c. from a farmer, when four of those who appeared most active, and that were identified by other farmers, who exhibited charges against them, were sent by an escort to the prison at Oswestry for further examination, and who were all committed to our county gaol on Tuesday last, under the guard of a detachment of the Oswestry Cavalry, together with a labourer, whom information was laid against as being the receiver of the money collected and who was apprehended near Bronygarth Lime Kilns, at two o'clock on Sunday morning by a party of the same corps who had volunteered their services on the occasion. The others were permitted to separate, and have not again re-assembled; but warrants, we hear, are put against some other persons who have been otherwise active in promoting the insurrection.

### *3.21 The execution of two rioters*

*Shrewsbury Chronicle*, 29 May 1801.

On Friday se'nnight were executed on Cardiff Heath, pursuant to their sentence, Samuel Hill and Aaron Williams, two of the Merthyr rioters, who had been capitally convicted at the late Great Sessions of the County of Glamorgan. – They both behaved with the greatest penitence, and seemed fully confident, through the merits of their Redeemer, of having had pardon and forgiveness. – Aaron Williams, during the course of his prayers, before they were turned off, observed "that they were going to suffer for hundreds," Samuel Hill replied, "yes, for thousands, but I never knew so happy a day as this in the course of my life."

## 4 *The* Salopian Journal

*The* Salopian Journal, *which appeared on Wednesdays, was founded in 1794 by a consortium of owners and published by J. and W. Eddowes (who also brought out Welsh almanacs and literature). Loudly proclaiming its loyalism, it set out to compete with the* Shrewsbury Chronicle, *but was only moderately successful in the 1790s. It contained both Welsh and English-language poetry as well as news from Wales, but appeared to focus more on the market on the English side of the border.*

### *4.1 The editors defend the new paper against accusations of Jacobinism*

*Salopian Journal*, 12 February 1794.

*The encouragements which the Editors of the* Salopian Journal *have experienced, calls for their warmest and most grateful acknowledgments: the demand for their second number exceeded their most sanguine expectations, and they were obliged to put it to press a second time.*

*They beg leave to assure their kind and indulgent readers, that, animated by this success, their best and unremitting endeavours will be exerted to deserve it. The great Question of* War *or* Peace *being now decided, and the supplies voted in Parliament, they hope soon to have more room for miscellaneous matter; and to carry into execution that part of their Plan, which, from the overflow of Political Information, it has hitherto been out of their power to find a place for.*

*Much pains, they find, have been taken by* unfounded Insinuations *of* Disaffection *and* Jacobinical Principles, *to prejudice their Undertaking. Their Paper will furnish the best answer to these Imputations; Imputations which no Man who knows the Parties concerned as Proprietors, will dare to avow: and they have the satisfaction of knowing it to be an undoubted Fact, that to the baseness of such an attack, they are indebted for many Friends, whom they have the honour to number among their zealous Supporters.*

### *4.2 The Supplementary Militia Act*

*Salopian Journal*, 25 January 1797.

For the Salopian Journal.

BROTHER BRITONS,

I HAVE heard that some of you are dissatisfied about the new levies proposed for the DEFENCE of the KINGDOM against FOREIGN INVASION: this must be from not having had the business properly explained to you; or rather, perhaps from having it, (by those who are your greatest enemies, I mean under the mask of Friendship) purposely misrepresented to you. I shall therefore concisely tell you what the Acts are, and call upon any one, not to contradict me only, but to prove that I am wrong.

First, with Regard to

*The Supplementary Militia Act.*

The Person drawn, or his Substitute, is to be trained and exercised for twenty days *within the County*, for which he will receive *one shilling* a day and *his Family be maintained at his own Home*, by an Order of a Magistrate upon the Parish Officers.

If the allotted man does not chuse to serve personally, he may by joining with his neighbours who will be in his lot, in subscribing from *two shillings and sixpence to five shillings* apiece, raise money enough to pay a Substitute a Bounty of One Guinea, or at most a Guinea and half, to serve for him.

If a Substitute, therefore, receive only one Guinea from the balloted man, he gets above *two shillings* a day for himself, besides having his family maintained at his own home.

When this is properly considered, let me ask, Where is the labouring man or mechanic, that would not have his income benefitted, by serving either as a Substitute or a balloted man? Where is the Briton, that would not wish himself to be the fortunate man drawn? Where is the true-born Englishman, that would shrink from stepping forward to serve his country in the hour of need, to defend his own bread and cheese, and eat it himself, rather than let a ferocious enemy eat it from him?

This is all, my brother Briton, that is required from you, till the enemy shall dare to intrude into this hallowed land, ever yet preserved sacred to the abode of REAL Liberty, that precious gift, received by us from our Ancestors, and SHALL BE transmitted untarnished to our Posterity – Britons have said it – Heaven hath confirmed the sacred declaration.

If the enemy should be bold enough to invade this happy Island, what is next required of this Militia? Why, – Not to go out of the Island, but to repel him and make him repent of his temerity.

*I will give you the Clause from the Act by and by.*

And would any true-born Englishman object to it? – If he were not drawn as a Militia Man, would he not offer his best services, under those who are able to conduct him to that part of this happy abode of *real* Liberty, where he can best serve himself, his wife and children, by defending his country? If not would it not be more desireable for him to know how to use his powers best for his Country's and thereby his own good, than have it to learn at the last moment? This is the Clause:

"Provided always, and be it further enacted, That neither the whole or any part of the Militia directed by this Act to be raised and maintained, shall, ON ANY ACCOUNT, be carried or ordered to go out of Great Britain."

*Next with regard to the Cavalry.*

The owners of every 10 Horses used for riding or drawing chaises, are to equip and furnish one man and one horse, and this at the expense of about *five shillings each*, for his coat, pantaloons, half-boots, cap and feather – to do what? Why to be called together to muster in their own Hundred, not often-er perhaps than *once* in *twelve months*, perhaps not at all; and this will take him up a few hours some morning, and he goes to his own home at night: – And this is all required of the Cavalry, except in case of actual Invasion; when, as I before stated with regard to the Supplementary Militia, he, and every other man, deserving the name of Englishman, will join the general armed Force of the kingdom, in the common defence of everything sacred and dear to him as a Briton.

Lastly, with respect to

*The Augmentation of the Army.*

The men to be raised under this Act, by the Parishes, in proportion to the number of Houses paying the Window Tax are to be drafted into the regular regiments, to serve as his Majesty's other regular forces do, with this material difference only, that they are to serve *only* for the present war & *one month* after the determination thereof, when the Cavalry and Supplementary Militia will also be discharged.

Thus you see the Government of the Country have wisely planned a mode for our defence, in case of necessity, in the cheapest, easiest, and least troublesome manner to us; for which we ought all of us to give them our grateful acknowledgments, and cheerfully acquiesce in their recommendation.

This plan is calculated to include the different classes of society; the first is upon the population of the country in general; the second is upon those who keep horses for riding or drawing chaises; and the last is upon the more opulent, who live in houses that are charged to the window tax – and *not upon the Poor.*

Thus you see every part of society is called upon in the way best suited to its condition and situation, to exert its strength and ability for the preservation of the whole; and he who is not eager to press forward to enrol himself in the service of such a country, instead of endeavouring to avail himself of some exemption he might possibly have a claim to, but ought to conceal, (and which in age or indigence would entitle him to commiseration and respect) does not, in my opinion, merit the name of Briton, or deserve the blessings he enjoys.

I shall conclude this address with the good old Song of George Alexander Stevens, upon the ORIGIN OF ENGLISH LIBERTY, which, I hope those who have heard it, as well as such of you as have not, will sing in the present and many a succeeding happy year.

Your real friend and well–wisher

*A true Antient Briton.*

### *4.3 Reports of the French landing from the London Gazettes*

*Salopian Journal*, 1 March 1797.

*London Gazettes Extraordinary.*
*Whitehall, February* 25.

A letter this day received by the Duke of Portland from Lord Milford, Lord Lieutenant for the county of Pembroke, dated Haverfordwest, February 23, five P.M. contains information that two frigates, a corvette and a lugger, appeared off the coast of Pembrokeshire the 22nd inst. and on the evening of that day disembarked some troops, reported by deserters to be about 1200, but without field pieces.

It appears that the most active exertions were made by the Lord Lieutenant and gentlemen of the county, and its neighbourhood, in taking proper measures on this occasion; and that the greatest zeal and loyalty were manifested by all ranks of people, who crowded to offer their services against the enemy.

*Extract of a Letter from Lieutenant Colonel Orchard, commanding the North Devon Volunteers, to the Duke of Portland, dated Hartland Abbey, February 23, 1797.*

I think it my duty to state to your Grace, that I yesterday received an express from Ilfracombe, mentioning that there were three French frigates off that place; (these are the same vessels mentioned in the above letter of Lord Milford) that they had scuttled several merchantmen, and were attempting to destroy the shipping in the harbour. They begged that I would immediately order the North Devon Regiment of Volunteers under my command to march to their assistance. In consequence of this representation, I ordered the men to get ready to march as soon as possible. I have great satisfaction in saying, that in four hours I found every officer and man that was ordered on the parade at Bideford (fifteen miles from home) ready and willing to march to any place they should be commanded to go to. I cannot express the satisfaction I felt on seeing the men so willing to defend their King and Country, at the same time as silent, orderly and sober as might be expected at a morning parade of an old regiment. The greatest exertions were made by ALL descriptions of people to assist, and to render every service in their power. As I was preparing to march, I received an account from Ilfracombe, that the French ships were gone from the coast, and that tranquility was restored again to the town. How far the report was well founded I cannot possibly say; but as this affair may be misrepresented and exaggerated, I trust your Grace will excuse my troubling you with this letter; and I flatter myself must give you pleasure to hear of the loyalty of this neighbourhood, and that the behaviour of the Volunteers and Inhabitants will meet the approbation of his Majesty.

A Second Gazette Extraordinary, published on Sunday, contains Extracts of two letters from Lord Milford: the first stating that the French ships had sailed, leaving 300 men behind; the second, that the whole of the French troops, amounting to near 1200 men, had surrendered, and were on Friday last on their march to Haverfordwest.

A third Gazette Extraordinary was published on Monday, containing the following letter from Lord Cawdor to his Grace the Duke of Portland.

*Fishguard, Friday, Feb.* 24, 1797.

MY LORD,

In consequence of having received information, on Wednesday night at eleven o'clock, that three large ships of war and a lugger had anchored in a small Roadsted, upon the coast in the neighbourhood of this town, I proceeded immediately, with a detachment of the Cardigan Militia, and all the provincial force I could collect, to the place. I soon gained positive intelligence that they had disembarked about 1200 men, but no cannon. Upon the night's setting in, a French officer, whom I found to be the second in command, came in with a letter, a copy of which I have the honour to inclose to your Grace, together with my answer; in consequence of which they determined to surrender themselves prisoners of war, and accordingly laid down their arms this day at two o'clock.

I cannot at this moment inform your Grace of the exact number of prisoners, but I believe it to be their whole force. It is my intention to march them this night to Haverfordwest, where I shall make the best distribution in my power. The frigates, corvette, and lugger, got under weigh yesterday evening, and were this morning entirely out of sight.

The fatigue we have experienced will, I trust, excuse me to your Grace for not giving a more particular detail; but my anxiety to do justice to the officers and men I had the honor to command, will induce me to attend your Grace with as little delay as possible to state their merits, and at the same time to give you every information in my power upon the subject.

The spirit of loyalty which has pervaded all ranks of people throughout this country, is infinitely beyond what I can express.

I am, &c. CAWDOR.

## 4.4 *A letter on the trial of the Dissenters accused of assisting the French at Fishguard*

*Salopian Journal*, 20 September 1797.

*A letter from Haverfordwest, dated Sept 10th, says,*

"The trials of the two prisoners confined in our gaol for high treason,[25] for joining with and assisting the French upon their landing at Fishguard, were brought on at our great sessions here. The solicitor for the crown came from London; and the Council for the prosecution were, the Attorney-General of the circuit, Mr Phillips, Mr Serjeant Williams, Mr Touchet, and Mr Dancey; for the prisoners, Mr Milles and Mr Blackstone. The two prisoners were brought up to plead to their indictments on Tuesday. Mr Milles took some objections to the form of them, at the same time declaring his determination, and that of the prisoners, to bring on the trials, and not to interpose any delay. The Judges over-ruled the objections, and

Thursday morning, at seven, was fixed for the trials. The public expectation had been much raised, and more than 140 gentlemen were summoned upon the Jury. – A large additional number of persons were sworn in as constables, and every precaution was taken to preserve the peace. At seven the court assembled, and the Jury were called, and after many challenges and some debate between the council and court upon points as they arose, a most respectable Jury were sworn; Mr Barlow, the Member for Pembroke, was the foreman. The Attorney-General made a very impressive and dispassionate speech, stating the evidence most distinctly which he should bring against the prisoners; and after having examined two or three witnesses relating to the apprehension of the prisoners, called one of the French prisoners to prove the facts which he had stated. – He was American, and could speak very good English. He refused to answer any question relative to the proceeding in the camp, or to the prisoner at the bar – saying, that he would stay and hear what the other Frenchmen would say, and then he would say as they did. Many attempts were made to get the facts from him, but in vain. The council for the prosecution then attempted to go into an examination of what had passed from him before the Justice of the Peace and the Grand Jury. This was resisted by the Council for the Prisoner; and very ably and eloquently argued, that the Council were heard upon a variety of questions which occurred in this part of the trial, when the Judges rejected the evidence, and would not allow from the papers a question to be put to him. As they could not get any thing more from him, he was dismissed, and the examination of two or three of the Frenchmen, who did speak out, affected the prisoner so little, that the Council for the Prosecution upon consultation with each other relinquished the prosecution. The other prisoner was then brought to trial. Against him the evidence was still slighter, and that prosecution was given up in less than an hour.

It seemed to be the universal opinion, that the Frenchmen were a set of most wicked and abandoned wretches, who, whether from motives and hopes of interest, or from a desire to raise confusion in the country, had been forward to say, what they thought would please the multitude, and would with as little scruple have sworn away the lives of the natives, as they would, by their invasion and arms, have plundered and assassinated them.

It is much to be hoped that the animosity of parties will subside in this country, and as the brave Welshmen gained much honour by their spirit and activity in resisting and overpowering the invaders, that they will continue for ever united in the same patriotic and truly honourable purpose, whatever may be their difference of sentiment in the general politics of their country, or in the exercise of their religion."

## 5 *The* Chester Chronicle

*The* Chester Chronicle, *founded as the* Chester Chronicle; or Commercial Intelligencer *in 1775 and renamed* Chester Chronicle and Cheshire and North Wales Advertiser *in 1792, was edited by the radical William Cowdroy for proprietor John Fletcher from 1785 and appeared on a Friday. It is the only weekly with clear radical leanings in this selection. In the 1790s, it was a major arena for the exchange of radical ideas between England and Wales, and a willing receptacle for radical texts from Wales and in the Welsh language.*

### *5.1 A report of the Gwyneddigion eisteddfod of May 1790*

*Chester Chronicle*, 11 June 1790.

At the meeting of the Welch bards which was held at St Asaph, in Flintshire, on the 25th and 26th ult. the silver medal and chair for the best poem on a given subject, viz. LIBERTY, was adjudged, by the Gwyneddigion Society, in London, to Mr. David Thomas, of Waun-fawr, near Caernarvon, otherwise called by the bards, Dafydd Ddu o Eryri. On one side of the medal is an inscription, complimenting the bard; and on the reverse, Britannia, kneeling by an altar, on which incense is burning, as if supplicating heaven for the preservation of her rights and liberties; over the altar an emblem of heavenly rays, signifying the acceptance of the oblation, with this motto "*Gwreichionen gre ei chynnydd*" (A strong Spark to kindle). Likewise, the silver medal, for the best production on LIBERTY in prose, was adjudged by the said society, to Mr. Walter Davies, near Llanvillin, otherwise called by the bards, Gwallter Mechain, ab Gwerfyl. On one side of the medal is the head of Cambria, with some emblems of liberty, and on the reverse, a lion defending Britannia (who resembles a child grasping venomous serpents) against foreign enemies, with this motto "*Trech iawn na gormes*." (Overcoming is better than Oppression). The chair for the best writer on extempore subjects, was adjudged to Mr. Thomas Edwards, of Nant, who is now deservedly honoured with the title of "Shakespear of Wales" – On being chaired, he delivered the following eulogy:

Eisteddais, cefais im cofion, Gadair<br>
Gwag ydyw balchio;<br>
Ond er hynny, dew heno<br>
I fagu'r trwst, – fi gae'r tro.

Er clwm clod, iawn fod yn fardd,
A honni nerth hunan urdd,
Gwell yw cael, gwiw allu cerdd,
Dawn a chan, a Duw'n ei chwrdd.

(I sat, I received for my memories, a Chair
it is vain to boast;
but nevertheless, tonight
to the sound of great applause it was my turn.

For the melody of praise, it is good to be a poet,
and claim the strength of self-dignity,
it is better to get, true skill of poetry,
talent and song, and God meeting it.)

The silver medal (given by the St. Asaph gentlemen) for the best singer, with the harp, was adjudged (tho' with much difficulty) to Mr. John Jones, of St. Asaph, a reputed son of Vulcan; but 'tis not unnatural to suspect, from the merits of this gentleman, Apollo must have honoured Venus with a visit in Vulcan's absence. – Too much praise cannot be given to the rest of the singers, particularly Mr. Roberts Foulks, of St. Asaph. Their vocal strains lasted *thirteen hours* before the umpires could place the *bays* upon the brow of the conqueror.

## 5.2 *The burning of Thomas Paine's effigy*

*Chester Chronicle*, 11 January 1793.

That miserable martyr, poor Paine, agreeably to the present fashion of the day, was chaired by proxy, in this city, on Wednesday last, and paraded, on the shoulders of four loyal hirelings, thro' the principal streets of the city, attended by two or three hundred boys. The habiliments of the effigy were furnished from the constitutional wardrobes of several of the friends of peace and good order; – a coat from one, a waistcoat from another, a pair of combustibles[26] from a third – and the sapient head of a man of the law transferred his whig to the man of straw, giving the figure at least the appearance of wisdom. After a pleasant promenade, the gentlemen halted at the Cross, where the philosopher was placed, and a few dogs were brought to tear and bark at him – a mode of refutation almost as intelligible as some others with which the pens of politicians have honour'd the world. – They at last committed his rebellious remains as a burnt-offering to the blazing ordeal of a bonefire; where it was with no small difficulty they were consumed – one proof at least that he is not of a very inflammable nature. It is but justice to add, that the persons employed conducted themselves with as much regularity as the rationality of the scene would admit of, and that they seem'd to have sense enough to be heartily ashamed of the task imposed upon them.

*Chester Chronicle*, 8 February 1793.

The effigy of Paine was committed to the ordeal of a bonfire, at Nantwich, a few days ago. Here, as in most other places, the scene was conducted by a description of people for whom reason and common sense must feel no other sensation than that of pity. The respectable part of the town, to their credit, discountenanced it.

## *5.3 A declaration of loyalty*

*Chester Chronicle*, 18 January 1793.

*Wrexham, January* 14, 1793.

At a most numerous and respectable meeting of the inhabitants of every description, within the Hundred of Bromfield, in the county of Denbigh, held at the Town-hall, in Wrexham, on Monday the 14th instant, the following declaration and resolutions were unanimously agreed to:

WE, the gentlemen, clergy, freeholders, and other inhabitants of the town of Wrexham, and the rest of the Hundred of Bromfield, should feel ourselves unworthy of the many blessings and advantages we enjoy as Britons; of the liberty of which we are so justly proud; of that pure religion, in support of which our ancestors were ready to shed their blood; and of those wise and equal laws, which the greatest cannot transgress with impunity, and which afford protection and security to the meanest; were we to neglect, in this critical period, uniting with the rest of the nation, in expressing our most zealous attachment to a constitution from which we derive such transcendent benefits, and our firm determination to support and defend it with our lives and fortune.

We see with abhorrence the artful efforts of men, desperate in their fortunes, and profligate in their principles, to delude and reduce the lower ranks of our fellow-subjects from their duty and allegiance, terrifying them with grievances which have no existence, and holding out advantages which are equally visionary.

Our abhorrence is kindled into the warmest resentment, when we see these sowers of sedition instigated and supported by our natural and inveterate enemies, the French; a people who, for centuries past, have been using every engine of open force, and secret artifice, to draw us under the yoke of arbitrary power and religious tyranny, and who would now persuade us to throw off all religion, and involve ourselves in their present state of anarchy and wretchedness. These are the enemies we are called upon to resist, and, we trust, no further arguments are necessary to unite our countrymen in such a cause. Britain will never suffer herself to be the dupe of French manners, and French politics. Upon these principles, and for these ends, it is unanimously resolved.

*First.* That we form an association for the support of our present established government, under a King, House of Lords, and House of Commons.

*Secondly.* That men of all ranks and descriptions in this town and hundred, be invited to join with us, as in one common cause, since the present calamitous situation of France is a convincing proof, that those levelling principles which bring ruin and destruction of property upon the rich, must, sooner or later, produce famine, slaughter, and desolation, amongst the poor.

*Thirdly.* That we all will, in our several stations, jointly and individually, use every effort in our power to support and assist the civil magistrates in suppressing all riotous and disorderly assemblies, all treasonable and seditious publications, and all other attempts whatsoever to disturb the public peace.

*Fourthly.* That the underwritten be a committee for carrying into execution these resolutions.

Mr. Hughes
Mr. Penson
Mr. Eddowes
Rev. Edward Edwards
Sir W. W. Wynne
Mr. Edwards
Mr. Sidebotham
Mr. Langford
Richard Myddleton, esq.
Mr. Brown
W. Wilkinson, esq.
Mr. Ellis
Rev. G. Warrington
John Evans, esq.
The Dean of St. Asaph
Danvers Gartside, esq.
Rev. W. Brown
Ed. Lloyd Lloyd, esq.
Captain Jones
Mr. Taylor
J. Meller, esq.
Mr. Samuel
Mr. Edwards
Rev. T. Youde
Richard Meredith, esq.
Mr. Woollam
Rev. J. Jenkins
Dr. Puleston

W. Williams, esq.
Rev. J. H. W. Eyton
Sir F. Cunliffe
Mr. T. Evans
Ed. Rowlands, esq.
Captain Chadwick
Mr. Matthews
Philip Yorke, esq.
Rev. S. Strong
W. Robert, esq.
Mr. Marsh
W. Lloyd, esq.
Rogers Kenyon, esq.
John Jones, esq.
Robert Griffiths, esq.
Rev. J. Yale
Mr. Crewe

Rev. W. Williams
Mr. D. Parry
Mr. Moore Williams
Mr. Kenrick
Mr. Wynne
J. Humberstone Cawdor, esq.
Rev. Robert Price
Rev. R. Saunders
Rev. J. Denman
Randle Jones, esq.
Jolin Jones, esq.
Earl Grosvenor
Rev. C. A. Wighton
Rev. Mr. Lewis
Mr. Hutchinson
Richard Lloyd, esq.

W. D. SHIPLEY, CHAIRMAN[27]

The following resolution was then proposed, seconded, and unanimously agreed to: – [*Fifthly.*] That the thanks of this meeting be given to the Dean of St. Asaph, for his ready compliance with our wishes in calling this meeting, for his spirited conduct in the chair, and for his truly loyal, and no less patriotic, speech on the occasion.

*Sixthly.* That the above resolutions be inserted in The Star, The General Evening Post, and in the two Chester papers.

### *5.4 An anti-war poem*

*Chester Chronicle*, 25 July 1794.

ODE,
ON CONVERTING A SWORD INTO A PRUNING HOOK
BY EDWARD WILLIAMS.[28]

FELL weapon, that in ruthless hand,
Of warrior fierce, or despot King,
Hast long career'd o'er every land,
Hast heard th'embattled clangor's ring;

Wrench'd from the grasp of lawless pride,
With reeking gore no longer dy'd,
I bear thee now to rural shades,
Where nought of hell-born War invades;
Where plum'd Ambition feels her little soul;
And, hiding from the face of day,
That dawns from Heav'n, and drives away
Those fiends that love eternal night,
She, with rude yell, blasphemes the sons of light,
That bid her dreadful arm no more the world controul.

I saw the tyrant on her throne,
With wrathful eyes and venom'd breath,
Enjoy the world's unceasing groan,
And boast, unsham'd, her fields of death;
When through the skies her banners wav'd,
When drunk with blood her legions rav'd,
Her priest invok'd the realms above,
Dar'd at thy throne, thou God of Love,
Call for the thunders of thy mighty will,
To storm around the guiltless head,
To strike a peaceful brother dead;
While blasphemies employed his tongue,
The gorgeous temple with loud echoes rung;
I felt my shudd'ring soul with deepest horror chill.

I saw the victor's dreadful day –
He, through the world, in regal robe,
Tore to renown his gory way;
With carnage zon'd th'affrighted globe:
Whilst from huge towns involv'd in flame,
The monster claim'd immortal fame,
What lamentable shrieks arose,
In all th'excess of direst woes!
Loud was the sycophant's applauding voice:
Together throng'd the sceptred band,
Hymn'd by the friends of ev'ry land;
How mourn'd my soul, to hear the tale
Of sad humanity's unpitied wail!
And each imperial dome with horrid shouts rejoice!

But hear from Heav'n the dread command –
It gives to speed that awful hour.
When from oppression's trembling hand,
Must fall th'insulting rod of power;
Long vers'd in mysteries of war,
She scyth'd her huge triumphant car;
Her lance, with look infuriate hurl'd,
Bade fell destruction sweep the world;
She wing'd her Churchill's name[29] from poll to poll:
Now brought before th'eternal throne,
Where truth prevails, all hearts are known,
She, self-condemn'd, with horrid call,
Bids on her head the rocks and mountains fall,
To shield her from the wrath whose venging thunders roll.

Dark Error's code no more enthrals,
Its vile infatuations end;
Aloud the trump of Reason calls;
The nations hear! the worlds attend!
Detesting now the craft of Kings,
Man from his hand the weapon flings,
Hides it in whelming deeps afar,
And learns no more the trade of War;
But lives with Nature, on th'uncity'd plain:
Long has this earth a captive mourn'd,
But days of old are now return'd,
We Pride's rude arm no longer feel,
No longer bleed beneath Oppression's heel;
For Truth to Love and Peace restores the world again.

The dawn is up, the lucid morn,
I carol in its golden skies;
The muse, on eagle-pinions borne,
Through rapture's realm prophetic flies:
The battle's rage is heard no more,
Hush'd is the storm on ev'ry shore;
See lambs and lions in the mead
Together play, together feed,

Crop the fresh herbage of perennial Spring;
From eyes that bless the glorious day
The scalding tears are wip'd away;
Raise high the song! 'tis Heav'n inspires!
In chorus joining with seraphic lyres,
We crown the Prince of Peace – he reigns th'Eternal King!

### *5.5 A loyalist poetic competition*

*Chester Chronicle*, 1 August 1794.

Congress of British Bards, lately assembled, determined to give the muses a *broadside* in honour of Admiral Howe, by composing an English Ode on that glorious event.[30] – However well a Welsh Pegasus may amble over its native mountains, 'tis rather unfortunate that there are few but what are confoundedly lame the instant they attempt to shew their paces over an English course: – Of this the reader will judge, when he has stretched his eye over a brace of couplets of the following (adjudged the *best*!) composition from the pen of Mr. C. Jones, of Bodfary – When we speak of the few who go smoothly over an English soil, our minds naturally apply to the first of those few Anglo-British Bards – our much-valued friend, LLWYD; – but, alas! *his* Pegasus has been long *tied to the manger*!

Come, brave sailors, fill the glasses –
Let's chorus join – God save the King!
To welcome our lovely lasses,
Another bowl now, waiter, bring.

Health to the King we'll drink all round,
And Prince of Wales, notorious found,
The Duke of York be more abound,
Queen Charlotte so, and Howe the same.

Long may the King successful stand,
Cause sincere subjects all obey;
To govern ALL, both sea and land,
While combin'd arms in spirit sway.

Honour the King is gracious good –
  Repeat this chorus four times ten,
To welcome all the Royal blood;
  And forty times repeat again.

If we forbear a heavy blows –
  By force of war on jovial crew;
Began with pleasure, gain applause,
  Since first of June our joys renew.

Stout Alexander, on ocean,
  With fortitude was martial try'd;
Yet fought away with might and main –
  Heroic commander seem'd the guide.

From port to port our cannons roar –
  We fancy, for to fence with France:
Her fleet so shall keep distant shore,
  In doleful dump to jump and dance.

Britons, prepare your songs, prepare,
  To praise hot actions, bloody wounds;
Loudly, loudly, sound the echoing air!
  Let virtue be with glory crown'd.

### *5.6 A threatening letter and the editor's reply*

*Chester Chronicle*, 21 November 1794.

The following is a literal copy of a letter (the original of which may be seen at the printing-office) sent, a few days ago, thro' the Chester post-office, to the person whose name appears on the superscription:

"Knowing you to be a rueful Jacobin I beg leave to inform you it is my intention to shoot you the first time I see you out at night therefore be careful of yourself.

I am Yours, A Detester of all Democrats, Christlington, Nov. 5, 1794, Julias Percian.

I have been in your company frequently at Flookersbrook, where I have heard you discourse on politics.

Mr. Cowdroy, at Mr. Fletcher's, printer, Chester."

If being a firm friend to peace, and consequently to the best interests of humanity and his country, entitles a man to the appellation of a Jacobine, the person to whom the above letter is addressed feels a conscious pride in being honoured with the title. To the unknown writer (whoever he may be) he bears no enmity; – the only motion of his mind is that of pity for a deluded fellow-being who can so far forget the character of a man as to insidiously threaten the life of another, merely because he may wish to promote the happiness of Englishmen, by the constitutional enjoyment of those liberties, which the writer perhaps has not an understanding to comprehend, nor, it is certain, sensibility to feel and appreciate.

As this is not the first time that the law has been recently violated, perhaps by the same hand, in the writing of letters of a similar complexion, we insert the following clause from the act of parliament of the 27th George II. – from a regard for the life of this misguided man:

"*If any person or persons, from and after the first day of May, 1754, shall knowingly send any letter or letters, threatening to kill or murder any of his Majesty's subject or subjects, every person so offending, being thereof lawfully convicted, shall be adjudged guilty of felony, without benefit of clergy.*"

### *5.7 An anti-war poem from Denbigh*

*Chester Chronicle*, 21 August 1795.

For the Chester Chronicle.

*Dum haec in animo meo revolvo effundo Lacrymas.*
(While I consider these things I shed Tears.)

Off to old Neptune's briny deep,
  From worldly sorrows free,
The man of pity walks to weep,
  And sings, O Want! of thee.

Thy pallid mien, and ghastly form,
  Have fought our northern shore;
For here the herdsman droops forlorn,
  Here starve the humble poor.

For want of bread the infant cries;
  The father hangs his head;
The mother fills the air with sighs,
  And wou'd her child were dead!

Rather than see its infant form
  Become a pray to thee,
"I'd hurl it headlong to the storm,
  And die in misery!"

Such, haughty War, thy poignant woes,
  To thee such scenes belong;
The painful Muse wou'd thee disclose
  In simple, artless song.

But yesterday, I saw with dread,
  A sight that drove me wild,
A mother gathering chaff for bread,
  To feed her hungry child:

Around her knees the trembling babe,
  Its eyes uplifted high,
The mother bade its form to save
  From grim-eye'd Poverty.

Oh God of mercies! loud I cry'd,
  From whence can this arise?
From War, from War, I deeply sigh'd,
  From War, that rends the skies.

Pity 'tis, then, that such a curse
  Shou'd hurt our happy isle;
Shou'd drain the nation's thread-worn purse,
  Or drown the fair one's smile.

Oh! soon again may Peace appear,
  And Concord's milder beam;
To glad each swift, revolving year,
  To cherish and redeem.

May Gallia's plains and Albion's shore,
No jarring discord prove!
May distant nations live once more
In kind and mutual love?

*Denbigh, Aug.* 14, 1795.

## *5.8 Two anti-war letters*

*Chester Chronicle*, 21 August 1795.

MR. PRINTER,
Should you think the following lines worthy of the attention of any of your numerous readers, you are at liberty to publish them.

JUVENIS

*Welsh Pool, Aug.* 3, 1795.
MUCH has been said of late of the necessity of persevering in the war, in which we are unhappily involved, in order to maintain the Christian religion. I apprehend, if the advocates for such principles were to pay a little attention to the history of Christianity, they would find, that its wholesome precepts were never inculcated by the edge of the sword, and that its mild doctrines were never enforced by the mouth of the cannon.

Craft and violence, injustice and cruelty, have been commonly used in the founding, supporting, and extending, of secular kingdoms. The Roman Empire was founded and grew to its height, in blood. But these are principles which Christ abhorred, as utterly repugnant to the mild and gracious designs of his gospel. The principal persons employed by Princes, to establish, maintain, and extend their dominions, are – not persons the most remarkable for integrity and benevolence, for piety and philanthropy; but those who are most eminent for political prudence, or martial bravery; for secret intrigue, or open hostility – those who are best qualified to persuade by eloquence, to circumvent by cunning, or to subdue by force. But was Christianity ever propagated by these means? The most illustrious instruments employed by the Prince of Peace in erecting his kingdom, were of a character quite the reverse. They were chiefly selected from the lower orders of life, and called from occupations deemed mean. Uneducated in the courts of royalty, in the schools of learning, or in the field of war; they were strangers to the finesse of politicians, and little acquainted with Gentile philosophy. So ignorant were they of sciences called liberal, so unpolite in their address, and uncanonical in their garb, that multitudes, called Christians, it is highly probable, would be ashamed to give them a hearing, were they now present among us; unless the public attention were first excited by the exercise of their miraculous powers. – Yes by the instrumentality of those unlettered arid plain men, did the Prince of Peace establish his kingdom, in making war upon Satan's Empire, evangelical truths, and spiritual gifts, laborious preaching and ardent prayer, fortitude, patience and holy examples, were the arms they used. Such were the militia, and such the armour, employed in spreading Christianity at first; and these are the means, I am persuaded, in the use of which we can promise ourselves any success in repelling our adversaries.

*Chester Chronicle*, 25 September 1795.

To the Printer of the Chester Chronicle.

SIR,

After so many noble, brave and flourishing soldiers, of every description and character, have fallen victims to the destructive sword; after having spent millions of money in the prosecution of a war, the termination of which will behold, in all probability, disappointment and loss of property; still however, against treason, principle, and the dictates of our religion, will ministers persevere in their obstinacy, and with unchristian-like apathy, devote their fellow-creatures to blood and slaughter! – Where must be the feelings of that man, who reflects, that he is the fatal cause of hastening a poor unfortunate brother to a sudden, premature death! But, in these days, inhumanity seems to be fashionable, and reason banished. The distresses of the private individual are overlooked and forgotten; the emaciated soldier, and the weather-beaten sailor are suffered to languish in pain and want, whilst ministers at home are hourly projecting schemes to add to the number of the afflicted. To politics I am a stranger, but to humanity a friend. I do not say that this war is either a just or an unjust one; I do not assert that it began in policy, or will end in ruin; I could only wish that the lives of our fellow-creatures might not be wantonly sported with, and that the blood-stained sword might once more be safely lodged in the scabbard, unmolested and useless. But, if it must devastate the earth, if its baneful point must penetrate the human heart, and shed innocent blood; what, in the name of peace, must become of those poor creatures, who, when they have lost the dearest pledges of their love, their husbands and children, have not wherewithal to purchase bread, already sufficiently scarce, to support the cravings of Nature? Independently of their natural feelings and afflictions, they have sufficient reason to complain: every article of life is dear and scarce, not a morsel of bread is to be procured without money, the very prospect of which they have lost in the death of their friends and relations. Many unhappy wretches, I well know, have, in many towns, procured the necessaries of life for themselves and children, upon the credit that their husbands will return home, loaded with riches and honour. But how often are they disappointed! The next ship perhaps brings the melancholy tidings, that their husbands are no more, – Where, then, O ye unfortunate females will ye fly for succour and relief? Where is the hand that will administer comfort, or pour its stores to relieve you? A prey to all the stings and tortures of want, neglected, despised, and without credit, they are reduced, perhaps, to a state of abject despondency, or what is still worse, to a state of prostitution, whose frightful concomitants are misery, disease, and death. Peace be then to your shades! May the God of mercy have pity upon your souls! But if one creature, as we are often times tempted to believe, must be made answerable for another, what can they say in vindication of themselves, who are daily the painters of such a scene as this? They are sinners indeed. Let them figure to themselves the penitent sinner at the last moment of existence, when life is trembling upon her lips, and reflect, at the same time, that war has brought her to such a state, and they perhaps, will weep. Some latent spark of sensibility may then revive, and the tear of contrition may be the means of saving an unhappy country from ruin, expence, and destruction.

There is another argument, equally, perhaps, as cogent, and drawn from the Holy Scriptures, which in my opinion, should deter men from rashly engaging in any war, whether just or unjust. We are expressly commanded not to shed the blood of a fellow-creature; and most certainly every man is a fellow-creature, whether Frenchman, Mahometan, or Jew. But in opposition to this, you will say, that the Israelites, and various other nations, were frequently, if not continually, engaged in carrying on wars; and you will undoubtedly say nothing but what has truth for its foundation. But it should be here observed, that our ancestors were by far less cultivated; they had not such a refined notion of morality as we entertain; and Revelation had not exhibited to their view a blessed Redeemer, compassionate, merciful, and forgiving. Taught by his humble example, and humiliating degradation, that all sublunary things are vain and transitory; that the utmost extent of our ambition should be a future state; that we should forgive our enemies, and embrace our foes, let peace once more assert her empire, and diffuse her blessings over the whole earth. But if the war must still be carried on; if the prayers and earnest entreaties of thousands must be heard in vain, and the cries of the distressed must be unnoticed; yet the individual, and the man of private character, is supported by the cheering reflection, that he is not the author of it, nor the fatal instrument by which so many innocent men are rudely cast into the bowels of the earth, or bosom of the deep. Comforted by a consciousness of his innocence, though he lives in a state of obscurity, he lives in ease and quiet, unembrued with the blood of any man. Whether the event of the war be prosperous or otherwise, it will be indifferent to him, though he must, at the same time, rejoice, that the effusion of human blood is stopped, and carnage is no more.

Many and various are the opinions of men, about the policy of the present war, and many, no doubt are hastily prompted, from motives of prejudice, and ill-judged malice, to reprobate it in the most bitter and illiberal terms of rancour. I, however, tread upon no such grounds, which, at best, must be unstable and tottering. He who is actuated by such motives, will one moment barely contradict what he asserted another; he may be persuaded, by the force of eloquence, or description, to forego and condemn a doctrine, which he once held in the highest administration and esteem; and, in short, such a man may be truly said to have no sound and permanent will of his own. You yourself, sir, must be sensible, from your general knowledge and intercourse with mankind, that there are numbers in the world, who expressly answer to this character, and must be well aware that little credit can be given to their opinion and assertions. But the man who declares himself with candour and impartiality; who, without supporting any man's party, or violating the dictates of his conscience, professes himself to be the enemy of the present war, from motives of purest conviction and benevolence, is entitled to public malice, and public approbation. Independency of opinion, indeed, so far from being in the least degree blameable, is noble and praise worthy; it shews man in his own light, indisguised by the foreign and adventitious garb of ringing dissimulation. The man who assumes such a character, or is naturally possessed of it, can never be sufficiently despised; he is a dangerous companion, and secret foe; he listens, with attentive avidity, to the sentiments of all men, without adopting a single one of his own; he is artful, cunning, and malicious. The man of independence, on the other hand (I mean independency of opinion) acts on nobler principles; he is the greatest ornament to society, the most substantial friend of man, and the most zealous advocate for truth. What he speaks, he speaks from principle; and never propagates any opinion, which is not founded upon truth, justice, and benevolence. Actuated by such motives alone, and wounded by the repeated attacks that have been made upon my sensibility, by the late unparalleled effusion of blood, I declare myself the enemy of the present war; and did but mankind in general feel one half as much as I do for the distressed objects it has occasioned, and will, in all probability, occasion, they would detest its policy, and despise its author.

*North Wales, Sept.* 4.

### *5.9 Advertisement for a radical Welsh periodical*

*Chester Chronicle*, 25 December 1795.

ER BUDD Y CYMRY:
Ar fyrr y cyhoeddir,
GWERTH PEDAIR CEINIOG, Rhifyn I.
(I'w barhau yn fisol)
O'r
GEIRGRAWN,
Neu GYLCHYNOL DRYSORFA GWYBODAETH;
YN CYNNWYS
Hynafiaethau; crefyddol athrawiaethau; bywgraffiadau; marwolaethau; gwybodaeth eglwysaidd a dinasaidd; newyddion tramor a chartrefol; chwedlau neullduol; caniadau, emynau, ac awdlau buddiol, &c. &c.
GAN D. DAVIES, TREFFYNNON
"Gwell gwybodaeth nag aur,
"Y doethion a lloriant wybodaeth."

ANNERCHIAD

Nid yw'r goruwchwylwyr yn anturio cymmeryd y gorchwyl hyn mewn llaw, oddiar wagdyb o'u bod yn meddu gwell cymmwysiadau, neu ysfa o ymddangos yn fwy dysgedig, nag eraill: ond oddiar chwennychiad crŷf i fod o ryw fydd cyffredinol i'w cydwladwyr; oddiar ddrych-olwg ar ddefnyddioldeb cyhoeddiadau cylchynol ymhlith eu cymydogion, y Saeson, ac ar y dygn anwybodaeth, ar dû-dew Dywyllwch sy'n dannedig dros ran fawr o'n gwlad gynhenid; oddiar ystyriaeth, mae'r achos pennaf deall y Saeson ar y Cymry uniaith yw, nid diffyg o gymmwysderau yn y naill mwy na'r llall, ond yn unig diffyg o foddion gwybodaeth; ac oddiar dyb mae'r ddyfais oreu i ledu gwybodaeth gyffredinol am bethau, yw cylchynol lyfrannau, gan eu bod yn cynnwys amrywiaeth defnyddiau, ac yn isel o werth. Gall cantoedd gyrraedd a darllain llyfrau o werth môr rhesymmol, a *Phedair ceiniog*, bob mis, nad oes ganthynt nag arian i brynu na hamdden i ddarllain llyfrau mwy. Er y bydd y goruwchwylwyr yn amcanu bob amser, gwneuthur dewisiad o'r defnyddiau mwya' cymmhwys i foddhau yn gystal ag adeiladu, nid idynt, ar yr un pryd, heb ragweled y bydd rhai o bob grâdd yn beio ar eu gwaith; er hynny anturiant ei ddwyn yn y blaen, gan obeithio y bydd eu hymegniad dros ddaioni, ac adeiladaeth cyffredinol eu cywleidiadon un-iaith, nid yn unig yn dderbyniol gan bob ewyllysiwr da i'r *cymry*, a'r *iaith frytanaidd*; ond o leshad parhaus i laweroedd, trwy fod yn offerynnol i chwalu ymaith y gaddug anwybodaeth sy'n gorchuddio Cymru; i ddadwreiddio difräwch sydd yn serchiadau y werin, am gyrraedd "doniau dysg"; ac i fywhau 'mofynniad a myfyrdod yn eu plith. Ni bydd i ymadroddion llibeiddus a sarrug i gael ymddangos yn y Geirgrawn; eithr bydd yn agored i bawb (gan nad yw i gael ei gyfyngu i unrhyw blaid) i fynegi eu meddyliau am bethau crefyddol a dinasaidd, ond iddynt eu hamlygu mewn yspryd addfwynder a chariad.

☞ Byddir yn rhwymedig i'r gwybedyddion, ac eraill, sy'n chwennych cefnogi a chynnorthwyo'r gwaith, a danfonner eu henwau, ac hefyd ddefnyddiau priodol, ar frŷs, at y cyhoeddwr y Nhreffynnon.

*** Bydd Y Geirgrawn ar werth gan E. Carnes, Llyfrwerthwr y' Nhreffynnon; a chan werthwyr Llyfrau y' mhob trêf y' Nghymru. – A chan G. Sael, Rhif. 192, Strand, Llundain.

D. S. Rhaid cyfarwyddo'r llythyrau – "*To the Editor of the Welsh Magazine, Holywell, Flintshire.*"

(FOR THE BENEFIT OF THE WELSH:
Published soon,
WORTH FOUR PENCE, Number I.
(To be continued monthly)
Of the
GEIRGRAWN,
Or SERIAL TREASURY OF KNOWLEDGE;
CONTAINING
Antiquities; religious philosophies; biographies; obituaries; information about church and state; foreign and home news; curious tales; poems, hymns, and beneficial odes, &c. &c.
BY D. DAVIES, HOLYWELL
"Knowledge is better than gold,
The wise lay the foundation of knowledge."

ADDRESS

The editors do not venture to take this task in hand, because of a vain notion that they are possessed of better qualifications, or an urge to appear more learned than others: but from a strong desire to be of some general benefit to their compatriots; from a view of the usefulness of serial publications amidst their neighbours, the English, and of the profound ignorance and the pitch-black Darkness which is spread over a large part of our native land; from a consideration that the main reason of the Englishman's understanding over the monolingual Welsh is not a lack of qualifications in one more than the other, but the lack of means of knowledge; and from the belief that the best vehicle for spreading general knowledge of things are the serial booklets, since they contain a variety of matter and are low in cost. Hundreds can reach and read books of a value as reasonable as *Four pence* every month, who do not have the money to buy nor the leisure to read more substantial books. Though the editors will aim at all times at choosing the matter deemed most appropriate to please as well as edify, they are not, at the same time, without the foresight that some of every station will find fault with their work; nevertheless they venture to take it on, hoping that their striving for the benefit and the general edification of their monolingual compatriots is not only well-received by every well-wisher of the *Welsh people* and the *British language* but of lasting advantage to many, by being an instrument for dispersing the fog of ignorance which envelopes Wales; for uprooting the apathy which is in the affections of the people about achieving the "talents of learning"; and for inspiring curiosity and contemplation among them. Sneaky and bitter expressions will not be allowed to appear in the Geirgrawn; but it will be open to everybody (as it is not restricted to any faction) to express their thoughts on religious and political matters, as long as they convey them in a spirit of tenderness and love.

☞ We shall be bound to the learned, and others, who desire to back and support the work, and they should send their names, and also appropriate materials, in haste, to the publisher at Holywell.

*** The Geirgrawn will be for sale from E. Carnes, Bookseller in Holywell, and from the sellers of Books in every town in Wales. – And from G. Sael, Number 192, Strand, London.

N. B. Letters must be addressed – "*To the Editor of the Welsh Magazine, Holywell, Flintshire.*")

## *5.10 Two letters from a Flintshire magistrate on the price of grain*

*Chester Chronicle*, 19 February 1796.

To the Right Hon. WILLIAM PITT.

Sir, I took the liberty last November of stating to you the disturbances here, occasioned by the dearness of corn, and the farmers sending it out of the neighbourhood, the markets being thereby unsupplied, the poor deprived of bread, either from the scarcity, or the price being above their reach. – I sent you the resolutions of a meeting on the occasion in Cheshire, manly, forcible, and eminent, characteristic of the gentlemen who attended; and also those of the adjoining county, of a very different complexion. – It is very hard, the farmer says, that he dare not send his property where he pleases, consistent with the law. – It is more so, says the industrious mechanic and labourer, to starve us by so doing; double our wages – as every necessary of life is doubled, and we shall be able to procure them – or if you don't like that expedient, fix the price of grain for a limited time, suppose wheat at 9s. barley at 5s. oats 3s. Winchester measure. – I have been a farmer myself, and no inconsiderable one, and will take upon me to say, that the farmer may get rich at those prices, and no disadvantage to the most extensive views in agriculture; and he must also allow that his most sanguine expectations, when he entered upon his farm, did not exceed those prices.

Until something of this kind is done the numerous evils which now exist I fear will continue; begin to punish, fill the gaols with delinquents, for stopping the removal of corn out of the neighbourhood, their families must be kept by their respective parishes – Will this be for the good of the community at large? "A consummation to be wished?" – The remedy will be worse than the disease. – Making the obstruction to remove corn felony, &c. did not operate as the least restraint, perhaps it might act as provocation to the mistaken multitude mild measure might possibly pacify. – That some measures may be devised to stop tumult and disorder is the most ardent wish of

A Flintshire Magistrate. Feb. 11 1796.

N.B. Since I wrote the above, my house has been beset by a vast concourse of persons, of all descriptions, to know the event of a complaint to me by a man who had sent a load of 21 hobbets of barley to a kiln in town, which was followed by a multitude of women, and brought back into the market, and unloaded by the instigation, and under the specious pretence of the person renting the toll of the market, or having toll thereof. The owner offered to sell the barley, but they would neither buy it nor suffer him to take it away. I sent to the commanding officer of the Rutland Fencibles for his assistance, and he very politely, and instantly, had a party ready; but whilst the owner was with me, it was lodged in the toll-shop, whence he was afraid to remove it, lest the kiln should be taken down, and left for the next market day. The matter was thus abated without violence or expense, except the exaction of toll.

What accumulating mischiefs grow from one existing evil, which emboldens me to repeat what I before suggested, of the prices of corn, as the only means for remedy. Something must be done to remove the insupportable burden on the poor. Avert dreaded consequences, and strike at the root of the existing evil, and that cannot be detrimental to any description of men. The late edict of mixing wheat and barley, I fear, defeats itself. The number of families, in most of the parishes of Wales, is about five who eat bread of barley alone, to one who used to eat wheaten; but now, such who can get it, think they have a sanction to eat it mixed. Barley sold, last week, at 17d. wheat at 40s. a hobbet. It is high time for *every man* to put his hand to his plough, to stop this torrent of extortion.

*Chester Chronicle*, 26 February 1796.

To the Right Hon. WILLIAM PITT,

Sir, I am happy in the honour of informing you, that the opinion I presumed to address to you, in these dangerous times in which we are all involved, have met, in my Neighbourhood, with entire approbation. I have also complaints from a few in several counties, wishing my hints may be noticed, and that "*general peace and harmony be restored and plenty resume its reign.*" – It will, without a doubt, restore us peace and quietness, more especially if some addition was made, to able labourers in husbandry; the common price is 16s. a day, and if advanced to 18d. they would be upon as good a footing as the smaller Farmers, and by that advance Agriculture would meet with no check for want of labourers, as the pleasurable employment, the healthiness, ease, and safety attending their labour (the wages being ample) would secure to the Farmer the preference. Any remedy suggested, by ascertaining the produce and consumption of corn in the Kingdom, is too remote; immediate relief is wanted, hunger is keen, and amusing delays whet the edge of the tool we should avoid. I am, Sir, your and the public's obedient servant, A Flintshire Magistrate.

## *5.11 A Welsh anti-fast-day hymn with translation*

*Chester Chronicle*, 4 March 1796.

### *A WELSH HYMN,*
### TO BE SUNG ON THE FAST-DAY.[31]

O! Dylodion isel Frî,
Mae'n rhaid i chwî, ymprydio,
Cym'rwch FARA i chwi yn Ddrŷch;
Ni chewch ond edrych arno.

Mae Cyhoeddiad wedi bod,
Am gadw Diwrnod ympryd,
Dyna'r ffordd sydd fwyaf rhâd
I borthi gwlad, newynllyd.

Mae'r Esgobion uchel nôd,
Ar Bysgod, am ymbesgi,
Ai da y'w rhain i Enaid Dŷn,
Efo Menyn, wedi ei doddi.

Cofied pawb sydd yn y Fro,
Weddio gyda'r Brenin
Rhag ofn bod Dynion drwg yn haid
O *Ddiawliaid* yn ei ddilin.[32]

O! Benaethi'ed gwael ei ffydd,
Ach Crefydd, er eich cryfed.
Gweddio am rwydeb yn y Byd,
I Ladd eich cyd Greadurie'd.

Rhai o'r geiriau gorau sydd,
Y'w Bywyd RHYDD a CHARIAD
Cofiwch un; fu yn rhoddi Parch
I was yr arch-offeiriad.

I. I. Glân y Gors.

*We shall, if possible, present our numerous readers with a translation of the above in English, in our next.*

*Chester Chronicle*, 11 March 1796.

*TRANSLATION of the WELSH HYMN*,
INSERTED IN OUR LAST.

Ye hapless Sons of humble life,
Who ne'er spire to feast,
Now distant eye the bread you want,
But must not dare to taste.

The Royal Mandate now ordains,
For sin an expiation,
To fast, for that's the cheapest way,
To feed a starving nation.

Our Bishops of exalted rank
Will feast on butter'd fish –
Can this evasion save the soul,
Mere changing of a dish?

Let all in Britain's ample bounds,
For George's welfare pray; –
That Heav'n may crush the horrid crew
That would their Sovereign slay.[32]

Yet powerful chiefs, RELIGION – FAITH –
Own not such sanguine features;
'Tis vain, they cry, to ask for aid
To kill your fellow creatures.

Remember ONE, who, void of wrath,
Could Malchas's* ear replace;
Who taught us, as his Father's will,
LOVE, CHARITY and PEACE.

* The servant of the High Priest.

### 5.12 *A poem claiming the Duke of Norfolk for Wales*

*Chester Chronicle*, 1 April 1796.

The following verses were composed on the occasion of the Duke of Norfolk[33] dining with the Society of Antient Britons on St. David's Day. After dinner, his Grace, in a neat and appropriate speech, informed the society, he had the honour of being a descendant from our noble Welsh Patriot, OWAIN GLYNDŴR.[34]

Holl Feirddion urddasol, sydd buddiol ei bod
I'r gwych Ddûc o *Norfolk*, yn glymog rhowch glod
Am Ddweud yn ardderchog ddŷn Talog fel Tŵr
Ei fod o Waedoliaeth; OWAIN GLYNDŴR.

Dyna hen Gymro, fu'n llunio gwellâd;
Un hynod iw ddeffol, i amddiffyn ei wlad
Ei wŷr, oedd ai Saethau yn gweu yn y gwynt
I ddiffodd gorthrymder, hen gaethder oedd gynt.

E gododd y Brenhin a'i Fyddin oedd fawr,
Ar fed'r lladd Cymru, ai llethu nhw ir llawr,
Nid oedd ganddo gwedyn, iw ganlyn, un gŵr,
Oedd deilwng i daro ac OWAIN GLYNDŴR.

Rhyfela am gyfiawnder, a'i hyder ei hun
(Rhyfedd) am RYDDID gadernid y Dŷn.
Mae'n gwladwr o *Norfolk* yn enwog iawn ŵr;
O ran meddwl! yn debyg, i OWAIN GLYNDŴR.

*Llundain, Mawrth 15.* I. I. Glan y Gors.

(All you dignified Bards, whose existence is beneficial
to the great Duke of *Norfolk* forcefully give your praise
for Saying splendidly, Strapping man like a Tower,
that he is of the Bloodline of OWEN GLENDOWER.

There's an old Welshman who was a reformer,
an excellent one to choose, to defend his country
his men made their Arrows weave in the wind
to wipe out oppression, the old bondage there before.

The King arose and his Army was large,
intending to kill Welshmen and crush them down;
he did not have, then, in his following, one man,
who was worthy of clashing with OWEN GLENDOWER.

Warring for justice, and his own hope
(marvellous) for LIBERTY was the Man's strength.
Our compatriot from *Norfolk* is a very famous man;
in spirit very similar to OWEN GLENDOWER.

*London, March 15.* I. I. Glan y Gors.)[35]

### *5.13 The Fishguard landing*

*Chester Chronicle*, 3 March 1797.

The above Gazette[36] is not very clear or explicit; the letter from Lieutenant-Colonel Orchard being inserted last, and without explanation, led many people to imagine that the French had landed, and had reimbarked.

The circumstances of this miserable attempt were so incomprehensible, that though the force was insignificant, the public mind was tortured with its own imaginations. No rational motive could be conceived for the landing of a set of troops without artillery or provisions, in a barren spot so strong by nature as to render their escape impossible. The first idea which presented itself to every military mind was, that it was the preface to some real attack in another quarter, and that this was to be viewed as a mere feint to distract the attention, and waste the spirits of the country.

A little reflection, however, exposed the fallacy of this conjecture. It was too contemptible a manoeuvre for a feint. They could not flatter themselves that the appearance of three or four frigates on the Welsh coast would have seduced ministers into the folly of exposing the British fleet to the danger of being locked up by a West wind in St. George's channel, when a few frigates might secure us against any insult they might offer. It was impossible therefore to account for the enterprise in any satisfactory manner, and ingenuity racked itself in vain speculations.

It was, however, some consolation, that on this occasion great alacrity was displayed. In consequence of this information that a small squadron, answering the description of this, had sailed from Brest, a squadron of frigates was sent to cruize in the Bristol channel; and a lugger was stationed in Milford-haven. This lugger gave the alarm. The commander sent one lieutenant to announce the news to the frigates in Bristol channel, and another was dispatched express to London with letters to the Admiralty, while he himself sailed to Cork to appraise Admiral Kingsmill.

It is very pleasing to hear of the zeal with which the natives of Wales poured down from their mountains to resist this inroad. It appears that above 3000 countrymen and miners assembled, armed with forks, scythes, and other ready weapons, besides the militia and volunteers of Pembroke and Cardigan. Lord Cawdor took the command, but not being a military man, he submitted to the directions of Capt. Mansel, who put a little fort at Fiskard [*sic*] into a good state of defence, and took such judicious positions as soon convinced the French that they had no choice left but to lay down their arms – the French vessels having disappeared off the coast. The only difficulty he found was to restrain the impetuosity of the mountaineers, who fell upon the French without order, indeed, but with irresistible fury. – Some few of them were killed by this irregular attack: but on the arrival of the militia and volunteers, the invaders surrendered prisoners of war.

### *5.14 A satirical Welsh litany*

*Chester Chronicle*, 6 August 1797.

A NEW WELSH LITANY,

*To be sung or said in Churches, Chapels, Methodist Meetings, or any other Meeting that will think proper to take it into use.*

GWRANDAWED y nef; ar ychydig o Gymru,
Sy'n chwenych danfon ochenaid i fynu;
Cyn i ni fyned, i gyflwr truenus
*Gwared ni, gwared ni, Arglwydd daionus.*

Rhag diodde caledi o achos cam gyfreth
Rhag Twyllwyr a lladron i drin y llywodreth
Rhag pobl ddideimlad, a meddwl gorthrymus
*Gwared ni, gwared ni, Arglwydd daionus.*

Rhag Balchder, a newyn, a Rhyfel a'i thwrw
Rhag offrwm yn'r eglwys tros enaid y Marw.
Rhag rhoi *wye Pasg*, i bregethwyr anfedrus
*Gwared ni, gwared ni, Arglwydd daionus.*

Rhag Gorychwylwyr, sy'n codi ar y Tiro'dd,
I wasgu ar y gwan, a ysbailio eu *meistradodd*
Rhag porthi cwn, a bwyd yr anghenus
*Gwared ni, gwared ni, Arglwydd daionus.*

Rhag llid, a chynfigen, a henddu [*sic*], gelynion,
Rhag ymelyd [*sic*] mewn arfau; i dywallt gwaed Dynion,
Rhag Treth y goleini, sy rad a haelionus;[37]
*Gwared ni, gwared ni, Arglwydd daionus.*

Rhag offeiriadau ystyfnig a meddwon
Rhag Esgob o'r creigiau a'i *lygaid yn dduon*
Rhag Puteinied mewn braint, tywysogion anhwylus
*Gwared ni, gwared ni, Arglwydd daionus.*

Rhag holl hen chwedle eglwys y RHUFEN
Rhag llichio dwr, i wyneb Plant bychen
Rhag bob can-grefydd [*sic*] sy'n twyllo'r aneallus
*Gwared ni, gwared ni, Arglwydd daionus.*

Rhag gwneuthur niwed i un gradd o ddynion
Rhag myned o'n hwylie i ganlyn bon'ddigion
Rhag meddwl am rwydeb, mewn rhyfel wradwyddus
*Gwared ni, gwared ni, Arglwydd daionus.*

I. I. GLAN Y GORS
*Llundain, Gorphena* 19.

(LET the heavens listen to a few Welshmen,
who desire to send a sigh upwards;
before we descend to a pitiful state,
*spare us, spare us good Lord.*

From suffering hardship because of injustice,
from Deceivers and thieves to handle the government,
from unfeeling people, with an oppressive intent,
*spare us, spare us good Lord.*

From Pride, and famine, and War and its tumult,
from offerings in the church for the souls of the Dead,
from giving *Easter eggs* to unskilled preachers,
*spare us, spare us good Lord.*

From Stewards who raise money on the Lands,
to press on the weak and despoil their *masters*,
from feeding dogs with the food of the needy,
*spare us, spare us good Lord.*

From rage, and envy, and the guile of enemies,
from taking up arms; to shed the blood of Men,
from the Tax on light, which is free and bountiful;[37]
*spare us, spare us good Lord.*

From stubborn and drunken priests
from a Bishop from the rocks and *his black eyes*,
from Whores in high places, intractable princes,
*spare us, spare us good Lord.*

From all the old tales of the church of ROME,
from splashing water in the face of small Children,
from every heresy which deceives the ignorant,
*spare us, spare us good Lord.*

From causing harm to any rank of man,
from going out of our minds to follow the aristocracy,
from thinking of success, in a shameful war,
*spare us, spare us good Lord.*

I. I. GLAN Y GORS
*London, July* 19.)

## *5.15 A patriotic appeal*

*Chester Chronicle*, 11 May 1798.

THE GHOST OF LLEWELLYN.[38]
SUMMIT OF PEN Y CARNEDD, HALF PAST 12 O'CLOCK,
MONDAY NIGHT.

FRIENDS AND FELLOW COUNTRYMEN,
The tranquil slumber I have now enjoyed for a period exceeding 500 years having been of late disturbed by dreams of the most confused and disorderly kind, I rise from the tomb, actuated by superior necessity, to lay before you a few plain truths, and to warn you of the dangers with which you are encompassed. As I have taken my station on the Summit of this well-known rock which bears my name, I shall thence have an opportunity of seeing clearly whatever is passing below, and of affording you such occasional assistance as you may wish to receive, and my separate state of being will enable me to bestow.

Since I was cut off in the prime of life, fighting for the liberties of my country, a wiser and happier system of intercourse with England has succeeded the national jealousies and antipathies of that barbarous period in which I existed: with what sincere satisfaction do I now see you governed by the same wholesome laws, participating the same blessings, and enjoying in common with her all the comforts and conveniences of civilized life. Amidst the various vicissitudes of human life, amidst the rise and fall of empires, after a succession of events, which, at different periods, have agitated and disturbed the world, Great Britain, I observe, though sometimes partially overwhelmed, has always risen superior to the shock, and seemed to gather strength from each convulsion. I see her now just in the zenith of her prosperity, assailed by an unheard-of monster, calling itself a nation, which, after having torn limb from limb nearly every nation in the world is now preparing to finish its sanguinary repast, and gorge its savage gluttony on the entrails of my beloved countrymen. But mark!

"Be lion mettled, proud; and take no care
Who chases, who frets, and who conspirers are,
England shall never conquered be."[39]

It gave me sincere pleasure to hear of the loyal and unanimous meeting which took place on Saturday last at Carnarvon, and my spirit rose at hearing the manly and decisive resolutions which passed on that occasion. I doubt not but that your next meeting will be marked with the same patriotism and the same spirit. It is my duty, however, to inform you, that the situation in which you are relatively placed, is more dangerous than you seem to imagine. You do not want courage, but you want energy; you want to see your danger, in order to take the necessary steps to guard against it. The truth must not be concealed. Consider for a moment, that if the French succeeded in reducing the sister kingdom, you will have to contend with the united force of France and Ireland on your own defenceless and unprotected coasts. The idea is dreadful. But let your vigour increase with the increasing danger, and

> "Llangciau'r Eryri ai gwyn gyll, ai ynnill hi."
> (The young men of Snowdonia with their white hazelnut rods,
> will win it.)[40]

I call upon you rich ones to open your purses, and furnish the means with which Providence has entrusted you (to avert this calamity) with an unsparing hand. I call upon the Clergy as a numerous and respectable body, who by their influence with the lower classes, may furnish the most important aid, to come forward with their *personal services*. – No exemptions should be allowed, but to such as are actually engaged in the discharge of parochial duty, and even those might enrol themselves to serve within certain limits. Should any person chuse to claim an exemption, let him purchase it with a sum of money to be laid out in arming and accoutreing the rest. With all the respect I owe to the gravity of that profession, and for the expediency of subordination to the higher powers in every station of life, I cannot see the necessity of applying to your Bishop for permission to arm yourselves at this present most eventful period. Will you ask permission to arm yourselves when Hannibal has crossed the Alps? – What! Will you ask permission to defend your lives, your fortunes, and your families, from the lawless gripe of Gallic aggression? No!

Here I must say a word or two on the score of employing substitutes. Should any person by reason of age, sickness, or infirmity, wish to claim an exemption from personal service, let him, as I just now observed, purchase that exemption with *money*. Let him remember, that neither age, sickness, nor infirmity, will screen him from French insolence, and French barbarism. By employing substitutes, the country may be deprived of their services as volunteers; you will convert into a mercenary traffic what ought to be considered as an honourable distinction, and by teaching others to expect the same, you will damp the rising spirit of the country.

I call upon you who are landlords over a numerous tenantry, to use your utmost influence to convince your dependants of the dangers which threaten them. Tell them, that in the black catalogue of human misery, the last victim of French aggrandizement and unprincipled ambition, was a nation assimilated in manners, customs, and simplicity of life, nearly to their own, who, leading a quiet and pastoral life, amidst their hitherto impenetrable mountains and fastnesses,[41] unvexed with all the cares and vexations inseparable from a state of opulence, yet gifted abundantly, like yourselves, with the two principal sources of human felicity, "Sufficiency and content;" tell them they are no more. Deluded by the fair promises of their hypocritical friends, and lulled into a state of fatal security, they were convinced of their error when it was too late to repair it; and presented themselves an easy conquest to the swords of the enemies of mankind.

> "Accipe nunc Danaum insidias, et crimine ab uno disce omnes."
> (Learn now the wiles of the Greeks, and from one crime learn what they are all like.)[42]

Whilst I am now speaking, I see, in that devoted country, groups of miserable victims, in all the attitudes of horror and despair; I see anarchy, murder, atheism, and rapine, stalking triumphant over those fields so lately the abode of innocence and peace; I see the altars of religion overthrown; I see helpless infirmity sinking beneath the blow of the cruel assassin; I see the guilty son lifting up his parricidal hand against the bosom of his aged parents; I see modesty and virtue dragged from its sanctuary, and brutally violated; I see the crying infant lifting up its little hands, to implore mercy for its ravished mother, whilst a monster in a human form tears it from her breast, and dashes it on the pavement with grinning ferocity.

> – – – – – – – – – – – – "Oh! But that I am forbid
> To tell the secrets of my prison-house,
> I could a tale unfold, whose lightest word
> Would harrow up thy soul, freeze thy young blood,
> Make thy two eyes like stars start from their spheres,
> Thy knotty and combined locks to part,
> And each particular hair to stand on end,
> Like quills upon the fretful porcupine:
> But this eternal blazon must not be
> To ears of flesh and blood; list, list, oh! List,
> If thou didst every thy dear country love."[43]

Let this suffice for the present; I shall visit you soon again, and remember, if I perceive any backwardness, my spirit will chase, and I will not spare you: on your passage to the hall of your next meeting, cast up your eyes at that venerable and majestic structure opposite to you! That proud monument of the unconquerable spirit of your ancestors, and be not degenerate! Let the motto, inscribed on your standard, be "Liberty or Death." I will hover over you in the day of battle, nor will I ever desert you, till you prove yourselves unworthy of my protection. And now

> "The glow-worm shews the matin to be near,
> And 'gins to pale his uneffectual fire;
> Adieu! Adieu! Adieu! Remember me."[44]

GHOST OF LLEWELLYN.

### *5.16 A Welsh elegy for David Samwell*

*Chester Chronicle*, 28 December 1798.

The following VERSES were composed on the death of Mr. DAVID SAMWELL, Bard, and Surgeon of the Royal Navy for upwards of twenty years, who died, after a short illness, at his own house in Fetter-lane, London, the 22d ultimo.[45]

> TROSTAF ymdanodd tristyd, – am gyfaill
> A gofiaf trwy mywyd:
> SAMWELL, a gadd ei symyd,
> E alleu fod; yn well ei fyd.
>
> Aeth gwychder mwynder o'n mysg, – a dirfawr
> Y darfu cywrainddysg
> Y meddig; a roe im addysg,
> Ym menydd Dafydd roedd dysg.
>
> O fiewn tri-mis, bu'n tramwy – TRE BARIS*
> Yn beraidd ei arlwy.
> Ni cheir nerth, na chynorthwy,
> Rhesymau maith, SAMWELL mwy.

* Mr. Samwell was sent to France, by order of Government, to be surgeon to the English prisoners. He, being fond of genius wherever he found it, got himself acquainted at Paris with Miss Helen Maria Williams, Thomas Paine, Count Zenobio, &c. of whom he related many curious anecdotes.[46]

Ar ddyfroedd mor[oedd] mawrion – yr Indiaid,
A'i rhandir echryslon
Bu amgylch,† ogylch eigion
Ddiwair hynt, y ddaear hon.

Iawn y bu'n haeddu, enw bonheddig,
A dawn ddwys gadarn, dyn addysgedig:
Ow! golli Prydydd, gallu prawedig
Terfyn aniddan; tyrfa WYNEDDIG.‡

Taro a braw, tori brîg, – eu doniau,
A difai foddau, DAFYDD DDU § FEDDIG.

I. I. GLAN Y GORS. *Llundain, Rhagfyr* 15.

(A sadness has enveloped me for a friend
whom I will remember throughout my life:
SAMWELL, who has been taken away,
he may be in a better world.

Greatness, tenderness have gone from our midst, and gone is
the great learning
of the doctor who gave me education,
in Dafydd's brain was learning.

Three months ago, he was bestriding – the TOWN of PARIS*
enjoying fine fare.
There is no strength or help,
or the deep reasoning of SAMWELL any longer.

† Alluding to his voyage round the world with Captain Cook.
‡ The Gwyneddigion Society, of which he was a distinguished and valuable member.
§ His Bardic name.

* Mr. Samwell was sent to France, by order of Government, to be surgeon to the English prisoners. He, being fond of genius wherever he found it, got himself acquainted at Paris with Miss Helen Maria Williams, Thomas Paine, Count Zenobio, &c. of whom he related many curious anecdotes.[46]

On the depths of the great seas of the Indians,
and the awful region
he sailed all around the seas†
of this earth on a fine voyage.

He well deserved a noble name,
and the deep and solid talent of the learned man:
Oh! to lose a Poet, with a proven skill
a comfortless end for the GWYNEDDIGION‡ crowd.

A shocking blow has broken the top of their talents,
and his flawless manners, BLACK DAFYDD THE DOCTOR.§

I. I. GLAN Y GORS.
*London, December* 15.)

*5.17 St David's Day celebrations*

*Chester Chronicle*, 6 March 1801.

*ANTIENT BRITONS.*

Monday being the Anniversary of the establishment of the Society of Antient Britons, for supporting the Welsh Charity School, erected in Gray's Inn Road, London, The President, Vice-Presidents, Treasurers, Governors and Subscribers, assembled at the school in the morning, and went in procession from thence through St. James's square, to Carlton House, and then to St. Martin's Church, where the prayers were read in the Welsh language, and an excellent sermon was preached by the Bishop of Norwich. The collection at the Church amounted to 28l. 8s. 9d. The company afterwards adjourned to the Crown and Anchor, where they dined. The Duke of Rutland, President of the Anniversary, was in the Chair. His Grace, after dinner, announced the amendment which, in the course of the day, had taken place in his Majesty's health. This intelligence was received with that loyalty which characterises the Antient Britons. His Majesty's health, together with that of the Royal Family, the President, Sir Watkin Williams

† Alluding to his voyage round the world with Captain Cook.
‡ The Gwyneddigion Society, of which he was a distinguished and valuable member.
§ His Bardic name.

Wynne, and many other appropriate toasts, were given. The Prince of Wales sent his annual donation of one hundred guineas, a similar sum was given by his Grace of Rutland; fifty guineas, an annual gift by Sir W. W. Wynne, and other liberal donations, from twenty pounds to forty guineas, were made by the Vice-President, Treasurers, and other Governors and Officers of the Society. The money collected at the different tables amounted to 202l. 15s. 6d.; and the whole collection of the day amounted to 882l. 9s. 3d., which is 200l. more than the collection of last year; and 100l. more than the highest of the preceding collections. Some Welsh songs were sung after dinner and Jones, the Prince's Harper,[47] played some airs most delightfully. – The Duke of Rutland made a very neat and appropriate speech on his health being drank; and Sir Thomas Mostyn accepted the office of President for the ensuing year. The whole business of the day was conducted with equal propriety and spirit.

It was also celebrated in Liverpool the same day, by the Brodorion Society, who met in the Assembly-room, Marble-street, where they were joined by a very numerous body of Cambrian Britons, from whence they went in procession to St. Paul's Church, with their banner flying, preceded by the Rev. L. Pughe, Evan Williams, Esq., and Mr W. Jones, the President of the Society, and attended by a complete band of music (the Scotch, who handsomely offered their services on this occasion) playing God Save the King, Rule Britannia, &c. &c.; whilst in church, and after the prayers for the King and Parliament, they sung the loyal air of God Save the King in a melodious tone, after which a sermon, suitably adapted to the occasion, was delivered by the Rev. L. Pughe, from Hebrews c.xiii.v.1. – "Let brotherly love continue." They then proceeded along Old-hall street, and in passing the Exchange were saluted by several Gentlemen, their appearance being truly pleasing; then along Castle-street, Lord-street and Paradise-street, to Cleveland square, where they dispersed in classes to five different reputable Welsh houses (in consequence of not being able to get a house which would contain such a number for the festival of the day) where excellent dinners, and plenty of *cwrw da* [good beer] were provided, Wrexham ale being the order of the day. The meeting was attended by a number of native bards, harps, &c. and, to the great credit of Mr. Pughe and the President, Mr. Jones, they visited the different houses about eight o'clock, and we are happy to say, that they found the companies sober and peaceable, enjoying themselves with the greatest harmony and unanimity, not a single discordant word having been uttered during the whole day; this is the more honourable, when it is considered that this society has only been instituted twelve months, and that it now contains upwards of 200 members, who contribute 1s. per month, and are now able to assist their brethren in illness or infirmity with 8s. per week. Much to the credit of the Antient Britons, the Mayor and Corporation have testified their approbation and respect of so charitable and benevolent an institution. It is supposed upwards of 2000 persons attended divine service. Their procession was truly worthy of praise and being nouvelle, attracted the attention of several thousands of spectators. The banner which was displayed before them, was a very elegant painting and did credit to the ingenious artist who executed it, Mr. John Fearnall. It represented Cambria seated in a retired posture, at the great entrance of Carnarvon Castle, having in her left hand the Prince of Wales's banner, and her right hand bearing a shield, supported by a cherub; on the shield are two bands, in salutation and round the same is their motto, "*Parhaed Brawdgarwch*", [i.e. Let brotherly love continue] – it also had a distant view of the sea, bounded by huge rocks, on which a Druid is seated, under an oak tree which altogether had a very brilliant appearance.

### *5.18 A letter on allegations of atrocities in Ireland*

*Chester Chronicle*, 4 December 1801.

TO THE EDITOR OF THE COURIER [*sic*]

SIR,

Having lately read a publication entitled *A History of the Rebellion in Ireland* in the year 1798, &c., by the Rev. J. Gordon, which contains, among many other misrepresentations and inaccuracies, the following paragraph in page 212, viz. "Some soldiers of the Ancient British Regiment cut open the body of Father Michael Murphy, after the battle of Arklow, took out his heart, roasted the body, and oiled their boots with the grease which dripped from it." – I feel that I should be wanting in gratitude to those brave men whom I had once the honour to command, and with whom I personally served during the whole of the Battle of Arklow above-mentioned, did I not take the earliest opportunity of declaring, that no soldier of the Ancient British Fencible Cavalry ever touched any part of the remains of Father Michael Murphy; And consequently the whole of the above anecdote is a gross calumny, totally destitute of any foundation.

WATKIN WILLIAMS WYNNE,
Late Col. of the Ancient British Fencible Cavalry.

## *6* Adams's Weekly Courant

*Founded in 1732 by John Adams and run by a succession of descendents of the family until 1821,* Adams's Weekly Courant *was the older and more conservative of the two Chester weeklies. It contained less Welsh and Welsh-language material than the* Shrewsbury Chronicle *or the* Chester Chronicle, *but did not reject loyalist contributions from Welsh poets and notables. It was published on Tuesdays.*

### *6.1 An ode to Anglesey*

*Adams's Weekly Courant*, 6 November 1792.

THE BANKS OF THE MENAI. AN ODE INSCRIBED TO THE DRUIDICAL SOCIETY OF ANGLESEY

Melys o ynys inni, – yw Mona
A'i mynych dew deri;
Glan dw'r hallt e'i Glyndir hi
Gardd Eden y gerdd ydi. Iolo.

(A sweet island to us is Mona
and its plentiful sturdy oaks;
the shore of the salt water is her Vale,
she is the Garden of Eden of song. Iolo.)

BEHOLD the fair testaceous shore,
Which oft was stain'd with human gore:
Methinks aerial forms surround,
As guardians of the fairy ground:
Loth to disturb the Druids solemn shade,
I softly glide along the verdant glade.

Surprizing beauties strike my eyes,
From land and water, earth and skies;
The rural scene, the prospect bright,
Rush now spontaneous on my sight:
Here Nature's works, how beautious and how great!
Where the wise patriots find a sweet retreat.

Here, Inspiration's tribe, before,
Excell'd in deep prophetic lore;
In yonder antiquated cell,
The white-rob'd virgins lov'd to dwell;
There ancient bards consum'd their midnight oil,
Enwrapt in thought or bent on mystic toil.

Here liv'd CASWALLON,* bold and brave,
Who spurn'd the terrors of the grave;
Here GWALCHMAI† tun'd his nervous lays,
And sung the conquests of his days:
Heroes of old, who wore the martial wreath,
And gain'd true honour in the fields of death!
Let all, who in their paths succeed,
Excel in ev'ry godlike deed.

Ye men, who claim the honor'd line,
The spark of genius cause to shine;
Transfer young Merit's fairest bloom
To regions far beyond the tomb:
Let Britons of the Tudor's race
Enjoy the philosophic blaze,
Each bosom warm in Freedom's cause,
And yet obedient to the laws:
Let Reason on the throne preside,
To curb Licentiousness and Pride:
Then shall your fame extend from pole to pole,
Your well-known worth to distant ages roll.

D. DDU ERYRI

### *6.2 The burning of Thomas Paine's effigy*

*Adams's Weekly Courant*, 15 January 1793.

We continue to receive accounts of the general martyrdom which Paine has suffered, by proxy, in nearly all the neighbouring towns. On Wednesday,

* Cassibellanus.
† Gwalchmai ap Meilir.

his effigy, with a dagger, smeared with blood, in one hand, and his libel in the other, was paraded thro' the streets of this city; and having been rudely treated with stones and mud by the indignant spectators, it was committed to the flames, at the Cross, amidst the loyal shouts of the multitude.

*Adams's Weekly Courant*, 22 January 1793.

Saturday se'nnight a number of people assembled at Chepstow, in order to see an effigy of Citizen Paine hanged on a gallows, which was prepared 50 feet high. For want of care in properly fixing the gallows, the whole apparatus, with the suspended citizen on it, suddenly fell down, and falling on one of the spectators, so much bruised him that he expired soon after.

### *6.3 Rioting in Denbighshire*

*Adams's Weekly Courant*, 21 April 1795.

*Extract of a letter from Denbigh, dated April 18*

"At a meeting of the magistrates of this county, assembled at this place, in the course of the last week, it was resolved, to invite persons of every rank, who were well-wishers to good order, to attend, for the purpose of apprehending John, of Aeddryn, in the parish of Llangwm, and such other of the rioters as inhabit the upper parts of the county of Denbigh, and who had opposed the due execution of the laws, in a tumultuous manner, at Denbigh, on the first instant; accordingly the acting magistrates, and a large company of gentlemen and tradesmen, together with the most reputable farmers, attended by two companies of the Somerset House Fencibles (who have so eminently distinguished themselves for their civility and good behaviour, wherever they have been quartered) set off from the town of Denbigh, at midnight, on Thursday last, for Cerrig y Druidion and the adjoining parishes; and after apprehending some of the most desperate of the rioters (though not the principal) the company, amounting to more than one hundred persons (exclusive of the officers and soldiers, who likewise partook of the repast) were most hospitably entertained by the Rector of Cerrig y Druidion; from thence attended by one company of the horse, the magistrates, and a great number of the persons assembled, proceeded to the parish of Gwtherin, at which place six more of the delinquents were taken up, and conducted through Llansannan to Denbigh. – Early on Friday morning a party of the Cardigan militia (to do duty at Denbigh, in the absence of the Fencibles) together with many gentlemen, marched from Ruthin to Denbigh, and in their route apprehended two more of the rioters. – At first a later hour had been fixed upon to leave Denbigh, but some of the gentlemen of the neighbourhood having met at the house of one of the magistrates, it was deemed more eligible to leave Denbigh at or before midnight: had not this alteration in the plan taken place, the company would have been more numerous, many persons having assembled at Denbigh at a later hour in the morning, some of whom returned home again; as it was, most of the gentlemen of the neighbourhood, of any consequence and property, were present; and the absence of those, who were not actually prevented by indisposition, and who sent not their representatives, cannot be accounted for, – as a general and firm resolution to preserve the *public peace, and enforce the due execution of the laws, universally obtains amongst all orders of the higher and middling classes of people throughout that county.*"

### *6.4 A Latin loyalist poem from Anglesey*

*Adams's Weekly Courant*, 12 May 1795.

FOR THE CHESTER COURANT

EPIGRAM ON THE FRENCH REVOLUTIONARY WISDOM.

GALLICA quid tandem profert sapientia? profert
Nil nisi nequitiam, stultitiamque suam.
Qui cædis fuerant avidi, rerumque novarum,
Quam misere insidiis hi periêre suis!
Istane libertas vera est, ubi sola voluntas
Et cuncta et cunctos pro ratione regit?
Libertas vera est, ubi leges juraque regnant;
At libertatem hanc Anglia sola tenet.
O fortunatos Anglos, sua si bona norint!
Hanc libertatem nil nisi mors adimet!

*Beaumaris, May 2, 1795* MONENSIS[48]

(What, ultimately, does Gallic wisdom bring forth?
It brings forth nothing except wickedness and its own folly.
Those who had been eager for slaughter and for new things,
how wretchedly they have perished from their own treacheries!

Is this liberty of yours true liberty, where only the will
rules all things and all men in place of reason?
True liberty is where laws and rights rule;
but that liberty England alone maintains.
Oh! fortunate English, if only they recognized their own blessing!
This liberty nothing but death will remove.

*Beaumaris, May 2, 1795* MONENSIS[48])

## *6.5 The Fishguard landing*

*Adams's Weekly Courant*, 14 March 1797.

We have received numerous accounts from various parts of South Wales, respecting the late hostile attempt of the enemy: and they all concur in stating the zeal and spirit with which the brave descendants of the Ancient Britons exerted themselves on the occasion. The roads were covered with both men and women; and those who could not procure fire-arms, furnished themselves with scythes, reaping hooks, and pitchforks. They attached themselves to the few military then in that quarter, and boldly advanced with them against the enemy, who were strongly posted on a high mountain and behind a large rock. It was with great difficulty Lord Cawdor could prevent these brave peasants from rushing in upon their invaders, during the parley that preceded their surrender.

Several coasting vessels having, subsequent to the above affair, appeared during the night close to shore carrying lights, it was conjectured that the enemy were about to land a reinforcement; and expresses were sent from Haverfordwest to Caermarthen and Bristol for military assistance. On this second alarm, the country again rose in a mass, and above 5000 of them among whom were a body of colliers with their pick-axes, set out instantly for the general rendezvous.

### *6.6 An appeal for the reinforcing of coastal defences*

*Adams's Weekly Courant*, 14 March 1797.

To the PRINTER of the CHESTER COURANT.

Sir,

The following is a copy of a letter to his Grace, the Duke of Portland, his Majesty's Principal Secretary of State for the home department. If you can afford it room in your excellent paper, the writer begs its insertion therein.

MY LORD,

I CONCEIVE it to be the essential duty of every man who professes a firm zeal and attachment to his King and Country, and more especially so at such an alarming and portentous crisis as the present, not only to afford to his country the aid of his understanding, but also in a spirited and patriotic manner, such as can be produced by any corporal service and exertion. – Impressed with this idea, I beg leave to submit to your Lordship's consideration the recent daring disembarkation of the French on the coast of South Wales, and to the alarm it has consequently excited in this part of the principality. In what point of view to consider, or what was the intrinsic Object of this expedition, I am at a loss to say, and indeed, I should humbly conceive that it would be by no means impolitic that it should be investigated with every degree of nice, scrupulous, and critical precision. The circumstance of so formidable a force of the enemy having, perpetrated no act of depredation, commenced no military operations, and without making even the smallest resistance, submitting themselves prisoners of war, is a matter awfully obscure. The most obvious interpretation that can be given to it is, that it is a most diabolical artifice and design of the French, to disencumber their nation of the innumerable licentious, depraved, and lawless kind of intemperate ruffians, and barbarous assassins with which it unfortunately too luxuriantly abounds. This race of brutes, for to call such a degenerated and irrational set of beings a race of men would be degrading those who fall under the latter denomination, have been seemingly deluded to endure their captivity with an idea that an invasion of this kingdom is feasible; and that their countrymen will march in triumphant procession to emancipate and lead them on to participate in their career of future glory. It is with horror and detestation I contemplate on that day, and when I paint it to the imagination with horror, I behold this prostituted gang becoming expert instruments in attempting to disseminate and instill into the minds of a good, virtuous, and obedient people their execrable system, opinion, and sentiment of republicanism, tyranny, oppression, rapine, and every species of vice and depravity which this happy nation is and I trust never will suffer itself by their nefarious seducement to be acquainted with. The general and most predominant sentiment with us is, that if proper precautions were taken by government to repel any attempt that should be made to invade this part of the principality, that such an attempt would terminate in the ruin and destruction of the enemy; but if those precautions are not adopted, the spirit of alarm most necessarily increase, while we see our coast unprotected and open to any violence which the enemy's ships may think proper to offer us. Concerned and solicitous for the security and protection of a defenceless country, I would propose the barracks and fortifications should be erected on such parts of the coasts of the counties of Carnarvon and Anglesey, as are accessible to the enemy, and that a certain number of frigates should cruise in a proper latitude, to embarrass their operations, and to annoy and molest them when they should attempt a disembarkation. If this squadron should find that of the enemy too powerful for them to encounter, they could place themselves under the protection of those fortifications, or fall to any other quarter, to give intelligence of the enemy. Should the enemy be able to accomplish their design, surely, my Lord, the common feelings of humanity would be a powerful consideration to induce your Lordship, and others in the administration of this kingdom, to exert yourselves in our defence. I feel, my Lord, with conscious satisfaction, that the gentlemen and commonalty of this part of the principality, after the example of their ancestors, to whose imitation they have invariably aspired, actuated by a spirit of unchangeable constancy, loyalty, and the love of honourable danger in a generous cause, will step forward with alacrity, and demonstrate the most distinguished promptitude to be exercised at stated times, and to undergo an easy and liberal discipline, for the purpose of rendering their services to their sovereign and the constitution for which they profess such enthusiastic reverence and admiration, and which is to venerable in the eyes of every worthy mind in the principality of Wales.

My Lord, I have the honour to be, Your Lordships most obedient humble servant.

A FRIEND TO HIS COUNTRY.

CARNARVON, *March* 1, 1797.

## 7 Cylch-grawn Cynmraeg

*This quarterly was the first radical periodical to appear in the Welsh language. Founded and edited by the Baptist minister and anti-slavery campaigner Morgan John Rhys from February 1793, it ran to five numbers, of which the last indicates that a change to a bimonthly was intended. The last issue was published in February 1794. It underwent several changes of name and appeared in two locations, Trefeca and Carmarthen. The editor emigrated to America in August 1794.*

### 7.1 *First instalment of an essay on government*

*Cylch-grawn Cynmraeg; Neu Drysorfa Gwybodaeth*, Rhifyn Cyntaf . . . am Chwefror 1793 (Welsh Magazine; or Treasury of Knowledge, the First Number . . . for February 1793), 42–5.

Am LYWODRAETH.

POB llywodraeth, yn ddechreuol, sy'n deilliaw oddi wrth yr hwn a greodd, ac sy'n cynnal a chyflawni pob peth, yn ol ei ddoethineb a'i ewyllys ei hun; ond, o ran y *dull* o lywodraethu, mae hynny wedi adael i ddynion i'w ddewis fal creaduriaid rhesymmol. Awdur trefn yw Duw: ac y mae pob math o anrhefn yn dymchwelyd ei gyfreithiau cyfiawn, eglur, a phur; gellir galw beth bynnag sydd wrthwyneb i hyn, yn *draws-lywodraeth*. Pob teulu a chymdeithas, a ddysg yr angenrheidrwydd o lywodraeth, ac ufudd-dod i'r gyfraith: er y dichon fod mewn teuluoedd wahanol ddull o reolaeth, etto, pan fyddont yn cydsynnio yn ngwneuthuriad cyfreithiau, rhaid ufudd-hau iddynt, hyd nes gwelont yn well eu newid, chwanegu at, neu dynnu oddi wrthynt. – Mae'r awdurdod hon yn ddifai gan bob teulu; – heb achos i'w gymmydog ofyn, Pa beth yr wyt yn ei wneuthur? – Heb lywodraeth, ni byddai'r byd ond cymmysgfa o annibendod; (oddi eithr dileu trosedd o hono) pob math o ormes ac anrhefn a dardda o'r ffynnon, *pechod*. Ac fal yr amlha anwiredd, yr amlha traws-arglwyddiaeth, hyd oni chyflawnir mesur yr anwiredd. Na ryfedded neb ddywedyd o honom, "Pob llywodraeth yn ddechreuol sy'n deilliaw oddi wrth Duw." Ie, pe dywedem fod llywodraeth Pharao, wrth ei orchymyn, ni cham-synniem lawer, canys "I hyn yma y'th gyfodais, medd yr Arglwydd."[49] Wrth alwad JEHOFAH y goresgynnodd Nebucodonozor Judea: a gwas Duw ydoedd Cyrus drachefn, i'w gwaredu. Ni buasai gan *Pilat* awdurdod ar Iesu, ond fal y rhoddwyd iddo; ac ni's gallasai'r milwyr dan Titus, lai nâ dinystrio'r deml yn Jerusalem; canys yr oedd Crist wedi rhag-ddywedyd "Na adewid yno garreg ar garreg."[50] Gwahanol amserau, sy'n galw am wahanol lywodraeth, weithiau'n dyner, weithiau'n greulon. Duw yn taro'r ddaear â barn, ac fal yr ymostyngo ei bobl, mae yn ymweled â hwynt mewn trugaredd. – Rhaid i Babyddiaeth a Mahometaniaeth gael eu dileu o'r byd; ond ni wyddom yn iawn pa fodd, na phwy fydd yr offerynau; rhagor nâ'u bod yn offerynau cyfiawnder a chreulondeb. – Yr Arglwydd sy'n teyrnasu. Mae hynny yn ddigon i'r duwiol. "Ymddarostynged pob enaid i'r awdurdodau goruchel, canys nid oes awdurdod, ond oddi wrth Dduw; a'r awdurdodau *sydd*, gan Dduw maent wedi hordeinio. Telwch gan hynny i bawb eu dyledion: teyrnged i'r hwn y mae teyrnged yn ddyledus, toll i'r hwn y mae toll; ofn i'r hwn y mae ofn; parch i'r hwn y mae parch yn *ddyledus*. Rhoddwch yr eiddo Cesar i Cesar, a'r eiddo Duw i Dduw. Ie, ofnwch Dduw, ac anrhydeddwch y brenin."[51] Ond gwybyddwch, nad yw hyn mewn un mesur yn dinystrio'r hawl sydd gan bob dyn, fal aelod o'r gymdeithas, i fod a *llais*, yn newisiad y swyddwyr gwladol; eithr ein dysgu i ufuddhau i'r awdurdodau sydd mewn *bod* yn y cyfamser; a hynny ddim ymhellach, nag y bo gair yr Arglwydd yn rheol i'n hufudd-dod: os amgen, dioddefodd y *merthyron* i gyd yn ofer.

Ond nid yw'n *cylch* ni, i sôn llawer am lywodraeth; ein diben yw, yn fwyaf neillduol, roddi hanes, (yn ei dro) am drefn llywodraethau'r byd, &c. ac ni a ddechreuwn gartref, trwy roddi portreiad byrr, o lywodraeth Lloegr, yr hon sydd fal tri-phlyg, yn cynnwys Un bennaeth (*Monarchy*) yn y brenin. Pendefigaeth (*Aristocracy*) yn yr arglwyddi, a gwladwriaeth, (*Democracy*) yn y cyffredin.[52] – Mae'r awdurdod o wneud cyfreithiau, a chodi trethi, yn gysylltiedig yn y tri: ond gan y senedd gyffredin yn unig mae'r awdurdod i enwi'r pethau a drethir, &c. ac ni all yr arglwyddi newid *bil* yr arian, heb ei wrthod a'i anfon yn ol drachefn i'r senedd gyffredin. – Os derbyn yr arglwyddi'r *biliau*, fe ddichon y brenin eu gwrthod; ond os derbyn hwynt, mae'n gosod ei sêl wrthynt: yn ganlynol, mae'r gyfraith mewn grym.

– Mae'n perthyn i'r brenin gyhoeddi rhyfel, a gwneud heddwch; danfon neu dderbyn cenhadau – creu swyddwyr, galw ynghyd, oedi, a gollwng ymaith y *Parliament*; rhoi teitlau o anrhydedd, a chreu rhagor o arglwyddi, gwneud ammodau â theyrnasoedd eraill, gwneuthur arian. Efe yw (*generalissimo*) pen cadpen yr holl fyddinoedd ar dir, a'r llyngesau ar y môr. Efe sy'n dewis, enwi, appwyntio swyddwyr uchel-radd; yn trefnu'r holl drysordai, cestyll, ymddiffynfaoedd, aberoedd, porth-laddoedd. Y Militia hefyd sydd dan ei awdurdod; yr holl gynghorwyr, dadleuwyr, swyddogion y'stad, a barnwyr cyfiawnder a osodir ganddo, ac yn pardynu'r neb a fynno; geill naill ai maddeu'r trosedd neu leihau'r gosp.

Ei fawrhydi, hefyd, yw goruchel-ben yr eglwys sefydledig, yn Lloegr, rhysgwydd, a rhoddwr yr holl esgobaethau. Trwy yr awdurdod hwn y dichon alw cymmanfaoedd (*synods*) eu gohirio a'u gollwng ymaith. Creu arch-esgobion, esgobion, deans, &c. ac yn oruchwyliwr ar y colegau a'r brenhinol ysgolion, &c. cymmaint yw'r anrhydedd a ddangosir iddo gan ei ddeiliaid, a'u bod yn bennoeth, nid yn unig yn ei ŵydd; ond hefyd pan na fyddo yn bresennol, os bydd yn y lle gadair frenhinol: yn y cyfarchiad cyntaf, mae pawb yn penlinio o'i flaen, ac yn derbyn ei orchmynion felly. Mewn perthynas i berson y brenin, mae'r gyfraith yn ei gyfrif yn uchel-frad, (*high-treason*) i feddwl neu fwriadu niweid iddo. Mae'r gyfraith hefyd yn cyfrif iddo ben arglwyddiaeth, perffeithrwydd mewn meddwl a gweithred. – Ni all y brenin wneud dim allan o'i le, (meddant) am nad yw'n gwneud dim heb ei gynghoriaid; ac y mae ymhob man ar yr un waith, am fod ei weision yno yn gwasanaethu ei swyddau.

Pan byddo'r brenin yn galw ei *Barliament* ynghyd, mae'n eu cyfarfod y tro cyntaf yn Nhŷ'r arglwyddi, yn ei wisg frenhinol, a'i goron ar ei ben: yna ei fawrhydi, neu'r arglwydd Canghellwr, a draetha achos y cyfarfod, yngwydd yr arglwyddi ysprydawl a thymhorawl, a'r senedd gyffredin. – Yna maent yn myned ynghyd â gorchwylion y deyrnas, gwneuthur cyfreithiau, diddymmu eraill, &c. Nifer yr arglwyddi yw 236, yn y senedd-dŷ uchaf – nifer y marchogion yn y senedd-dŷ isaf yw 558. Yn y rhifedi cyntaf yr ydys yn cyfrif 16 o arglwyddi'r Alban, ac yn yr olaf 45 o farchogion yr Alban, a 24 o farchogion Cynmru.

Gellir profi nad oes nemmawr o wledydd i'w cystadlu â Brudain fawr; mae'n atteb arwyddoccad y gair, sef, *Brô-dêg*, a honno yn llawn o ychen, gwartheg, a defaid; gwenith, haidd, a phob rhyw lafur; gerddi dymunol a phob rhyw ffrwythau. – Mynyddoedd yn llawn o fwyn-gloddiau, arian, copr, haiarn a phlwm. Afonydd a chornentydd yn dyfrhau'r glynnoedd, ac yn sirioli'r maesydd ar eu ffordd i'r *weilgi*; yr *Eos*, yn ymbyngcio gyd â'r mân adar, ym mrig y dymunol goedydd, nes yw'r gelltydd yn barod i ddawnsio wrth eu muwsic. Mae pob peth yn y deyrnas hon (ond y dyn anniolchgar) yn gosod allan ogoniant y Creawdwr, ac yn cyhoeddi'n uchel, mai efe sydd Dduw. – Mae'r môr yn ein hamgylchu; â llongau Brudain yn britho'r cenfor, o'r naill Begwn i'r llall, ac yn dwyn eu gwerthfawr farsiandaeth i bob porthladd, at gyfoethogi'n gwlad. Ie, gellir yn gyfiawn honni pe b'ai Brudain ond byw heb ryfel, a'r bobl yn gweled bod yn dda i ddiwygio eu bucheddau: y byddai'n baradwys i'w thrigolion. Onid hynod ei bod yn gallu talu, dwy fyrddiwn ar bymtheg o bunnau, o drethi, yn y flwyddyn, ac etto fod digon o arian yn y deyrnas!

Ac oni bae difrawch y Cynmro, gallai ei enedigol wlad fod yn un o'r gwledydd mwyaf ardderchog dan y nef. Pa le mae'r fath borthladdoedd? Aber-dau-gleddyf, &c. Pa le mae'r fath fynyddoedd godidog, llawn o fwyn-gloddiau, haiarn, copr, plwm, a glô? Pa le mae'r fath frôydd glân-deg, llawn o lafur, ac anifeiliaid pedwar carnol, digon i borthi'r deg cymmaint o drigolion? Pa le mae'r fath ffynhonnau rhinweddol, ac afonydd llawn o bysgod, a'r môr yn fwy nâ hanner amgylchynu'n tir? Pa ham gan hynny na ellid gwneud Cynmru fal gwlad Canaan gynt, yn cnydio ar ei chanfed? Ie, pa'm na sefydlid ar frys, bob math o weith-dai ynddi? at drin y gwlan, cotton, haiarn, copr, tin, &c. ac yna fe redai golud trwyddi, fal y mae'r afonydd yn rheged tu a'r môr. (I'w Barhau).

(Of GOVERNMENT.

EVERY government, in the beginning, emanates from him who created and who maintains and accomplishes everything, according to his own wisdom and his will; but as regards the *method* of governing, that is left to men to choose as creatures endowed with reason. The author of order is God: and every kind of disorder overturns his just, clear and pure laws; whatever is contrary to this may be called *tyranny*. Every family and society teaches the necessity of government, and obedience to the law. Though there may be different methods of ruling in families, yet, when they agree in the making of laws, they must be obeyed, until they see fit to change them, add to them, or take away from them. – This authority properly rests with each family; – without cause for its neighbour to ask, What are you doing? – Without government the world would be nothing but a hotch-potch of confusion; (unless crime were deleted from it) all kinds of oppression and disorder have one source, *sin*. And as untruth spreads, so does tyranny, until the measure of the untruth is complete. Let none wonder at our saying, "Every government, in the beginning, emanates from God." Yeah, if we said that the Pharaoh ruled by His command, we would not be much mistaken, because "Even for this same purpose have I raised thee up, said the Lord."[49] It was by order of JEHOVAH that Nebuchadnezzar conquered Judaea: and Cyrus, who delivered it, was also the Lord's servant. *Pilate* only had authority over Jesus, because it was given him; and the soldiers under Titus could not but destroy the temple in Jerusalem; for Christ had foretold, "There shall not be left here one stone upon another."[50] Different times call for different governments, sometimes gentle, sometimes cruel. God strikes the earth with judgement, but as His people submit themselves, He visits them in mercy. – Catholicism and Mahometism must be deleted out from the world; but we do not know clearly in what manner, or who will be the instruments; any more than that they will be instruments of justice and cruelty. – It is the Lord who reigns. This is enough for the godly. "Submit yourselves to every ordinance of man for the Lord's sake . . . For so is the will of God. Render therefore to all their dues: tribute to whom tribute is due; custom to whom custom; fear to whom fear; honour to whom honour. Render to Caesar the things that are Caesar's, and to God the things that are God's. Yeah, fear God and honour the king."[51] But you should know, that this does not in the least abolish every man's right, as a member of society, to have a *voice* in the choice of officers of state; but rather, it teaches us to obey the authorities which are in *existence* at the time; and that no further than the Lord's word is the rule of our obedience: otherwise, the *martyrs* all suffered in vain.

But it is not our *scope* to talk much about government as such; our aim is, more particularly, to give the history, (each in its turn) of the system of the governments of the world, &c. and we shall begin at home, by presenting a short description of the government of England, which is as if threefold, containing Monarchy in the king. Aristocracy in the lords, and Democracy in the commons.[52] – The authority to make laws and raise taxes is connected in all three: but only the common parliament has the authority to decide the things which are to be taxed, &c. and the lords cannot change the *bill* of the money without refusing it and sending it back to the common parliament. – If the lords accept the *bills*, the king may yet refuse them; but if he accepts them, he sets his seal on them: as a result, the law is in force. – It appertains to the king to declare war and make peace; send or receive ambassadors – create officials, summon, adjourn or dissolve *Parliament*; award honorary titles, and create more lords, agree treaties with other realms and make money. He is the (*generalissimo*) commander in chief of all the armies on land and the fleets on sea. He chooses, names and appoints high-ranking officials; governs all treasuries, castles, fortifications, estuaries, and ports. The Militia is also under his authority; all councillors, advocates, estate officials and judges of justice are installed by him, and he can pardon whoever he wants; he can either forgive the crime or reduce the punishment.

His majesty is also the head of the established church in England, patron and giver of all the bishoprics. By this authority he can call synods, adjourn them or dissolve them. [He can] create archbishops, bishops, deans, &c. and oversee the colleges and the royal schools, &c. Such is the respect shown to him by his subjects, that they are bare-headed, not only in his presence; but also when he is not present if there is a royal chair in the location: at the first greeting, every man kneels before him, and receives his commands thus. In relation to the king's person, the law counts it as high treason to purpose or intend an injury to him. The law also ascribes to him overlordship, and perfection in thought and action. – The king can do no wrong, (they say) because he does nothing without his councillors; and he is everywhere at the same time, because his servants there fulfil his offices.

When the king calls his *Parliament* together, he first meets them in the House of Lords, in his royal robes, with his crown on his head: then his majesty or the lord Chancellor declares the reason for the meeting, in the presence of the spiritual and secular lords, and the common parliament. – Then they go about the tasks of the kingdom, make laws, abolish others, &c. The number of the lords is 236, in the higher house of parliament – the number of knights in the lower house of parliament is 558. The first number includes 16 lords from Scotland, and the last, 45 knights from Scotland and 24 knights from Wales.

It can be proved that there are but few countries to compete with Great Britain; it answers the meaning of the word, namely, *Fair-country*, one which is full of oxen, cattle, and sheep; wheat, barley, and every kind of corn; pleasant gardens and every kind of fruits. – Mountains full of ore-mines, silver, copper, iron and lead. Rivers and streams water the vales, and refresh the plains on their way to the *ocean*; the *Nightingale* trills with the other birds, on the branches of the pleasant forests, until the hillsides are ready to dance to their music. Every thing in this kingdom (except the ungrateful man) sets outs the glory of the Creator, and proclaims aloud that he is God. – The seas surround us; and Britain's ships speckle the ocean, from one pole to the other, carrying their valuable merchandise to every port, to enrich our country. Yeah, one can justly claim that if only Britain lived without war, and if the people saw fit to reform their lives: it would be a paradise for its inhabitants. Is it not it remarkable that it can pay seventeen million pounds of tax per year, and yet there is enough money in the kingdom?

And were it not for the apathy of the Welshman, his native country could be one of the most glorious countries under heaven. Where else are such ports? Milford Haven, &c. Where else are such magnificent mountains, full of ore-mines, iron, copper, lead and coal? Where else are such comely vales, full of corn, and four-hoofed animals, enough to feed ten times the inhabitants? Where else are such healing wells, and rivers full of fish, and the sea more than half encircling our land? Why, then, could Wales not be made as the land of Canaan of yore, increasing yields a hundred-fold? Yeah, why should every kind of factory not be established in it forthwith? For treating wool, cotton, iron, copper, tin, &c., and then wealth would run through it, as the rivers run towards the sea. (To be continued.))

### *7.2 Religious liberty*

*Cylchgrawn Cynmraeg.* Rhifyn II. Am Mai, 1793 (Welsh Magazine. Number II. For May, 1793), 90.

TRI PHETH A GADWODD DUW IDDO EI HUN.

PAN oedd y *Jesuits* yn annog STEPHEN Brenin *Poland*,[53] i erlid y *Protestaniaid.* Attebodd, "Na feiddiai; fod *tri pheth a gadwodd Duw iddo ei hun*: GALLU CREADIGOL, – GWYBODAETH O'R PETHAU I DDYFOD, AC AWDURDOD AR GYDWYBOD." Am hynny ni all'sai lai na rhoddi gogyfuwch ryddid i'w holl ddeiliaid.

(THREE THINGS WHICH GOD KEPT TO HIMSELF.

WHEN the *Jesuits* were urging STEPHEN King of *Poland*,[53] to persecute the *Protestants.* He answered, "He could not; that there were *three things which God kept to himself*: The CREATIVE POWER, – A KNOWLEDGE OF THE THINGS TO COME, AND AUTHORITY OVER CONSCIENCE." And therefore, he could not but give equal liberty to all his subjects.)

### *7.3 Prince Madog's speech on leaving Wales*

*Cylchgrawn Cynmraeg.* Rhifyn II. Am Mai, 1793 (Welsh Magazine. Number II. For May, 1793), 103–4.

MADAWG AB OWAIN GWYNEDD *yn ymadaw â* CHYNMRU.[54]

FY nghydymdeithion! syniwch, dyma ein llongau wedi ein cychwnu i'n hantur; dacw greigiau a bryniau, gwlad a'n maethodd yn diflannu o'n golwg! y rhai sydd gynnrych o derfysgau ei thrigolion. Y terfysgau hyn a'n cymhellodd i ffoi o honi dros byth; ond ein golygon yn glynu yn hiraethus arni, sydd yn dangaws mai anhawdd diffawdd yr hoffder a gynneued yn ein calonau am ein hên gartref – O! na allem ni fyfyriaw am wynfyd *Cynmru* rhag llaw! Yn y lle hynny braidd na welwn y' nghaddug yr amser ar ddyfod amryw gysgodion ofnadwy, o drais, gorthrymder, a thrueni, yn tyfu mewn grym i'w blinaw! Bellach diflanoedd o'n golwg! Fy nghyfeillion, dyma ni yn awr ar daith ein gobaith; dylynwn y llwybyr a drefna rhagluniaeth drwy y dyfnder. – Hawddamawr i ti y defnydd diddarfod o ryfeddawd a myfyrdawd! – Hawddamawr i ti yr eigion lliosawg! tonau yr hwn sydd yn trosi eu gilydd ymaith mal cenedlaethau dynion, a chwedl rhynawd bach o amser a ydynt yn foddi i anghof tragywyddawl! – Dy ddyfroedd yn bwhwman a amgylchant holl gyffiniau y byd, megis terfyn rhwng cenedloedd rhag rhyfel, ac er digonoldeb ac iechyd dynion.

O mor ogoneddus! mor arswydus yw y golygiadau a ddangosi di! Pa'r un a wnelom ai edrych arnat yn dy dawelwch, pan fo haul y bore yn gorwynu dy lyfnder – neu pan yw ei lwybyr echwydd wedi ei euraw yn ddisglaer, a'th wyneb digrych yn adlewyrchu gwychder yr entyrch! – pan fo y dryghin gorddu yn rhwygaw y morgymmlawdd, a'r doniau yn terfysgu a'r cymmylau, – pan fo angeu yn dwyn cyrch ar y corwynt, – a dynoliaeth yn bwrw dagrau diles tros y morwr yn ei flinder! –

Etto, y dyfnder tramawr! dy wyneb yn unig a welwn – Pwy a dreiddia ddirgelion dy lywodraeth? Pa lygad a ymwel a'th greigiau a'th ogofau anfeidrawl, y sydd gyflawn o fywyd a thyfiant? – neu chwilied yr amrywiaethau sydd a'u tegwch ar wasgar dros dy geuedd arswydus?

Mae y meddwl yn tynnu tan lwyth ei amgyffrediadau, – ac wrth ystyried dy lanw â thrai, y rhai er dechreuad amser ni bu arnynt ball, O, fal y mae yn ymgiliaw wrth ystyr yr Hollalluawg a osodoedd dy seiliau mor ddiogel, a llais yr hwn a sefydloedd y terfynau sydd yn attal dy donau beilchion!

Fy nghyfeillion! Yr hwn a drefnoedd y gogoniant y sydd o'n hamgylch sydd hefyd yn cynnal yr awel dêg, gan yr hon y rhedwn yn mlaen; yr hwn a'n harwain drwy yr holl gyfyngderau, i ganfod mwy rhyfeddodau; ac o'r diwedd i gyfanneddu gwlad sydd â thuedd ieuenctyd y crëedigaeth yn ei thirioni.

(MADOG AB OWAIN GWYNEDD *leaving* WALES.[54]

MY companions! behold, here our ships have set us out on our adventure; yonder the rocks and hills of the country which nourished us are disappearing from our sight! those which are exemplary of the conflicts of her inhabitants. It is these conflicts which forced us to flee her forever; but our eyes cling longingly to her, which shows that it is difficult to extinguish the love kindled in our hearts for our old home – Oh! that we could contemplate the paradise of *Wales* evermore! Instead we just discern in the mists of the time to come sundry terrible shadows of violence, oppression and sorrow, growing in force to trouble her! Now she has disappeared from our sight! My friends, here we are on the journey of our hope; we follow the path through the depths marked out by providence. – Hail to you, perennial subject of wonder and contemplation! – Hail to you the vast ocean! the waves of which chase each other like generations of men, and in the space of a moment they sink to eternal oblivion! – Your rolling waters surround all the regions of the world, like a boundary between nations against war, and for the abundance and the health of men.

Oh how magnificent! how terrible are the views you display! Whatever we do, whether looking at you in your stillness, when the morning sun brightens your sleekness – or when his noon path is painted dazzling gold, and your smooth face reflects the magnificence of the zenith! – when the dark storm splits the surging sea, and the waves contend with the clouds, – when death drives the hurricane on, – and mankind sheds vain tears over the seaman in his misery! –

Yet, the vast depth! it is your face alone we see – Who will explore the secrets of your dominion? What eye will visit your immeasurable rocks and caves, which are full of life and vegetation? – or search the diversity whose fairness is scattered across your terrible void?

The mind withdraws under the weight of its conceptions, – and as it ponders your tides, those which have not ceased since the beginning of time, Oh, how it retreats from the purpose of the Almighty who set your foundations so safely, and the voice of Him who set the bounds which hold back your proud waves!

My friends! He who arranged the magnificence which is around us also sustains the fair wind which drives us on; he will lead us through all afflictions, to discover more wonders; and in the end to inhabit a land which has something of the youth of the creation in its pleasantness.)

### *7.4 The search for the descendants of Prince Madog in America*

*Cylchgrawn Cynmraeg*. Rhifyn II. Am Mai, 1793 (Welsh Magazine. Number II. For May, 1793), 104–5.

TAITH JOHN EVANS AT Y MADAWGWYS.

Yn niwedd mis *Medi* o'r flwyddyn aeth heibio cychwynoedd JOHN EVANS, llanc o *Arfon*, ar ei daith i ymweled a'r *Madawgwys*, sef yr hên Gynmry, o hiliogaeth Madawg ab Owain, a'i gymdeithas, a amadawsant o Gynmru yn y flwyddyn 1170; y sawl sydd yn awr yn cyfanneddu y'nghanol yr *America* Ogleddawl. Yn ol y llythyrau diweddaf a dderbyniwyd oddi wrth y gwr ieuanc hwnw, gwedi y mawr ganmoliaeth o'i dderbyniad yn *Baltimore*, y mae yn rhoi hanes ei fod yn dechreu ei daith oddi yno tua *Kentuckey*, 800 milltir i fynu yn y wlad, yn niwedd *Ionawr*; ac ei fod wedi cael hyfforddiant at wr a fuasai yn mhlith yr *Indiaid Cynmreig*, fal y maent yn eu galw. Oddiwrth yr hyn a glywyd gan *John Evans*, mae yn ddigon tebyg ei fod wedi cyrhaedd bro y *Madogion* cyn yr amser hyn.

(THE JOURNEY OF JOHN EVANS TO THE MADOGANS.

At the end of *September* of the year which has passed, JOHN EVANS, a young man from *Arvon*, set out on his journey to visit the *Madogans*, that is the old Welsh of the race of Madog ab Owain and his companions, who left Wales in the year 1170; those who now live in the centre of North *America*. According to the latest letters received from that young man, following the great praise of his reception in *Baltimore*, he reports that he is setting out from there towards *Kentucky*, 800 miles up in the country, at the end of *January*; and that he has had direction from a man who had been among the *Welsh Indians*, as they call them. From what was heard from *John Evans*, it is quite probable that he has reached the land of the *Madogans* by now.)

## *7.5 News from the Continent*

*Cylchgrawn Cynmraeg*. Rhifyn II. Am Mai, 1793 (Welsh Magazine. Number II. For May, 1793), 119–20.

### ARWYDDION YR AMSERAU,

WRTH sylwi ar drefn y rhôd, parod ydym i waeddi allan, "O olwyn –!" Yn ein barn ni, mae terfysgoedd *Ewrop* yn tynnu at ryw amser nodedig, a bair syndod i'r byd. *Peidiwch, a gwybyddwch mai myfi sydd* DDUW. *Sefwch yn llonydd, a gwelwch iechydwriaeth yr* ARGLWYDD.[55] – Ni wyddys etto pa le, neu pa fodd, y try'r olwyn. Meddwl rhai, os gorchfygir *Ffraingc*, "na chyttuna'r *galluoedd cysylltiedig*, â'u gilydd". Y mae'n sicr na fu'r fath gyngrair, er dechreuad y byd. – Eglwys *Rhufain*, eglwys *Groeg*, eglwys *Loegr*, *Lutheriaid*, *Calfinistiaid*, *Arminiaid*, &c, &c. sy'n dwyn i'n cof yr haiarn a'r pridd yn nhraed y ddelw. *Dan*. ii.[56]

Mae rhyw *ddieflyn*, wedi myned yn yspryd celwyddog, i enau'r bobl, fal y mae'n anhawdd adrodd newyddion yn yr amser presennol. – Yr ydym yn barod i alw'r oes hon, *Yr oes gelwyddog*. Bu'r bobl yn ddiweddar, agos a gorphwyllo; ac ni's gwyddom, yn iawn, pa un a ydynt wedi dyfod i'w iawn bwyll, ai peidio; gobeithio bydd i dynerwch yr hâf dymheru eu meddyliau – ac yr hauant lai o anwireddau ar eu cymmydogion wrth deithio ar hyd y wlad – Da fyddai i bawb ystyried mai'r "*hyn a hauo dyn, hynny hefyd a fed efe*,"[57] a chofied yr hwn na attalio ei dafod (rhag dywedyd celwydd) mai *ofer yw ei grefydd*.

Gyd â'n bod yn rhybuddio'n cydwladwyr, i ochelyd y tafod celwyddog, mae'n angenrheidiol iddynt fod ar eu gwyliadwriaeth i ymgadw rhag dwylo ysgeler, ni bu erioed, o bosibl, fwy o bîg-ladron cyfrwys. – Ac os para y rhyfel yn hir, gellir disgwyl y cynhyddant; – canys y mae llawer o filoedd o bob math o grefftwyr, yn ddiweddar, wedi cael eu bwrw allan o waith, trwy fod y terfysg yn attal masnach. – Y marsiandwyr, siopwyr, &c. &c. a'r cyfnewidwyr arian (*Bangcwyr*) sydd yn torri wrth y * * * *.[58] Y mae'n gofyn i'r *Cynmro* edrych yn ofalus pa bapur a gymmero yn lle arian. – Ond weithian ni gawn roi ychydig o hanes y byd.

Y mae'r *Ffrancod* wedi cael eu gyrru o wlad *Belgia*, dan ymerodraeth *Germani*, ac o *Holland*. Trodd blaenor eu llu, *Dumourier*,[59] yn fradwr; a gwnaeth dro digrif â'r rhai a anfonodd y gymmanfa giwdawdol* i'w gymmeryd, sef eu hanfon yn garcharwyr i'r gelynion. – Y mae ef eî hun a llawer o'r rhai a drodd gyd âg ef, yn bresennol, gyd â'r *Awstriaid*. Y mae *Mentz*, dinas gadarn o eiddo'r ymerawdwr, etto yn meddiant y *Ffrancod*. – Ac y mae'r penciwdawd (*general*) CUSTINE,[60] a'i wyr yn ymladd yn gethin yn y wlad honno. – Nid yw'r byddinoedd cysylltiedig wedi myned nemmawr i dir *Ffraingc* – Bu brwydr boeth yn ddiweddar, ymha un yr oedd ail fab ein brenin, y Duc o *York*, wrth ben ei fyddin, gyd â'r *Prwsiaid*, a'r *Germaniaid*, &c. &c.[61] Lladdwyd llawer o bob ochr – ond llawer mwy, meddant, o'r *Ffrancod* – Y mae rhan fawr o dalaith brenin *Sardinia*, sef *Savoy*, a *Phiedmont*, yn meddiant y *Ffrancod* etto. – Ac y mae'r Penciwdawd *Biron*,[62] yn dywedyd fod ei fyddin yn anorchfygol yno. –

Nid oes nemmawr o deyrnasoedd a thaleithiau *Ewrop*, nad ydynt mewn rhyfel â'r Ffrancod. Mae ymerodres *Rwssia* yn bygwth y *Swedeniaid*, os na ddeuant i'r cyngrair. – Mae *Portugal* wedi uno â'r rhai a soniasom yn y rhifyn cyntaf – a gwaeth nâ'r cwbl, i lywodraeth bresennol *Ffraingc*, yw eu bod mor rhannedig yn eu plith eu hunain. – Y mae llawer iawn o'r *Brython*,[63] ac eraill, wedi codi gwrthryfel yn *Lludaw*, (*Brittany*) ac yn debyg o gynnyddu yn lliosawg, meddant – Os gall y *Saeson* dirio attynt, i'w cynnorthwyo, tebygid y dinystriant y *Ffrancod* ar fyrr. Pe baent genedl o *gawri*, nid oes bosibl iddynt sefyll yn erbyn cynnifer teyrnas, &c. heb fod rhagluniaeth o'u tu.

Nid oes dim arwyddion (hyd yn hyn, beth bynnag) y bydd i'r *Americaniaid* uno gyd âg un blaid, yn y rhyfel bresennol – Mae'n arswydus meddwl fod cynnifer o'n cyd greaduriaid yn cael eu rhifo bob dydd i'r cleddyf. – Pwy

* National Convention.

bynnag a ennillo'r frwydr, miloedd sy'n gorfod marw; a llawer o honynt yn ddigon amharod. Wrth sylwi ar greulondeb rhyfeloedd, a chyd-ymdeimlo â'r trueiniaid sy'n dioddef; yr ydym yn barod i ddymuno, "Fod yr holl fyd yn *Gwaceriaid* – ." Nid yw yn gyfreithlon, yn ein barn ni, fod neb crist'nogion a llaw mewn rhyfel ymhellach nâ hunan ymddiffyniad. – Gweddill anghrist – ffrwyth pechod, ydyw rhyfeloedd yn *Ewrop* – a gwyn fyd, na chaid y bwystfil dan draed; mal y *troi'd y cleddyf a'r waywffon yn swch ac yn bladur.*[64]

Achosion y *Poliaid* sy'n debyg o ddibennu'n athrist. – Y mae ymerodres *Rwssia* wedi cyduno, mae'n debyg, â brenin *Prwsia*, i rannu eu gwlad rhyngddynt, a gadael i'w brenin tyner, a hwythau i dorri eu calon dan iau caethiwed. – Ond yr ydym yn gobeithio y bydd i FRENHIN y nef ddadleu cwyn y gorthrymedig, trwy roddi rhyddid cyfreithlon i holl ddynol ryw. –

> "Trwy'r byd, nid tristyd y tro, cu ryddid,
> Caredig a lwyddo;
> Rhag i gwmmwl dwl yn do
> A chaddug ei orchuddio."[65]

Mae dadleu diogel wedi bod yn ddiweddar, yn y senedd gyffredin, mewn perthynas i gynnyrchioliad cyfreithlon y deyrnas hon. Dywedir "ei bod yn amherffaith mewn pedwar peth neillduol. Nattur cynnyrchiolaeth, y deiliaid, y dull ar diben. Eu bod o rhan ei nattur wedi colli'r cydpwys angenrheidiol i'r ddwy gaingc arall o'r lywodraeth; o ran y deiliaid, nad oes dim *llais* yn newisiad eu seneddwyr, gan y rhan fwyaf o'r deyrnas – mai dynion ddylai gael eu cynnyrchioli, ac nid hen drefydd pydron yn *Gerniw* (*Cornwal*) &c. &c. heb braidd neb yn byw ynddynt – tra mae'r trefydd mwyaf poblog yn *Lloegr* heb anfon un marchog i'r Senedd-dŷ – O ran y dull o ddewis Senedd-wyr, &c. ei fod wedi myned mor llygredig, fal y mae'n fynych yn waradwydd i ddynoliaeth – Mal y gwel pob dyn synhwyrol, wrth y meddwi, y gwobrau, a'r trais sydd wrth ddewis marchogion. Trwy fod y moddion fal hyn yn cael ei gwneud yn ddieffaith, nid yw diben cynnyrchiolaeth yn cael ei atteb fal y dylai. – Nid yw'r amherffeithrwydd hwn yn hanfodol, yn y drefn sefydledig, eithr llygredigaeth sydd wedi dyfod i mewn trwy amrywiol ddamweiniau: nid oes nemmawr o amser er pan sefydlwyd y senedd gyffredin i eistedd dros saith mlynedd – ac nid llawer mwy er pan daethant oddiwrth newid y seneddwyr bob blwyddyn, i'w newid bob tair blynedd – Yn nheyrnasiad Harry'r chweched y collwyd y fraint hon."

Terfynwn y tro hwn, gan ddywedyd, – *Byw, fyddo'n Brenin; duwiol, fyddo'i deulu, doeth, fyddo'i gynghoriaid; union, fyddo'n Seneddwyr; cyfiawn, fyddo'n barnwyr; diwygio, wnelo'n gwlad; heddwch, gaffo'r byd.* Amen.

(SIGNS OF THE TIMES,

OBSERVING the state of the world, we are ready to cry out, "Oh wheel [of fortune] –!" In our opinion, the upheavals in *Europe* are drawing to an appointed time which will astonish the world. *Be still, and know that I am* GOD. *Stand still, and see the salvation of the* LORD.[55] – It is not known yet where, or which way, the wheel will turn. Some think, if *France* is conquered, "that the *allied forces* will disagree with each other". There surely has not been such an alliance since the beginning of the world. – The church of *Rome*, the church of *Greece*, the church of *England*, *Lutherans*, *Calvinists*, *Arminians*, &c, &c, which brings to our mind the iron and the soil in the feet of the statue. *Dan.* ii.[56]

Some *devil* has become a lying spirit in people's mouths, so that it is difficult to report news in the present time. – We are prepared to call this age *The age of lies*. The people have recently been close to losing their senses; and we do not know for sure if they have come to their right senses or not; we hope that the mildness of summer will temper their thoughts – and that they will spread fewer untruths among their neighbours as they travel the country. – It would be good for everybody to consider that "*whatsoever a man soweth, that shall he also reap*,"[57] and let him who cannot hold his tongue (from telling a lie), remember that *his faith is in vain*.

As well as warning our compatriots to be ware of the lying tongue, it is necessary for them to be on their look-out to keep away from wicked hands. There never were, possibly, more cunning petty thieves. – And if this war lasts long, one can expect them to increase; – because many thousands of all kinds of craftsmen have recently been thrown out of work, since the conflict prevents trade. – The merchants, shopkeepers, &c., and the money changers (*Bankers*) who are cutting the * * * *.[58] The *Welshman* has to be careful what paper he takes instead of silver money. – But now, we shall give a bit of world news.

The *French* have been driven out of *Belgium*, under the *German* empire, and out of *Holland*. The leader of their force, *Dumourier*,[59] has turned traitor. He played a funny trick on those whom the National Convention had sent to take him, by sending them as prisoners to the enemies. – He himself and many of those who turned with him are at present with the *Austrians*. *Mentz*, a fortified city belonging to the emperor is still in the possession of the *French*. – And general CUSTINE,[60] and his men are fighting fiercely in that country. – The allied armies have hardly advanced on to *French* soil. – Recently, there was a great battle, at which the second son of our king, the Duke of *York*, led his army with the *Prussians*, and the *Germans*, &c., &c.[61] Many were killed on each side – but many more, they say, of the

*French*. – A great part of the state of the king of *Sardinia*, namely *Savoy*, and *Piedmont*, is still in possession of the *French*. – And General *Biron*[62] says that his army there is invincible. –

There is hardly any kingdom or state in *Europe* which is not at war with the French. The empress of *Russia* threatens the *Swedish*, if they do not join the alliance. – *Portugal* has joined those which we mentioned in the first number – and worst of all, for the present government of *France*, is that they are so divided among themselves. – Many *Britons*,[63] and others, have risen in revolt in *Brittany* and are likely to increase greatly in numbers, they say. – If the *English* can land there to assist them, they are likely to destroy the *French* shortly. Even if they were a nation of *giants*, it is not possible for them to stand against so many kingdoms, &c., without providence being on their side.

There are no signs (at the moment anyway) that the *Americans* will join either side in the present war. – It is terrible to think that so many of our fellow-creatures fall to the sword every day. – Whoever wins the battle, thousands must die; and many of them unwilling enough. Observing the cruelty of wars, and empathizing with the poor wretches in their suffering, we are ready to wish, "That the whole world were *Quakers* – ." It is not right, in our opinion, that any Christian should have a hand in war further than for self-defence. – The wars in *Europe* are the refuse of antichrist – the fruit of sin – and it would be a blessing if the beast were trampled under foot; so that the *swords and the spears might be turned into ploughshares and pruning hooks*.[64]

The affairs of the Poles are likely to end sadly. – The empress of *Russia* seems to have agreed with the king of *Prussia*, to divide their country between them and to let their gentle king and them break their hearts under the yoke of bondage. – But we hope that the KING of heaven will take up the complaint of the oppressed, by granting just liberty to all mankind. –

> "May dear liberty prosper throughout the world,
> happy event;
> lest a dense cloud of darkness
> should cover it over."[65]

In the common parliament, there has recently been considerable debate in relation to the lawful representation of this kingdom. It is said that "it is imperfect in four things in particular. The nature of representation, the subjects, the manner and the purpose. That as regards its nature it has lost the weight which needs to be equal to the two other branches of government; as regards the subjects, the largest part of the kingdom has no *voice* in the choice of their Members of Parliament – it is people who should be represented, and not rotten old boroughs in *Cornwall* &c., &c., with hardly anybody living in them – while the most populous towns in *England* do not send a single knight to Parliament. – As regards the manner of selecting Members of Parliament, &c., that its has become so corrupt, that often it is a disgrace to mankind. – As every sensible man can see from the drunkenness, the bribery and the violence which occur while selecting the knights. Since the methods are thus rendered ineffectual, the purpose of representation is not answered as it should be. – This imperfection is not inherent in the established order, but rather corruption has crept in through various accidents: it is not long since the common parliament started sitting for seven years – and not much longer since they ceased changing the Members of Parliament every year, and moved to every three years – This privilege was lost in the reign of Henry the Sixth."

We shall close this time by saying, – *May our King live*; *may his family be godly*; *may his councillors be wise*; *may our Members of Parliament be righteous*; *may our judges be just*; *may our country reform*; *may the world have peace*. Amen.)

## 7.6 *The Enlightenment of the Welsh*

*Cylchgrawn Cymraeg: Neu, Drysorfa Gwybodaeth*. Am Awst 1793 (Rhifyn III) (Welsh Magazine: Or, Treasury of Knowledge. For August 1793 [Number III]), 121–6.

GYMRO HAWDDGAR,

WELE y trydydd Rhifyn yn ei gylch yn dy annerch: y mae'n dwyn goleuni i'th dŷ; na ddigia wrtho, canys nid yw yn meddwl dy dramgcwyddo, eithr dy hyfforddi'n raddol mewn pob gwybodaeth ddefnyddiol: os gweli ynddo rai pethau anhawdd eu deall, darllain hwynt drachefn a thrachefn, a gofyn i'th gymmydog deallus beth yw ystyr neu arwyddoccad y peth neu'r peth.

Nid yw'r Cymry yn yr oes ddiweddaf wedi gweled fawr lyfrau yn y iaith Gymraeg ond llyfrau crefyddol, am hynny y mae'r geiriau a'r llyfrau sy'n trin am naturiaethau a chyfreithiau yn fwy dieithr iddynt. Amcan a diben y *Drysorfa Gwybodaeth* yw goleuo'r wlad mewn pethau naturiol yn gystal ac ysbrydol. Y mae'r Cyhoeddwyr yn rhwymedig i'r dysgedigion haelionus, o bob enw, sydd yn addaw eu cynnorthwyo â defnyddiau defnyddiol ar bob testun. Nid oes ond dau beth yn attal y *Cylchgrawn* rhag cymmeryd lle yn gyffredinol trwy Gymru; hynny yw, yr anhawsdra o'u dosbarthu a chasglu'r arian am danynt. At ddiwygio hyn, y mae'r Cyhoeddwyr yn gobeithio y bydd i un neu ddau ag sy'n caru eu gwlad un-iaith a lles cyffredin, i gymmeryd rhan o'r gwaith a'r baich arnynt ymhob cwrr o Gymru; a dymunol fyddai cael un o bob plaid neu *sect* o grefyddwyr, fel y byddo rhagfarn i gael ei chadw i lawr. Y mae'r Cyhoeddwyr wedi cael eu cyhuddo ar gam eisioes, am nad oes rhagor ynghyd â'r gorchwyl, canys fel y dywedodd Mr *J. Griffith*,[66] "Y mae gormod o ddynion annysgedig, a dysgedig hefyd, na's gallant roi gair da i ddim ond eu heiddo'u hunain." – Meddyliodd rhai, am ein bod wedi cyffwrdd ag yspryd erledigaethus *Calfin*, mai condemnio eu holl athrawiaeth oedd ein hamcan, ond mae'n eglur i'r darllenydd ystyriol, nad oes dim rhagor yn cael ei amcanu nâ gosod allan yr atgasrwydd o ysbryd erledigaethus, a'r ynfydrwydd o fod dynion yn galw eu hunain ar enw neb heblaw Crist.

Pe baem yn sylwi ar yr amrywiol leisiau sydd yn y byd, nid elem fawr ymlaen yn ffordd y bywyd; y mae un yn gwaeddi yn erbyn *Arminius*, a'r llall yn erbyn *Arius*, a'r trydydd yn gwaeddi'n groch fod y diafol yn well nâ Dr. *Priestley*, a'r pedwarydd yn tyngu nad oes braidd ddim gwahaniaeth rhwng *Sosiniaeth* a *Sabeliaeth*; y pummed a haera fod *Trinitarieth* yn fwy atgas nâ dim, am fod yr athrawiaeth hon yn gwneud tri Duw; o'r hyn lleiaf, ei bod yn llysenwi Duw, trwy ei alw'n Ddrindod o Bersonau: ho! ho! medd y chweched, ofer siarad sydd gennych i gyd: yr ydych fel adeiladwyr twr Babel yn methu deall eich gilydd. Wele'n ddigon siwr medd y seithfed, yr wyf yn meddwl mai gwell fyddai diddymmu'r holl bleidiau, a dechreu byd o'r newydd, a galw Duw yn Dduw, a christ'nogion yn grist'nogion; a pheidio cyfrif neb yn grist'nogion ond y cyfryw sy'n caru Crist a chadw ei orchymynion. Am fod goruchwilwyr y Cylchgrawn yn rhy debyg i'r hwn a lafarodd ddiweddaf, yn peidio dyrchafu un blaid yn uwch nâ'r llall, y mae amryw, o bob *sect*, yn eu diystyru; ond fe fydd i'r doeth, a'r diduedd o bob enw, eu cynnorthwyo tra safont dros *y gwir yn erbyn y byd*.[67]

Ar ddymuniad llawer o'n darllenwyr, ni gawn osod, yn y Rhifyn nesaf o flaen y Cymro, yr amrywiol farnau y mae'n clywed dadleu yn eu cylch, fel y gallo wybod rhyw beth am danynt.

* * * * * *

*At* GYHOEDDWYR Y CYLCHGRAWN CYMRAEG, *a phob* CYMRO *Diledryw, yng* NGWYNEDD *a* DEHEUBARTH, *Annerch.*

WRTH ystyried mor ymddifaid yw'r Cymry un-iaith, o bob math o freintiau a chynnorthwyon, i'r diben o'u hyfforddi a'u gwneuthur yn hyddysg a gwybodus mewn *dysg chelfyddyd*, &c. a lleied a fu'r ymgais tu ag at eu coleddu a'u meithrin mewn dysg a doniau, peth rhyfedd na buasem yn waeth y ddelw arnom nag ydym. Foneddigion Cymru, o hil Bruthon,[68] cyfodwch eich pennau i'r lan, ac ymysgydwch lwch y ddaear oddi wrthych, a sefwch ar eich traed fel ceiri o blaid eich cenedl, y sydd wedi gorwedd yn rhy hir o amser, ysywaeth, dan gaddug anwybodaeth a difrawch: mae'n llawn bryd i chwi weithian roddi llaw o gymmorth i'r gwerinos tlodion. Anrhydedd gwlad yw ei thrigolion: a pha anrhydedd a fyddai i wlad yn y byd, pe byddai ei mynyddau oll yn aur pur, a'i holl ddyffrynnau yn dwyn i fynu ddim ond pob math o ffrwythau melus-bêr, a llysiau pêr-arogl a holl drigolion y wlad honno yn deillion; ac heb archwaeth ganddynt, na ffroenau i arogli'r llysiau arogl-bêr hynny. – Mae Madam *Haelioni* yn llefain weithiau wrth eich drysau, gan ymbil arnoch fod yn fwy llaw agored: a hwythau'r ddwy dduwies ardderchog, nid amgen *Doethineb* a *Gwybodaeth*, sy'n erchi arnoch godi eich golygon tu ag i fynu, fel y gweloch bethau yn eu lliwiau priodol eu hun; ac hefyd, roddi clust i wrando ar lef y trueiniaid sy'n erfyn am borth a chynnorthwy, fel y canfyddo y trueiniaid tlodion yr amrywiol ryfeddodau y sydd bob dydd yn eu hamgylchynu o bob parth. Och! och! ystyriwch eu cwynfan, ac na fyddwch gernfyddariaid mwy.

Dyma'r *Cylchgrawn Cymraeg* wedi dangos ei bîg i'r byd, (rhwydd hynt iddo) yr hwn, os tŷf mewn grym ac oedran, a all fod yn foddion i agor llygaid ambell ddall, a gwneuthur iddo weled o bell ac yn eglur, ac unioni esgeiriau ceimion llawer gwr cloff, a'i osod yn syth ar eu draed, fel y gallo lammu dros ffosydd a llaid cyfeiliorni. Deuwch holl foneddigion Cymru, a phawb eraill a garo iaith a lles cyffredin ein cenedl, yn un galon, a rhoddwch faeth addaflawn i'r *Maban*, rhag iddo ef, er caffael o hono ei esgor, yn berchen pedwar aelod a phen, ac yn berchen genau yn medru llafaru yn groyw yn y dydd y ganed ef, ac yn berchen hefyd ar afrifed o lygaid brithion, bolwynion ac amrantau duon, ac wynebpryd siriolwyn iddo, megis yn gwenu ar bawb, ac heb ewyllysio drwg i neb, na chanddo gynfigen i lwyddiant neb, o ba radd bynnag a sefyllfa y bont, ac y mae ei freichiau ar led yn barod i gofleidio yr hyn a rodder iddo, o barth bynnag y deuant; etto, er hyn, oni's rhodder maeth prydlawn a chyfaddas iddo, dihoeni a marw a wna, a hynny yn unig o ddiffyg gwell achles ac ymgeledd.

Nid yw cenedl y Cymry un gronyn llai eu synwyr, eu medr, a'u parodrwydd i dderbyn addysg nag ydoedd Cenhedloedd eraill, a lewyrchasant mor odidowgwych mewn dysg a chelfyddyd. Pwy a ymddisgleiriasant ac a lewyrchasant yn fwy medrus wiw a gorddoethion mewn pob math o ddysg a chelfyddyd, nâ'r Groegiaid? A changen ydym ninnau o'r genedl honno, medd *Brut y Brenhinoedd*, a 'sgrifenwyd gan *Tyssilio*, o *Fon*,[69] er's mwy nâ naw can mlynedd a aethant heibio; pa fodd bynnag am hynny, ac o ba fan a chenedl bynnag y deryw ac yr hannoedd y Bruthon, mae'n wir eu bod yn berchen cynheddfau anianol mor ehelaeth ag un genedl arall dan ffurfafen y nefoedd.

Haelioni'r boneddigion, a phennaduriaid, a fu yn foddion i gyfodi llawer gwr gwych megis o'r llwch; ac na buasai iddo ef byth ddangos ei ragor gampau, heb gymmorth ac haelioni eraill. Mae llawer o'r meini gwerthfawr-occaf, pan eu cloddier o'r gloddfa, yn edrych yn wrthun, afluniaidd, a geirwon, ac nid llawer o ragor rhyngddynt yn eu hymddangosiad cyntaf â *maen llwyd y rhych*; ond pan eu llyfnhaer, ac eu dylower, trwy gelfyddyd y crefftwr cywreinllaw, braidd na serenant olygon y neb a graffo arnynt. Yr un ffunud, y mae llawer plentyn tlawd, pe'u coleddid ef mewn ffordd addas, yn berchen cystal cynheddfau, pwyll, synwyr, ac ymgyffrediadau â neb o ddynolryw. Mae llawer gwr gwisgi na's medr, gan falchedd, a choeg rodres, gymmaint a throi ei olygon tu ag i wared, a chan faint ei anystyriaeth a'i ynfydrwydd: yn ei dyb ef, nid yw'r gwerinos ddim amgen nag ysgribliaid wedi eu trefnu gan ragluniaeth i ddim arall onid trin a thrafod y dom: ac er ei holl rodres a'i ymhonni o'i ddysg a'i wybodaeth; wedi'r cwbl, fe allai, fod y bachgen llymmaf a thlottaf yn ei wasanaeth ef, yn berchen deg cymmaint o synwyr mam (chwedl y bobl) nag a fedd ef; ond yn unig ei fod ef wedi dysgu rhyw swrn o bethau ar ei dafod-leferydd, a'u pwyo fel â phistl i'w fiol ynfyd.

Rhifydd-deb a elwid gynt yn *Llawforwyn pob celfyddyd*; felly etto, a phwy all dreiddio ond i ychydig o wybodaeth mewn neb rhyw gaingc o'r celfydd-ydau heb fod yn fedrus a hyddysg mewn rhifyddiaeth? Yr hon, ond ei defnyddio yn gyfaddas, a all fod yn fuddiol, ac yn ganllaw i arwain ei pherchennog yn fedrusach yn holl oruchwilion a negeseuau'r bywyd hwn: ïe, anhawdd fyddai, heb gymmorth *hon*, ddeall llawer man o'r ysgrythur lân. Mae'n fuddiol i'r llafurwr i gadw ei gyfrifon a chylch yr amseroedd; i'r cybydd i rifo ei god a llog ei arian; i fasnachwyr a marchnadyddion i gyfartalu eu masnachyddiaeth; i'r morwr i hyfforddio ei fordwy, ac adnabod llwybr ei long yn y cefn-fôr garw mal ar dir goleu; i'r crefftwr cywrein-ddoeth i gymmedroli ei amrywiol beirianau yn eu lleoedd priodol; i'r physygwr a'r philosophydd, ac ymholyddion pethau anianol, i chwilio allan ddefnydd ac ansawdd pethau o berfeddion daear hyd yn mro'r Nifwl a Chaergwdron; i'r prydydd i rifo odlau ei gynghanedd, ac i gadw cyssondeb ar fesur; i'r cyfreithwr i rifo ei filiau, a gwneuthur uniondeb rhwng gwr a'i gymmydog; i'r ustus, rhag i'r cyfreithwr, a'r trethwr chwantus, â'u biliau twyllodrus orthrymmu'r wlad; i'r penswyddogion a goruchwilwyr y deyrnas i drefnu achosion y wladwriaeth; i'r cadpeniaid i drefnu a gosod eu milwyr yn drefnus mewn câd ar faes, a thalu i bob un ei ddogn o fwyd a chyflog; ac i'r brenin i reoli ei ddeiliaid; ac nid oes un dyn, o ba radd a sefyllfa bynnag y bo, o'r brenin i'r cardottyn, nad rhaid iddo wrth ryw gyfran o ddeall-dwriaeth mewn rhifyddeb. Gan hynny, beth meddwch chwi, fy eneidiau gwynion? oni fyddai odfa ac adeg dêg i chwi neillduo rhyw ddosparth fechan o'ch CYLCHGRAWN i'r diben o addysgu a hyfforddi y Cymry un-iaith yn amrywiol geingciau rhifyddiaeth? Gan ddechrau yn gyntaf ar ei chyn-seiliau; ac oddi yno arwain y disgybl, o gam i gam, ac o res i res, o ganghenau isaf rhifyddeb; gan ei holrain yn fanol o fon i frig; a chyfleu y cyfryw ddosparthiadau, modd y galler eu rhwymo yn un llyfr cryno wrtho ei hun? Ac os byddwch yn awyddus i annog y gwaith yn y blaen, ac i dderbyn y cynnyg, byddaf yn bob cynnorthwy i chwi ag y fyddo yn fy ngallu.

*Yr wyf yr eiddoch,*

*A charwr fy ngwlad a'm cenedl,*

BRUTTWN BACH.[70]

* * * * * *

## *OLYSGRIFEN*

Chwi soniasoch yn yr ail Rhifyn o'r Cylchgrawn, y byddai yn dda ac yn dderbyniol ganthoch gaffael rhyw gyfran o drioedd ynys Prydain:[71] rhag nad ydych yn hyspys pa fath beth ydynt, deallwch mai math o hanes ein hynafiaid ydyw. A chyn y gellid ei ddeall ef yn iawn trwyddo, (onid gan un o fil) byddai raid mwy o nodau ar bob tu dalen o hono, nag a lanwai y bedwaredd ran o'r Cylchgrawn. Fe 'sgrifenodd Mr. *Lewis Morris* nodau helaeth ar y trioedd,[72] ac hefyd ar sylwiadau Mr. *Robert Fychan*,[73] gynt o'r *Hengwrt*, ar yr unrhyw; ond y mae'r holl waith yn *Saesonaeg*; ac nid wyf fi yn meddwl y byddai fudd na dywenydd yn y byd ei gyhoeddi. Yr *Eulogium Brittaniæ*[74] a soniasoch, yr un peth ydyw a *Brut y Brenhinoedd*, ond ei fod wedi ei lygru yn anfad gan ddwylaw budron *Galffrid*[75] a *Nennius*.[76] *Galffrid* a'i cyfieithodd i'r *Lladin* allan o *Frut y Brenhinoedd* gan *Tyssilo* 350 o flynyddau wedi marw'r awdwr; ac ym mhen yspaid 350 o flynyddoedd eraill, *Nennius* a'i hargraphodd yn yr *Almain*, dan yr enw *Eulogium Brittaniæ*, a garw yr anffurf a wnaeth ef arno; ni's gadodd ef gymmaint a brenin, pennadur, gwlad, na dinas, heb eu llysenwi, ïe, yn oed *Arthur* ei hun a ddifenwodd efe, yr hyn a barodd i *Baxter*[77] ac eraill daeru yn haerllug nad yw'r cwbl a ddywedir am y milwr dewr-wych hwnnw, ond chwedlau gwneuthur, ac na bu'r fath ddyn erioed. Ond y mae nodau Mr. *Lewis Morris* a'r *Baxter's Glossery* wedi bwrw ei holl wag-siarad gyd â'r gwynt, ac wedi diseilio a bwrw i'r llawr yr holl waith a fu gan elynion ein cenedl er gwrthbrofi *Brut y Brenhinoedd*, a phob hanes arall o'r eiddom.

* * * * * *

## LLYTHYR AT Y CYMRY.

Garedigion,

WELE, fy anwyl Gydwladwyr, dyma Gylchgrawn cymraeg neu Drysorfa Gwybodaeth ar gychwyniad; yr wyf yn hyderu y bydd yn foddion i daenu gwybodaeth fuddiol, drwy holl Gymry; os nad ydyw'r gwaith yn llwyr ddifai, y mae'r amcan yn ganmoladwy, ac yn haeddu achles, cynnorthwy a derbyniad gan bob gwir Gymro. Pa fwy anfoesgarwch ar ddŷn na gwadu ei fam naturiol, yr hon a'i hymddûg, a honi perthynas ag Estrones? Pa faint gwell yw cyflwr yr hwn sy'n gwadu neu'n diystyru iaith ei fam, Bernwch chwi. – O gan hynny, chwychwi Ddysgedigion [a] Gwybodyddion, deffrowch yn unfryd, a rhoddwch ryw gyfran o'ch dysgeidiaeth allan i'r Byd, fel y byddo eraill yn well erddi; felly y gwnewch gymmwynas i'ch cyd-wladwyr, ac yr attebwch ddiben eich anfoniad i'r Byd. – Ow, Ow! A gaiff pob cenedl ragori ar y Cymry, mewn dysg a gwybodaeth? Na atto Duw. Pe buasai'r dysgedigion gynt mor ddifraw a chysglyd, a rhai sydd yn myned dan Enw dysgawdwyr yn yr oes hon, nyni a fuasem heddyw yn ymbalfalu mewn dugn anwybodaeth a thywyllwch dudew; ond y mae gennym gyfleusdra têg yn awr, a gochelwn er dim ei gam-arferu. – Chwychwi Gymry uniaith, trigolion Gwlad *Camber*[78] na esgeuluswch yr adeg brydlawn hon, ac na wrthodwch wybodaeth a diddanwch sylweddol, na adewch i falchder na chybydd-dod eich lluddias rhag derbyn y cynnygiad amserol hwn; drwy'r cyfryw foddion a hyn, y gall y Bugail mynyddig ddyfod mor ddoeth a'r Dinasydd tewglyd, y moddion hyn a ddichon eich arwain at ddiddanwch a bery, pan fyddo cybyddion a thyrchod, a'u haur a'u harian yn cyd-losgi; ond ysgatfydd y dywed rhai ohonoch, nad ydych yn deall Cymraeg yn dda, ond eich bod yn cael bob gwybodaeth ddymunol mewn llyfrau seisnig: caniattewch i'm ddywedyd; os nad ydych yn deall Cymraeg; mwyaf yn y Byd y cywilydd, ac os nad oes ond chwychwi yn unig yn deall saisneg &c. pa beth a ddaw o'r Cymry uniaith? O na fyddwch mor angharedig ac anghymmwynasgar a gadael iddynt fyw a marw mewn anwybodaeth, mae'n resyn eich bod yn diystyru eich Iaith gynhenid, Iaith yr hon a roddes i chwi faeth a sugn, Iaith y Wlad, ymha un yr agorasoch gyntaf eich amrantau i weled goleu dydd. Pa leshâd yw i chwi fod yn gydnabyddus mewn gwledydd pellenig ac yn ddieithr gartref. O chwychwi, feibion anffyddlon *Cambria*, gwridwch a chywilyddiwch am y gwall, – wrth fyfyrio ar brydferthwch yr Iaith Gymraeg, y torodd un Bardd allan ac y cant fal hyn:

"Iaith bêr, Iaith Gomer,[79] Iaith gymen, – Iaith lwys
Iaith lesol i'w pherchen;
Iaith, a'i gwaith o wyth gwythen,
Iaith a saif, er eitha sen."

Ysgatfydd y rhyfyga rhywun ddywedyd nad oes dim a dal edrych arno yn yr Iaith Gymraeg; ond pwy bynag a chwilio yn ddyfal a genfydd ynddi drysorion o ryfeddod i'r Byd. –

Drwg genyf glywed fod rhai o honoch yn achwyn fod y Cylchgrawn yn rhy lawn o Dduwioldeb, eraill yn chwenych ychwaneg o Ganiadau, Hynafiaeth, newyddion &c. Gymry anwyl, rhoddwch heibio yr holl wrthddadleuon diles hyn, ac ystyriwch, mai adeiladaeth gyffredinol, sydd fwyaf defnyddfawr i'r Byd, y peth a fo yn ddiflas gan un a all fod yn gymmeradwy gan y llall: nid un saig a foddia bob archwaeth. – Bellach myfi a gymmeraf fy nghenad, gan obeithio y gwelir, y rhan fwyaf o'm Cyd-wladwyr, 'yn cyd-fawrhau doniau dysg; Diddan gofleidio addysg."

Wyf,
(Ewyllysiwr da im Gwlad am Iaith,)
Llanfair Bettws Geraint, ym Môn, D. THOMAS.
*Gorphenhaf* 15. 1793.

(AMIABLE WELSHMAN,
HERE is the third Number addressing you in its turn: it enlightens your house; do not be displeased with it, because it does not intend to offend you, but to educate you gradually in all branches of useful knowledge: if you see in it some things which are difficult to understand, read them again and again, and ask your intelligent neighbour what the meaning or the significance of this or the other is.

The Welsh have not seen many books in the Welsh language in this recent age apart from religious books, therefore the words and books which treat natural sciences and laws are more unfamiliar to them. The aim and purpose of the *Treasury of Knowledge* is to enlighten the country in things natural as well as spiritual. The Publishers are indebted to the generous learned men, of all denominations, who promise to support them with useful material on every subject. Only two things prevent the *Magazine* from taking its place through Wales generally; these are, the difficulty of distributing it and of collecting the money for it. In order to amend this, the Publishers hope that in every corner of Wales one or two who love their fellow Welsh-speakers and the common weal will take on part of the work and of the burden; and it would be desirable to have one of every religious faction or *sect*, so that prejudice may be kept at bay. The Publishers have already been falsely accused, because there are not more involved with the undertaking, for, as Mr *J. Griffith*[66] said, "There are too many unlearned and learned men who cannot say a good word about anything, but what belongs to themselves." – Some thought, because we have touched upon the persecuting spirit of *Calvin*, that our aim was to condemn his whole teaching, but it is clear to the thoughtful reader that the aim was only to set out the hatefulness of a persecuting spirit, and the folly that men should call themselves by any other name than that of Christ.

If we paid attention to all the various voices in the world, we would not make much headway on the road to salvation; one cries out against *Arminius*, and the other against *Arius*, and the third shouts angrily that the devil is better than Dr. *Priestley*, and the fourth swears that there is hardly any difference between *Socinianism* and *Sabellianism*; the fifth maintains that *Trinitarianism* is more odious than anything else, because this philosophy makes three Gods; at least, that it mocks God by calling him a Trinity of People: ho! ho! says the sixth, you are all talking in vain: you are like the builders of the tower of Babel unable to understand each other. Now indeed, says the seventh, in my opinion it would be better to abolish all the factions, and start afresh, and call God God, and Christians Christians; and not count anyone a Christian but those who love Christ and keep his commands. Because the editors of the *Magazine* are too similar to the last speaker, refraining from promoting one faction above another, some of each *sect* condemn them; but the wise and the unbiased of every denomination will assist them while they stand for *the truth against the world*.[67]

Following the wish of many of our readers, in the next Number, we will place before the Welshman the various opinions which he hears being debated, so that he may know something about them.)

* * * * * *

(*To the* PUBLISHERS OF THE WELSH MAGAZINE, *and every Pure* WELSHMAN, *in* GWYNEDD *and the* SOUTH, *an Address.*

WHEN it is considered how bereft the monolingual Welshmen are of all kinds of advantages and aids for the purpose of their instruction and of making them knowledgeable in *learning, the arts*, &c., and how small the attempts to cultivate them and foster them in learning and talents have been, it is strange that our condition is not worse than it is. Gentlemen of Wales, of the British race,[68] lift up your heads and shake off the dust of the earth, and stand up for your nation like giants who, regrettably, have lain for too long under a mist of ignorance and apathy: it is high time now for you to lend a supporting hand to the poor commoners. The honour of a country are its inhabitants: and what kind of honour would a land possess, if its mountains were all of pure gold and its vales all produced only delicious fruit and fragrant herbs, if all the inhabitants of that country were blind, with no sense of taste, or nostrils to smell these fragrant herbs. – Madame *Generosity* sometimes cries at your doors, imploring you to be more liberal; and also the two excellent goddesses, none other than *Wisdom* and *Knowledge*, beseech you to turn your eyes upwards, so that you may see things in their true colours; and also to lend an ear to listen to the cries of the poor wretches who beg for succour and assistance, so that the wretched poor may discover the various wonders which surround them daily on every side. Woe! woe! consider their lament and do not be stone-deaf any more.

Now the *Welsh Magazine* has shown itself to the world, (may its journey be easy), and if it grows in strength and age, it could be a means to open the eyes of a few blind men and make them see far and clear, and to straighten the crooked legs of many a lame man and put him upright on his feet, so that he may leap over the ditches and the mud of error. Come, all gentlemen of Wales, and everybody else who loves the language and the common weal of our nation, of one heart, and give abundant nourishment to the *Infant*, so that he does not die. He has been born, possesses four limbs and a head, and a mouth that could talk clearly the day he was born, and he also possesses countless speckled bulging eyes, and black eyelashes, and a pleasant face, as if smiling at everybody and wishing no harm to anyone, nor does he envy anyone their success, from whatever station of life they may be, and his arms are open ready to embrace what is offered him, from whatever part it may come; nevertheless, if he is not given timely and appropriate nourishment, he will sicken and die, and that only for want of better support and care.

The nation of the Welsh have no less reason, ability or readiness to receive education than other Nations which have succeeded so brilliantly in learning and the arts. Who shone and flourished more splendidly and sagaciously in all fields of learning and the arts than the Greeks? And we are a branch of that nation, says *The History of the Kings of Britain* written by *Tyssilio* of Anglesey[69] more than nine hundred years ago; however that may be, and from whatever place and nation the Briton came and derived, it is true that the innate qualities they possess are as abundant as those of any other nation under the firmament.

It was the generosity of the nobility and the sovereigns which were the means of raising many a fine man as if from the dust; and he would never have been able to show his talents without the assistance and generosity of others. Many of the most precious stones, when they are first dug up from the mine, look ugly, deformed and rough, and in their first appearance there is not much difference between them and the *grey stone of the furrow*; but when they are smoothed and polished by the dexterous hands of the skilful craftsman, they almost dazzle the eyes of whoever gazes on them. In the same way, many a poor child, if cultivated appropriately, is possessed of abilities, intelligence, reason and comprehension equal to those of any other member of mankind. There is many a sprightly fellow who cannot, out of pride and vain ostentation, so much as turn his sight downwards, and because of his thoughtlessness and his foolishness the common people are, in his opinion, no more than animals, ordained by providence only to work the dung. And despite all his pomp and his claim to learning and knowledge, it may well be after all that the poorest and most ragged boy in his service possesses ten times more common sense (as the people say) than he; but that he has learnt a good deal of things by rote and ground them as if with a pestle in his foolish bowl.

Numeracy used to be called the *Handmaiden of all arts*; so it is still, and who could penetrate but a little way into any branch of the arts without being skilled and learned in arithmetic? Arithmetic, used properly, may be beneficial and a guide to lead its owner more expertly in all the undertakings and affairs of this life: indeed, without it, it would be difficult to understand many passages of the Holy Scripture. It is useful for the labourer in keeping his accounts and the cycle of the seasons; for the miser to count his pouch and the interest on his money; for merchants and salesmen to balance their trade; for the sailor to expedite his voyage and to know the way of his ship on the rough ocean as he would on plain earth; for the skilled craftsman to adjust his various machines in their appropriate places; for the physicist and the philosopher, and investigators of natural things, to search out the material nature and quality of things from the bowels of the earth as far as the Planetary mists and the Milky Way; for the poet to count the rhymes of his *cynghanedd*, and to keep his metre consistent; for the lawyer to count his bills and ensure equity between a man and his neighbour; for the justice, lest the lawyer and the greedy taxman with their deceitful bills oppress the country; for the chief officials and stewards of the kingdom to order the affairs of the state; for the generals to arrange and place their soldiers in good order on the battle-field, and pay each their share of food and salary; and for the king to rule his subjects. And there is no man, of whatever standing and grade in life, from the king to the beggar, who does not need some understanding of arithmetic. Therefore, what say you, my sweet friends? would this not be an opportunity and a good time to put aside a small part of your MAGAZINE for the purpose of instructing the monolingual Welshmen in the various branches of arithmetic? Beginning first with its foundations, and from there leading the pupil step by step, and from rung to rung from the lowest branches of arithmetic; following it carefully from the root to the branch; and arranging these sections so that they may be bound as a neat book on its own? And if you are eager to encourage this work and to accept the offer, I will assist you in any way I can.

*I am yours,*

*And a lover of my country and my nation,*

The LITTLE BRITON.[70]

* * * * * *

## POSTSCRIPT

In the second Number of the Magazine, you mentioned that it would be good and well-received by you to obtain a part of the triads of the isle of Britain:[71] in case you do not know what they are, understand that they are a kind of history of our ancestors. And before one can understand it properly throughout (and not by one in a thousand) there would have to be more notes on every page of it than would fill a quarter of the Magazine. Mr. *Lewis Morris*[72] wrote extensive notes on the triads, and also on the observations of Mr. *Robert Fychan*,[73] formerly of Hengwrt, on the same; but the whole work is in *English*; and I do not think there would be any benefit or pleasure in the world in publishing it. The *Eulogium Brittaniæ*[74] which you mentioned is the same thing as *Brut y Brenhinoedd*, but that it has been villainously corrupted by the dirty hands of *Galffrid*[75] and *Nennius*.[76] *Galffrid* translated it into *Latin* from *Brut y Brenhinoedd* by *Tyssilo* 350 years after the author's death; and within a further 350 years later, *Nennius* printed it in *Germany* under the title *Eulogium Brittaniæ*, and he mutilated it harshly; he did not leave so much as one king, chief, country or city without misnaming it, yes, he even dishonoured *Arthur* himself, which caused *Baxter*[77] and others to assert arrogantly that all the things which are said about that valiant soldier are nothing but fabricated tales and that such a man never existed. But Mr. *Lewis Morris*'s notes on *Baxter's Glossery* have scattered all his empty talk to the wind, and have undermined and thrown down all the work done by the enemies of our nation to disprove *Brut y Brenhinoedd*, and every other history of ours.

* * * * * *

## LETTER TO THE WELSH.

Friends,

MY dear Compatriots, here is the beginning of the Welsh Magazine or Treasury of Knowledge; I am confident that it will be a means of spreading useful knowledge throughout all of Wales; if the work is not entirely faultless, the aim is praiseworthy and deserves succour, assistance and acceptance from every true Welshman. What greater immorality is there in a man than to disown his natural mother, who gave birth to him, and claim a relationship with a Foreigner? How much better is the state of him who disowns or neglects the language of his mother, you judge. – Oh, therefore, you, learned and knowledgeable Men, wake up unanimously, and give some part of your learning to the World, so that others may be better for it; thus you will do your compatriots a service and fulfil the purpose for which you were sent to this World. – Oh, Oh! Shall every nation excel over the Welsh in learning and knowledge? God forbid. If the learned men of yore had been as indifferent and sleepy as those who go by the Name of teachers in this age, we would today be groping about in dire ignorance and thick black darkness; but we have a fair opportunity now, and let us avoid its misuse at all cost. – You monolingual Welshmen, inhabitants of the Land of *Camber*,[78] do not miss this timely opportunity, and do not reject substantial knowledge and comfort, do not allow pride and miserliness to prevent you from accepting this timely offer; through such means the mountain Shepherd can become as wise as the comfortable Town-dweller, these means may lead you to lasting comfort, when misers and hogs burn together with their gold and their silver; but perhaps some of you say that they do not understand Welsh well, but that you get all desirable knowledge in English books: allow me to say; if you do not understand Welsh; more in the World is your shame, and if only you understand English &c., what will become of the monolingual Welsh? Oh, do not be so unkind and disobliging as to let them live and die in ignorance. It is a pity that you scorn your native Language, the Language of her who nourished and suckled you, the Language of the Country in which you first opened your eyelashes to see the light of day. Of what advantage to you is it to be acquainted with far-flung countries and foreign at home? Oh, you unfaithful sons of *Cambria*, blush and be ashamed of this negligence, – on contemplating the beauty of the Welsh Language, one poet broke into the following song:

"Sweet Language, Language of Gomer,[79] accomplished Language,
fair Language
and a beneficial Language to its owner;
a language which is formed of eight-fold stock,
a Language which will withstand utmost rebuke."

Perhaps somebody will dare say that there is nothing which is worth looking at in the Welsh Language; but whoever searches diligently will discover treasures of wonder to the World. – I am sorry to hear that some of you complain that the Magazine is too full of Piety, others covet more Poetry, Antiquity, news, &c. Dear Welshmen, throw aside all these useless counter-arguments and consider that general edification is most useful to the World, the thing which is disagreeable to one is acceptable to another: the same dish is not to every taste. – I shall now take my leave, hoping that the majority of my Compatriots will be seen "extolling together the virtues of learning; Happily embracing education."

I am,
(A Well-wisher to my Country and my Language,)
Llanfair Bettws Geraint, on Anglesey, D. THOMAS.
*July* 15. 1793.)

## 7.7 *Against the Established Church*

*Cylchgrawn Cymraeg: Neu, Drysorfa Gwybodaeth.* Am Awst 1793 (Rhifyn III) (Welsh Magazine: Or, Treasury of Knowledge. For August 1793 [Number III]), 147–9.

At Orychwylwyr y Cylchgrawn

Mi dybygwn fod eich amcan i ddiwreiddio coel-grefydd ac anghrediniaeth o'r wlad. Llwyddo wneloch. Yr ydwyf wedi hir alaru, wrth weled cymmaint o weddill pabyddiaeth yn aros yn Nghymru ymhlith *pob* plaid. Nid ydwyf yn bwriadu rhoddi drwg absen i neb mwy nai gilydd. Chwilied pob un ei dŷ ei hun. Nid oes dim yn fwy argyhoeddiadol na *gollwng y goleuni* i'r tŷ, ac yna gadel pob perchen enaid i farnu drosto ei hun; – ond fel y dywed y bardd.

"Ni phaid yr offeiriaid offeru – Eneidiau
A'u nadel iawn gredu,
Fel ffyddlon weision IESU;
A rhoi coel yw eiriau cû.

Nid preiliaid, neu 'ffeiriaid, neu fferen, – ddylem
Ni ddilyn yn llawen.
MAB DUW, nid *pab*, yw'n PEN
Cyd-bwys i fod yn Cad-pen,

Mor ddoethed, Cryfed yw crefydd, – y duwiol
Sy'n dewis, y wir ffydd;
O ddwled yw'r addolydd,
A âd, i'r offeiriad* ei ffydd.

Ni âd un 'Ffeiriad na Pharao,† – i'r Haulwen
Wiw lawen oleuo;
*Ond* llu'r *fagddu*, ni all rwysdro,
Yr Haul fru, a *hawl* y fro.

* Peidied neb a meddwl mai offeriaid eglwys Rhufain, ac eglwys Loegr, yn unig, a feddylir, eithr pob Pregethwr, a Chynghorwr, nad yw yn rhybuddio ei wrandawyr i roddi heibio draddodiadau dynion, a barnu dros eu hunain, trwy gymmeryd gair yr ARGLWYDD yn unig reol iddynt.

† Gellir cymmwyso'r farddoniaeth at draws-lywodraeth *ddinasaidd* yn gystal âg *eglwysaidd*. – Y mae rhyddid dinasaidd ac eglwysaidd yn wastad yn cyd-fyned; ac yn sefyll, neu syrthio gyd â'u gilydd: er nad oes un berthynas (fel y breuddwydia rhai) rhwng eglwys a llywodraeth wladol: etto mae awdwr rhyddid wedi cysylltu, hawl naturiol, ac ysprydol, ei greaduriaid mor agos, yn y byd hwn, fel na ellir byth mo'i gwahanu. Yr ydwyf ymhell oddiwrth farnu, ei fod yn anghenraid cael eglwys sefydledig trwy'r gyfraith, mewn un gwlad: ïe mor belled, fel ag yr ydwyf yn meddwl mae'r diystyrwch mwyaf ar grefydd CRIST (yr hwn a ddywedodd NID YW FY NHEYRNAS I O'R BYD HWN) yw amcanyd ei syfydlu dan un dull neu enw trwy gyfreithiau dynol. Gadael pob crefydd i sefyll neu syrthio trwy eu proffeswyr ei hun yw'r ffordd oreu. Os na thal crefydd ei chynnal yn *fyw* gan eu phroffeswyr, heb gymmorth y llywodraeth; – cystal ei gadael i *farw*. Y mae Dr Adam Smith wedi dangos yn ddigon eglur fod pob plaid o bobl yn fwy zelog dros eu crefydd ac yn ei chadw'n fwy pur pan y maent yn cael eu gadael iddynt eu hunain, heb i'r lywodraeth ymyraeth â hwynt. – Yr oedd *Hume* ac eraill o'r deistiaid yn fawr dros grefydd sefydledig. A pha'm? am ei bod yn porthi diogi'r offeiriad fel nad oedd achos iddynt lafurio nac ymdrechu i argyhoeddi dynion o wirionedd y grefydd grist'nogol.

Mae'n eglyr i fi, na waeth ar y ddaear pa grefydd fyddo wedi ei sefydlu, mewn gwlad, os bydd elw iw gael trwy broffesu'r grefydd honno, caiff ddigon o ganlynwyr. Pe byddid i sefydlu Jupiter yn Dduw yn Mhrydain, a threfnyd Esgobion ac offeiriaid i weini iddo; ond rhoi digon o gyflog, caid gormod o weision yn fuan. – Y mae gormod

Ceiff caethion, deillion, o dywyllwch, – olwg
Ar haulwen diddanwch;
Daw dyddiau llawn dedwyddwch;
Ar waelion llwydion y llwch.

Hêd llawer o hâd dulluan, – ar gil
O'r golau mwyneidd lan:
Gwell gan ynfyd, fyglyd fan,
O'r golwg, dan rhyw geulan. – "

Ynys Gotha: PHILO RECTUM.
*Gorphenhaf* 1793.

O.Y. "Er i arthod ac eryrod,
Gyd â llewod, godi'n lluoedd;
Byth ni lwyddant, pan ryfelant,
O dra nwyfiant, â Duw'r nefoedd."

o ddynion drwg ymhob gwlad, yn caru bydr elw a byw yn segur – ac nid yw crefydd sefydledig dan ba enw bynnag y byddo da i ddim arall, ar wn i, ond porthi'r cyfryw. – Y ffordd oreu i buro'r eglwys yw sychu'r ffrwd o lygredigaeth sydd yn cynal y fath bysgod aflan ynddi. – Gweddi dda iawn ac angenrheidiol i'w chofio ydyw, "Nag arwain ni i brofedigaeth." A da fyddai i bawb ystyried fod yr hwn sydd ai wyntyll yn ei law, "*Yn dyfod i lwyr lanhâu ei lawr dyrnu.*"[80] Ni thrig cymmaint ag ŷsyn arno ond y gwenith *o bob plaid*, a erys – Ni byddai golled yn y byd i'r duwiol yn yr eglwys sefydledig eu bod yn gorfod ymddibynu ar eu brodyr duwiol eraill, am eu cynhaliaeth. Gwell o lawer fyddai iddyn gynghori'r llywodraeth, i roddi'r holl arian sydd yn myned ar gynal esgobion ac offeiriaid i dalu dyled y goron, rhag ofn i'r trethi fyned yn rhy drwm i'r werin gyffredin i'w dwyn, ac yna fe fydd y canlyniad yn ofidus i lawer, ag sydd yn caru llwyddiant y wlad, a heddwch y deyrnas. – Yr ydwyf o'm calon yn caru heddwch, ac yn dymuno daioni i bob dyn byw – Fy nyledswydd, fel cristion, yw porthi ngelyn ac mi dybygwn mai fy hoff waith fyddai gwneud hynny – ond rhaid rho'i fynu, yr ydwyf yn clywed y taranau yn ddychrynllyd draw, ac wrth ystyriaid mor afiachus mae'n awyr ninau wedi bod er's llawer amser, yr ydwyf yn ofni i'r trwst dorri uwch fy mhen, *Ffown i'r noddfa* – Byddwch wych o gyhoeddwyr a Dosbarthwyr Gwybodaeth. Os bydd i gymmaint a hyn gael lle yn eich trydydd rhifyn, o bosibl bydd i chwi gael clywed etto oddiwrth PHILO RECTUM.

(To the EDITORS of the MAGAZINE

I suppose that your aim is to root out superstition and unbelief from the country. MAY YOU SUCCEED. I have long been grieved to see so many remnants of Catholicism among *every* faction in Wales. I do not intend to attack any one in particular. Let everybody search their own house. There is nothing more convincing than *letting the light* into the house, and then letting each owner of a soul judge for themselves – but as the poet says.

"The priests do not cease to shackle Souls
and to prevent them from truly believing,
as faithful servants of JESUS;
and from trusting in his kind words.

It is not prelates or priests or the mass that we
should follow joyfully.
The SON OF GOD, not the *pope*, is our HEAD,
even-handed to be our Captain,

So wise and strong is the religion of the godly
who choose the true faith;
Oh! how foolish is the worshipper
who leaves his faith to the priest.*

No Priest or Pharaoh† will allow the good
joyful light of the sun to shine;
*but* the host of *hell* cannot hinder
the Sun above and the *right* of the land.

* Let nobody think that only the priests of the church of Rome and the church of England are meant, but every *Preacher* and *Exhorter* who does not warn his listeners to put aside the traditions of men and judge for themselves by taking the word of the LORD as their only rule.

† The poetry may be applied to *political* as well as *religious* tyranny. – Political and religious liberty always go together; and stand or fall with each other: although there is no relationship (as some dream) between church and state government; nevertheless the author of liberty has linked together the natural and spiritual rights of his creatures so closely, in this world, that they can never be separated. I am far from the opinion that it is necessary to have a church established by law in a country; yes, so far that I think it is the highest contempt towards the religion of CHRIST (who said MY KINGDOM IS NOT OF THIS WORLD) to attempt to establish it in one manner or name through human laws. The best way is to let every religion stand or fall through its practitioners. If a religion is not worth keeping *alive* by its practitioners without the help of the government, it

From darkness, slaves and blind men will have sight
of the sunshine of comfort;
days full of happiness will come
to the lowly grey ones of the dust.

Many of the owl's offspring fly into hiding
from the gentle light above:
a madman prefers a suffocating place,
to be out of sight, under some bank. – "

The Isle of Gotha: PHILO RECTUM.
*July* 1793.

P. S. "Though bears and eagles,
together with lions rise in throngs;
they will never succeed when they wage war
wantonly on God in heaven.")

is just as well to let it *die.* Dr Adam Smith has shown clearly enough that every denomination of people is more zealous for its religion and keeps it purer if it is left to its own devices, without government interference. – *Hume* and other deists were much in favour of an established faith. And why? Because it feeds the laziness of priests so that they have no cause to labour or endeavour to convince men of the truth of the Christian faith.

It is clear to me that it does not matter in the least what religion is established in a country if profit is to be had by professing that religion, it will have enough followers. If one established Jupiter as a God in Britain and organized Bishops and priests to serve him, as long as the wages were enough, there would soon be plenty of servants. – There are too many wicked men in every country who love filthy lucre and an idle life – and an established religion under whatever name it may be is good for nothing else, to my mind, than to feed their like. – The best way of cleansing the church is to dry the stream of corruption in which this kind of unclean fish is sustained. – A very good and necessary prayer to remember is, "Lead us not into temptation." And it would be good for everybody to consider that he whose fan is in his hand, "*is coming to thoroughly purge his floor.*"[80] Not one grain of chaff will be left on it, but the wheat *of every denomination* will remain. – It would be no loss at all to the pious in the established church that they must depend on their other pious brothers for their support. It would be much better for them to advise the government to spend all the money which goes on supporting bishops and priests to pay off the crown debt, in case the taxes become too heavy for the common people to bear, the result of which would be sad for many who love the prosperity of the country and the peace of the kingdom. – From the depth of my heart I love peace and wish well to every man. – It is my duty, as a Christian, to feed my enemy and I think that doing so would be my favourite task – but it must be given up. I hear the awful thunder yonder, and considering how unhealthy our air has been for a long time, I fear that the storm will break above my head. *Let us flee to the sanctuary.* – Farewell, publishers and Distributors of Knowledge. If as much as this will find a place in your third number, you will possibly hear again from PHILO RECTUM.

*7.8 America's example to the world*

*Cylchgrawn Cymraeg: Neu, Drysorfa Gwybodaeth.* Am Awst 1793 (Rhifyn III) (Welsh Magazine: Or, Treasury of Knowledge. For August 1793 [Number III]), 164–6.

*Ychydig o Ddesgrifiad* KENTUCKY, *y Dalaith newydd yn* AMERICA.[81]

. . . *Yr oedd un pregethwr mawr, yn ddiweddar, yn Llundain, yn dywedyd fel hyn,* "Fod yr happusrwydd o ddysgu i'r byd y gwersi pwysig canlynol yn perthyn i Unol lywodraeth America."

1. "Fod yn bossibl i wlad fawr ac chang gael ei llywodraethu gan drefn wladwriaethol heb un *monarch* nac arglwyddiaeth."
2. "Fod yn hawdd cynnal addoliad cyhoeddus heb un grefydd sefydledig; ac mai gadael pawb i farnu drostynt eu hunain mewn achosion crefyddol, ac addoli Duw yn ol goleuni eu cydwybodau eu hunain, yw'r ddoeth ineb fwyaf."
3. "Mai gosod pawb enwau (neu sectau) yn gyd-radd yw'r ffordd gyntaf i ddinystrio pob math o genfigen, cynnen, rhagfarn, erledigaeth, ac anioddefgarwch – ac i dueddu dynion yn effeithiol i blannu heddwch, cariad, ac ewyllys da yn y wladwriaeth."
4. "Gall eglwys a gwladwriaeth (*church and state*) eill dau, fod a llwyddo, heb eu cyssylltu a'u cymmysgu â'u gilydd, am fod prawf wedi ei gael y dichon llywodraeth ddinasaidd fyw heb un cynnorthwy oddiwrth yr eglwys."
5. "Fod newid y gosp o ddihenyddiad, i waith caled, a charcharu, yn tueddu i attal drygioni yn llawer gwell nâ chospi dynion â marwolaeth braidd am bob bai."
6. "Pa fwyaf tyner a chyfiawn y byddo llywodraeth, mwyaf dedwydd a boddlon y bydd y bobl; a bod y fath lywodraeth nid yn wanach, eithr yn gadarnach ac yn fwy effeithiol nâ'r lywodraeth ormesol, ac nid mewn cymmaint o berygl i gael ei dadymchwelyd." Ac yn –
7. "Fod derbyn yr Iuddewon i freintiau dinasyddion eraill ymhell oddi wrth fod yn niweidiol, fel y bernyd gynt."

"Nid yw hyn," meddai'n hawdwr, "ond ychydig o'r gwersi rhagorol ag y mae'r *Unol-lywodraeth* wedi ei ddysgu i ddynolryw;" ac y mae'n gorfoleddu wrth feddwl am yr amser, ac yn gobeithio nad yw ymhell,

"Pan y byddo'r holl fyd i ddysgu ac ymarferyd y gwersi hyn yn fwy perffaith nac y maent etto yn *America* ei hun." –Y mae'n ymfawrhau fod *America* yn enedigol wlad iddo, y wlad gyntaf fydd wedi sefydlu gwir ryddid crefyddol a dinasaidd, ar sail cyfiawnder a gogyfuwchder o ran breintiau*. –

(*A little bit of a Description of* KENTUCKY, *the new State in* AMERICA.[81]

. . . *A great preacher recently said the following in London*, "That the blessedness of teaching the world the following important lessons pertains to the United government of America."

1. "That it is possible for a big and wide country to be governed by a republican system without any *monarch* or aristocracy."
2. "That it is easy to sustain public worship without any established religion; and that it is wisest to leave everybody to judge for themselves in religious matters and to worship God according to the light of their own consciences."
3. "That making every denomination (or sect) equal is the best way of destroying all manner of envy, strife, prejudice, persecution and intolerance – and to incline men effectively to plant peace, love and good will in the state."
4. "That church and state can both exist and succeed without linking and mixing them together, as proof has now been had that a civil government can live without any assistance from the church."
5. "That changing the punishment of execution to hard labour and imprisonment tends to prevent evil much better than punishing men with death for almost every misdemeanour."
6. "That the gentler and more just a government, the happier and the more contented the people will be; and that this kind of government is not weaker, but stronger and more effective than an oppressive government, and not in as much danger of being overthrown." And –
7. "That receiving the Jews into the rights of other citizens is far from being harmful, as was formerly judged."

"These are," says our author, "only some of the excellent lessons which the *United-government* has taught mankind;" and he rejoices in thinking of the time and hoping that it is not far off,

"When the whole world will learn and practise these lessons more perfectly than they are yet in *America* itself." – He prides himself that *America* is his native country, the first country which will have established true

* See an Oration on the Discovery of America, By Elhanan Winchester. – This was taken from the Gentleman's Mag. for May 1793.

religious and political liberty on the basis of justice and equality as regards rights.* –)

### *7.9 Home and foreign news*

*Cylchgrawn Cymraeg: Neu, Drysorfa Gwybodaeth.* Am Awst 1793 (Rhifyn III) (Welsh Magazine: Or, Treasury of Knowledge. For August 1793 [Number III]), 178–84.

NEWYDDION PELLENIG A CHARTREFOL.

DAETH can myrddiwn un cant a deugain o filoedd, a dau cant a phymtheg a deugain o *fwsheli* o lafur, y rhan fwyaf yn wenith, o *America Ogleddol* i *Frydain* y flwyddyn ddiweddaf.

Daeth hefyd un myrddiwn pedwar cant a thrugain a naw o filoedd, a saith cant ac ugain o *fareli* o gann (*flour*) ynghyd â biscuit, rice, &c. Daeth hefyd beth anferth o bob math o goed, wedi eu llifo, ac heb eu llifo, a llawer iawn o gig moch, a chig eidion, &c. Y mae hyn, gyd â llawer o bethau eraill, yn dangos llwyddiant neillduol y wlad honno. *Star.*

Yn yr eisteddfod ddiweddar, yn nhre' *Derby*, dygwyd dau ddyn ger bron y llys am werthu gwaith Mr. *Paine* ar Ddynol Hawl (*Rights of Man.*) Mynnodd y rheithwyr (*jury*) ddarllain y llyfr, a chwedi ei ystyried yn fanol, barnasant nad oedd y gwerthwyr yn euog. – *Not guilty.*

Dygwyd gwr yn *Llundain*, (Mr. *Wood*) o flaen y llys, am argraphu annerchiad *Paine* at yr annerchwyr:[82] – cafodd y rheithwyr eu hanfon gan arglwydd *Kenyon* ddwy waith i ystyried yr achos, a chwedi aros yn hir bob tro, barnasant fod y dyn yn euog o argraphu'r llyfr, eithr nad oedd yn euog o un gosp. Er bod rhai'n cael myned yn rhydd, y mae llawer yn cael eu carcharu am argraphu a gwerthu gwaith y gwr uchod.

Dywedir fod y rhyfel presennol yn sefyll i'r deyrnas hon mewn pymtheg cant o bynnau bob awr, yr hyn sydd yn un fil ar bymtheg ar ugain o bynnau yn y dydd, ac yn dair myrddiwn ar ddeg ac un cant a deugain o filoedd yn y flwyddyn. – Pe b'ai ond para un flwyddyn, hi fydd wedi gosod chwech can mil o bynnau yn y flwyddyn o dreth ar y deyrnas hon dros byth. Dyma'r fendith o fyned i ryfel!

Mae hanes arall yn dywedyd, fod pedwar ugain a deg o filoedd o *guineas* caled yn myned allan o'r deyrnas bob dydd at gynnal y byddinoedd sy'n

* See an Oration on the Discovery of America, By Elhanan Winchester. – This was taken from the Gentleman's Mag. for May 1793.

ymladd yn erbyn *Ffraingc*: nid yw ddim yn ddigon i *Frydain* gynnal ei byddinoedd ei hun, ond rhaid cynnal byddinoedd brenin *Sardinia*, a'r *Hanofeiriaid*, a thywysog *Hesse Cassel*, &c.

Dywedir i un o *spies Lloegr* gael ei ddal yn *Ffraingc* a pheth anferth o arian gyd ag ef, i'w rhannu rhwng y bobl aflonydd yn *Ffraingc*, i'r diben i geisio dadymchwelyd y llywodraeth newydd; ac y maent wedi cyhoeddi yn senedd *Paris*, fod *Pitt* yn elyn dynolryw.

Y mae *Marrat*, un o aelodau'r senedd-dŷ (*convention*) yn *Paris* wedi ei ladd gan *Sharlette Corde*,[83] benyw hŷ, a ddaeth o *Normandy* gyd â bwriad i'w ddihenyddio, am ei fod yn elyn brenhinoedd: cyflwynwyd hi atto fel pe buasai ar neges, a hi a'i brathodd â chyllell fel y bu farw. Yr ydoedd yn gorfoleddu yn y weithred, am ei bod wedi achub ei gwlad oddiwrth ddyn ag oedd wedi bod yn achos, meddai hi, a llawer eraill, o ran fawr o'r terfysg a'r creulondeb yn *Ffraingc*. Tra fu yn y carchar, ac o flaen y barnwr, ymddygodd gyd âr gwroldeb mwyaf: yr oedd, hyd yn oed, ei golwg yn peri syndod i bawb. Wedi ei chondemnio aeth gyd â sirioldeb ryfedd i'r *scaffold*, i gael torri ei phen gan y *gullotine*; math o gyllell fawr, wrth *spring*, at dorri pennau dynion o bwrpas yn *Ffraingc* – Yr oedd y *Marrat* hwn, mae'n debyg yn un o'r *Jacobins** mwyaf yn Paris ac, o bossibl, yn dymuno'n dda i'r wlad.

Dywedir fod terfysg anghyffredin ymhlith y *Ffrangcod* yn ddiweddar, eu bod mor rannedig yn eu plith eu hunain, fel na wyddant yn iawn beth i'w wneud – Y mae *Gaston*[84] a'i fyddin yn *Llydaw Brittany*, yn para i waeddi am frenin; ac er iddynt gael brwydr ddrwg unwaith neu ddwy, a lladd peth garw o honynt, y maent, drachefn, wedi adfywio a churo'r gwladwriaethwyr (*republicans*) yn lew. – Y mae trigolion *Marseilles*, tre' fawr ar lan môr y Canoldir, wedi codi yn erbyn y senedd yn Paris, a llawer eraill gyd â hwynt, am eu bod wedi carcharu'r dynion doethaf meddant, a mwyaf tyner yn y senedd-dŷ. – Y mae'r rhai'n a'r penciwdawd *Wimpfen*,[85] yn meddwl sobru rhai o honynt. – Tra maent fel hyn yn lladd eu gilydd gartref, mae holl bwerau *Ewrop* yn eu herbyn, oddieithr y *Daniaid*, a'r *Swedeniaid*, a'r Duc o *Tuscany*. Y mae'r byddinoedd cyssylltiedig yn dywedyd, fod yn rhaid i'r diweddaf uno â hwynt. Y mae'r *Spaniaid* wedi dyfod i mewn i *Ffraingc*, ac y mae byddinoedd cyssylltiedig *Germani*, *Prwsia*, *Holland*, a *Lloegr*, gwedi cymmeryd tair tre' oddi arnynt yn ddiweddar, sef *Conde*, *Mentz*, a *Valensiens*; trefydd caerog cadarn, a safasant yn hir i ryfeddu yn erbyn cynnifer o elynion. – Bu'r cyntaf agos a newynu cyn rhoi fynu, a bu lladdfa dynion echrydus o flaen yr ail – Cafodd y drydedd ei chwilfriwio'n erchyll, a'i llosgi, y rhan

* Y mae'r *Jacobins* yn cael eu galw felly am eu bod yn cyfarfod mewn eglwys ag oedd gynt yn perthyn i'r *Jacobin Convent*, lle'r oedd sect o Bapistiaid; ond yn y cyfnewidiad, fe'u rhoddwyd fel lle i ddadleu am achos y deyrnas, &c. Mae llefydd o'r fath ymhob tre' yn *Ffraingc* ar y cyfnewidiad, *revolution*.

fwyaf, gan dân gwyllt, cyn ildo i'r byddinoedd oedd yn ei hamgylchynu; o'r diwedd rhoddodd i fynu ar dilerau anrhydeddus, i'r Duc o *York*, ail fab ein brenin. –Y mae ef a'i fyddin yn awr yn *Ffraingc*, yn meddwl myned i wersyllu *Dunkirk*, tre' fawr arall, ar gyfer afon *Llundain*. Yn awr yw'r pryd i'w byddinoedd cyssylltiedig i wneud eu goreu i ddifetha *Ffraingc*; canys os gall y Ffrangcod ond dala ychydig o fisoedd yn hwy, o bossibl yr unant â'u gilydd, ac yna fe fydd mor anhawdd eu gorchfygu, ag attal yr haul i godi. Y cwbl sydd i'w ddywedyd, ac a ddymunem ni ei ddweud mewn perthynas i'r rhyfel rhyfeddol hwn, yw, "Yr Arglwydd sydd yn teyrnasu," Efe sydd Wr o ryfel, ac y mae lle i feddwl y rhyfela ef yn y diwedd o blaid y cyfiawn, er y gall y diniweid ddioddef llawer. Dyledswydd y Cymry, fel pob cenedl arall, yw deffroi i gyfiawnder, ac ystyried yn ddwys, pa un a ydyw'r barn yn hongian uwch eu pen hwythau ai peidio; nid beio a melldithio'r *Ffrangcod*, ond ymgadw rhag bod yn euog o'u pechodau, a diwygio'n bucheddau yw'r ffordd i ymgadw rhag y gospedigaeth. Mae'n sicr na all y deyrnas hon ddim dihangyd rhag barn Duw, os na edifarha a diwygio ar frys: nid oes un ffordd arall wedi adael trwy ba un mae'n rhaid i ni fod yn gadwedig.

Y mae'r *Cwaceriaid*, wrth roi hanes eu herledigaeth, yn dywedyd, Fod saith mil a saith cant a naw o bynnau wedi eu cymmeryd ar gam oddi wrthynt y flwyddyn ddiweddaf yn *Mrydain* a'r *Iwerddon*, a hynny gan mwyaf at wasanaeth eglwys *Loegr*. Y mae'r corph hyn yn ystyried pob math o dreth a osodir arnynt at wasanaeth yr eglwys yn erledigaeth, ac yn neillduol y degwm, ni fynnant ei dalu er neb; eu hatteb i'r offeiriad yn gyffredin yw, Dim gwaith, dim tâl: *No work, no pay*; hynny yw, nid ydynt yn gweithio dim iddynt hwy; ac am hynny, y maent yn barnu, y dylai pob meistr dalu ei was ei hun.

Daeth newydd fod y *Ffrangcod* yn curo'r *Spaniaid* yn ddrwg. Nid yw ddim yn wir fod y frenhines a mab y brenin wedi eu lladd.

Y mae rhai o'r *Gwyddelod* wedi bod yn anesmwyth o blegid y trethi a'r degymmau, &c. Cododd llawer o'r gwerinos mewn un man, a derw i'r milwyr ladd llawer o honynt; yr ydys yn ofni, na fydd y *Gwyddelod* ddim yn esmwyth yn hir iawn, heb ragor o ryddid – Y mae'r Papistiaid wedi cael llawer rhagor o ryddid yn y flwyddyn ddiweddaf nag o'r blaen, fel y maent yn bresennol mewn gwell sefyllfa nâ'r Ymneillduwyr yn y deyrnas hon; etto i gyd nid oes dim lle i feddwl y gorphwysant ne's byddont ogyfuwch mewn breintiau â'r Protestaniaid. Nid oes un ffordd i ddinystrio eiddigedd a chynnen, heb osod pob plaid o grefyddwyr ogyfuwch eu braint yng olwg y llywodraeth.

Daeth y newydd i mewn heddyw, *Awst* 21, 1793, fod yr Americaniaid yn debyg o uno â'r *Ffrangcod* yn y rhyfel presennol; os felly, fe fydd miloedd etto allan o waith, a'r deyrnas hon yn debyg o fod yn prysuro i'w dinystr ei hun. Pwy na weddia, Yr Arglwydd a roddo heddwch?

Daeth y newydd hefyd fod y gwrthryfelwyr yn *Llydaw Brittany*, wedi cael y gwaethaf, a bod penciwdawd *Wimpfen* wedi ffoi, a'i fyddin wedi gwasgaru; bod y *Ffrangcod* yn uno i dderbyn y sefydliad, (*constitution*) newydd; bod pob peth wedi digwydd yn dawel yno, y degfed o *Awst*, pan oedd y cenhadau yn cyfarfod i wneud coffadwriaeth o'r cyfnewidiad a gymmerodd le y flwyddyn ddiweddaf.[86] Y mae'r llythyr a gafwyd yn *Ffraingc*, oddiwrth *Pitt*, wedi cynhyrfu senedd *Paris* yn anghyffredin: y maent yn dywedyd fod llywodraeth Lloegr yn ymddwyn yn deilwng o fwrddwyr tu ag attynt, trwy hirio cynnifer o ddynion yn ddirgelaidd i yrru'r wlad ben-ben, ac i ladd eu gilydd. Os ydyw'r hanes yn wir, mae'n waradwydd i ddynoliaeth fod neb yn ymarferyd â'r fath ddichellion, hyd yn oed i ddinystrio eu gelynion.

(FOREIGN AND HOME NEWS.

ONE hundred million one hundred and forty thousand and two hundred and fifty-five *bushels* of grain, the greater part of it wheat, came from *North America* to *Britain* last year.

There also came one million four hundred and sixty-nine thousand and seven hundred and twenty barrels of *flour* together with biscuit, rice, &c. There also came huge quantities of all kinds of sawn and unsawn wood, and much pork, beef, &c. This and many other things show the great prosperity of that country. *Star.*

In the recent session in the town of *Derby*, two men were brought before the court for selling the work of Mr. *Paine* on *Rights of Man*. The jury insisted on reading the book, and having considered it in detail, judged that the sellers were *Not guilty*.

A man in *London* (Mr. *Wood*) was brought before the court for printing *Paine*'s address to the addressers:[82] – twice the jury was sent by Lord *Kenyon* to consider the case, and having tarried long each time, they judged that the man was guilty of printing the book, but that he did not deserve any punishment. Although some go free, many are imprisoned for printing and selling the works of the above man.

It is said that the present war costs this kingdom fifteen hundred pounds every hour, which is thirty-six thousand pounds a day, and thirteen million one hundred and forty thousand a year. – If it lasts only a year, it will have placed six hundred thousand pounds of tax on this kingdom forever. This is the blessing of going to war!

Another story says that ninety thousand hard *guineas* leave the kingdom every day to sustain the armies which are fighting against *France*: it is not enough for *Britain* to sustain its own armies, but it must sustain the armies of the king of *Sardinia*, the *Hanoverians*, and the prince of *Hesse Cassel*, &c.

It is said that one of the *English spies* was caught in *France* with an enormous sum of money on him to share between the discontented people in *France*, with the aim of trying to overthrow the new government; and in the convention in *Paris* they have declared Pitt an enemy of mankind.

*Marrat*, one of the members of the convention in *Paris*, has been killed by *Sharlette Corde*[83] an audacious woman who came from *Normandy* with the intention of assassinating him because he was an enemy of kings: she was introduced to him as if she had a message, and she stabbed him with a knife so that he died. She rejoiced in the deed, because she had saved her country from a man who had been the cause, so said she and many others, of a great part of the disturbances and the cruelty in *France*. While she was in prison and before the judge, she behaved with the utmost courage: even her appearance surprised everybody. Having been condemned she went to the *scaffold* with remarkable cheerfulness to have her head cut off by the *guillotine*; a kind of large knife attached to a spring, designed for cutting off people's heads in *France* – This *Marrat* is said to have been one of the foremost *Jacobins** in Paris and possibly meant well for the country.

It is said that there has been extraordinary disorder among the *French* recently, that they are so divided among themselves that they do not know what to do. – *Gaston*[84] and his army in *Brittany* continue to shout for a king; and though they had a bad battle once or twice, and an awful number of them were killed, they have revived again and beaten the republicans valiantly. – The inhabitants of *Marseilles*, a large town on the coast of the Mediterranean, have risen against the convention in Paris, and many others with them, because they have imprisoned the wisest, they say, and most humane men of the convention. – These and the general *Wimpfen*[85] intend to sober some of them up. – While they kill each other like this at home, all the powers of *Europe* are against them, except the *Danes*, the *Swedes* and the Duke of *Tuscany*. The allied armies say that the latter must join them. The *Spaniards* have progressed into *France*, and the allied armies of *Germany*, *Prussia*, *Holland* and *England* have taken three towns from them recently, namely *Conde*, *Mentz*, and *Valenciennes*; strongly fortified towns which withstood such a large number of enemies astonishingly long. – The first nearly starved before giving up, and there was a dreadful slaughter of men before the second – The third was battered terribly and the larger part burnt by

* The *Jacobins* are so called because they meet in a church which formerly belonged to the *Jacobin Convent* of a sect of Papists; but in the revolution it was put as a place to discuss matters of the realm &c. Such places exist in every town in *France* since the revolution.

a raging fire, before yielding to the armies which were surrounding it; in the end it capitulated to the Duke of *York*, the second son of our king, on honourable terms. – He and his army are now in *France*, planning to besiege *Dunkirk*, another large town opposite the river of *London*. Now is the time for the allied armies to do their best to destroy *France*; because if the *French* can but hold out a few more months, perhaps they will unite with each other and then it will be as difficult to overcome them as it would be to prevent the sun from rising. All that is to be said and that we wish to say about this remarkable war is, "The Lord reigns," He is a Man of war, and there is reason to believe that in the end he will wage war on behalf of the just, although the innocent may suffer much. The duty of the Welsh, like every other nation, is to wake up to justice, and to consider earnestly whether or not the judgement hangs over their heads; not to blame and curse the *French*, but to refrain from being guilty of their sins, and to reform our lives is the way to avoid the punishment. It is certain that this kingdom cannot escape God's judgement if it does not repent and reform in haste: there is no other way left through which we must be saved.

The *Quakers*, giving an account of their persecution, say that seven thousand seven hundred and nine pounds were wrongly taken from them last year in *Britain* and *Ireland*, and this mainly for the use of the church of *England*. This body considers every kind of tax which is placed on them for the use of the church as persecution, and particularly the tithe, which they do not wish to pay on any account; generally, their answer to the priests is, No work, no pay; that is, they don't do anything for them and therefore they judge that every master should pay his own servant.

News came that the *French* have badly defeated the *Spanish*. It is not true that the queen and the king's son have been killed.

Some of the *Irish* have been restless because of the taxes, the tithes, &c. In one place many of the common people rose up and the soldiers killed many of them; it is feared that the *Irish* will not be calm for long without more liberty – The Papists have gained much more liberty in the last year than before, so that they are at present in a better position than the Dissenters in this kingdom; but still there is no reason to think that they will rest until they have equal status with the Protestants. Jealousy and strife may not be vanquished without giving every religious sect equal status in the eyes of the government.

Today, *August* 21, 1793, news came in that the Americans are likely to join the *French* side in the present war; if so, thousands more will be out of work, and this kingdom is likely to hasten towards its own destruction. Who would not pray, may The Lord grant peace?

News also came that the rebels in *Brittany* have been defeated, and that general *Wimpfen* has fled and his army has dispersed; that the *French* are uniting to accept the new constitution; that everything has happened quietly there, on the tenth of *August* when the representatives met to commemorate the revolution which took place last year.[86] The letter from *Pitt* which was received in *France* has infuriated the convention in *Paris* uncommonly: they say that the government of England, by secretly hiring so many men to foment civil war in the country so that they kill each other, is behaving in a manner worthy of murderers towards them. If this story is true, then it is a disgrace to mankind that anyone should employ such plots, even to destroy their enemies.)

### *7.10 A poem denouncing the traitor Dumourier*

*Cylchgrawn Cymraeg: Neu Drysorfa Gwybodaeth* (Rhifyn IV) (Welsh Magazine: Or, Treasury of Knowledge [Number IV]) (1793), 234.

YSGRIFEN-FEDD (*Epitaph*) i'r Bradwr DUMOURIER.[87]

Y Diras Suddas⊥ a soddir – i warth,
A'i wyrthiau ni chofir;
Y filain mwy ni folir;
I'r dom yr a DUMORIR.

'Sgrifen ei dommen* fydd, 'Dyma – ngwely
Oer, gwaeledd, lle pydra;
Sa' draw, can oes y drewa;
Cerdd o'r plwy rhag cwrdd â'r pla.'

(EPITAPH to the Traitor DUMOURIER.[87]

The Wicked Judas will be sunk in shame,
and his virtues will not be remembered;
the villain will no longer be praised;
DUMORIR will go to the dung-heap.

⊥ Judas.

* Tumulus, tomb, and tommen, are derived from the same root, and bear the same signification.

The writing on his tomb will be, 'Here is my bed
cold and wretched, where I rot;
keep away, I will stink for a hundred ages;
go from this parish lest you catch the plague.')

### *7.11 The execution of Marie Antoinette*

*Cylchgrawn Cymraeg: Neu Drysorfa Gwybodaeth* (Rhifyn IV) (Welsh Magazine: Or, Treasury of Knowledge [Number IV]) (1793), 237–8.

DIHENYDDIAD BRENHINES FFRAINGC.

Y Dywysoges anffortenus hon a ddioddefodd dan gyllell y guillotine dydd merchur yr unfed ar bymtheg o Hydref. Gwedi cael ei chondemnio'r dydd gynt ger bron y frawdle yn Paris, fel *yn euog o gydfwriadu a chyd-weithredu mewn amrywiol bethau dichellgar yn erbyn rhyddid Ffraingc; – o fod yn cadw cyngweddiad â gelynion y wladwriaeth; – o fod yn gyfrannog mewn bradwriaeth i gyfodi rhyfel ddinasaidd ynghalon y wladwriaeth, trwy arfogi dinasyddion yn erbyn eu gilydd.*

Llawer iawn o bethau eraill, rhy faith i ni eu gosod i lawr, a osodwyd yn erbyn Marie Antoinette, o Loraine ac Austria, a gweddw Louis Capet, (fel y geilw'r Ffrangcod hi). Yr oedd y cyhyddwr yn dwyn y cwbl a wyddai am dani (os nid ragor) er dechreu'r cyfnewidiad; fel y diafol, fe fedrai goffa ei beiau i gyd o'i mhebyd, ond nid oedd gyd ag ef un drugaredd i roddi iddi. Y mae'n sicr wrth yr hanes gyffredin ei bod yn fenyw falch ormesol, ac yn cael ei chasau gan y rhan fwyaf o'u hen ddeiliaid; etto i gyd, fe debygsid, mai peth doeth a chanmoladwy a fuasai i'r Ffrangcod roi trugaredd iddi hi a'i gwr. Ond mae'n debyg fod rhyw law oruchel yn gwaeddi, Dial! dial! o bossibl, ar yr holl deulu.

Y mae'r Duc de Orleans, cefnder y brenin, wedi cael torri ei ben ar ol y frenhines, a'i holl feddianau, y rhai gynt oedd yn werth cant a hanner o filoedd o bunau, yn y flwyddyn, wedi eu cymmeryd at ddefnydd y llywodraeth.

Daeth Mr. Erskine, yr hwn oeddem yn ei ddisgwyl er's talm, o Rufain, i Lundain, dydd Iau'r 14 o'r mis hwn, â diolchgarwch y llys pabaidd i'r deyrnas hon am uno yn y rhyfel yn erbyn Ffraingc. – *Star.*

Y mae'r newyddion diweddaf o Ffraingc yn gosod allan greulondeb y blaid sydd yn llywodraethu yno'n bresennol, mewn modd arswydus: y mae'n sicr na all neb eu hymddiffyn. Yr unig beth y gall dynion ymgysuro ynddo yw hyn, na pharhaodd un lywodraeth greulon yn hir erioed: y mae yn difetha ei hun. Y cwbl a ellir ei ddywedyd am eu creulondeb yw, eu bod yn offerynau cymmwys i ddiwreiddio pabyddiaeth o'r byd; ac y mae'n ddigon tebyg mai hwynt yw'r bobl y mae'r Hollalluog wedi godi i hynny.

Y mae'r offeiriaid yn Ffraingc yn rhoi i fynu eu swyddau yn feunyddiol. Y maent yn ysgrifennu at y senedd na thwyllant ddim o'r bobl mwyach; eu bod yn ddigon hir yn gaeth-weision i goel-grefydd eu hunain; eu bod yn awr yn gweled yn eglur, nad oes dim a all foddio Duw ond gwneuthur cyfiawnder a hoffi trugaredd; eu bod yn rhoddi i fynu eu holl elw eglwysaidd, ac yn myned i fyw fel dynion eraill.

Y mae peth anferthol o seintiau aur ac arian, &c. yn cael eu hanfon o'r holl eglwysi, trwy Ffraingc, i'r fathfa, (*mint*) i gael eu gwneud yn arian at gynnal y rhyfel.

(THE EXECUTION OF THE QUEEN OF FRANCE.

THIS unfortunate Princess suffered under the knife of the guillotine on Wednesday, the sixteenth October. The day before, she had been condemned before the court in Paris, and found *guilty of conspiring and collaborating in various nefarious schemes against the liberty of France; – of communicating with the enemies of the republic; – of participating in treason to raise civil war in the heart of the republic by arming citizens against each other.*

Many other things, too many for us to set down here, were brought against Marie Antoinette of Lorraine and Austria, and the widow of Louis Capet, (as the French call her). The prosecutor brought up everything he knew about her (if not more) since the beginning of the revolution; like the devil he was able to remember all her vices from her childhood, but he did not show her any mercy. It is certain according to the common account that she was a proud and tyrannical woman, who was hated by the majority of her former subjects; nevertheless, it would surely have been wise and praiseworthy if the French had shown her and her husband mercy. But it is likely that some divine authority is calling, Revenge! revenge! perhaps on the whole family.

The Duke of Orleans, the king's cousin, had his head cut off after the queen, and all his estate, which was worth a hundred and fifty thousand pounds a year, has been taken for the use of the government.

Mr. Erskine, whom we had expected for a long time, came from Rome to London on Thursday 14 of this month, with the gratitude of the papal court to this kingdom for joining in the war against France. – *Star.*

The latest news from France sets out the cruelty of the party which governs there at present in a terrible manner: it is certain that no one can defend them. People can only find comfort in the knowledge that no cruel government ever lasted long: it destroys itself. All that can be said about their cruelty is that they are suitable instruments of eradicating papism from the world; and that it is likely that they are the people the Almighty has raised up for this purpose.

The priests in France are daily giving up their offices. They are writing to the convention that they will no longer deceive the people; that they themselves have been slaves to superstition long enough; that they see clearly now that nothing can please God but to do justice and to cherish mercy; that they are giving up all their church profits and are going to live like other people.

An enormous number of gold and silver saints, &c., are being sent from all the churches throughout France to the mint in order to create money to support the war.)

## *7.12 The demise of the periodical*

*Welsh Magazine. Y Cylchgrawn; Neu Drysorfa Gwybodaeth*, Am Ionawr a Chwefror (For January and February) 1794, i–ii.

*Y Cyhoeddwyr at eu Gohebwyr, a'r Cymry'n gyffredin.*

Gydwladwyr hynaws gwnaethom ein goreu ar eich gwasanaethu'n ddiduedd dros y flwyddyn a aeth heibio; ond o ddiffyg cael yr annogaeth ofynnol yn y rhifyn diweddaf, sef digon o rhagdalwyr i'n cynnorthwyo i fyned trwy draul yr argraffwasg, rhaid rhoi i fynu, er maint ein hawydd i wasanaethu, ac amcanyd goleuo'n cydgreaduriaid. Dywedwyd am weddw gynt, "yr hyn a allodd hon hi a'i gwnaeth." Felly ninnau ymdrechasom i ddosparthu'r Cylchgrawn mor gyflawn ac y medrem trwy Gymru, etto i gyd fe fethwyd ei anfon i lawer parth o eisiau cyfleusdra. Os gellir trefnyd rhyw ffordd i gyflwyno'r fath lyfr gyd a brys trwy'r Gogledd a'r Dê, o bosibl y bydd i ryw rai sy'n caru eu gwlad, i fyned ynghyd a'r gorchwyl o argraffu COFIADUR CYMRAEG, pris *Tair Ceiniog*, i'w ddosparthu bob pythefnos yn y Deheudir, a phob mis trwy'r Gogledd, pris *Chwe' Cheiniog*. – Os ceir annogaeth i argraffu'r fath lyfr a hwn, dealled y Cymro mae Hanesion, Newyddion a Dadleuon y Senedd fydd ei gynnwysiad, ynghyd a rhyw ychydig o Farddoniaeth ac a fyddo'n gymmwysiadol at yr amserau. Bydded i'r Cymry ystyried yr amnaid hon, a deffroi i gynnorthwyo'r fath orchwyl; a chofied pawb, os aiff y gwaith ymlaen, na fydd dim dadleuon crefyddol i gael lle ynddo, ond pob math o hanesion am rhyfeloedd, &c. &c. fel y byddo'r Cymro'n cael ei gadw'n fyw i ystyried Arwyddion yr Amserau, ac i farnu drosto ei hun, beth sydd uniawn. Os ceir dynion ffyddlon yn amryw barthau Cymru, a attebo am gynnifer o'r *Cofiadur* dros flwyddyn, ag a ddigolledo'r Goruchwilwyr, y mae'n debyg y bydd rhai yn Nghaerfyrddin yn barod i fyned â'r gwaith ymlaen. – Fe dderbyn y dosparthwyr presennol enwau, ac fe dderbynir llythyrau digost yn ddiolchgar, ond eu cyfarwyddo *To the Editors of the* WELSH REMEMBRANCER, *Carmarthen.*

Y mae'n ddrwg gan Gyhoeddwyr y Cylchgrawn eu bod wedi gorfod gadael cynnifer o lythyrau eu Gohebwyr heb eu hargraffu, daeth rhai o honynt i mewn yn rhy ddiweddar – megis Pryssur heb Ddiolch a Thrafferth heb Gais. – Gwrthododd yr argraffydd eraill megis Cywydd ar Gyflwr Brydain, ac Atteb dysgedig a chywrain G. Owen i Tudur Glustfain a Bleddyn fin pladur o eisiau llythyrennau Groeg, &c. Gwrthodwyd Voltaire ar Rhyfel am fod y Deist yn dweud gormod o wir ar y rhith grist'nogion. – Y mae Siamas Wynedd a'i Bregethwr Bol-clawdd[88] wedi bod yn agos a thynnu'r wlad yn ein pen, er hynny ni chawsom ond un atteb iddo, yr hwn sydd yn trin Siamas o'i goryn i'w sawdl fel na edrych'sai cigfran arno mwy; pe buasem yn argraffu y llythyr sydd yn amddiffyn y pregethwyr bol-clawdd, ac yn galw'r hwn sydd yn ei beio yn flaidd rheibus a bwystfil bol-gorddiog. Yr ydym hefyd wedi derbyn cosfa erchyll i Siamas oddi wrth ei hen gyfaill *moesol*; am roddi lle i Araith y Brenin ac Areithiau Seneddwyr, gorfod arnom adael eraill ar ol – Japheth bump synwyr a Gomer ddau sens –[89] Chwedlau Callineb – Llythyr Philadelphus – Ail Lythyr R. E. Caernarfon – Hanes Astronomyddiaeth &c. a gollwyd o ddwylaw'r argraffydd – Yr oedd Credo Emanuel Swedenbourg[90] yn rhy hir i gael yn bresennol, felly'r oedd Cywydd Prydydd hir pan yn nhir Cent –[91] Gorphwysodd y Llythyr a'r Cywydd ac sy'n ymbil am un o Fiblau mawr y Parch. Mr. Peter Williams,[92] yn llaw'r argraffydd ynghyd a Hanes o holl Argraffiadau'r Bibl Gymraeg. Y mae amrywiol bethau eraill mewn llaw gan y Goruchwilwyr. Dylai Llythyr W. W. gael ei argraffu'n llyfr Bychan; a Derbyniasant yn ddiweddar ddau Lyfr mewn hen 'sgrifen, yn cynnwys rhan fawr o hanes yr hen Gymry, er pan ddaethant gyntaf i'r ynys hon. Pe buasent yn cael annogaeth i fyned a'r gwaith ymlaen, gallasai rhoi llawer o ddywenydd i'r hen Frython. O bosibl gall rhai o'r erthyglau uchod gael lle yn y *Cofiadur Cymraeg*. Gan ddymuno pob llwyddiant i'r cyfryw waith i fyned ymlaen, yr ydym yn terfynu, gan gymmeryd ein cennad mewn modd diolchgar oddiwrth y cyffredin am ddim cymmorth a gawsom, gan y rhan hynaws o honynt. – Gan brinder amser y mae'r Cyhoeddwyr yn gorfod dymuno i'r Darllenydd ddiwygio dim gwallau ag a welo a'i bin ysgrifennu.

*(The Publishers to their Correspondents, and the Welsh in general.*

Genial compatriots, we did our best to serve you impartially over the year which has gone by; but for want of getting the necessary encouragement for the last number, that is enough subscribers to to help us defray the cost of publishing, we must give up, despite our great desire to serve and our intent to enlighten our fellow creatures. It was once said of a widow, "she did what she could." Thus we, too, strove to distribute the Magazine as fully as we could throughout Wales, yet for want of expediency, we failed to send it to many areas. If some way of speedily distributing this kind of book throughout the North and the South can be organized, some who love their country may go ahead with the undertaking of printing a WELSH REMEMBRANCER, price *Three Pence*, to be distributed every fortnight in the South, and every month in the North, price *Six Pence*. – If encouragement to publish this kind of book is met with, the Welshman may assume that its content will be true Accounts, News and Parliamentary debates, together with a little Poetry appropriate for the times. Let the Welsh heed this signal and wake up to assist this kind of undertaking; and let each remember that if the work does go ahead, religious debates will have no place in it, but rather all manner of accounts of wars, &c. &c. so that the Welshman will be kept abreast to heed the Signs of the Times and to judge for himself what is right. If faithful men can be found in the various parts of Wales, who would be answerable for as many copies of the *Remembrancer* over a year as would reimburse the Editors, it is likely that some in Carmarthen will be prepared to go ahead with the project. – The present distributors will gratefully receive names and franked letters, as long as they are addressed *To the Editors of the* WELSH REMEMBRANCER, *Carmarthen*.

The Publishers of the Magazine are sorry that they have had to leave so many of their Correspondents' letters unpublished. Some of them came in too late – like Busy without Thanks and Trouble without Seeking. – The publisher refused others, such as the *Cywydd* on the State of Britain, and G. Owen's learned and and subtle Answer to Tudur Eavesdrop and Bleddyn scythe-edge for want of Greek letters, &c. Voltaire on War was refused, because the Deist pronounced too much truth on the pretend Christians. – Siamas Wynedd and his Hedgerow Preacher[88] have nearly set the whole country against us, though we only had one answer to it, which dresses Siamas down from head to toe so that not even a raven would look at him anymore if we published the letter, which defends the hedgerow preachers, and calls the one who faults them a ravenous wolf and a stomach-churning beast. We have also received an awful beating for Siamas from his old *moral* friend; for giving space to the King's Speech and the Speeches of the

Parliamentarians, we had to leave out others – Japheth five senses and Gomer two senses –[89] the Tales of Wisdom – the Letter of Philadelphus – the Second Letter from R. E. Caernarvon – the History of Astronomy &c. which was lost from the hands of the printer – The Credo of Emanuel Swedenbourg[90] was too long to have in at present, and so was the *Cywydd* of the Prydydd Hir when he was in Kent –[91] The Letter and the *Cywydd* which beg for one of the big Bibles of the Rev. Mr. Peter Williams[92] remained in the hands of the printer, together with a History of all Editions of the Welsh Bible. The Editors have various others things in hand. The Letter by W. W. should be printed as a Small book; and we recently Received two Books in old handwriting, which contain a large part of the history of the ancient Welsh, since they first came to this island. If they had encouragement to go ahead with the project, they could give the old Briton much pleasure. It is possible that some of the above articles could find a place in the *Welsh Remembrancer.* Wishing this project every success for the future, we conclude, taking our leave from the public with gratitude for the help we received from the kinder part of it. – For lack of time, the Publisher must ask the Reader to correct any misprints he sees with his writing pen.)

## *8* Y Drysorfa Gymmysgedig

*This Welsh-language quarterly, founded and edited by the weaver and first Unitarian minister of Wales, Tomos Glyn Cothi, ran to three numbers, published from summer 1795 to the beginning of 1796 at Carmarthen. It contained a significant number of translations and adaptations from the English radical press. In 1801 its editor was sentenced to two years imprisonment for sedition.*

### *8.1 Ecumenical appeal by the editor*

*The Miscellaneous Repository: Neu, Y Drysorfa Gymmysgedig*, Rhifyn Cyntaf . . . am y Chwarter Haf (First Number . . . for the Summer Quarter) 1795, 6–7.

MYFYRDODAU ar GREFYDD.

YR addoliad o Dduw, â'r galon ac â'r gwefusau, a chyflawniad cydwybodol o'n dyledswydd y naill tu ag at y llall a wnai ddynol-ryw yn frodyr, a'r byd yn deml. Dyfais dynion dichellgar, gwallgofus ac anonest, yw cymmell eu tybiau ar eraill, megis gwirioneddau diamheuol. Oddi wrth Dduw y mae moesoldeb yn deilliaw. Y mae'r athrawiaeth o burdan wedi costio myrddiynau o fywydau; ond y broffes wirioneddol hon o ffydd, YR WYF YN CARU DUW, AC MI DDYLWN WNEUTHUR DAIONI I FY NGHYD-GREADURIAID, ni fu yn achos o un ymryson er seiliad y byd. Am hynny tyred yn nês fy Undodwr rhesymol; fy anwyl Grynwr (Quaker); fy Medyddiwr crediniol gwresog; fy Mhresbeterian prudd; fy Esgobwr ysmala! Deuwch chwi Fethodistiaid a Duwiolion; deuwch hyd yn oed Bapistiaid! A gadewch i ni syrthio i lawr bawb oll o flaen y Bod goruchaf, gan diolch iddo am angenrheidiau'r bywyd, gan ymdrechu ei adnabod â'r deall, ei addoli â'r galon. Yn ôl ymostwng o un fryd yn y modd hwn ger bron y Bod anfeidrol, gadewch i ni swpperu ynghyd gyd ag ewyllys da y naill at y llall, fel cymdeithas rinweddol.

(CONTEMPLATIONS ON RELIGION

IT is the worship of God with heart and lips, and the conscientious performance of our duty one towards another which would make mankind brothers and the world a temple. It is the device of crafty, mad and dishonest men to press their beliefs on others as indisputable truths. Morality derives from God. The doctrine of purgatory has cost myriads of lives; but this true profession of faith, I LOVE GOD, AND I SHOULD DO GOOD TO MY FELLOW-CREATURES, has never given cause for dissension since the foundation of the world. Therefore, come closer my rational Unitarian; my dear Quaker; my warm-hearted convinced Baptist; my grave Presbyterian; my smart Episcopalian! Come, you Methodists and Pietists; come even Papists! And let us each and all kneel down before the supreme Being, thanking him for the necessities of life, endeavouring to know him with the intellect and to worship him with the heart. After submitting ourselves in this manner and in accord before the infinite Being, let us have supper together with good will towards one another, like a virtuous society.)

## *8.2 A fast-day prayer*

*The Miscellaneous Repository: Neu, Y Drysorfa Gymmysgedig*, Rhifyn Cyntaf . . . am y Chwarter Haf (First Number . . . for the Summer Quarter) 1795, 13–15.

GWEDDI i'w harfer gan y bobl a fyddo yn byw dan lywodraeth greulon drahaus, ar ddydd ympryd.[93]

O Tydi yr hwn wyt Oruwch-lywodraethwr yr ehangder! At bwy y deuwn ond attat ti ein Creawdwr, ein Tad a'n Duw. Ni alwn arnat yn ein cyfyngderau, O Arglwydd; ni osodwn ein achwynion ger dy fron; ac ni dywalltwn ein blinder i f'ynwes ein Duw. Yr ydym yn cael ein cystuddio yn fawr, ac a fydd i ni ddim llefain arnat? Adfyd a thrueni sydd yn gorchuddio wyneb y ddaear, fel y mae y dyfroedd yn toi'r mor. Treiswyr sydd yn sychedu am waed, yn anrheithio'r byd, ac yn gwasgaru anghyfannedd-dra dros y gwledydd. Megis creaduriaid ysglyfaethus, y maent yn ymhyfrydu mewn lladdfeydd, y maent yn gosod y dinasoedd yn garneddau, ac yn distrywio preswylfeydd dy bobl; y gwastadedd sydd yn cael ei orchguddio gan gyrph, neu gelaneddau'r meirwon; a'r dyffrynoedd yn cael eu golchi gan afonydd o waed. Och'neidiau chwerwon, 'sgrechau poenydiol y miloedd sydd yn ymdroi mewn llewygon nyddiadol ac arteithiau marwolaeth, a drywanant yr awyr, ac a lefant arnat ti am ddialedd ar eu dinystrwyr. Llef gwaed sydd i fynu attat; cynddaredd uffern sydd ar led yn y byd; gwallgof cythreuliaid sydd yn aflonyddu ein llysoedd; y tlawd sy'n llefain yn yr heolydd am fara, a rhai cyfiawn y ddaear mewn caethiwed; y byd sydd yn och'neidio dan bwys gorthrymder, ac nid oes neb a rydd gymmorth ond tydi, O Dduw. Pa hyd? O Arglwydd, pa hyd y bydd i ti gyd-ddwyn a drygioni meibion creulondeb a thrais, anrheithwyr trahaus y ddaear, y rhai, yn eistedd yn y lleoedd uchel, er nad ydynt ond dynion, a ymddyrchafant uwchlaw pob peth, ac a gymmerant arnynt mai duwiau ydynt: gan honni hawl i'r awdurdod hwnnw ac sydd yn perthynu yn unig i'r Hollalluog. Dywedant y gair, a miloedd a leddir ger eu bronnau. A ydyw mesur eu hanwiredd etto heb ei gyflawni? Pa hyd y bydd i'th ddialedd gael ei attal? Gwrando ein gweddiau, O Dduw'r trugaredd a'r tosturi! Tosturia wrth gyflwr gresynus dy greaduriaid; achub ddyn rhag dinystr. O! attal ffyrnigrwydd y rhai sydd yn ymbesgi ar waed, gan ym-hyfrydu i gamddefnyddio eu hawdurdod; a thraflyngcu tammaid y tlawd, a myned yn foethus ar lafur dy bobl; y rhai a wawdiant wrth ein blinfyd, ac a'n diystyrrant yn ein trueni. O, cymmer ymaith y cleddyf dinystriol o'u dwylaw, a gwared y byd o dan orthrymder a gallu treiswyr! O dysg ddoethineb i'th bobl, bydded iddynt gyrraedd gwybodaeth, fel y byddo iddynt edrych gyd a dychryn ac atgasrwydd ar ddifrod ac anrhaith traws-lywodraethwyr; a'u gyrru hwynt bendramwnwgl oddi ar orseddfeingciau eu hawdurdod; bydded i ddynolryw arfer y pwerau hynny ac sydd yn perthynu iddynt, i'r diben i ddwyn yn ol y rhydd-did hwnnw, ac sydd yn rhodd nattur a rhodd Duw, a meddiant enwedigol dyn, a'r hyn a fawryga ac a addurna ei nattur, ac a'i gwna ef yn ddelw ei Greawdwr.

Gwrando ni, yr ydym yn attolwg arnat, O tydi yr hwn a lywodraethi yn y nefoedd, yr hwn wyt Drefnwr mawr pob digwyddiadau, yr hwn wyt Ben-llywydd mawr yr holl fydoedd, a Thad tirion a chyffredinol pawb o'th greaduraid! O gwrando, ac atteb ni yn ein deisyfiadau hyn, O achub y tlawd o law'r gorthrymmydd; rhyddha'r caethion o'u caethiwed, a gwared y byd o dan law gormeswyr. Gwna i bawb fod yn feddiannol ar yr hawl naturiol honno, o'th addoli di, a thywallt dylanwadau duwiol eu heneidiau allan ger dy fron, yn y ffordd y mae eu cydwybodau yn eu cyfarwyddo a'r ffordd a gymmeradwyi di, heb neb i'w haflonyddu neu wneuthur iddynt arswydo: a bydded i'r tlawd gael mwynhau cysuron ei lafur caled, heb neb yn beiddio crafangu y tammaid o'i enau.

Yr ydym yn ostyngedig yn cyflwyno y deisyfiadau hyn ger dy fron yn enw, a thrwy Gyfryngdod Iesu Grist ein Iachawdwr, trwy yr hwn i ti y byddo *mawl*, gallu ac awdurdod. *Amen.*

(A PRAYER to be used by those people who live under a cruel and tyrannical government, on a day of fast.[93]

Oh, you Supreme Governor of the universe! To whom shall we come but to you our Creator, our Father and our God. We call upon you in our afflictions, Oh Lord; we lay our complaints before you; and we pour our sorrows into the bosom of our God. We are greatly afflicted, and shall we not cry unto you? Misery and wretchedness cover the face of the earth as the waters cover the sea. Tyrants, thirsting for blood, ravage the world and spread desolation over the lands. Like beasts of prey, they delight in carnage, they reduce the cities to piles of rubble, and destroy the habitations of your people; the plains are covered with bodies, or the carcasses of the dead; and the valleys are awash with rivers of blood. The bitter groans, agonized shrieks of the thousands who writhe in twisting pangs and agonies of death, pierce the air and cry out to you for vengeance upon their destroyers. The cry of the blood is up unto you; the fury of hell is abroad in the world; the rage of devils abuses our courts; the poor cry in the streets for bread, and the righteous of the earth are in chains; the world groans under the weight of oppression, and there is none to give help but you, Oh God. How long? Oh Lord, how long will you bear with the wickedness of the sons of cruelty and violence, the tyrannical despoilers of the world, those who are sitting in the high places, though they are only men, who elevate themselves above everything, and who pretend that they are gods: claiming the authority which pertains only to the Almighty. They speak the word, and thousands are killed before them. Is the measure of their iniquity not fulfilled yet? How long will your vengeance be withheld? Hear our prayers, Oh God of mercy and compassion! Have pity on the wretched state of your creatures; save man from destruction. Oh! stay the fury of those who gorge themselves on blood while delighting in abusing their authority; who devour the morsel of the poor, and grow fat with the labour of your people; those who jeer at our affliction, and who disdain us in our misery. Oh, take the destructive sword from their hands, and deliver the world from oppression and the power of tyrants! Oh, teach your people wisdom, may they get knowledge, so that they may look with horror and hatred at the ravages and devastation of despots; and hurl them headlong from the thrones of their authority; may mankind use those powers which belong to them in order to recover the freedom that is the gift of nature and the gift of God, and man's particular possession, and which ennobles and adorns his nature and makes him the image of his Creator.

Hear us, we beseech thee, Oh you who rules in the heavens, who is the great Arbitrator of all events, who is the great Sovereign of all worlds, and the kindly and universal Father of all of your creatures! Oh, hear and answer us in these our requests, Oh, save the poor from the hand of the oppressor; free the slaves from their bondage, and deliver the world from the hands of tyrants. Let all be in possession of the natural right to worship you and pour out the pious effusions of their souls before you in the manner which their consciences dictate and the way of which you approve, with none to molest them or make them afraid: and may the poor enjoy the comforts of their hard labour, with none daring to claw the morsel from their mouths.

We humbly offer these supplications to you, in the name, and through the Mediation of Jesus Christ our Saviour, through whom may you have *praise*, power and authority. *Amen.*)

## *8.3 A fast-day hymn*

*The Miscellaneous Repository: Neu, Y Drysorfa Gymmysgedig*, Rhifyn Cyntaf . . . am y Chwarter Haf (First Number . . . for the Summer Quarter) 1795, 16–18.

HYMN i'w chanu ar ddydd ympryd gan gyfeillion dynolryw.[94]

1 DY farnau Ior ac uchel lef
Cyhoeddant ddial Duw y nef;
Trwy Ewrop oll, O! gwasgar mae
Rhyfeloedd ffyrnig, cri a gwae!

2 Clywn swn y canon erchyll syn,
A dynol-waed fel llawer llyn!
Clywn lef ein brodyr dan eu clwy',
A chyd ymdeimlo wnawn â hwy.

3 Mae difrod hyll a garw'i wedd,
Trwy'r tan, a'r glas ddinystriol gledd;
Trefydd a'u llon drigolion llawn,
Sydd 'nawr mewn modd truenus iawn.

4 Dinasoedd mawr oedd hardd a gwych,
Sydd yn garneddau gwael eu drych!
A holl drigolion y rhai'n sydd
Yn feirw – clwyfus – neu yn brudd!

5 'Sglyfaethwyr sy'n ymdroi mewn gwa'd,
Gan 'speilio heddwch pob rhyw wlad;
Mor helaeth eu 'sgelerder 'nawr,
Mae'n llanw'r byd a dychryn mawr.

6 Tra rhodio'r anghenfilod hyn,
Bydd dychryn a thrueni syn:
Pa bryd y bydd i'w gwaed, pa bryd,
Roi tâl am lwyr anrheithio'r byd.

7 Oes terfyn i'w cynddaredd chwith,
Neu ddrygau etto i dd'od i'n plith?
Gan dreiswyr drwg uffernol lin,
Fel aethlyd bla, dinystriol blin.

8 O Dduw y lluoedd bydd o'n plaid,
Bydd nawdd a chymmorth in' wrth raid;
O cadw'th ddelw, Duw y grâs
Rhag difrod rhyfel treiswyr câs.

9 Yn bendramwnwgl bŵr i lawr,
Holl dreiswyr byd mewn munud awr;
O! gwasgar, Hollalluog Dad,
Y rhai sy'n pesgi ar ddynol-waed.

10 Yna daw heddwch i bob gradd,
Yn lle gorthrymder llym a lladd;
A'r holl fyd fel cyd-blant yn byw,
Yn deulu mawr i ti ein Duw.

11 Yna caiff caethion fyn'd yn rhydd,
O'u bron, 'nol bod yn hir yn brudd,
A mwynhau'r breintiau hyfryd hael,
Appwyntiodd nattur i ddyn gael.

12 Yna ceiff pawb o ddynolryw,
Dy foli di o hyd, ein Duw;
A'th gyfrif *di* ein Brenin doeth,
A chashau treiswyr d'orsedd goeth.

13 Ni fydd erlidwyr wrth eu chwant,
I ladd a blino'th anwyl blant,
Am gredu yr Efengyl lon,
A gostwng i reolau hon.

14 Y ddae'r a rydd ei ffrwythau da,
Yr hwsmon hefyd a'i mwynha;
Ac nid rhoi hwn heb gael ei flâs
I besgi ysglyfaethwyr câs.

15 Ac ni bydd bleiddiaid haid ddi-hedd,
Uffernol gŵn, a'u ffyrnig wedd,
Na locust i anrheithio'r tir,
Ond llwyddiant a llonyddwch hir.

16 Ni fydd balch tlws, i flino'r tlawd,
Neu drin heb fri oedrannus frawd:
Ond er cysuro'r claf a'r gwan,
Bydd pawb yn rhwydd; yn gwneud eu rhan.

17 O deued y bendithion hyn,
Ar frys yn lle gorthrymder syn;
Tanned y rhai'n dros dir a môr,
I bawb yn llawn dan haul a llo'r.

18 Hyn yw ein cais â chalon brudd,
Yn unig hyn yw gwaith y dydd;
Gyr dreiswyr drwg i lawr o'u bron,
Bendithia'r byd â heddwch llon.

(A HYMN to be sung on the fast-day by the friends of mankind.[94]

1 YOUR judgements, Lord, loudly
announce the vengeance of the God of heaven;
throughout all Europe, Oh! cry and woe,
fierce wars are scattered.

2 Dazed, we hear the terrible roar of the cannon,
and human blood as many a lake!
we hear our wounded brothers' cries,
and sympathize with them.

3 There is ugly destruction of terrible appearance
by the fire and the grey destructive sword;
towns and their contented inhabitants
are all now in a very wretched state.

4 Great cities which were beautiful and splendid
are heaps of stones of miserable appearance!
And all their inhabitants are
dead – wounded – or mournful!

5 Predators are wallowing in blood,
despoiling the peace of every country;
so widespread is their wickedness now,
it fills the world with great dread.

6 While these monsters are roaming
there will be dread and stunned misery:
when, Oh, when, will their blood
pay for utterly ravaging the world?

7 Is there an end to their sinister rage,
or are more evils yet to come amongst us?
By tyrants of infernal descent,
like a grievous destructive plague.

8 Oh, God of hosts be on our side,
be our succour and aid in need;
Oh, save your image, God of grace,
from the destructive war of evil tyrants.

9 Throw down headlong
all the tyrants of the world in an instant;
Oh! disperse, Almighty Father,
those who grow fat on human blood.

10 Then peace will come to every station,
instead of harsh oppression and killing;
and all the world will live as fellow-children,
as a big family for you our God.

11 Then slaves will be allowed to go free,
altogether, after long sadness,
and enjoy the lovely, generous rights
which nature appointed for man to have.

12 Then every member of mankind
may worship you continuously, our God;
and claim *you* as our wise King,
and hate those who violate your pure throne.

13 There'll be no persecutors to murder and molest
your beloved children at will,
for believing the happy Gospel,
and submitting to its commands.

14 The earth will give its good fruits,
and the husbandman, too, will be able to enjoy them;
and not pass them on, without having a taste,
to fatten evil predators.

15 And there'll be no pack of warlike wolves,
hounds of hell, with savage demeanour,
nor locusts to despoil the land,
only long prosperity and happiness.

16 There'll be no proud dandy to harass the poor,
or treat the aged brother without dignity:
but to comfort the sick and weak,
all will be ready, doing their part.

17 Oh, may these blessings come,
without delay in place of stupefying oppression;
let them extend across land and sea,
fully to all under sun and moon.

18 This is our request with heavy heart,
this only is this day's task;
hurl evil despots down altogether,
bless the world with contented peace.)

## *8.4 A prayer for liberty*

*The Miscellaneous Repository: Neu, Y Drysorfa Gymmysgedig*, Rhifyn Cyntaf . . . am y Chwarter Haf (First Number . . . for the Summer Quarter) 1795, 18–19.

GWEDDI arall i'w harfer gan gyfeillion dynolryw ar ddiwedd addoliad.

O Tydi Drefnwr Hollalluog pob digwyddiadau, yr hwn wyt yn llywodraethu ym mrenhiniaeth dynion, ac a'u rhoddi i'r neb y mynnech.* Edrych ar dy greadur DYN yn yr amser peryglus a phwysfawr hwn: attal y llifogydd mawrion o waed dynol ac sydd yn boddi y ddaear wrth ewyllys brenhinoedd CRISTIANOGOL, y tu hwnt i bob esampl yn yr oesoedd mwyaf creulon, barbaraidd, anwybodus a thywyll. Siomma ddychymmygion pawb o ddifrodwyr gwaedlyd ddynolryw ac sydd yn ymgyssylltu yn erbyn rhydd-did a gwybodaeth, y rhai ydynt wir *synagog satan,* a dychwel eu calonnau, diddymma bob egwyddor o greulondeb gwladol ym mhob dwyfron; fel na byddo creulondeb rhyfel a chelanedd yn aros ond yn unig mewn hanes, fel coffadwriaeth arswydus am ffyrnigrwydd a chreulondeb dyn! Gostwng dy glust at lef cystuddiol yr *Affrican* tlawd, a gwobrwya ef â blynyddoedd o ddiddanwch, *yn lle y blynyddoedd y gwelodd ddrygfyd.* Cadarnha a chysura ferthyron gogoneddus gwirionedd, dynoliaeth, a rhydd-did, pa un bynnag ai mewn rhwymau neu mewn alltudiaeth. Lliosoga rifedi eu canlynwyr fel y byddo i genhedlaethau i ddyfod eu galw yn wynfydedig! Diffodd fflam ynfyd coel-grefydd a genhedlwyd yn ffos ddrewedig dichellion offeiriadol, trais, ac erledigaeth, trwy lewyrch mwy disglair a hyfryd haul cyfiawnder, sef crefydd bur a dihalog Iesu Grist!

Rhwym bob cnawd ynghyd â rhwymyn cariad efangylaidd a brawdgarwch, a haelioni. Effeithiola bawb calonnau â'r yspryd cyd-ymdeimladwy hwnnw o *Undeb*, *Heddwch*, a *Chydgordiad. Amen.*

(Another PRAYER to be used by the friends of mankind at the end of worship.

Oh, you Almighty Arbitrator of all events, you who rules in the kingdom of men and gives them to whoever you wish.* Look at your creature MAN in this dangerous and important time: stem the great floods of human blood which, beyond any example from the cruellest, darkest, most barbaric

* Dan. iv. 35.

and ignorant ages, drown the earth by the will of CHRISTIAN kings. Disappoint the designs of all the bloody despoilers of mankind who join forces against liberty and knowledge, they are the true *assembly of satan*, and turn their hearts, dissolve every rudiment of political cruelty in every bosom; so that the cruelty of war and carnage remain only in history, a terrible memorial of the ferocity and cruelty of man! Incline your ear to the distressed wail of the poor *African*, and reward him with years of comfort *instead of the years in which he experienced hardship*. Strengthen and comfort the glorious martyrs of truth, mankind and liberty, whether in chains or in exile. Multiply the numbers of their adherents so that generations to come may call them blessed! Extinguish the insane flame of superstition which was conceived in the stinking pit of priestcraft, oppression and persecution, through the brighter and lovelier radiance of the sun of justice that is the pure and undefiled religion of Jesus Christ!

Bind all flesh together with the bonds of evangelical love and fraternity and generosity. Infuse each heart with that sympathizing spirit of *Unity*, *Peace*, and *Harmony*. *Amen*.)

### *8.5 A poem in praise of the Welsh language*

*The Miscellaneous Repository: Neu, Y Drysorfa Gymmysgedig*, Rhifyn Cyntaf . . . am y Chwarter Haf (First Number . . . for the Summer Quarter) 1795, 43.

ENGLYN i'r IAITH GYMRAEG.

Iaith doethion mwynion manawl; Iaith Brydain,
Iaith brodyr synhwyrawl;
Iaith y byd, Iaith wybodawl,
Cedwch hon, cyhyd a'ch hawl.

L. W.

(*ENGLYN* to the WELSH LANGUAGE

The Language of gentle, diligent sages; the Language of Britain,
the Language of rational brothers;
a Language of the world, a Language of knowledge,
keep it, as long as your right.

L. W.)

### *8.6 A sermon on the early church*

*The Miscellaneous Repository: Neu Y Drysorfa Gymmysgedig*, Rhifyn III, 1796, 115–27.

GWIR NATTUR EGLWYS CRIST,
A'R AMMHOSIBLRWYDD O'I BOD MEWN PERYGL:
SEF, PREGETH AR MAT. xvi. 18.
*Ar y graig hon yr adeiladaf fy eglwys, a phyrth uffern ni's gorchfygant hi.*

EIN Iachawdwr, wedi gwneuthur amryw wyrthiau, mewn tystiolaeth o'i anfoniad dwyfol, oedd yn ewyllysgar i wybod a oedd y profiadau a roddodd ef yn cael eu heffaith briodol, trwy dywys dynion i gasglu, eu bod hwynt yn brofiadau sicr mai efe oedd y Messiah. Efe a ofynnodd i'w ddisgyblion, gan ddywedyd, "Pwy y mae dynion yn dywedyd fy mod i Mab y dyn." . . . Simon Pedr a attebodd ac a ddywedodd, "Ti yw'r Crist, Mab y Duw byw," hynny yw, Tydi yw y Messias, y Prophwyd oedd yn cael ei ddisgwyl i ddyfod i'r byd." . . . Pedr a roddodd y fath ddarluniad cymmwys o Grist, fel yr attebodd ein Harglwydd ac a ddywedodd wrtho, "Gwyn dy fyd di Simon mab Jona: canys nid cig a gwaed a ddatguddiodd hyn i ti, ond fy Nhad yr hwn sydd yn y nefoedd; ac yr ydwyf finneu yn dywedyd i ti, mai ti yw Pedr, ac ar y graig hon yr adeiladaf fy EGLWYS, a phyrth uffern ni's gorchfygant hi." Hynny yw, Gwyn eich byd, ddarfod i chwi ffurfio y meddwl hwn am danaf, a hynny nid yn ddi-sail, ond oddi ar argyhoeddiad, na's gallaswn wneuthur y gwyrthiau a welsoch, neu ddysgu yr athrawiaeth a glywsoch, oni buasai i mi gael fy awdurdodi a'm danfon gan fy Nhad nefol i'm swydd. A hyn yr wyf yn sicrhau i chwi, mai y gyffes hon o ffydd a wnaethoch yn awr, a chrediniaeth o'r erthygl hwn, mai fi yw y Messia, yw y gwirionedd sylfaenol, ar yr hwn y bydd i'm crefydd gael ei sefydlu: a pa beth bynnag a fyddo ymdrechiadau ei gelynion i rwystro ei thaeniad a'i derbyniad yn y byd, fe fydd iddi fyned ar gynnydd ac yn y diwedd lwyddo yn erbyn pob gwrthwynebiadau.

Hyn yw meddwl amlwg y testun. Ond gan fod arferiad o eiriau heb glymmu meddwl eglur a phendant wrthynt, yn rhoddi achlysur i'r cyfeiliornadau mwyaf chwythig, a gwyrdroad o'r pethau mwyaf union; ac yn gymmaint ac nad oes un peth o bosibl wedi cael ei gyfnewid yn fwy o'i briodol ystyr nac arwyddoccâd y gair *Eglwys,* fe fydd i mi yn yr ymadrodd canlynol ystyried yn gyntaf feddwl ysgrythurol y gair *Eglwys*, ac yn ail mi geisiaf ddangos yn ol dywediad ein Iachawdwr na fydd iddi gael ei gorchfygu.

Yn gyntaf, Y gair *Eglwys,* yn yr ysgrythur, ac mewn awdwyr eraill,* sydd yn wastad yn arwyddoccau *cynnulleidfa* neu *gymmanfa.* Pa le bynnag yr oedd nifer fawr, neu fechan, o Grist'nogion yn ymgynnull ynghyd, y cyfarfod neu'r cynhulliad oedd yn cael ei alw *eglwys*; a'r enw oedd yn cael ei gymmeryd oddi wrth y *bobl* oedd yn cyfarfod, ac nid oddi wrth *le* eu cyfarfod. Nid rhyw nifer fechan mewn cydmariaeth o'r bobl o herwydd rhyw swydd yn eu plith, ond yr holl gynnulleidfa oedd yn gwneuthur i fynu yr *eglwys* hon . . .

Fel nad oedd un lle yn fwy cyssegredig na'r llall gyfarfod ynddo, felly nid oedd neb yn cael eu dethol allan i fod yn feddiannol ar un gradd o awdurdod goruwch y lleill: eithr gogyfuwchdra cyffredinol oedd yn cymmeryd lle yn eu plith. Nid oeddynt yn cydnabod un pen ond Crist. Fe'i gelwir ef *pen yr* EGLWYS,‡ sef pawb crist'nogion. Ac i ddangos y cyd-raddiaeth perffaith a ddylai fod rhwng yr aelodau, hwy a elwir yn frodyr, "Un yw eich Athraw chwi sef Christ: a chwithau oll *brodyr* ydych."† "Mi a fynnwn i chwi wybod," medd Paul, "mai pen pob gwr yw Crist."‖ Nid oedd neb uwch nac ef mewn pethau crefyddol. Nid oedd yr apostolion eu hunain yn meddiannu un awdurdod ond yr hyn oedd yn perthyn i'w dwyfol anfoniad; yr awdurdod i wneuthur gwyrthiau, prophwydo a llefaru a thafodau. Ac yr oedd hyd yn oed yr awdurdod hyn yn cael ei gyfrannu gan yr apostolion i grist'nogion yn gyffredinol, ac nid oedd yn cael ei gyfyngu i ryw swyddwyr neillduol yn eu plith . . . Y cymhwysderau angenrheidiol at gyflawni y swyddi mwyaf pwysig yn yr eglwys oedd oedran, duwioldeb a challineb; ac mor bell ac y gallai y pwerau o gyngor, esampl a difrifwch fyned, yr oeddynt ar eu rhydd-did i'w harfer hyd yr eithaf: ond nid oeddynt yn feddiannol ar unrhyw oruchafiaeth neu lywodraeth ysprydol; a lle na byddai yr efengyl mewn modd uniongyrch yn perthynu, nid oedd gan yr apostolion a'r henaduriaid ddim awdurdod uwchlaw crist'nogion eraill yn gyffredinol . . .

Dyma yr hanes sydd gennym am yr eglwys a sefydlodd Crist, yr hon, o herwydd ei duwioldeb a'i symlrwydd, a allai haeddu cael ei mawrygu gennym. Ac os cydmarwn *hon* âg eglwysi diweddar, ei chymhwysder a'i manteision uwchlaw y gosodiadau dynol hynny, nag ê, mi fum agos a dywedyd, ei gwrthwynebiad hollol iddynt, a ymddangosai yn rhy amlwg i'w wadu. . . . Yr ammodau o dderbyniad i eglwys yn awr nid ydynt mor esmwyth. Llawer o bethau a ofynir eu credu nad ydynt yn yr efengyl, cyn

* Εκκλησία, ym mysg y Groegiaid oedd yn arwyddoccau cymmanfa yn cael ei galw ar achos cyhoeddus i drefnu cyfreithiau, &c. Æschines passim, &c.

‡ Colos. i. 18.

† Mat. xxiii. 8.

‖ 1 Cor. xi. 3.

y caffo un ei dderbyn iddi. Ni's gall gan hynny gael ei "phregethu i bob creadur," yn yr ystyr helaeth ac y gorchymynwyd, gan fod llawer yn gwrthod dyfod i mewn iddi, o achos yr erthyglau a chwanegwyd atti. Nid oedd un math o urdd o ddynion y rhai a gymmerent iddynt eu hunain awdurdod dros yr eglwys, neu yr hyn ydym yn alw yn awr gwyr llen. Ond i bob Creadur y rhoddwyd gras yn ol mesur dawn Crist.‡ Mewn graddau mwy yn wir i rai nac eraill, ac i'r unig ddiben o "berffeithio'r saint, i waith y weinidogaeth, i adeilad corph Crist;" nid i fod yn arglwyddi ar ffydd eraill, neu i arfer unrhyw bennaduriaeth ysprydol. Yr ydym yn darllen yn wir am henuriaid ac esgobion, neu olygwyr y rhai oedd i edrych dros ymddygiad y dychweledigion crist'nogol, a'r rhai trwy eu hoedran oeddynt gymmwysaf i chwanegu cadernid eu hesiampl at dduwioldeb eu hyfforddiadau. . . . Yr apostolion a'r pregethwyr cyntaf oeddynt yn cymmeryd baich arnynt, ond nid swydd o awdurdod a llywodraeth; yr oeddynt yn well ac yn dlottach nac eraill, nid arglwyddi a meistriaid ar eraill. Y swyddwyr a dybir yn awr sydd angenrheidiol ydynt lawer yn fwy lliosog na'r rhai yn y prif amseroedd, ac mor fyr o gyrraedd defnyddioldeb y rhai hynny.* . . .

Wedi ystyried meddwl ysgrythurol y gair *Eglwys,* mi ddangosaf yn yr ail le, yn ol tystiolaeth ein Iachawdwr, na's geill fod mewn perygl, neu na fydd iddi gael ei gorchfygu.

Pe buasai bawb eglwysydd yn cael eu hadeiladu â'r un defnyddiau ag *eglwys Crist,* ni fuasai byth achwyniad eu bod mewn perygl, nac achos ofni eu cwymp. Y graig ar yr hon yr adeiladwyd *eglwys Crist* oedd, mai efe oedd "y Crist Mab y Duw byw." Hi wrthsefodd ddifrod amser, rhythrad y llifogydd, a ffyrnigrwydd y tymhestloedd a ymosodasant arni, ac nid oedd dim yn abl ei siglo, canys yr oedd wedi ei hadeiladu ar y "graig."‡ Fe ddywedir am eglwysi eraill iddynt gael eu hadeiladu ar ol hyn wrth yr un ffurf. Ond y perygl yr hwn y maent ynddo, a'u sefyllfa ddadfeiledig sydd yn brawf eglur mai ar sail, a dull wahanol y maent wedi cael eu ffurfio. Yr apostol a ddywedodd wrthym, "Sylfaen arall ni's gall neb ei gosod heblaw yr hon a osodwyd; yr hon yw Iesu Grist."[95] Yn awr y mae yn sicr, i rai geisio gosod sylfaen dra gwahanol, ac adeiladu arni. Llawer o erthyglau hollawl wrthwyneb i grist'nogrwydd, a niweidiol i'r cyfryw, sydd yn cael edrych arnynt

‡ Ephes. iv. 11, 12.

* In our common idea of the English church, the body of the people is hardly included. It is supposed to consist of the King, as supreme head; of Arch-bishops, Bishops, Priests, Deacons, Deans, Arch deacons, Convocations, Chancellors, Treasurers, Precentors, Prebendaries, Canons, Petty Canons, Rectors, Vicars, Curates, Chaplains, Choristers, Organists, Parish Clerks, Vergers, Sextons, &c. Vide Robertson's Attempt to explain the words Reason, Substance, &c. page 171.

‡ Luc vi. 48.

fel ei gwirioneddau sylfaenol; ond gan eu bod yn groes i reswm a Gair Duw, nid oes i ni ddisgwyl y bydd iddo ef arfer ei allu i'w sefydlu. Y sylfaen a osodwyd gan yr apostolion a'r prophwydi, a saif yn ddiysgog; ond, "Os adeilada neb ar y sylfaen hon – coed, gwair, sofl, gwaith pob dyn a wneir yn amlwg; canys y dydd a'i dengys, o blegid trwy dân y datguddir ef, a'r tân a brawf waith pawb, pa fath ydyw."† Lle byddo dychymmygion ffuantus dynion yn cael eu gosod yn lle gair Duw, neu lle byddo athrawiaethau anysgrythurol yn cael eu 'chwanegu atto, fe ymddengys yn amlwg gwaith pwy ydyw. Dirgelwch a dadguddiad – tywyllwch a goleuni, sydd mor wrthwyneb y naill i'r llall fel na's gall neb fod mewn camsynied yn eu cylch, os bydd iddynt ond gwneuthur defnydd o'u cynheddfau deallus; a phan wnelont ddefnyddio'u cynheddfau mewn chwiliad o'r ysgrythyrau a chydmaru eu hopiniynau a'r maen-prawf hwn yna y prawf tanllyd a ddengys y coed, gwair a sofl, a'r holl adeilad o gyfeiliornadau a adeiladwyd dros oesoedd a ddiflanna ymaith megis gweledigaeth nos. Y fath eglwys anghristaidd hon a raid fod mewn perygl bob amser, ac nid yw ryfedd fod aelodau y fath eglwys yn wastad mewn dychryn o'i phlegid. Pe buasai unrhyw awdurdodau dynol yn abl rhoddi cymmorth iddi, hi gafodd bob amddiffyniad posibl oddi wrth y cyfryw. Y mae yn cael ei gwylied gan derfyniadau, *(restrictions)* ei hamddiffyn gan ddirwyau a chospedigaethau, ac yn EGLWYS SEFYDLEDIG TRWY Y GYFRAITH. Er yr holl gynhaliaeth hyn, y mae'n wastad mewn perygl o gael ei *gorchfygu*, ac yn galw am gymmorth. Y mae hyn yn eglur ddangos rhyw wendid mawr oddi *fewn,* gan ei bod yn cael ei diogelu mor dda oddi *allan!* – Mawr yw awdurdod y swyddwyr gwladol, ond nid oes un awdurdod a eill wneuthur cyfeiliornad yn wirionedd, neu ddal cyfreithiau afresymmol ac annoeth trwy nerth arfau creulondeb. Hwy allant ddistewi llais gwirionedd, ond nid ei lwyr *ddiffoddi*, hwy allant wobrwyo dynion i *broffesu* y gwrthddywediadau mwyaf ffiaidd, ond nid oes un awdurdod a eill wneuthur iddynt eu credu hwynt. – Y rhan amlaf o'r eglwysi sefydledig o sefydliad dynol, ydynt achos o fusgrellni, anwybodaeth a rhagrith yn eu proffeswyr, ac yn attaliadau i gynheddfau godidoccaf y meddwl, gan eu caethiwo i awdurdod offeiriadol a ffolineb. Nid yw Crefydd Crist yn sefyll mewn diffyg o'r fath gynhorthwy, hon a all ei chynnal ei hun trwy ei gallu ei hun, a'r prawf o'i gwirionedd ei hun. Nid yn unig hi wnaeth ei ffordd i'r byd *heb gymmorth* awdurdodau gwladol, ond hyd yn oed mewn *gwrthwynebiad* iddynt oll; a hyn pan yr oedd yn cael ei phregethu gan ychydig o bysgodwyr tlawd annysgedig a digyfeillion. Nid oedd gan y pregethwyr cyntaf hyn ddim gwobrwyon i'w cyfrannu, dim anrhydedd i'w roddi i'r diben o dynnu canlynwyr a'u cadw yn eu hachos.

† 1 Cor. iii. 11, 12, 13.

Yn y gwrthwyneb eu rhan sicr oedd rhwymau, carcharau, a marwolaeth. Ac er yr holl rwystrau hyn hwy aethant ymlaen yn yr ymdrech, heb un arfau, ond arfau gwirionedd, nac un diddanwch neu gysur ond cydwybod dda . . . Yn y modd hwn, er fod crist'nogrwydd yn agored i ymosodiadau ei gelynion cyhoeddus, â zel gamsyniol ei chyfeillion gau; y mae *wedi*, ac *yn* torri, dros bob anhawsderau, ac hyd yn oed yn cael nerth ychwanegol trwy wrthwynebiadau, ac yn profi rhagddywediad ein Iachawdwr, "na fydd i byrth uffern ei gorchfygu."

Oddi wrth yr hyn a ddywedwyd, y casgliadau hyn a ganlyn yn naturiol.

Yn gyntaf, Cyn y byddo i ni achwyn fod yr eglwys mewn *perygl*, neu yn debyg o gael ei *gorchfygu,* ni ddylem ystyried yn dda pa eglwys ydym yn feddwl. Os *eglwys Crist,* ein hofnau sydd ofer; o blegid y mae ein Harglwydd ei hun wedi dywedyd na fydd iddi gael ei gorchfygu. Ond os ydym yn bryderus am unrhyw eglwys arall, y mae sail ddigonol i'n hofnau; ac nid oes un ffordd i'w symmud hwynt, ond trwy ei gwneuthur mor gyffelyb i'r gyntaf ac yw bosibl, mewn disgyblaeth ac athrawiaeth; a dal yr un gyffes ffydd ac a gafodd ei chanmol mor rhagorol gan ein Iachawdwr, yr hon oedd yn unig hyn, "Mai Iesu yw'r Crist, Mab y Duw byw."

Yn ail, Fel ac y dywedodd Crist am ei deyrnas ef, nad oedd o'r byd hwn, felly ni's gall fod un math o gyngrair rhwng ei *eglwys ef* a theyrnasoedd y byd hwn. Cyffroeadau mawrion a raid gymmeryd lle, ac amser hir (y mae'n debygol) a raid fyned heibio, cyn y caffo y brophwydoliaeth fawr ei chyflawni, "Pan byddo i deyrnasoedd y byd ddyfod yn eiddo ein Harglwydd ni a'i Grist ef."* Hyd yn bresennol nid oes dim mwy o gydgordiad rhyngddynt nac sydd rhwng *gwirionedd* a *thwyll,* neu rhwng *Crist* a *Belial.* Canys mor annhebyg oedd "y ffydd a roddwyd unwaith i'r saint" i'r hon a gymmellwyd gan *Constantine,* fel nad oedd dim mor debygol i ddistrywio crist'nogrwydd a'r hyn *a sefydlwyd* gan awdurdodau y byd hwn, dan yr enw o grist'nogrwydd. Dirmyg yw meddwl fod gallu dwyfol yn sefyll mewn diffyg o gymmorth dynol.

Yn olaf, Cyfeillion goreu yr eglwys yw y rhai sydd yn ceisio ei hadnewyddu i'w phurdeb a'i symlrwydd dechreuol. Fel wedi ei gwreiddio, ei hadeiladu a'i chadarnhau yn y ffydd, y byddo yn eglwys ogoneddus heb arni na brycheuyn na chrychni, na dim o'r cyfryw; ond fel y byddo yn sanctaidd a difeius. A phan y byddo i hyn gymmeryd lle, ac nid gynt, hi all ddibrisio pob gelyn, a bod yn sicr na wnaiff pyrth uffern un *niwaid* iddi, neu fod yn *debyg* i'w *gorchfygu.*

I'r Brenin tragywyddol, anfarwol, anweledig, yr unig ddoeth Dduw, y byddo anrhydedd a gogoniant yn oes oesoedd. *Amen.*

* Dat. xi. 15.

## (THE TRUE NATURE OF THE CHURCH OF CHRIST, AND THE IMPOSSIBILITY OF IT BEING IN DANGER: THAT IS, A SERMON ON MAT. xvi. 18.

*Upon this rock I will build my church; and the gates of hell shall not prevail against it.*

Our Saviour, having performed various miracles as testimony of his divine mission, was eager to know if the experiences he conferred had their proper effect by leading men to conclude that they were sure proof that he was the Messiah. He asked his disciples, "Whom do men say that I the son of man am." . . . Simon Peter answered and said, "Thou art the Christ, the Son of the living God," that is, "You are the Messiah, the Prophet who was expected to come into this world." . . . Peter gave such a fitting description of Christ, that the Lord answered him and said, "Blessed art thou Simon Barjona: for flesh and blood hath not revealed it unto thee, but my Father, which is in heaven; and I say also unto thee that thou art Peter, and upon this rock I will build my CHURCH and the gates of hell shall not prevail against it." That is, Blessed are you, that you formed this opinion of me, and that not without foundation but through conviction, that I could not have performed the miracles you saw or taught the doctrines you heard if I had not been authorized and sent to my calling by my heavenly Father. And of this I assure you, that this profession of faith you made now, and the belief in this article, that I am the Messiah, is the fundamental truth on which my religion will be based: and whatever be the efforts of its enemies to prevent its proliferation and its reception in the world, it will increase and in the end succeed against all opposition.

This is the manifest meaning of the text. But since the use of words without having a clear and definite meaning attached to them occasions the most untoward errors and the perversion of the most precise things; and in so far as there is possibly not one thing which has been changed as much from its proper meaning as the word *Church,* I shall in the following discourse consider, firstly, the scriptural meaning of the word *Church* and, secondly, I shall attempt to show that, in the words of our Saviour, it will not be prevailed against.

Firstly, The word *Church,* in the scriptures and in other authors,* always signifies a *congregation* or *assembly.* Wherever a large, or a small, number of Christians assembled, the meeting or the congregation was called a *church*; and the name was taken from the *people* who were in the meeting, and not

* Εκκλησία amongst the Greeks signified an assembly called on a public matter to organize laws, &c. Æschines passim, &c.

from the *place* of the meeting. Not some comparatively small number of people from their midst because of some office, but the whole congregation made up this *church* . . .

Just as no place was more hallowed than another for meeting, so no one was chosen to be more deserving of a higher degree of authority over the others: rather, there was general equality in their midst. They did not acknowledge any leader but Christ. He is called the *head* of the CHURCH,‡ that is, of all Christians. And to show the perfect equality which should be between the members, they are called brothers, "One is your Master even Christ: and you are all *brethren*."† "I would have you know," said Paul, "that the head of every man is Christ."‖ Nobody was above him in religious matters. The apostles themselves did not have any authority beyond what pertained to their divine mission; the authority to perform miracles, to prophesy and to speak in tongues. And even this authority was shared with Christians in general by the apostles, and not restricted to some particular officials in their midst . . . The qualifications necessary for holding the most important offices in the church were age, godliness and wisdom; and as far as the power of advice, setting an example and gravity could go, they were at liberty to exercise them to the utmost: but they did not possess any spiritual superiority or governance; and where the gospel did not apply directly, the apostles and the elders did not have any authority over any other Christians generally . . .

This is the account we have of the church which Christ founded, and which, because of its godliness and its simplicity is deserving of our veneration. And if we compare *this* one with modern churches, its suitability and its advantages above these human inventions, nay I almost said its complete contrast to them, appears too obvious to deny . . . These days, the conditions of reception into a church are not as easy. Many of the things one is asked to believe before one is accepted into it are not in the gospel. It cannot therefore be preached "to every creature," in the wide sense which was commanded, since many refuse to join it because of the articles which were added to it. There was no order of men who took upon themselves authority over the church, or those whom we now call clergymen. Rather, grace was given to each Creature according to the measure of the gifts of Christ.‡ To a greater degree to some than others, indeed, and only "for the perfecting of the saints, for the work of the ministry, for the edifying of the body of Christ;" not to be masters over the faith of others or to

‡ Colos. i. 18.
† Mat. xxiii. 8 ('brethren' in the King James Bible).
‖ 1 Cor. xi. 3.
‡ Ephes. iv. 11, 12.

exert any spiritual supremacy. We read, indeed, of elders and bishops or guardians, who were to watch over the conduct of the Christian converts, and who by their age were most suitable to add the strength of their example to the piety of their instructions. . . . The apostles and the first preachers took this burden upon them, but not an office of authority and governance; they were better and poorer than others, not lords and masters over others. The officials who are now assumed to be necessary are much more numerous than of ancient times and fall so short of the effectiveness of those.* . . .

Having considered the scriptural meaning of the word *Church*, I shall show, secondly, that, according to the testimony of our Saviour, it cannot be in danger nor will it be vanquished.

If all churches had been built of the same material as the *church of Christ*, there would never have been a complaint that they are in danger, or reason to fear their fall. The rock on which the *church of Christ* was built was that he was "the Christ, Son of the living God." It has withstood the devastation of time, the onrush of the floods and the fierceness of the storms which have attacked it, and nothing could shake it, because it had been built on the "rock".‡ It is said about other churches that they were afterwards built in the same way. But the danger in which they are and their ruinous situation are clear proof that they were formed on a different basis and manner. The apostle told us, "For other foundation can no man lay than that is laid, which is Jesus Christ."[95] It is clear now that some attempt to lay down a very different foundation and build upon it. There are many articles wholly contrary to Christianity, and damaging to it, which are looked upon as fundamental truths, but since they are contrary to reason and the Word of God, it is not to be expected that he will use his powers to maintain them. The foundation laid by the apostles and the prophets will stand firm; but, "if any man build upon this foundation – wood, hay, stubble; every man's work shall be made manifest: for the day shall declare it, because it shall be revealed by fire; and the fire shall try every man's work of what sort it is."† Where the disingenuous imaginations of men are put in place of God's word or where unscriptural doctrines are added to it, it will become clear whose work it is. Mystery and revelation – darkness and light, are so different

* In our common idea of the English church, the body of the people is hardly included. It is supposed to consist of the King, as supreme head; of Arch-bishops, Bishops, Priests, Deacons, Deans, Arch deacons, Convocations, Chancellors, Treasurers, Precentors, Prebendaries, Canons, Petty Canons, Rectors, Vicars, Curates, Chaplains, Choristers, Organists, Parish Clerks, Vergers, Sextons, &c. Vide Robertson's Attempt to explain the words Reason, Substance, &c. page 171.

‡ Luke vi. 48.

† 1 Cor. iii. 11, 12, 13.

from one another that nobody can ever be mistaken about them if they but make use of their intellectual faculties; and when they use their faculties to search the scriptures and compare their opinions with this touchstone, then the fire test will show the wood, hay and stubble, and the whole building of errors built over ages will disappear like a nocturnal phantasm. This type of unchristian church must be in danger at all times, and it is no wonder that the members of such a church are always worried about it. If human authorities were able to give it any assistance, it has received every possible protection from them. It is minded by restrictions, defended by fines and punishments and it is a CHURCH ESTABLISHED by LAW. Despite all this support, it is always in danger of being *vanquished* and calls out for help. This clearly shows great weakness on the *inside*, since it is safeguarded so well from the *outside!* – Great is the authority of state officials, but no authority can turn error into the truth or uphold unreasonable and unwise laws by the strength of the weapons of cruelty. They can silence the voice of truth, but cannot wholly *extinguish* it, they can reward men for *professing* the most terrible contradictions, but there is no authority which can make them believe in them. – The majority of the churches founded by human establishment are the cause of debility, ignorance and hypocrisy in their adherents, and hindrances to the finest faculties of the mind, enslaving them under priestly authority and foolishness. The Faith of Christ does not suffer from lack of such succour; it can sustain itself by its own power and the proof of its own truth. Not only did it make its way into the world *without the help* of state authorities, but even *in opposition* to them all; and this when it was preached by only a few poor, unlearned and friendless fishermen. These first preachers had no rewards to dispense, or distinction to award in order to attract followers and keep them for their cause. On the contrary, their sure part was chains, prisons, and death. And despite all these obstructions they continued in the effort, without any weapons but the weapons of truth, or any consolation or comfort but a clear conscience. . . . In this way, though Christianity is open to attacks from its public enemies and the errant zeal of its false friends; it *has* and *is* breaking through all difficulties, and grows even stronger from obstructions, thus proving the prophesy of our Saviour that "the gates of hell shall not prevail against it."

From what has been said, these conclusions follow naturally.

Firstly, Before we complain that the church is in *danger* or likely to be *vanquished*, we should consider well what church we mean. If it is the *church of Christ*, our fears are unfounded; because our Lord himself said that it shall not be vanquished. But if we are worried about any other church, there is good ground for our fears; and there is no way of removing them, except through making it as similar to the first as possible, in discipline and doctrine; and to hold the same profession of faith which was praised so gloriously by our Saviour, and which was only, "That Jesus is the Christ, the Son of the living God."

Secondly, As Christ said about his kingdom that it was not of this world, so there cannot be any kind of alliance between *his church* and the kingdoms of this world. Great commotions must take place and a long time (probably) must pass before the great prophesy is fulfilled, when "The kingdoms of this world are become the kingdoms of our Lord and of his Christ."* Up to the present there is no more concord between the two than there is between *truth* and *deceit*, or between *Christ* and *Belial*. For the "faith which was once given to the saints" was so different to the one enforced by *Constantine,* that nothing was more likely to destroy Christianity than that which was *established* by the authorities of this world under the name of Christianity. It is contemptuous to believe that the divine power requires human assistance.

Lastly, The best friends of the church are those who attempt to restore it to its early purity and simplicity. So that rooted, built and reinforced in the faith, it may be a glorious church without any specks or wrinkles or the like; but holy and flawless. And when this takes place, and not before then, it will be able to disregard every foe and be sure that the gates of hell will not do it any *harm* or be *likely* to *vanquish* it.

May honour and glory be to the eternal, immortal, invisible King, the only wise God, forever and ever. *Amen.*)

* Rev. xi. 15.

## *9* Y Geirgrawn

*This monthly was the most regularly issued of the three radical Welsh periodicals of the 1790s. Edited by the Independent minister David Davies of Holywell and published by Minshull at Chester, it ran to nine numbers, which appeared between February and October 1796. It featured much original material, most notably a sustained discussion of the most important radical Welsh pamphlet to appear in the 1790s,* Seren tan Gwmmwl. *Its abrupt demise – the last issue featured poetry and prose that were 'to be continued' – was rumoured to have been caused by political pressure on the editor.*

### *9.1 A letter from America*

*Y Geirgrawn: Neu Drysorfa Gwybodaeth.* Am Chwefror, 1796. Rhif. I (The Magazine: Or Treasury of Knowledge. For February, 1796. No. I), 9–14.

LLYTHYR ODDIWRTH MORGAN AP JOAN RHYS.
AT ROBERT ROBERTS, CAEREFROG NEWYDD.

CLYWAIS y neithwr dy fod ar gychwyn tu a gwlad dy enedigaeth. Parodd y newydd i mi beth anesmwythder, rhag it' hwylio cyn i mi gyrraedd *Caerefrog Newydd.*

Yr ydwyf ar fy nhaith yn cyrchu tu ag atti, er's mwy na mis. Gadewais wlad yr *Indiaid* i'r gogledd orllewin o'r afon *Ohio* o gylch canol gorphenaf. Yr oeddwn yn bwriadu, fel y gwyddot; myned heibio i *Detroit*, a'r llynau gogleddol i *Loegr Newydd*: Eithr attaliodd ymddugiad atgas rhai o swyddogion Lloegr hen, sy'n byw yn *Canada*, i'm fyned i'r ffordd honno. Y mae pobl yr Unol Daleithau, yn bresennol yn debyg i wneud cyngrair heddychol a'r holl Indiaid o fewn eu cyffyniau; ond nid yw llys Brydain ddim yn hoffi'r fath waith; y maent wedi gwneud dim a fedrent i attal yr Indiaid i ddyfod i'r cyngrair. Y mae *cwn y rhyfel* yn sychedu o hyd am waed, ac am yrru'r holl fyd ben ben; i'r diben iddynt gael brashau eu hunain yn Nhinystr ereill, ond 'e ddywed y ddihareb gymraeg, "a dymuno ddrwg i'w gymmydog iddo ei hun y daw." Nid hwyrach, na ddarostyngir balchedd yr hon sydd wedi ymdecau, ac ymchwyddo, gan alw ei hun yn "*frenhines y gwledydd.* Pa hwya byddo Duw cyn taro, llwyr y dial pan y delo."

Yr ydwyf gwedi danfon amrywiol o lythyrau at y Cymry ond rhag ofn eu bod heb eu derbyn, mi roddaf i ti hanes fer o'm taith, er pan gadewaist fi yn *Savannah.* Yn ol ymdeithio o gylch dau fis yn *Georgia* a *S. Carolina*, mi groesais y mynydd glas a'r mynydd moel, i'r dalaith newydd a elwir *Cumberland.* Oddi yno mi aethym i *Kentucky.* Y mae'r wlad ffrwythlon hon yn y rhan fwyaf o bethau yn atteb i'r portreiad a argrephais yn gymraeg. Hynod y cynnylliad sydd iddi i o bob cwr o America. Nid wrth y cantoedd, ond wrth y miloedd, y mae dieithriaid yn ffrydio iddi, bob blwyddyn. Y mae hyn yn gosod allan werthfawrogrwydd y wlad, yn well nag y dichon un iaith ddadgan ei gogoniant. Mewn ychydig flynyddau, gyd a diwydrwydd, a bendithion cyffredin rhagluniaeth, yn y wlad hon, 'e aiff y *bwth* yn *balas,* ac fe gyferfydd y tlawd a'r cyfoethog wrth yr un bwrdd, i fwyta danteithion y tir.

Nid wyt' ddim i ddyall wrth hyn, fy mod yn canmol pob rhan o *Kentucky.* Y mae yma, fel llefydd ereill, dir drwg, a llawer o bethau annymunol. Ni ddylai neb bwrcasu tir yn *America* heb ei weled, yn gyntaf, a gwybod fod ei *deitl* yn dda. Y mae llawer o bobl fel y Diafol, yn myned beunydd oddi-amgylch, gan geisio pwy bynnag a allont lyngcu. Y maent yn cymmeryd *dieithraid* i mewn, ond, nid fel y gorch'mynnodd *Crist iddynt gael eu cymmeryd i mewn!*

O *Kentucky* mi es i'r sefydliadau newydd, draw i'r afon *Ohio.* Mi hwyliais i fynu, ac i wared i'r afon hon, o gylch tri chan' milldir. Y mae peth mawr o'r tir i'r gogledd orllewyn i'r afon, mor fras, a ffrwythlon, o bosibl, ag un rhan o'r byd, ac mewn amryw ystyriaethau yn well lle, i wneud sefydliad, na'r deheu orllewyn i'r afon. *Un peth* mae *teitl* y tir yn sicr o fod yn dda, am fod yn rhaid ei gael yn union oddiwrth *Congress,* neu o'r pellaf ar yr ail neu'r drydydd law. *Peth arall,* nid oes dim fath beth a dwyn *caethweision* dros yr afon, yr hyn sy'n cael ei oddef yn rhai o'r taleithau, er mawr wradwydd i ddynoliaeth. – Y mae'r gogledd-orllewyn i'r afon hefyd yn cael ei dwfrhau yn well na *Chentucky.* Y mae'r holl afonydd sydd yn rhedeg i'r *Ohio* i'r gorllewyn Ogledd yn tarddu'n agos i'r llynau gogleddol, yr hun a wnaiff y wlad mewn ystyr masnachol yn werthfawr i ryfeddu, am y gellir dwyn pob math o ddefnyddiau, i mewn ac allan o'r wlad, ar hyd yr afonydd. Y mae yn y wlad hon hefyd, yn ol myned y'mhell i mewn iddi, y fath wair-glodydd, a meusydd mawrion, fel na fydd mewn ystyriaeth ddim trafferth ar y sefydlwyr i lanhau a chwrteithio'r tir, &c. Ond rhaid i mi dewi. Mi a'th glywaf yn dywedyd, "Y mae'r Indiaid yna:" digon gwir y maent yn byw y'mhell i fynu i'r wlad: mi fym' dros dair wythnos yn ei plith. Yr oedd yn *Greenville,* lle mae byddin yr unol daleithau, rhwng chwech a saith cant o Indiaid yn gwneud heddwch gyda'r Penciwdawd, *Wayne.*[96] Yr oedd mwy o Bennaethiaid y llwythau (*chiefs*) wedi cyfarfod ynghyd, nag ar un achlyssur o'r fath, yn y wlad hyn o'r blaen. Mae'r heddwch yn debyg o gael ei sefydlu a'r sail cyfiawnder, ac y mae lle i obeithio y bydd yn barhaus. Y mae 'rhan fwyaf o'r Indiaid wedi blino rhyfela a'r Unol daleithau. Mi gefais gyfleisdra i ymddiddan a rhai o honynt, am bethau crefyddol. 'E debygid eu bod yn foddlon i dderbyn gwybodaeth. Mi bregethais o flaen y Penciwdawd, unwaith, ar y pwngc o anfon cenhadau i'w plith. Nid oes nemawr o gynnygion wedi cael eu gwneud etto, i anfon yr Efengyl i blith y truainiaid hyn. Gwell gan lawer o bregethwyr yn ein dyddiau ni syrthio allan a'u gilydd, ac ymgomio ynghylch pyngciau na ddeallant byth, na chadw gorch'-mynnion Crist: "Ewch a dysgwch yr holl genhedloedd – Pregethwch yr Efengyl i bob creadur," &c. O na bai holl weinidogion Jesu yn fwy tebyg i'r Angel a welodd Joan "*yn ehedeg y'nhanol y nêf.*"[97] Mae'r MORAFIAID wedi bod yn gryn ddiwyd, ac y mae amryw o'u disgyblion y'mhlith yr Indiaid gogleddol. Gobeithio nad yw'r dydd ddim y'mhell, pan y bydd i "rhai sydd y'mro a chysgod angau weled goleuni mawr."[98]

Doed yr Indiaid at yr Orsedd;
Doed y negro dua 'i liw;
Doed pob llwyth, ac Iaith, o bobloedd,
Doe'nt yn fuan at eu Duw:
Doed i dderbyn Iechydwriaeth,
Doed i ganmol am y gwa'd,
Doed pob enw 'nawr ar unwaith,
I seinio iechydwriaeth râd.

Ond yma yr wyt' yn barod i ofyn, 'a ddichon y Cymry sefydlu'n ddiogel a diofn drâw i'r afon *Ohio*? O'm rhan fy hun nid wyf yn gweled llawer mwy o berygl yno, na rhan arall –Y mae yno filoedd o bobl wedi sefydlu'n barod, a'r trefydd yn lliosogi'n rhyfedd ar yr afon *Ohio*. 'E fydd milwyr yn cael eu cadw mewn llefydd caerog sydd wedi'u hadeiladu trwy'r anialwch: a thra fyddo'r Indiaid yn heddychol, maent yn cael eu cyfrif y cyfeillion goreu. Mewn blwyddyn neu ddwy 'e fydd y wlad mor lliosog, fel na fydd dim mwy o ofn yr Indiaid ar y trigolion sy'n byw ar yr *Ohio*, nag sydd ar drigolion *Philadelphia*.

Os bydd y Cymry yn chwennych gwladychu gyd a'u gilydd, ac yn dewis myned i'r gorllewin – yr wyf wedi golygu tyddyn o dir, ar yr afon *Ohio*, a'r afon, *Big Miami*, o gylch *Lat.* 38½. Y mae yma le i gael *dau can'mill o erwi*, heb un erw ddrwg, o bosibl, ynddynt, – ac ni bydd y pellaf ddim chwaneg na deg milldir oddiwrth un o'r ddwy afon. Y mae mewn sefyllfa rhagorol i osod *Tref* neu ddwy, i lawr; ac y mae i lawer math o gelfyddydwyr, yn barod, fwy o anogaeth yn y wlad hon, nag un lle arall yn America, ac mae cyflogau da yn gyffredin i bob math o weithwyr, a'r ym borth am lai na hanner y prîs y ceir e' yn Nhrefydd yr *Atlantic*. Nid oes dim golwg y bydd yr ymborth yn ddryd yn y wlad hyn, yn ein hoes ni: Canys mae'r tir mor ffrwythlon, ac y dyg pob erw gymmeint a dwy neu dair, mewn un lle arall a wn i am dano.

Yr wyf wedi clywed fod rhai o'r Cymry wedi cychwyn i'r rhan ogleddol o dalaith *Caerefrog Newydd* (New York). Yr wyf yn barnu yr edifarhant cyn natolig, canys, yn ol yr hanes, y mae'r gauaf lawer galetach, a hwy yno, nag ar yr *wyddfa*. Ni ddylai'r Cymry, yn fy marn i, ddim myn'd i le gwaeth na'u gwlad eu hunain. Rwy'n meddwl fod y *climate* goreu yn America i'w gyfarfod o Lat. 37. i 40. Os eir y'mhellach i'r dê', neu i'r gogledd, mae naill neu'r hâf, neu'r gauaf yn rhy hir i'r *Europëaid*. Mewn perthynas i wrês yr hâf – mae'n agos mor frwd i'r gogledd a'r dê', dros ychydig, yn y wlad hyn: ond nid yw'r oerni ddim felly yn y gauaf. Gan hynny, gwell debygaf yw sefydlu mewn gwlad iachus, lle byddo'r gauaf yn fyr. Ond yn lle llythyr, 'e gymmerai lyfr bychan, i osod allan ragoriaeth rhai llefydd yn y wlad hyn ar y lleill. Yr wyf yn bwriadu cyn gynted ac y caffwyf amser, rhoi hanes yr holl daleithau, eu sefyllfa, Swyl, Marsiandiaith, &c. &c. o flaen y Cymry, fel y gallo pob un farnu dros ei hun – Fel un a gafodd drugaredd i deithio o gylch pedair mil o filldiroedd, yn y byd newydd, yr wyf yn bwriadu teithio o gylch dwy o filldiroedd yn chwaneg trwy Loegr Newydd, &c. ac yna mi argraphaf hanes mor ddiduedd ac a fedrwyf, o'r holl wlad: daioni a drygioni ei thrigolion, &c.

* * * * * *

Mi ddymunaf lwyddiant i ti ar dy daith i *Frydain*. Cofia fi'n garedig at bob un fyddo'n gofyn am fy helynt, dywed wrthynt, fod bugail Israel wedi'm tywys trwy lawer o anialwch; ond mae'n debyg mae ffordd union ydoedd i'r ddinas, saer ac adeiladydd yr hon yw Duw. Yr ydwyf gwedi pregethu ar fy nhaith gyd â phob plaid, fal y byddai cyfleisdra'n rhoi. Er maint mae'r bwystfil *rhagfarn* yn rhûo, mae'n colli tir bob dydd mae'n gofyn iddo fod yn ddiwyd ronyn bach, canys mae ei amser yn agos.

Y mae *John Evans* gwedi myn'd o'r diwedd, i fynu i'r afon *Missouri*, ar ei helfa am yr Indiaid Cymraig. Fe gafodd ei gymmeryd gan yr *Hispaniaid* a'i osod yn y carchardu yn *St. Louis* ar y Mississipi. Trwy erfyniad Cymro a elwir *Jones* yn byw yn y lle, fe gafodd rhyddid. Yn agos i'r yn pryd y daeth y Barnwr *Turner*,[99] i ardal *Cahokia* a *Chascaske*,[100] ar yr afon *Mississipi* i gyflawni ei swydd dros y wlad i'r gogledd orllewin i'r afon *Ohio*. Ymwelodd Pen Llywydd St Louis ag ef, ac a fynegodd iddo, fod un *John Evans* gyd a hwynt yn meddwl myned i fynu i'r afon *Missouri*, a'i fod gwedi ei attal hyd oni chaffai wybod ei hanes a'i gennadwri. Yr oedd y *Barnwr Turner* wedi clywed am *John Evans*, ac yn gwybod rhywbeth o'i hanes – Fe erfyniodd gyda'r Penllywydd am ei adael i fyned y'mlaen ar ei daith – gan hyspysu os na fyddai iddo gyfarfod ar bobl yr oedd yn ymofyn, y byddai ei daith er bydd cyffredin i'r byd. Ar hyn, addawodd, nid yn unig, i oddef i *J. Evans* i fyned y'mlaen ar ei daith – ond rhoddi llythyrau iddo yn y iaith *Hispaneg*, *Ffrangeg*, a *Saesoneg*, i'w gyflwyno ar ei daith, ynghyd a'r cyfryw bethau, ag fyddai yn fuddiol iddo i'w rhoddi i'r Indiaid. Yn llynn, y mae'r pethau sy'n debyg o fod yn rhwystrau yn ein gyrru'n gynt ar ein taith. By'r *Barnwr Turner* mor fwyn a rhoddi pob cyfarwyddyd angenrheidiol i J. E. mewn perthynas i'w ymddugiad gyda'r *Indiaid*, – cadw ei ddydd lyfr, &c. fel y mae'n fwy tebyg o lwyddo'n bresennol nag erioed. Cyn ei ddychweliad, y mae i ddilyn yr afon *Missouri* hyd at ei tharddiad; i ymweled ar mynydd Tan; ac os gall, ddwyn prawf ei fod wedi cyffwrdd ar *Mor heddycholl*, (Pacific Ocean) 'e fydd iddo dderbyn dwy fil o *ddolrs* [*sic*] oddiwrth Lywodraeth yr Hispain. Yn llynn, y mae'r Cymro, os caiff einios i ddychwelyd o'i daith pa un wnelo a'i llwyddo ai peidio, mewn perthynas i'r Indiaid cymraig, yn debyg o gael bywoliaeth gyssurus yn niwedd ei oes. 'E fydd ei ddydd goffadwriaeth os cadw 'fe hi'n daclus, yn werth rhai can'oedd o byn'au iddo. Mi fym' mewn cyfrinach ac un o'r Americaniaid sydd wedi cychwyn yn ddiweddar i'r afon *Missouri*, ac i aros i fasnach gyda'r Indiaid rhai blynyddau. Rhoddais iddo amryw o eiriau cymraeg a saesoneg fel os digwydd iddo gyfarfod a neb o'r cymry, y byddo iddo ei adnabod. Y mae wedi bod, yn barod mewn cyfrinach a mwy o Indiaid nag un dyn gwyn yn y wlad. Y mae'n ofni nad oes dim o'r fath bobl i'w cael. Hyn sydd si[ŵ]r fod llawer o Indiaid gwynnion yn byw y'mhell ar yr afon *Missouri* ac yn byw yn fwy tacclus na'r Indiaid yn gyffredinol. Bydd wych; a'r hwn sydd yn dal y mor y'nghledr ei law a'th gadwo, ag a'th ddygo'n ddihangol nid yn unig i dir Cymru, on[d] i dir y bywyd. Y mae'n ddrwg gennyf ddywedyd fod achos Duw'n bresennol yn America yn rhwyfo yn erbyn ffrwd o anghrediniaeth – gad iddo mae'n debyg fod yn rhaid dihoeni, hyd yn oed, sylfeini *Babylon goelgrefyddol*, cyn adeiladu'r Jerusalem newydd "Pan ddel mab y dyn a gaiff e' ffydd (y'mhawb) ar y ddaear?"[101] Trwy drugaredd yr wyf yn cael lle i obeithio, na fy'm taith ddim yn ofer yn yr Arglwydd, y tro hwn.

I Dduw, ag i air ei ras i'th och'mynaf,
Ydwyf dy ffyddlon gyfeill,
M. AP JOAN RHYS,

DINAS WASHINGTON,
AWST 21, 1795.

## (LETTER FROM MORGAN AP JOAN RHYS. TO ROBERT ROBERTS, NEW YORK.

I HEARD last night that you were about to set out for the land of your birth. The news caused me some uneasiness, lest you sail before I reached *New York*.

I have been on my journey heading towards it, for more than a month. I left the land of the *Indians* to the north-west of the *Ohio* river around the middle of July. I had intended, as you know, to go past *Detroit*, and the lakes to the north of *New England*: But the hateful behaviour of some of the officials of old England who live in *Canada* prevented me from going that way. The people of the United States are presently likely to make a peaceful accord with all the Indians within their borders; but the British court does not like such a course; they have done everything they can to prevent the Indians joining the alliance. The *dogs of war* thirst always for blood, and to drive the whole world head to head; so that they may fatten themselves on the Destruction of others, but the Welsh proverb says, "who wishes ill to his neighbour, it will come to himself." The pride of her who has made herself fair, and who has inflated herself, calling herself "*the queen of countries*", will surely be subdued. "The longer God takes before striking, the more complete will be the vengeance when it comes."

I have sent various letters to the Welsh but in case they have not received them, I will give you a short history of my journey since you left me in *Savannah*. After travelling about two months in *Georgia* and *S. Carolina*, I crossed the blue mountain and the bald mountain, to the new state that is called *Cumberland*. From there I went to *Kentucky*. This fertile land meets the description I published in Welsh in most things. The influx into it from every corner of America is wondrous. Strangers stream there, not by the hundreds, but by the thousands, every year. This shows the value of the land better that any language can express its glory. In a few years, with diligence, and the common blessings of providence, in this country, the *cottage* will become a *palace*, and the poor and the rich will meet at the same table, to eat the delicacies of the land.

You are not to understand by this that I praise every region of *Kentucky*. There are here, as in other places, bad land and many undesirable things. No-one should purchase land in *America* without seeing it first and knowing that its *title* is good. There are many people going about like the Devil every day, trying to swallow whoever they can. They take *strangers* in, but not as *Christ* commanded *that they should be taken in!*

From *Kentucky* I went to the new settlements across the river *Ohio*. I sailed up and down this river for about three hundred miles. Much of the land to the north-west of the river is as rich, and fertile, perhaps, as any region of the world, and is, from many points of view, a better place to make a settlement than to the south-west of the river. *For one thing* the *title* of the land is sure to be good, because it must be got directly from *Congress*, or at the furthest at second or third hand. *For another thing*, there is no such thing as taking *slaves* across the river, something which is tolerated in some of the states, to the great disgrace of mankind. – The north-west of the river is also better watered than *Kentucky*. All the rivers which run to the *Ohio* to the North-west spring from close to the northern lakes, which makes the country extremely valuable in a mercantile sense, for it is possible to carry all sorts of materials in and out of the country along the rivers. In this country there are also, after going far into it, such pastures and great fields that there is, in a way, no problem for the settlers of clearing and fertilizing the land, &c. But I must be quiet. I hear you say, "The Indians are there:" true enough, they live far up in the country; I spent over three weeks among them. In *Greenville*, where the United States' army is, there were between six and seven hundred Indians making peace with the General, *Wayne*.[96] There were more tribal Chiefs met together than on any occasion of this kind before in this country. The peace is likely to be settled on the basis of justice, and there is room to hope that it will be permanent. The majority of the Indians have tired of fighting with the United States. I had the opportunity of discoursing with some of them on religious matters. It would appear that they are willing to receive knowledge. I preached in front of the General once on the subject of sending missionaries amongst them. Not many attempts have yet been made to send the Gospel among these unfortunates. In our days, many preachers would prefer to fall out with each other and converse about subjects that they will never understand than to keep Christ's commandments: "Go and teach all the nations – Preach the Gospel to every creature," &c. If only all the servants of Jesus were more like the Angel that John saw "*flying in the midst of heaven*."[97] The MORAVIANS have been quite diligent, and there are several of their disciples among the northern Indians. Hopefully the day is not far when "to them which sat in the region and shadow of death light is sprung up."[98]

Come the Indian to the Throne;
come the negro of the blackest colour;
come every tribe, and Language, of people,
come they soon to their God:
come they to receive Salvation,
come they to praise for the blood,

come every denomination now at once
to proclaim gracious salvation.

But here you are ready to ask, 'is it possible for the Welsh to settle safely and without fear across the river *Ohio*?' For my own part I do not see much more danger there than in any other region – There are thousands of people settled there already, and the towns on the river *Ohio* multiply amazingly. Soldiers will be kept in fortified places which are built throughout the wilderness: and whilst the Indians are peaceful, they are counted as the greatest friends. In a year or two the country will be so populous that the residents who live on the *Ohio* will fear the Indians no more than the inhabitants of *Philadelphia* do.

If the Welsh desire to settle with each other, and choose to go to the west – I have seen a croft of land, on the river *Ohio*, and the river *Great Miami*, about *Lat.* 38½. Here there is space to get *two hundred thousand acres* without one bad acre, perhaps, in it, – and the furthest will be no more than ten miles from one of the two rivers. It is in an excellent position to establish a *Town* or two; and for many kinds of craftsmen there is already more encouragement in this country than in any other place in America, and good salaries for every sort of worker are common, and the food is less than half the price that it is to be had for in the Towns of the *Atlantic*. It does not appear that food in this country will be expensive in our time: For the land is so fertile, and each acre will bring forth as much as two or three in any other place I know of.

I have heard that some of the Welsh have set out for the northern district of the state of *New York*. I judge that they will regret this before Christmas, for, according to the accounts, the winter is much harder and longer there than on *Snowdon*. The Welsh should not, in my opinion, go to a place worse than their own country. I think that the best *climate* in America is to be met from Lat. 37. to 40. If one goes further south or north, either the summer or the winter is too long for the *Europeans*. With regard to the heat of the summer – it is nearly as hot in the north as in the south in this country: but the cold is not like that in the winter. Therefore, I deem it better to settle in a healthy country where the winter is short. But instead of a letter it would take a small book to set out the excellence of some places in this country over the others. As soon as I have time I intend to put an account of all the states, their situations, Soil, Commerce, &c. &c. before the Welsh so that each may judge for himself – As one who had the good fortune to travel about four thousand miles in the new world, I intend to travel about two thousand miles more in New England, &c. and then

I will print as unbiased an account as I can of the whole country: the good and bad of its inhabitants, &c.

* * * * * *

I wish you success on your journey to *Britain*. Remember me kindly to everyone who asks after my affairs, tell them that Israel's shepherd has led me through many wildernesses; but it was probably a straight path to the city whose architect and builder is God. I have preached with every denomination on my journey, as opportunity arose. However much the beast of *prejudice* roars, it loses ground every day. It has to be busy for a little while yet, for its time is near.

*John Evans* has at last gone up the river *Missouri*, on his hunt for the Welsh Indians. He was taken by the *Spanish* and thrown into prison in *St Louis* on the Mississippi. Through the entreaties of a Welshman called *Jones* who lives in the area, he was given his freedom. About the same time Judge *Turner*[99] came to the *Cahokia* and *Kaskaskia* area,[100] on the river *Mississippi*, to fulfil his office for the country to the north-west of the river *Ohio*. The Governor of St Louis visited him and said to him that one *John Evans* was with them, who was intending to go up the river *Missouri*, and that he had stopped him until he got to know his story and his mission. *Judge Turner* had heard of *John Evans* and knew something of his story – He pleaded with the Governor to let him go ahead with his journey – pointing out that even if he did not meet with the people he was seeking, his journey would be of general benefit to the world. Thereupon, he promised not only to permit *J. Evans* to go ahead with his journey – but to give him letters in the *Spanish, French*, and *English* languages to present on his journey, along with such things as would be beneficial to him to give to the Indians. Thus, the things which appear as restraints drive us faster on our journey. *Judge Turner* was kind enough to give every necessary direction to J. E. as regards his conduct with the *Indians*, – to keep his journal, &c. so that he is more likely to succeed now than ever. Before his return, he is to follow the river *Missouri* to its source; to visit the Fire mountain; and, if he can bring proof that he has reached the *Pacific Ocean*, he will receive two thousand *dollars* from the Spanish Government. Thus, the Welshman, if he returns from his journey alive, whether he may succeed or not as regards the Welsh Indians, is likely to have a comfortable livelihood for the remainder of his life. His journal, if he keeps it neatly, will be worth some hundreds of pounds to him. I had private council with one of the Americans who recently left for the river *Missouri* to stay and trade with the Indians for some years. I gave him some Welsh and English words so that if he happens to meet any of the Welsh, he will recognize them. He has already communicated with more Indians than any white man in the country. He fears that no such people exist. It is certain that many white Indians live far along the river *Missouri* and live more cleanly than the Indians in general. Fare well; and may he who holds the sea in the palm of his hand keep you, and bring you safely not only to the land of Wales, but to the land of [eternal] life. I am sorry to say that the cause of God presently in America rows against a current of atheism – let it be, it seems that we must weaken even the foundations of *superstitious Babylon* before building the new Jerusalem. "When the Son of man cometh, shall he find faith (in everyone) on the earth?"[101] Thank goodness I have reason to believe that my journey was not vain in the Lord this time.

To God, and to the word of his grace I commend you,
I am your faithful friend,
M. AP JOAN RHYS,

WASHINGTON CITY,
AUGUST 21, 1795.)

### *9.2 An attack on* Seren tan Gwmmwl

*Y Geirgrawn: Neu Drysorfa Gwybodaeth.* Am Chwefror, 1796. Rhif. I (The Magazine: Or Treasury of Knowledge. For February, 1796. No. I), 16–21.

GOLWG BYR AR Y LLYFR A ELWIR *SEREN TAN GWMMWL* A GYHOEDDWYD YN *LLUNDAIN* YN Y FLWYDDYN, 1795.

MOLIANT am bob rhagluniaeth feunyddiol, sydd yn ymddangos y'mhlith dynion. Yr ydym yn darllain, ddarfod i *Syr Isaac Newton*, astudio, a rhoddi mawr wybodaeth i'r byd, yn berthynol i'r gelfyddyd *seryddaidd*, ond beth am hynny; dyma ddyn, wedi ymhwthio y'mhellach i ddirgelwch yr wybren gymmylog, nag a ddarfu *Newton* erioed; ac a daflodd i lawr i'n plith y fath *Seren* a'r y sydd yn goleuo yn y tywyllwch, megis *phosphorus*, ac yn dangos pethau buchain yn fawrion, a'r pethau pell yn agos. Nid wyf i ddim yn chwennych moliannu'r Llyfr a elwir *Seren tan gwmmwl*, rhag ofn eilwaith, i'r Awdwr happio gwisgo am dano'n wych ac anghofio am ei grys; ac ar y llaw arall, nid wyf am ei ddychanu'n fawr o'r achos, rhag ofn iddo lygoeri, yn ei ryfeddol, a'i wybodol ddoniau.

Y peth mwya gresynol gennyf; ydyw ei fod wedi ymddangos i'n plith mor druan, a hynny megis crippyl, braidd yn hollawl ymlusgo, wrth nerth baglau gwyr ereill.

Y mae'r awdwr yn dywedyd yn nechreu ei lyfr, fal hyn, medd ef; "Yr oedd Nimrod yn ddiammau, yn ddyn mileinig, a gwaedlyd, yn ol yr hanes mae'r 'scrythur yn ei roddi o hono." Dyma lle'r ydym yn dal yr awdwr, yn union yn ei ddechreuad, mewn rhwyd o anwiredd, a deued allan o honi os medr. Nid oes dim o'r fath hanes yn y'r yscrythyr, fod Nimrod yn ddyn mileinig a gwaedlyd, fal ag y mae'r awdwr, wedi ymmhonni, a dywedyd y fath beth yn ei anwybodaeth ac er ei gwylydd, ac i geisio tywyso dynionach y byd ar ol ei ynfydrwydd ef. Cymmaint o hanes am Nimrod, ac y sydd i'w gael yn yr ysgrythyr o'i ddechreu i'w ddiwedd, a welir yn 10*fed* bennod o *Genesis*, ac yn yr adnodau 8, 9, 10, ac yr wyf yn deisyf a'r y darllennydd, gymmeryd ei feibl, ac edrych a ydyw'r hanes, fal y mae'r awdwr yn dywedyd. Gwedi hyn, y mae'n dywedyd yn hynod o'r call, a feddyliwn, yn ei olwg ei hun.

Medd ef, "Cyn bod brenhinoedd nid oedd rhyfel; wrth hynny gellir meddwl, ped fae heb frenhinoedd, y byddai'r byd mewn heddwch, undeb a chariad." Yr un peth yw dywedyd, cyn bod dynion prysur heb ddiolch, nid oedd ymbleidiau, ac ymrysonau; ac yn yr [un] modd gellir meddwl, pe b'ai heb y fath ddynion, y byddai'r byd etto yn debyccach i fod mewn heddwch, undeb a chariad: a thra b'o dynion diddysg, penauryddion, a choeg-ddiriaid, yn ein plith y rhai sy'n ymyrru y'nhrefn Llywodraeth, ac yn trefnu Llys brenhin, a'u cabandai eu hunain gartref yn gwbl annhrefnus, nid oes le i ddisgwyl on'd blinder o'u hachos, o ddydd i ddydd. Ychydig y'mlaen, mae'r awdwr yn son, mor llawn o garcharion, oedd y *Bastille* yn Ffraingc gynt, a hynny medd ef, heb achos yn y byd ond son am ryddid a chyfiawnder; os gwir yw hyn, 'rwy'n cyffaddef ei fod yn resynus; ond os cymmerwn olwg manol ar Ffraingc, y pryd hyn, 'rwy'n meddwl y cawn weled, fod ei charchardai yn ddigon llawnion, a llawer, 'rwy'n ammau, o garcharwyr ynddynt, mor ddiachos ac yr oedd llawer gynt yn y *Bastille*: hefyd rwy'n meddwl, nad oes yn dyddiau hyn, un deyrnas yn Ewrop, oddi tan fwy gwg-ofn, a gorwch lywodraeth na Ffraingc. Ychydig y'mlaen wedi hyn, mae'r awdwr yn rhyfeddu fel yr oedd yr hen Israeliaid, yn eu dallineb, medd ef, yn gweiddi am frenhin; ac yn y fan hyn, mae wedi ceisio bod yn bur gyfrwys, ac fel pob gwrthgiliwr arall, yn cadw swn mawr ar ei dommen ei hun, a dewis rhyw ran, oedd at ei fwriad ef ei hun, o'r wythfed bennod o Lyfr cyntaf Samuel, ac heb son am y rhannau eraill o'r bennod, yr hyn sy'n ddigon i wrthdroi ei fynediad ef, a hynny, fal y dangosaf yn ganlynol.

Yn y rhan gyntaf o'r bennod hon, mae'r Israeliaid yn gofyn brenhin, o herwydd eu bod yn cael eu *haflywodraethu* gan feibion Samuel; felly mae miloedd o *bobl yn Ffraingc y dydd heddyw yn cwyno am frenhin; ac os ca' eu †gelynion, sef y pen Llwodraethwyr, afael ynddynt, hwy a gant yn fuan golli eu bywydau. Ond i sylwi'n fanylach ar y bennod.

Y mae'n dechreu fal hyn "Ac wedi heneiddio Samuel efe a osododd ei feibion yn farnwyr ar Israel, a'i feibion ni rodiasant yn ei ffyrdd ef, eithr troisant at gybydd-dra, a chymerasant wobrwy, a gwyrasant farn. Yna holl henuraid Israel a ymgasglasant, ac a ddaethant at Samuel i Ramah, ac a ddywedasant wrtho ef, weled, ti a heneiddiaist, a'th feibion ni rodiasant yn dy ffyrdd di; yn awr gosod arnom ni frenhin i'n barnu, megis yr holl genhedloedd. A'r ymadrodd fu ddrwg gan Samuel pan ddywedasant dyro i ni frenhin i'n barnu: a Samuel a weddiodd ar yr Arglwydd. A dywedodd yr Arglwydd wrth Samuel, gwrando ar lais y bobl, yn yr hyn oll a ddywedasant wrthit." Gwedi hyn, mae'r bennod yn adrodd dull y brenhin a deyrnasa arnynt, fel ag y mae'r awdwr wedi ei osod i lawr; a chwedi hynny, mae'r bennod yn diweddu fel hyn, "Er hynny, y bobl a wrthodasant wrando ar lais Samuel, ac a ddywedasant, nage, eithr brenhin fydd arnom ninnau hefyd, fal yr holl genhedloedd; a'n brenhin a'n barna ni, efe a â allan hefyd o'n blaen ni, ac efe a ymladd ein rhyfeloedd ni. A gwrandawodd Samuel holl eiriau y bobl, ac a'u hadroddodd hwynt lle y clybu'r Arglwydd. A dywedodd yr Arglwydd wrth Samuel, gwrando ar eu llais hwynt, *a gosod frenhin arnynt*." Y mae'n rhyfedd fod yr Awdwr yn dywedyd, fod yr Israeliaid yn eu *dallineb* yn gofyn brenhin, ac ar yr un pryd yn cael eu trawslywodraethu gan feibion Samuel: Pe buasent yn cael eu llywodraethu'n gyfiawn gan feibion Samuel, ac wrth hynny'n gofyn brenin, i lywodaethu arnynt, a hwythau eisus tan lywodraeth hynaws, yn wir, 'c f'asai hynny'n beth dallineb arnynt; a chan eu bod yn cael eu cam lywodraethu gan feibion Samuel, pa rai oeddynt yn cymmeryd gwobrwy, er mwyn gwyro barn, yr oeddynt y'marn y byd yn ddynion gwybodus, ac yn ceisio gwrthod eu cam: ac nid oeddynt chwaith ddim mor ddeillion, ac y mae'r awdwr yn ei ryfeddol oleuni, yn meddwl eu bod. I ddyfod y'mlaen, yn arafedd, gwedi hyn, 'rwy'n sylwi ar yr awdwr yn rhyfeddu na b'asai rhai o'r offeiriadau, yn cymmeryd testun i'w pregeth o'r bennod hon, y dydd ympryd diweddaf, ac, medd ef, "pe buasent yn gwneuthur hynny, ac yn dilyn yn agos i'w testyn, 'e f'asai raid iddynt ollwng y gath allan o'r cwd." Dyma hanes newydd i mi; ni chlywais i erioed o'r blaen, am offeiriadau yn cario cathod mewn cydau, nag yn enwedig yn y pulpud wrth bregethu: a chan na ddarfu'r offeiriadau, gymmeryd testun i'w pregeth, o'r bennod a soniwyd, y mae'r awdwr ei hun (diolch iddo!) yn cymmeryd ei destun yno, ac yn anturi rhoddi pwyth

* *Royalists in France.*

† *Democrats in France.*

yn e'u celfyddyd, ond chwi welsoch fal y dangosais ychydig o'r blaen, y fath gandryll-waith llygrynllyd, o wnaeth ar yr hyn a gymmerodd o'r beibl. O chwi *offeiriadau Pabaidd*, *Calfinistaidd*, *Lutheraidd*, a *Methodus*[t]*aidd*, glynwch yn eich llyfrau, a rhoddwch bwythau manylach na'r gwr hwn, yn y gelfyddyd! Paham y byddwch segur, a gadael i drychod dirio'r Winllan! Paham y byddwch ddistaw, a dulluan y tywyllwch yn bloeddio'n uwch na chwi?

Bellach mi ddaliaf sylw byr, ar yr hyn y mae'r awdwr yn son, am "goron brenhin, a chap ffwl;" ac 'rwy'n ei weled yn dywedyd fal hyn; medd ef, "os oes neb yn meddwl fod y dynion," hynny yw y brenhin a'r ffwl, "yn perchen cymmeint synwyr a digrifwch, un *heb* ei goron a'r llall *heb* ei gap," ac yma mae'n gofyn, "I ba beth mae'r cap a'r goron dda?" ac ar yr un anadl yn atteb, ac yn dywedyd mae i synnu pobl gyffredin, ac i'w hudo hwy i ymadael a'u harian; yn wir dyma chwedl y gwyr pob hen wrach am dano yn gystal a'r awdwr ei hun, ond etto diolch yn fawr i'r gwr, am y fath holiadau, ac attebion. Pe b'ai brenhin yn Lloegr heb ei goroni ni byddai ddim yn gymmwys i'w alwedigaeth. Ped fae dyn yn myned i neithior heb y wisg briodas am dano annheilwng fyddai'r olwg arno. Nid ydyw'r brenhin ddim yn coroni ei hunan, ond trwy orchymmyn y Senedd yr ydis yn gwneud hynny; a phob aelod yn y Senedd, sydd yn addef, ei fod yn deilwng goronog, ac yn ei barchu'n fawr, ac yn dywedyd ei fod yn brif golofn, – yn undeb y deyrnas; ac mae'n debygol, mae dyma'r dynion ffo[l] ffroen-uchol, y rhai mae'r awdwr yn crybwyll am danynt.

Ac etto ar y llaw arall, nid ydyw ffwl *Interlude* ar y daflod, neu'r *Stage* ddim yn edrych yn gymmwys i'w alwedigaeth, heb ei syrcyn brith a'i gap; felly y gwelir nad eill y brenhin ddim bod heb ei goron, na'r ffwl heb ei gap, i gyflawnu eu dyledswyddau. Rhyfedd mor ddifrifol mae'r awdwr wedi bod, ac yn ceiso ei dystiolaeth yn fynych o'r bibl, ac wrth hynny'n dywedyd cyn gystal, nad ydyw'r Hollalluog yn ewyllysio cydnabod neb yn frenhin, ond brenhin nef; ac ar yr un pryd mae'r hen Destament yn llawn o hanesion brenhinig, a llawer o honynt wedi eu heneinio'n frenhinoedd, trwy orchymmyn yr Arglwydd. Os edrych yr Awdwr yn y 15*fed*. bennod o Lyfr cyntaf Samuel, *adn*. y 17*eg*. fe ga' weled fal ag y mae Samuel yn dywedyd wrth Saul; fal hyn. "A Samuel a ddywedodd, ond pan oeddynt fychan yn dy olwg dy hun, y gwnaed di'n ben ar lwythau Israel, ac yr eneiniodd yr Arglwydd di yn frenhin ar Israel." Y mae'r awdwr yn dywedyd yn eglur, fod dynion yn canu mawl, i'r brenhin, ac yn ei addoli megis Duw; a chan hynny, medd ef, "nid oes ganddynt ond ychydig barch i frenhin y nef, ac onid ê, hwy a ddalient Sylw ar y geiriau "*Na fydded it Dduwiau eraill ger fy mron i*." Dyma'r awdwr wedi hir ymbalfalu yn y bibl, yn myn'd mor sanctaidd, a rhoddi un o'r deg gorchymmyn o'n blaen; a pheth rhyfedd hefyd na b'sai yn dangos i ni, heblaw hyn, rai o'r defodau sacramentaidd. Mae'n debygol mae'r un gorchymmyn yna ydyw un o'r pwythau, a osododd ef y'ngelfyddydd yr offeiriadau, fel ac y soniwyd o'r blaen. 'Rwyf inneu'n cofio fod rhyw un wedi peri anrhydeddu, ac ufyddhau i'r brenhin. Ymddwyn o honom yn ostyngedig, gan berchi pawb o'm gwell. Na wnelon niwed i neb ar air na gweithred. Bod yn gywyr ac yn union, y'mhob peth a wnelom &c. Y gwersi hyn nid hwyrach na byddant ddim yn dygymmod ac awdwr y SEREN TAN GWMMWL; Ond ar yr un pryd 'rwy'n gobeithio y byddant; eithr gwnaed ef a fynno a hwy, 'rwyf i'n haeru'n eofn, mae gwersi cymmwys i ddynion i'w cadw mewn côf ydynt. Etto yr ydym yn darllain, fod yr hen 'scrifennydd *St. Paul* yn peri talu teyrnged i'r hwn mae'n ddyledus, toll, i'r hwn mae toll, parch i'r hwn mae parch yn ddyledus. Yn y lle nesaf, 'rwy'n sylwi ar yr awdwr yn son am allu brenhin, Medd ef mae gan y brenhin allu i wneuthur rhyfel a'r deyrnas a fynno heb na chennad na chyngor gan undyn, a gwneuthur heddwch pan welo ef yn dda ei hun. Dyma ryw hanes rhyfedd yn wir, na wybym i erioed am dani o'r blaen. Yr ydym yn deall ddarfod i'n brenhin yn ddiweddar, ddanfon cennadwri i'r Senedd, (neu fal y dywed y Saeson Parliament,) a dywedyd ei fod yn ewyllysio gwneuthur Heddwch a'r Ffrancod, cyn gynted ag y gellir; ond os oes gan y brenhin, y fath allu, yn unig ynddo ei hun, fel ac y dywedoedd yr awdwr fod ni b'asai raid iddo ddim danfon i'r Senedd y fath gennadwriaeth, ond gwneuthur heddwch a'r Ffrangcod yn union, a hynny o honno ei hun; A chan ddarfod iddo ddanfon cennadwri felly, y mae'n eglur ddigon, nad all ef ddim gwneuthur cyngrair nag anghyngrair, ac un Llywodraeth ba bynnag, heb fod y senedd a llaw yn y gwaith: A phe b'ai ganddo allu i wneuthur rhyfel pan fynai, nid oes ganddo ddim gallu a hynny pan funai, i gael cymmeint ag *un geiniog* o'r *drysorfa*, heb genad y Senedd; ac wrth hynny pa fodd y dichon iddo gynnal ei ryfel? Mae'n rhy faith yn awr i'm olrhain gwaith yr awdwr o ben bwygilydd, ac y mae wedi scrifennu yn y fath gymmysgfa o annibendod, fal nad wyf i, ysywaeth yn deall mo hono, ac yr wyf yn haeru fod llawer o'i ddychmygion mor egwan, fell nad eill yr awdwr ddim dal atynt y'ngwyneb profedigaeth; ond ni wiw, ac hefyd mae'n ddiddiben, mynd i daro pob peth erthylaidd, a'r y sydd yn ymddangos i'n plith; nid oes ond gadael iddynt, fal llysiau diwreiddiog, ddihoeni o honynt eu hunain.

Yn y lle nesa, 'rwy'n sylwi ar yr awdwr yn gresynu fod un dyn yn gallu myn'd i'r Senedd-dy, ac sydd yn byw ar ei eiddo ei hunan. Ond yr wyf i'n meddwl mae fal hyn yr oedd yr awdwr yn tybied, a hynny yw fod yn resyn gan bob dyn sydd yn gwisgo cap ffwl, na b'ai lloegr yn cymmeryd ei dysgu gan y bwystfil a soniodd yr awdwr am dano; a chan Ffraingc: a chan America, pa sutt i lywodraethu. Pe byddai'r fath beth a hynny yn Lloegr, yna byddai'r hen ddihareb yn cael lle, "Yr oen yn dysgu i'r ddafad bori." Ond am yr Awdwr yn son am yr hen *Syr Watkin Williams Wynne*, a llinynau arffedogau merchaid, a'r cariad oedd rhwng *Dafydd ap Gwilym* a *Morfudd*,[102] nid ydynt ond Sothach islaw sylwi arnynt; Ac mae'n rhyfedd ddarfod i'r dysgawdwr, a scrifennwr trefn llywodraeth, halogi ei dafod, a difwyno ei ddwylaw, gyd â'r fath betheu.

Mi feddyliwn mae dyn, ydyw awdwr y SEREN TAN GWMMWL, tebyg i un a fai'n myned oddiamgylch y wlad, a digwydd iddo graffu a'r ryw adeilad wych, a cherfwaith cywrain arni, ac yntef yn dywedyd fod yr adeilad yn feius o'r topp i'r gwaelod, ac nad oedd modd i neb fyw ynddi, er bod bobl yn byw yno'n gwbl ddedwydd, y pryd hynny; Ond er hyn mae arno eisiau tynnu'r adeilad i lawr yn garnedd, a'r trueni yw, na wyr y dyn pa fodd i osod un garnedd yn ei lle tu ag at ei hail wneuthur yn drefnusach nac o'r blaen. Rwyf i'n meddwl mae breuddwydio a wnaeth yr awdwr ryw noson, ar y *newydd Loer*, ei fod yn 'scrifennu hanes brenhinoedd, ac yn dysgu iddynt drefn Llywodraeth, a phan ddefrodd, y'mha le'r oedd ef, ond yn eigion y ffurfafen, ac yn chwilio am seren tan gwmmwl; ac oddi yno ar fyr fe ddisgynnodd i lawr, trwy'r corwynt, fal llwttrach y ser, ac a geisiodd anrheithio gwlad cymru o gwrr bwygilydd. – Bellach, mae'n bryd i m' ddiweddu gyda diolch yn llaes i'r bwystfil, fal ac y mae'r awdwr yn ei henwi, ac medd ef, a ddaeth yma o'r America gythreilig, a dywedyd i ni ein hachau, mae lladron, ac ysbeilwyr, a llofruddion ydym ni, 'r Lloegeriaid, o'n dechreuad hyd heddyw. Ac y'mhellach yr wyf yn diolch nos a dydd, i awdwr y SEREN TAN GWMMWL am ddangos ei ryfeddol ddoniau: ac yr wyf yn gobeithio y gwna ef eilwaith, fal ag y mae wedi addo, fwrw yr hyn sydd yn ei geudod; Canys 'e fydd hynny'n oleuni i oleuo'r cymry, y rhai sy'n eistedd mewn tywyllwch, ac y'nghysgod mynyddau; ac hefyd a fydd yn lles, a gogoniant anfarwol iddo ef ei hun. Gwyn ein byd, gymry truain! dyma ddyn cymmwys iawn, (fal ag y soniodd am ei gymmwysder yn nechreu ei lyfr) gwedi dangos i ni ddull brenhinoedd, esgobion ac arglwyddi, yng-hyd a threfn Llywodraeth; ac wrth hynny fe ddangosodd ryw ychydig o'i ddull a'i wybodaeth ei hun, yn berthynol i drefn llywodraeth, a phwytho celfydd yr offeiriadau, ac am hynny oll bydded moliant iddo yn ein plith ni, o genhedlaeth hyd genhedlaeth, ac o amser i amser, hyd na byddo amser mwyach.

ANTAGONIST.

## (A SHORT VIEW OF THE BOOK WHICH IS CALLED *SEREN TAN GWMMWL* (A STAR UNDER A CLOUD) WHICH WAS PUBLISHED IN *LONDON* IN THE YEAR, 1795.

PRAISE be for every daily providence which appears among men. We read that *Sir Isaac Newton* studied and gave great knowledge to the world pertaining to the *astronomical* art, but what of that; here is a man who has pushed further into the secrets of the cloudy heavens than *Newton* ever did; and who threw down into our midst such a *Star* as shines in the darkness like *phosphorus*, and shows small things enlarged, and far things as near. I do not intend to praise the Book which is called *Seren tan Gwmmwl*, for fear that the Author again happens to dress himself finely and forget his shirt; and on the other hand I do not intend to lampoon him greatly because of it, lest he grow lukewarm in his marvellous and learned talents.

The most deplorable thing for me is that he has appeared among us so pitifully, and that like a cripple, almost entirely dragging himself, by the strength of other men's crutches.

The author says at the beginning of his book, like this, he says; "Nimrod was undoubtedly a vicious and bloody man, according to the account the scripture gives of him." Here we catch the author out, straightaway at the beginning, in a web of untruth, and let him come out of it if he can. There is no such account in the scripture that Nimrod was a vicious and bloody man, as the author has asserted and has thus said in his ignorance and to his shame and to attempt to lead the frail men of this world to follow his own madness. Such an account of Nimrod as is to be had in the scripture from its start to its end is seen in the 10th chapter of *Genesis*, and in the verses 8, 9, 10, and I urge the reader to take his bible and see if the account is as the author says. After this, he speaks remarkably sensibly, I think, in his own estimation.

He says, "Before there were kings there was no war; which may be taken to mean that if there were no kings, the world would be at peace, unity and love." It is the same thing to say, before there were busy men without thanks, there were no factions, and contentions; and in the [same] manner it can be thought that if there were no such men, the world would again be more likely to be at peace, unity and love: and while there are ignorant, headstrong and false wretches among us, who interfere with the order of Government and who put a king's Court in order while their own cabins at home are completely disorderly, there is nothing but trouble to be expected because of them from day to day. A little further on, the author mentions how full of prisoners the *Bastille* in France used to be, and that, he says, without any reason whatsoever except that they spoke of liberty and justice; if this is true, I admit it is a pity; but if we take a close look at France now, I think we may see that its prisons are full enough, and many of the prisoners in them, I suspect, as innocent as many of those formerly in the *Bastille*: I also think that these days there is not one kingdom in Europe more cowed and under a more authoritarian government than France. A little on from this, the author wonders at how the old Israelites in their blindness, he says, called for a king; and here he has tried to be quite cunning, and like other renegades makes a great noise on his own dung-heap, and has chosen some section which served his own purpose of the eighth chapter of the first Book of Samuel, and without mentioning the other parts of the chapter, which are enough to block his way, as I will show in the following.

In the first section of this chapter the Israelites ask for a king, because they are being *misgoverned* by the sons of Samuel; thousands of *people in France lament for for a king thus today; and if their †enemies, the chief Rulers, get hold of them, they will soon lose their lives. But to comment on the chapter in more detail.

It begins like this "And it came to pass, when Samuel was old, that he made his sons judges over Israel [. . .] And his sons walked not in his ways, but turned aside after lucre, and took bribes, and perverted judgement. Then all the elders of Israel gathered themselves together, and came to Samuel unto Ramah, and said unto him, Behold, thou art old, and thy sons walk not in thy ways: now make us a king to judge us like all the nations. But the thing displeased Samuel, when they said, Give us a king to judge us. And Samuel prayed unto the Lord. And the Lord said unto Samuel, Hearken unto the voice of the people in all that they say unto thee." After this, the chapter reports how the king will rule over them, as the author has set it down; and after that, the chapter ends like this, "Nevertheless the people refused to obey the voice of Samuel; and they said, Nay; but we will have a king over us; that we also may be like all the nations; and that our king may judge us, and go out before us, and fight our battles. And Samuel heard all the words of the people, and he rehearsed them in the ears of the Lord. And the Lord said to Samuel, Hearken unto their voice, and *make them a king*." It is strange that the Author says that the Israelites in their *blindness* asked for a king, and at the same time were being tyrannized by the sons of Samuel: If they were being governed justly by the sons of Samuel, and with that had asked for a king to rule them, and they already being under a genial government, truly that would be a touch of blindness

* *Royalists in France.*

† *Democrats in France.*

in them; and because they were being misgoverned by the sons of Samuel, who took bribes in order to pervert justice, they were, in the opinion of the world, wise men and trying to right their wrong: and neither were they as blind as the author in his strange interpretation thinks they were. To gradually move forward, after this I note the author wondering that no priests took the text of their sermons from this chapter on the last fast-day, and he says, "if they had done this, and had followed the text closely, they would have had to let the cat out of the bag." This is news to me; I have never heard of priests carrying cats in bags before, and especially not in the pulpit while preaching: and as these priests did not take the text of their sermon from the chapter mentioned, the author himself (thanks to him!) takes his text from there and ventures to add a stitch to their artwork, but you saw, as I showed you a little earlier, what a mangled mess he made of what he took from the bible. Oh you *Papist, Calvinist, Lutheran, and Methodist priests*, stick to your books in the art and make more detailed stitches than this man! Why do you remain idle, and allow swine to root up the Vineyard! Why are you silent, with the owl of darkness hooting louder then you?

Now I will remark briefly on that which the author mentions of "the king's crown, and the fool's cap"; and I see him speaking thus; he says, "if anyone thinks that the men," that is the king and the fool, "possess so much sense and wit, the one *without* his crown and the other *without* his cap," and here he asks, "What are the cap and the crown good for?" and in the same breath replies, and says that it is to stun ordinary people, and to entice them to part with their money; indeed this is a tale that every old hag knows as well as the author himself, but yet thanks to the man for such questions and answers. If the king of England were not crowned, he would not be fit for his calling. If a man were to go to a marriage feast without his wedding clothes on, his appearance would be inappropriate. The king does not crown himself, but it is done by the command of Parliament; and every Member of Parliament avows that he is rightfully crowned and greatly respects him and says that he is the chief pillar in the unity of the kingdom; and perhaps these are the foolish snobs whom the author mentions.

And yet on the other hand, the *Interlude* fool on the cart or the *Stage* does not look suited to his calling without his motley jerkin and his cap; so it can be seen that the king cannot be without his crown nor the fool without his cap to fulfil their duties. Strange how serious the author has been, often seeking his evidence in the bible, and accordingly saying as much as that the Almighty does not desire to acknowledge anyone as a king but the king of heaven; and at the same time the old Testament is full of royal histories, and many of them kings anointed at the Lord's command. If the Author were to look in the 15th chapter of the first Book of Samuel, *verse*

17, he will see that Samuel says to Saul; like this. "And Samuel said, When thou wast little in thine own sight, wast thou not made the head of the tribes of Israel, and the Lord anointed thee king over Israel?" The author says clearly that men sing praise to the king and worship him as a God; and with that, he says, "they have but little respect for the king of heaven, and if they did, they would take Note of the words "*Thou shalt have no Gods before me.*" Here the author, having long groped about in the bible, has become so holy as to put one of the ten commandments before us; and it is a strange thing that he does not also show us some of the sacramental rites in addition to this. This one commandment is probably one of the stitches that he put in the artwork of the priests, as was previously mentioned. I, too, remember that someone had bid us honour and obey the king. To conduct ourselves humbly, respecting all of our betters. That we shall not do harm to anyone by word or deed. To be right and true, in all that we do &c. These lessons, perhaps, will not agree with the author of the SEREN TAN GWMMWL; But at the same time I hope they will; but let him do what he will with them, I assert confidently that they are suitable lessons for men to remember. Again we read that the old writer *St. Paul* bids us pay tribute to whom it is owed, toll to whom toll is owed, respect to him who is owed respect. Next, I notice that the author speaks of the king's power. He says that the king has power to make war with any kingdom he wishes without permission or counsel from anybody, and to make peace when he himself sees fit. This is some strange tale indeed, which I never heard before. We understand that our king recently sent a message to the Senate, (or as the English say, Parliament,) to say that he desired to make Peace with the French as soon as possible; but if the king has such power himself alone as the author said, he would not have to send Parliament such a message, but make peace with the French directly and by himself; And as he has sent such a message, it is clear enough that he can make neither alliance nor disunion with any Government whatsoever, unless Parliament has a hand in the matter: And if he had the ability to make war when he desired, he would not have the power to take as much as *one penny* from the *treasury* when he wants to without the permission of Parliament; and thus, how would he be able to conduct his war? It is too tedious for me to trace the work of the author from one end to the other now, and he has written in such a hotchpotch of confusion that I cannot, alas, understand it, and I assert that many of his fantasies are so feeble that the author cannot maintain them under test; but it is unfitting and also pointless to strike out at every abortive thing which appears in our midst; they need only be left, like rootless vegetables, to wither of themselves.

Next, I note that the author deplores that any man can go to Parliament who lives from his own property. But I think that the author meant this, and that is that every man who wears a fool's cap thinks it a pity that England would not be taught by the monster of which the author spoke; and by France; and by America, how to govern. If there were such a thing as that in England, then there would be a place for the old saying, "The lamb teaching the sheep to graze." But as for the Author speaking of old *Sir Watkin Williams Wynne*, and the apron strings of girls, and the love that was between *Dafydd ap Gwilym* and *Morfudd*,[102] they are but Trash beneath comment; And it is strange that the teacher and the writer on governmental order should defile his tongue and dirty his hands with such things.

I think that the author of SEREN TAN GWMMWL is a man similar to one who goes about the country and happens to look at some wonderful building with fine carvings on it, and maintains that the building is faulty from top to bottom, and that there is no way for anyone to live in it, even though people lived there perfectly contentedly at that time. Nevertheless, he wants to reduce the building to rubble, and the pity is that the man does not know how to put one stone on another towards rebuilding it more neatly than before. I think that the author dreamt one night, at the *new Moon*, that he was writing the history of kings, and was teaching them the order of Government, and when he awoke, where was he but in the depths of the firmament, searching for a star under a cloud; and from there shortly he fell down, through the hurricane like star-dust and attempted to despoil the country of Wales from end to end. – Now, it is time for me to finish with a modest thank you to the monster, as the author calls it, saying that it came here from devilish America to inform us of our race, that we Englishmen are robbers and despoilers and murderers from our beginning to this day. And further, I am grateful night and day to the author of SEREN TAN GWMMWL for showing his wondrous talents; and I hope he will again, as he has promised, divulge what is in his bosom; For it will be a light to enlighten the Welsh, those who sit in the darkness, and in the shadow of mountains; and it will also be of benefit and immortal glory to him. Blessed are we, poor miserable Welsh! Here, a very competent man, (as he spoke of his competence at the beginning of his book) has shown us the way of kings, bishops and lords, together with the order of Government; and thus exhibited a little of his own way and knowledge pertaining to the order of government, and the skilful stitching of priests, and for all that let him be praised in our midst, from generation to generation, and from age to age, until the end of time.

ANTAGONIST.)

## *9.3 In defence of* Seren tan Gwmmwl

*Y Geirgrawn: Neu Drysorfa Gwybodaeth.* Am Mawrth, 1796. Rhif. II (The Magazine: Or Treasury of Knowledge. For March, 1796. No. II), 58–62.

### AT GYHOEDDWR Y GEIRGRAWN.

DDINESYDD,

Os na bydd awdwr y SEREN TAN GWMMWL yn gwel'd y Bregawthen a ymddangosodd yn y Rhifyn cyntaf o'r GEIRGRAWN yn werth ei atteb, byddaf yn *ddiolchgar* i'ch' am roddi yr atteb canlynol iddo.

### ATTEB I *ANTAGONIST* AM EI OLWG AR Y LLYFR A ELWIR SEREN TAN GWMMWL.

Ni fedraf mo'r dirnad o ba gongl i'r wlad y daeth dyn mor hyfedr a thydi allan; ond o ba le bynnag y daethost, ac y'mha le bynnag yr wyt, mae cyn hawsed dy adnabod, wrth dy ymadrodd, ag ydyw adnabod pren wrth ei ffrwyth. – Digwyddodd i minnau ddarllain y Llyfr a elwir, SEREN TAN GWMMWL, ond ni wn ddim am yr awdwr, yn berthynol i'w ymddygiad yn y byd, er i mi ei weled ddwywaith neu dair. Yr wyf yn tybied nad ydyw ond ieuangc, o ran oedran, ond henedd o ran Dealldwriaeth, Synwyr, a Dysg. Nid ydwyf yn bresennol am amddiffyn ond ychydig ar y awdwr, na'i Lyfr: y peth a'm cynhyrfodd fwya oedd dy atteb di, o ran cariad arnat, rhag ofn iti etto yn dy ddallineb, a'th anwybodaeth, a'th ryfygus dyb da, ohonot dy hun, neidio i orsedd Barn, ar ol i ti edliw i'r awdwr, i fod ef yn cerdded wrth faglau rhai eraill, a'i fod ef gwedi gwisgo am dano heb gofio am ei grys, (dyna fagl a ges dithau gan Dwm o'r Nant,[103]) a llawer o bethau eraill, digon ynfyd a direswm.

Yr ydwyt yn dywedyd, dy fod wedi dal yr awdwr mewn rhwyd o anwiredd, yn yr hanes a roddodd ef am *Nimrod*. I ddwyn ar ddeall i ti, fod yr awdwr wedi cofio am ei grys, ac am danat tithau hefyd cyn iddo son am *Nimrod*; chwennychwn i ti ddal sylw ar ei Ragymadrodd, sydd yn dechreu fel y canlyn. "Gan fod y Llyfryn yma yn debygol o dreinglo i ddwylaw rhai a fydd yn meddwl eu hunain yn ddoethion os medrant trwy addysg Geir-lyfrau ganfod bai ar waith eraill," &c. – Dyma dy hanes di dy hun, rhyfedd na buaset yn cymmeryd amynedd, i edrych a oedd dy hanes di yn ei le, cyn hedeg (fal Giar i ben twr o yd) i chwilio a oedd *Nimrod* yn waedlyd ai nid oedd. Pan f'o *Ceryddwyr* yn sylwi ar lyfr, hwy fyddant bob amser yn dechreu ar y rhagymadrodd, cyn myned i gorph y gwaith, yna y caent wybod meddwl yr awdwr; at ddealldwriaeth pa râdd o bobl yr oedd yn scrifennu. – Ond mi feddyliwn fod dy hanes di yn ei le yn y rhagymadrodd; o herwydd hynny rhaid yw dy esgeuluso am beidio a sylwi arno.

Yn y 10*fed* bennod o Genesis ar 8*fed* adnod yr ydys yn dywedyd am *Nimrod*, "efe a ddechreuodd fod yn gadarn ar y ddaear," – pa beth 'r wyti'n feddwl o'r gair *cadarn* nis gallafi ddeall: – Pa fodd yr aeth efe yn ddyn cadarn ar y ddaear? onid trwy orthrymu ei gydgreaduriaid? a f'asai tair talaith yn ymostwng iddo, ped f'asai yn ddyn llonydd, esmwyth a diniwed? Pa fodd hefyd yr aeth *Alexander Fawr* a *Julius Cæsar* yn wyr cedyrn ar y ddaear? Onid wrth hela, ac ymlid, a llâdd eu cyd-greaduriaid? ac nid oes le i ammau nad rhag ei ofn yr aeth *Nimrod* yn gadarn.

Ychydig ymlaen, yr wyt yn son, fod dynion pennau ryddion yn y byd yn ymyrru a *threfn Llywodraeth*; – A wyti yn meddwl, nad oes dim achos i neb, ond *Edmund Burke*, neu ryw *Locustiaid* o'r fath, ac sy'n byw ar eiddo'r wlad, wybod dim o reolaeth y Deyrnas, os byddant yn byw ynddi? rhaid i bob dyn rhesymol gyfaddef fod yn iawn i bawb a f'o'n talu treth gael llais yn y *Llywodraeth*: a gwybod hefyd, pa beth yr ydys yn ei wneud a'u harian. Meddyliais wrth dy ymadrodd fod yn fawr gennyt fod y *Bastille* yn *Ffraingc* wedi ei ddryllio, ac yr wyt yn ceisio dyw'yd fod Carcharau Ffraingc mor lawnion heddyw ac oedd y *Bastille*. Mae hynny yn beth a all fod; yr achos bod hen Garchar Ffraingc mor lawn oedd "son am Ryddid a Chyfiawnder;" a'r achos bod Carcharau *Ffraingc* yn bresennol mor lawnion yw, bod *Esgobion* ac *Offeiriadau Pabaidd*, a llawer o *gnafiaid* eraill yn ceisio cael *Brenhin* i gael iddynt hwy le i lechu yn ei gysgod, ac i speilio'r wlad fel arferol.

Yn nesaf, yr wyt yn dyw'yd nad oedd yr hen *Israeliaid* ddim mor deillion ag y mae'r awdwr yn dywedyd eu bod, ac wrth geisio goleuo'r hen *Israeliaid* ti ddangosaist gryn lawer o'th ddallineb, a'th dywyllwch dy hun. Dangosaf it ar fyr fod y wythfed bennod o *Samuel* o'i dechreu i'w diwedd yn gwirio geiriau awdwr y SEREN TAN GWMMWL. Dywedyd y mae "fod coron *frenhinol* agos y'mhob gwlad yn rhedeg o *aer* i *aer* pa un bynnag, ai *hen* ai ieuangc, ai ffol, ai synwyrol, &c. ac e wyr pob dyn (medd ef) nad ydyw synwyr a doniau, ddim yn rhedeg o *dad* i *fab*," &c.

Ped fuasai meibion *Samuel* yn dilyn lwybrau eu Tad, ac yn peidio a gwyro barn, a throi at gybydddra ni fuasai'n rhaid i'r *Israeliaid* fyned at Samuel i ofyn Brenhin; dyna dyst nad ydyw Synwyr yn rhedeg o dad i fab, ac yr oedd yr hen *Israeliaid* ynghanol eu tywyllwch wedi gweled hynny trwy brofiad. Rhyfedd yn wir dy fod yn ceisio dal allan nad oeddynt mewn dallineb, a chaddug anwybodaeth, pan oeddynt yn gweiddi am *frenhin*, ac yn troi at *dduwiau* dieithr, – ni ddichon i blant dynion fyned i fwy o ddallineb, na phan f'ont yn ymwrthod a'r gwir Dduw ac yn troi at *eulunaddoliaeth* – bellach cymmer dy ddewis, ai dechreu'r bennod, ai'r canol, ai'r diwedd, o herwydd y mae'r cwbl yn dy erbyn, ac yn dyst safadwy o'r gwirionedd sydd gynnwysedig yn y SEREN TAN GWMMWL.

Dywedaist fod yr awdwr yn cadw swn mawr ar ei dommen ei hûn: – ni chlywais i ddim son mai ar dommenod y bydd awdwyr llyfrau'n byw, mwy nag y clywaist tithau son fod *offeiriadau*, yn cludo *cathod* mewn *cydau*. Ond y mae y ddau ddywediad uchod yn cael eu harfer, er ys cantoedd o flynydd-oedd, a gwyr pob hen wrach (ond tydi) pa beth y maent yn ei feddwl, ac yr oedd gan yr awdwr gystal hawl i wneuthur arfer o'r naill, ag oedd gan tithau wneuthur arfer o'r llall. Mae'n rhy faith i'm atteb pob chwedl ynfyd a ddywedaist, am yr awdwr, rhag ofn i mi fyned a mwy na fy rhan yn y GEIRGRAWN, ac y mae diwedd dy ERTHYLIAD mor ddidrefn nad ydyw yn ddim werth atteb ond ychydig o honno; – weithiau yr wyt yn dywedyd fod yr awdwr yn tirio yn y Winllan, waith arall y mae efe yn ddulluan yn bloeddio'n uwch na'r *offeiriadau*, a phryd arall yn *breuddwydio*, ac yn tynnu adeilad i lawr, ac yn y cymmylau, ac yn Llwttrach y Ser, &c. Mae'r holl swn gwag yna, yn dangos yn eglur dy fod yn methu canfod "brychau yn llygaid dy frawd," ac o herwydd hynny yr wyt yn ei ddanfon i'r cymmylau, er mwyn cael dangos dy ynfydrwydd wrth ddywedyd ei fod ef wedi desgyn fal *Llwttrach y sêr* i lawr.

Soniaist hefyd am yr oen [yn] dysgu'r ddafad bori. *America* sydd yn awr yn ddrych i Brydain: Ai nid trwy ffoledd ein *Llywodraethwyr*, y collasom ni America? ac wedi hynny sylfaenwyd Llywodraeth yno trwy Gyfiawnder, amddiffynnwyd hi trwy Ryddid, a holl daranau gorthrymmedig Brydain nid allasant ei malurio. – Drych dychrynnedig i Reolwyr Brydain yw *Ffraingc*. LLYS VERSAILLES, ychydig o flynyddoedd a aeth heibio, oedd mor wych o wag ogoniant ac ydyw LLYS ST. IAGO yn bresennol. Mae gorthrymder a hen arferion Llysoedd yn myn'd allan o arfer, ac y mae balchder yn sicr o gael ei gwymp.

Er i ti ddangos cryn lawer o ynfydrwydd, ti haeddit beth parch o herwydd dy ddigrifwch. Pan mae'r awdwr yn dywedyd "nad ydyw *coron* a *chap ffwl* dda i ddim ond i *hudo pobl* i ymadael a'u harian," yr wyt tithau yn atteb yn hynod o'r call, "dyma chwedl a wyr pob hen wrach;" ac mewn man arall, pan y mae'r awdwr yn dywedyd fod "gan y Brenhin allu yn ei law ei hun, wneuthur rhyfel neu heddwch," meddi dithau "dyna hanes na wybym i erioed o'r blaen," gresun yn wir fod dyn mor anwybodus a thydi, yn meddwl myned yn farnwr ar Lyfrau; ond y mae hynny fal pob peth arall, ac y sydd yn y SEREN yn wir, ac y mae'n ddiammau gennyf y gwyr llawer o hen wrach-od fod hynny yn wir. – O ddysgedig Farnwr! pa fodd y digwyddodd i ti gyfaddef fod pob hen wrach yn ddoethach na'th'di: Ac i egluro ychwaneg ar bwngc arall e ddarfu it gam-ddirnad, – dyma y peth yw gollwng y *gâth* allan o'r cwd. Ti a soniaist am *Samuel* yn eneinio *Saul*, ond nid oedd Saul fawr well (yn ol yr hanes) wedi cael ei eneinio, mwy na gwyr eraill. – Ni *choronwyd* ac ni *eneiniwyd* erioed mo *Sior Washington*, etto e wnaeth ef fwy o ddaioni i'r byd (trwy dorri iau gorthrymder, – darostwng gorthrymwyr – uno talaithau – ymgeleddu moddion gwybodaeth, a'r celfyddydau – derchafu uniondeb, a helaethu heddwch) nag a wnaeth *holl* bennau coronog y *Byd.*

Y mae'r awdwr gwedi son gyd â dyledus barch am yr hen *Syr Watkin*, ac am yr *Ovid* gymreig *Dafydd ap Gwilym*: Yr wyt tithau gwedi rhyfygu galw'r hen enwau parchus hynny yn *Sothach*; Yr wyf yn meddwl mai gair hoff gennyt yw *Sothach* a *Sothachlyd*. F'allai fod mwy o sothach yn dy ben di nag o ddim arall felly nid gwiw disgwyl dim arall allan o hono. Yr wyt yn dy *Bregowthen* wedi dy alw dy hun yn *arglwydd*, yn *Sais*, ac yn gymro felly y mae yn anhawdd dy adnabod, a thithau yn methu dy adnabod dy hûn.

Ti ddywedaist hefyd fod gwaith yr awdwr wedi ei scrifennu yn gymmysgfa o annibendod, a'i fod wedi dywedyd amryw bethau, nad eill ef sefyll wrthynt y'ngwyneb profedigaeth. Er mwyn dangos iti, a dwyn a'r gof i'r cyffredin, nad ydyw'r awdwr ddim mor gibddall ac yr wyti yn haeru ei fod, chwenychwn roddi un pwngc o'i waith i lawr yma. – Pan mae yn son am *Esgobion tu dal* 37, – medd ef, "ond yn amser y dywygiad," "mi gymmerodd yr Esgobion hynod ofal rhag diwygio'r gyfraith, ac oedd mewn grym i godi tâl iddynt hwy, oddiar bob dûll" (enw) "o grefyddwyr, yn y deyrnas, a thrwy nerth y gyfraith uchod mae *Esgobion* ac *offeiriadau* yn cael lle i lechu y'ngysgod darnau o hen Furiau gwaedlyd Eglwys Rhyfain, pa rai mae mellt cyfiawnder, a Tharanau, arfau *Rhyddid* yn barod i ddryllio eu sylfaenau hwy ac i'w chwalu yn chwilfriw." Onid oes synwyr, a chadarnwch iaith, a llyfnder ymadrodd yn y pwngc uchod, yr wyf yn cyfaddef na wn i ddim pa le y maent. Mae hefyd (heblaw y Seren) Farddoniaeth o waith *J. Jones Glanygors* yn cael derbynniad, parch, a chlod trwy Gymru. I ddiweddu, os na fedri di wneuthur dim dy hun ond barnu ar waith pobl eraill, a chan dy fod wedi addo y ceir clywed oddiwrthyt ti etto, – paid a myn'd i'r ffurfafen, rhag ofn dy osod yn gydymaith i'r *Bol Haul*[104] wrth glin y bottwm gloyw, a'r cnâf pig; yr ydwyf yn meddwl mae'r pethau mwya cyfaddas at dy ddealldwriaeth yw hanes y *Trwstan*,&c.[105] bydd haws i ti gael clod am sylwi ar ryw Lyfrau haws eu rhwygo na'r SEREN TAN GWMMWL.

Ond cofia na raid iti ddim dywedyd i'r byd, yn rhagor, fod pob hen wrach yn ddoethach na thydi, mae y rhan fwyaf a ddarllenodd dy waith yn coelio hynny'n barod,

TUDUR.

*Ffynnon y Gwirionedd*
Mawrth 25n, 1796.

## (TO THE PUBLISHER OF THE GEIRGRAWN,

CITIZEN,

If the author of SEREN TAN GWMMWL (A STAR UNDER A CLOUD) does not find the Prattle which appeared in the first Number of the GEIRGRAWN worth answering, I would be *grateful* if you would give the following answer to it.

## ANSWER TO *ANTAGONIST* FOR HIS VIEW ON THE BOOK WHICH IS CALLED SEREN TAN GWMMWL.

I cannot discern from what corner of the country a man as expert as you came; but from wherever you came and wherever you are, it is as easy to recognize you by your expression as it is to know a tree by its fruit. – I also happened to read the Book that is called SEREN TAN GWMMWL, but I know nothing about the author with respect to his conduct in the world, although I have seen him two or three times. I suppose that he is but young as regards age, but old as regards Understanding, Sense, and Learning. At present I do not intend to defend the author or his Book but a little: the thing that troubled me most was your answer, out of love to you, lest again, in your blindness, and your ignorance, and your arrogant high opinion of yourself, you jump to the throne of Judgement, after you reproached the author that he walked with others' crutches, and that he had dressed himself forgetting his shirt, (that was a crutch that you got from Twm o'r Nant,[103]) and many other things, unreasonable and foolish enough.

You say that you caught the author in a net of untruth in the account he gave of *Nimrod*. To make it clear to you that the author has remembered his shirt and you as well before he spoke of *Nimrod*; I would like you to pay attention to his Introduction, which begins as follows. "As this Booklet is likely to fall into the hands of those who think themselves wise if they can, through Dictionary-learning, find fault with the work of others," &c. – This is your own story, strange that you did not have the patience to see if your history was in its place before flying (like a Hen to the top of a heap of corn) to find if *Nimrod* was bloody or if he was not. When *Critics* take note of a book, they will always start with the introduction before going to the body of the work, there they will get to know the intention of the author; for what level of understanding he was writing. – But I think that your story was in its place in the introduction; because of this you must be slighted for not taking note of it.

In the 10th chapter of Genesis and the 8th verse it is said of *Nimrod*, "he began to be a mighty one in the earth," – what you think of the word *mighty* I cannot understand: – How did he become a mighty man in the earth? if not through oppressing his fellow-creatures? would three provinces submit to him, if he were a quiet, easy and innocent man? How also did *Alexander the Great* and *Julius Cæsar* become mighty men on the earth? Was it not through chasing, and persecuting and killing their fellow-creatures? and there is no doubt that it was by making people afraid of him that *Nimrod* became mighty.

A little further on you mention that headstrong men in the world are interfering with the *order of Government*; – Do you think that there is no cause for anyone except *Edmund Burke* or some *Locusts* of that sort, who live on the wealth of the country, to know anything of the management of the Kingdom, if they live in it? Every reasonable man must admit that it is right for everyone who pays tax to have a voice in the *Government*; and also to know what is done with their money. I reckoned by your expression that you were concerned that the *Bastille* in *France* had been destroyed, and you attempt to say that the Prisons of *France* are as full today as was the *Bastille*. That may be so; the reason that the old French Prison was so full was "speaking of Liberty and Justice," and the reason that the French Prisons are so full at present is that *Bishops* and *Popish Priests*, and many other *knaves*, are trying to get a *King* so that they may skulk in his shadow, and despoil the country as they used to.

Next, you say that the old *Israelites* were not as blind as the author says they were, and while trying to enlighten the old *Israelites* you revealed a good deal of your own blindness and darkness. I will show you in short that the eighth chapter of *Samuel* from its beginning to its end confirms the words of the author of SEREN TAN GWMMWL. He says "that a *kingly* crown in almost every country runs from *heir* to *heir*, whether *old* or young, or foolish, or sensible, &c. and that every man knows (he says) that sense and talents do not run from *father* to *son*," &c.

If the sons of *Samuel* had followed in their Father's footsteps and had not perverted justice and turned to avarice, the *Israelites* would not have had to go to Samuel to ask for a King; that is evidence that Sense does not run from father to son, and the old *Israelites* in the midst of their darkness had seen that by experience. Strange indeed that you try to maintain that they were not in blindness and a fog of ignorance when they were clamouring for a *king* and turning to foreign *gods*, – it is not possible for the children of men to fall into more blindness than when they reject the true God and turn to *idolatry* – now take your choice whether it is the beginning of the chapter or the middle or the end, for the whole is against you and is a lasting witness to the truth which is contained in SEREN TAN GWMMWL.

You said that the author makes a great noise on his own dung-heap: – I never heard tell that the authors of books lived on dung-heaps any more than you heard tell that *priests* carried *cats* in *bags*. But the two sayings above have been used for hundreds of years and every old hag (except you) knows what they mean, and the author had as much right to use the one as you had to make use of the other. It is too tedious for me to answer every mad tale you told about the author, lest I take more than my fair share of the GEIRGRAWN, and the end of your ABORTION is so disorderly that it is not worth answering but a little of it; – sometimes you say that the author roots around in the Vineyard, another time he is an owl hooting louder than the *priests*, and another time he is *dreaming* and pulling down a building, and in the clouds, and in the Star-dust, &c. All this empty noise shows clearly that you cannot find "mote in your brother's eye," and therefore you send him to the clouds in order to show your madness by saying that he has fallen down like the *Star-dust.*

You also spoke of the lamb teaching the sheep to graze. *America* is now an example for Britain: Is it not through the foolishness of our *Governors* that we lost America? and after that a Government was established there through Justice, it was defended by Liberty and all the oppressive thunder of Britain could not shatter it. – *France* is a terrible example for the Rulers of Britain. THE COURT OF VERSAILLES was as full of vain splendour a few years ago as the COURT OF ST. JAMES is at present. The oppression and old customs of Courts are going out of use, and pride is sure to have its fall.

Although you have shown a great deal of foolishness, you deserve some respect because of your buffoonery. When the author says that "a *crown* and a *fool's cap* are good for nothing but to *entice people* to part with their money," you answer most sensibly "that is a tale that every old hag knows;" and in another place, when the author says that "the King has power in his own hand, to make war or peace," you say "there is a tale which I never heard before," it is a pity, indeed, that a man as ignorant as you intends to become a judge of Books; but this, like all other things which are in the SEREN, is true, and I do not doubt that many old hags know that to be true. – Oh learned Judge! how did you happen to admit that every old hag is wiser than you: And to explain further on another subject that you misapprehended, – this is what letting the *cat* out of the bag is. You spoke of *Samuel* anointing *Saul*, but Saul was not much better (according to the account) having been anointed, any more than other men. – *George Washington* was never *crowned* or *anointed*, yet he did more good for the world (through breaking the yoke of oppression, – bringing down oppressors – uniting states – fostering the means of knowledge, and the arts – promoting justice, and extending peace) than *all* the crowned heads of the *World*.

The author spoke with due respect about old *Sir Watkin*, and about the Welsh *Ovid, Dafydd ap Gwilym*: You dared call those respectable old names *Trash*; I think that *Trash* and *Trashy* are your favourite words. Perhaps there is more trash in your head than anything else so there is no point expecting anything else from it. In your *Prattling* you have called yourself a *lord*, an *Englishman*, and a Welshman so it is difficult to know you when you are unable to know yourself.

You also said that the author's writing is a hotchpotch of confusion, and that he said various things that he could not stand by under test. In order to show you and to remind the public that the author is not as stupid as you assert he is, I desire to put one topic of his work down here. – When he talks of *Bishops page* 37, – he says, "but in the time of the reformation," "the Bishops took great care not to reform the law which was in force to raise payment for them from every manner" (denomination) "of religious people in the realm and through the power of the above law *Bishops* and *priests* have room to lurk in the shadow of parts of the bloody old Walls of the Church of Rome, whose foundations the lightning of justice, and the Thunder, the weapons of *Liberty* are ready to destroy and smash to smithereens." If there is no sense and strength of language and smoothness of expression in the text above, I admit that I do not know where they are. Poetry by *J. Jones Glanygors* (as well as the Star) is also well received, respected and praised throughout Wales. To finish, if you cannot do anything yourself but judge other people's work, and as you have promised that we will hear from you again, – do not go to the firmament, in case you become a companion to Mr Pointy Belly[104] at the knee of the shining moon button and of the starry knave; I think that the things most appropriate to your understanding would be the history of the *Unfortunate*, &c.[105] it will be easier for you to win praise for taking note of some Books which are easier to maul than SEREN TAN GWMMWL.

But remember that you do not have to tell the world again that every old hag is wiser than you, the majority of those who have read your work believe that already,

TUDUR.

*The Fountain of Truth*
March 25th, 1796.)

### *9.4 News from the Continent*

*Y Geirgrawn: Neu Drysorfa Gwybodaeth.* Am Fai, 1796. Rhif. IV (The Magazine: Or Treasury of Knowledge. For May, 1796. No. IV), 125–6.

YR AMSERAU.

Y MAE annorchfygol fyddinoedd Ffraingc yn parhau i dorri trwy bob gwrthwynebiadau yn yr Eidal. Yr hen Benciwdawd *Beaulieu*,[106] Blaenor y fyddin Austro-Sardiniaidd, sy'n gorfod ffoi o flaen y *llangc* Ffrangaeg hwnnw *Buonaparte*. Y mae holl amrywiol Dalaithau yr Eidal yn analluog i'w wrth-sefyll; ac nid oes ganddynt yn bresennol un gobaith am ddiogelwch, ond trwy ddilyn siampl, brenhin Sardinia, a gwneud heddwch cyn gynted ag y gallont, ar yr ammodau a welo'r Ffrangcod fod yn dda i gynnyg iddynt. Y mae brenhin Sardinia (i'r hwn yr oedd Lloegr mor ynfyd a rhoi dau can mil o bunau yn y flwyddyn, tu ag at gynnal y rhyfel yn y blaen) wedi gwneuthur heddwch a'r Ffrangcod ar ammodau manteisiol i'r Wladwriaeth honno; y mae wedi rhoddi i fynu iddynt *Nice*, rhan o Dalaith *Piedmont*, a *Savoy*, talaith yn cynnwys tair mil, a phym cant a thri ugain a deuddeg o filldiroedd scwâr, dros byth; heblaw amrywiol o'i amddiffynfeudd tra parhao y rhyfel. Y mae Arch Dduc Parma, yn barod, wedi gwneud heddwch amserol a hwynt; ac y mae pob lle i gredu y gwna eraill ddilyn yr un mesurau ar fyr. Y mae ai Sancteiddrwydd y Pab, yn dechreu arswydo yn bresennol, ac nid heb achos; canys y mae ei diriogaethau mewn enbydrwydd. Efe a gyhoeddodd ympryd a gweddi dros Wyth awr a deugain, i eidduno'r Nefoedd am heddwch cyffredinol.

Yr ydym yn ofni y bydd mwy o barodrwydd yn y tramor awdurdodau cyngreiriol i wneuthur heddwch ar anwrthwynebol genedl Ffrengig, na Brudain Fawr; llwyddiant a dedwyddwch yr hon sy'n ymddibynnu ar hedd-wch. Yr ydys yn darogan llawer, y dyddiau hyn, y bydd rhyfel ar fyr rhyngom ni ac *America*: y mae gelyniaeth neullduol gan y werin bobl yno, yn erbyn Lloegr; a'u llef yn gyffredinol trwy'r talaithau yw "ymddialwn," &c.

Yr Arglwydd a brysuro'r amser, i'r cleddyfau i gael eu troi yn sychau a'r gwaew ffyn yn bladuriau, a'r cenhedloedd i beidio dysgu rhyfel mwyach.

(THE TIMES.

THE invincible armies of France continue to break through every opposition in Italy. The old General *Beaulieu*,[106] Leader of the Austro-Sardinian army, has to flee before that French *lad Buonaparte*. All the various States of Italy are unable to withstand him; and at present they have no hope of safety except to follow the example of the king of Sardinia and to make peace as soon as they can on the terms that the French see fit to offer them. The king of Sardinia (to whom England was so foolish as to give two hundred thousand pounds a year towards carrying on the war) has made peace with the French on terms which are favourable to that Republic; he has given up to them forever *Nice*, a part of the Region of *Piedmont*, and *Savoy*, a region containing three thousand five hundred and seventy-two square miles; as well as various of its fortresses while the war continues. The Archduke of Parma has already made a timely peace with them; and there is every reason to believe that others will follow the same measures shortly. His Holiness the Pope is presently growing frightened, and not without cause; for his lands are in great danger. He announced a fast and prayer for forty-eight hours, to implore the Heavens for a general peace.

We are afraid that the foreign allied powers will be more prepared to make peace with the irresistible French nation than Great Britain; whose success and prosperity depends on peace. It is much prophesied, these days, that there will shortly be war between us and *America*: the common people there have a particular animosity towards England; and their common cry throughout the states is "vengeance," &c.

May the Lord hasten the time when the swords will be turned into ploughshares and the spears into pruning hooks, and the nations will cease to counsel war anymore.)

### *9.5 A Welsh version of the 'Marseillaise'*

*Y Geirgrawn: Neu Drysorfa Gwybodaeth.* Am Fai, 1796. Rhif. IV (The Magazine: Or Treasury of Knowledge. For May, 1796. No. IV), 127–8.

*Ty y Crochenydd, Mai* 20, 1796.

DDINESYDD,

OS yw'r Gân ganlynol wrth eich bodd, y mae i chwi gyflawn ryddid i'w rhoddi yn y *Geirgrawn*. Am y cyfieithiad, nid oes gennyf ddim i'w ddywedyd, ond *barned y deallus*. Y mae lluoedd *anorchfygol* y Wladwriaeth Ffrangaeg yn ddyledus iddi, mewn mesur mawr, am eu buddugoliaethau ardderchoccaf. Yn ddiweddar, fe'i dadseiniwyd gan uchel fynyddoedd yr *Eidal*; a hi a gyrrhaeddodd Frudain, megis ar adenydd y gwynt. O bydd neb yn ei beio, gwneled ei gwell. Y mae iddo gyflawn roesaw o ran

GWILYM.

## CAN RHYDDID[107]
## YR HON A GENIR GAN FILWYR FFRAINGC WRTH FYNED I'R FRWYDR.

*Allonz enfans de la patriæ, &c.*

CHWI feibion Rhyddid daeth yr amser,
Ac wele myrdd yn galw i ma's!
O clywch ruddfannau plant gorthrymder,
Yn gwawdd i wisgo'r cleddyf glas!
A gaiff hyll dreiswyr, llawn drwg fwriad,
A'u byddin lôg (hull arfog lu!)
Ladd a dinystrio ar bob tû,
Er gwaedu o Ryddid, hêdd a chariad?
I'r maes! – I'r maes rai dewr!
Ein llawn ymroad fydd,
Ymlaen! – Ymlaen! awn oll yn un,
Am farw, neu fyw'n *rhydd*!

Clywch! Clywch y dymestl a'r taranau,
A'r rhyfel poeth yn gwasgu 'mlaen!
Ac wele'n meusydd a'n meddiannau,
A llawer dinas dêg a'r dan!
A gaiff b– –nh–n– –dd, a'u *cwn gwaedlyd*,
Eu harfau a'u lluoedd ar bob llaw,
Wneud ing a thrallod yma a thraw,
A Ninnau'n goddef heb ymsymmud?
I'r maes! – I'r maes! &c. &c.

Gormodedd balchder a chybydd-dod,
O gylch yr hyll orthrymwyr sydd;
Ac o chwant i arian ormod,
*Mesurant, gwerthant oleu'r dydd!!!*[108]
Fel Duwiau gwnant i'w caethion grymmu,
I'w parchu, a'u haddoli hwy:
Ond *dyn* yw *dyn*, a phwy sydd *fwy*?
A gant hwy'n hwyach ein gorthrymmu?
I'r maes! – I'r maes! &c. &c.

O crynwch, crynwch, euog dreiswyr;
Ac mwyach byth na lawenhewch;
A chwitheu hefyd gas fradychwyr
O ffrwyth eich llafur y bwyttewch:
Ac er i'ch hên fyddinoedd dawnus,
Guro ein hifaingc wyr i dre;
O'u llwch daw eraill yn eu lle,
I yrru'n oll eich lluoedd dawnus.
I'r maes! – I'r maes! &c. &c.

*A ninnau rodiwn yr un llwybrau
A phan na b'o'n cyfeillion mwy,
Ymaflwn yn ei hên gleddyfau
I'w dïal, neu i'w dilyn hwy
Wrth wel'd arwyddion eu gwroliaeth
A'u gwaed yn llifo ar hyd y llawr,
'E gwyd o'n mewn eiddigedd mawr
Am gyd-gyfrannu o'u marwolaeth.
I'r maes! I'r maes! &c. &c.

(*The Potter's House*, *May* 20, 1796.

CITIZEN,
IF the following Song is to your taste, you are at perfect liberty to put it in the *Geirgrawn*. About the translation, I have nothing to say but *let the knowledgeable judge*. The *invincible* forces of the French Republic are indebted to it, to a great extent, for their greatest victories. Lately, it has been echoed by the high mountains of *Italy*; and it reached Britain as if on the wings of the wind. If anyone should blame it, let him do it better. He is full welcome as far as GWILYM is concerned.

THE SONG OF LIBERTY[107]
WHICH IS SUNG BY THE SOLDIERS OF FRANCE
WHEN GOING TO BATTLE.
*Allonz enfans de la patriæ, &c.*

FOR YOU sons of Liberty the time has come,
and see the myriads calling out!

* Y Pennill hwn a genir gan y plant bychain.

Oh, hear the groans of the children of oppression,
an invitation to take up the grey sword!
Shall ugly tyrants, full of ill intention,
and their hired army (an ugly armed mob!)
get to kill and destroy everywhere,
to bleed Liberty, peace and love?
To the field! – To the field brave ones!
This our full devotion be,
forward! Forward! Let's all go as one,
to die or to live *free*!

Hear! Hear the tempest and bolts of thunder
and the raging war drawing close!
And see our fields and our possessions
and many a fair city on fire!
Shall k–ngs and their *bloodhounds*,
their weapons and their armies on every side
cause anguish and affliction far and wide,
while We motionlessly abide?
To the field! – To the field! &c. &c.

Excess pride and avarice
surround the ugly Tyrants;
and from unbounded greed for money
*they Measure, sell, the light of day!!!*[108]
Like Gods they bid their slaves bow down,
to revere and to worship them:
but *man* is *man*, and who is *more*?
And shall they continue to oppress us?
To the field! – To the field! &c. &c.

Oh, tremble, tremble, guilty tyrants;
and henceforth, never rejoice;
and you, as well, odious traitors
will eat of the fruit of your labour:
and though your old and seasoned armies
may beat our young men home;
from their ashes others will come in their stead
to overcome all your well-trained forces.
To the field! – To the field! &c. &c.

*And we shall follow the same paths,
and when our friends are no more,
we shall grasp their old swords
to avenge them or to follow them
observing the traces of their heroism
and their blood streaming over the ground,
a great zeal arises in us
to partake of their death.
To the field! – To the field! &c. &c.)

### *9.6 An attack on* Seren tan Gwmmwl *with a response by the editor*

*Y Geirgrawn: Neu Drysorfa Gwybodaeth.* Am Fehefin, 1796. Rhif. V (The Magazine: Or Treasury of Knowledge. For June, 1796. No.V), 144–6.

Y GOLYGWR,

MAE canlynwyr *Tom Paine*; (un o ba rai yw Sion Jones, Cyfieithydd y "Seren Tan Gwmmwl") yn llwyr elyniaethol i Frenhinoedd, Esgobion, Offeiriadon, Degymmau, a chrefydd sefydledig, (ïe yn fy marn i, y maent yn cashau, ac yn gwrthwynebu pob math o grefydd a Duwioldeb; fal ag y mae *Tom Paine* wedi gosod allan, yn eglur yn ei lyfr, a elwir, "*Age of Reason*," neu Oes Rheswm;) maent hefyd mor ynfyd, ac wyneb-galed, a thaeru mae brenhinoedd yw'r achosion o'r holl ryfeloedd sydd, ac a fu ar wyneb y ddaear; ond pe b'aent yn deall yr Ysgrythur Lân, neu yn adnabod eu calonau eu hunain, ac yn deimladwy o lygredigaeth eu hanian; hwy a gaent weled y Gwraidd a'r ffynnon o bob drygioni a phechod: "O ba le y mae rhyfeloedd, ac ymladdau (neu ymgynhénau) yn eich plith chwi? (medd yr apostol Jago) onid oddiwrth hyn, sef eich melus-chwantau, y rhai sydd yn rhyfela yn eich aelodau?"[109] Yr ydym yn darllain i "Abel ladd ei frawd, o genfigen,"[110] a bod "holl fwriad meddylfryd calon dyn, yn unig yn ddrygionus bob amser;"[111] a hyn, cyn bod, na brenhin, nac offeiriad, ar y ddaear: Mae'n rhaid fod rhyw ben ar bawb, os amgen, ni fydd dim trefn, na rheolaeth. Yn y cyn-oesoedd, yn amser y Patriarchiaid, neu hên Deidiau yr eglwys, yr oedd Duw yn gweled yn dda i lywodraethu'r ffyddloniaid, heb yr un brenhin; ond wedi talm o amser, hwy a rwgnachasant i'w erbyn; ac a ddeisyfiasant gael brenhin daearol i'w llywodraethu, (megis y cenhedloedd digrêd,) yn lle yr Arglwydd eu Duw: fal y gallwn weled yn helaethach, yn

* This Verse is sung by the small children.

Eglurhad y *Parch. Peter Williams*, ar yr viii *Bennod* o 1 *Sam.* "cymmerodd Israel achlysur, oddiwrth ddrwg-fucheddau meibion Samuel i geisio brenhin, ond nid da y gwanaethant; gwell fuasai disgwyl yn amyneddgar, wrth y brenhin tragwyddol, i drefnu iddynt farnwyr amgenach:" Ond nid oedd ceisio brenhin yn bechadurus; canys y mae Duw yn gwneuthur brenhinoedd (megis ac yr ydym yn darllain y'Mhrophwydoliaeth Esay xlix. 23) yn dad-maethod i'w eglwys; ac ni waharddodd Duw osod brenhin arnynt; eithr gorchymmynodd trwy *Foses*; os *gosodent*, i'w ddewis o blith eu brodyr; ac un o gynheddfau rhinweddol. Ond eu pechod oedd ei chwennych yn *ol arfer y cenhedloedd*, ac nid yn ol rheol y gair. Hefyd dymunasant gyfnewid trefn y Llywodraeth; ond nid oeddynt yn gofalu am ddiwygio moesau'r wlad-wriaeth. Pan gániattäodd Duw osod brenhin ar Israel, yn ol eu dymuniad, rhagddywedodd hefyd am y caledi a ddygent arnynt eu hunain, trwy hynny: felly, y gwelwn fod Duw yn dioddef pethau nad yw foddlon iddynt, a bod dynion trwy ddilyn eu hewyllys eu hunain, yn tynnu drygau ar eu pénau eu hunain: Gan hynny, ordinhad Duw sydd oreu y'mhob peth. Mae ein Harglwydd Bendigedig ei hun, yn tystiolaethu, y bydd rhyfeloedd, a son am ryfeloedd cyn diwedd y bŷd. "A phan glywoch sôn am ryfeloedd a therfysgoedd (medd efe) na chymmerwch fraw, canys *rhaid* i'r pethau hyn fod yn gyntaf:"[112] – Ni a welwn yma, fod yn angenrheidiol i ryfeloedd a therfysgoedd i ddigwydd yn y bŷd: Nid fal pethau dymunol, ni a ellwn feddwl; ond fal canlyniadau o'n pechodau, a llygredigaeth ein natur.

Yr ydwyf fi yn credu, y peru gair Duw hyd ddiwedd y byd: Mae pob peth ag sy'n scrifennedig ynddo, yn perthyn i ni, yn gystal a'n hynafiaid; a'r bobloedd at ba rai, y cyfarwyddwyd yr epistolau. Mae *St. Pedr* yn gorchymmyn i ni ofni Duw, ac anrhydeddu'r brenhin: A phe buasai yr Apostol yn rhagweled, y buasit yn torri pen pob brenhin cyn diwedd y byd; ni fuasai ef ddim yn rhoddi'r fath *orchymmyn i ni. Yr ydwyf yn gobeithio y bydd fy nghyd-wladwyr, y Cymry, yn fwy parod i wrando ar Apostol Duw, nag ar *Dwm Paine*, nac un o'i ganlynwyr terfysglyd aflonydd.

* Wrth edrych, yn fanwl, ar gyfrwymiad neu gyssylltiad geiriau *Pedr*, (*Pedr* ii. 13, 14, 17) a'u cymharu a'r hyn a ddywed *Paul*, (*Rhuf.* xiii. 1, 2, 3, 4, 5, 6, 7), e welir yn eglur, nad yw efe yn gorchymmyn i ni i anrhydeddu neb rhyw swyddogion gwladol, ond y rhai y mae anrhydedd a pharch yn ddyledus iddynt; sef y rhai hynny *ag sydd er dïal ar y drwg weithredwyr* (*h.y.* yn cyflawni, neu yn gosod y gyfraith mewn grym yn erbyn pob math ar anfoesoldeb, ac afreolaeth;) *ac er mawl i'r gweithredwyr da* (*h.y.* er cefnogrwydd a diogelwch i'r rhai ufudd a rhinweddol). Pan y mae Paul yn haeru fod "*yr awdurdodau sydd, wedi eu hordeinio gan Dduw*, a bod yr hwn *sydd yn ymosod yn erbyn yr awdurdod yn gwrth-wynebu ordinhäd Duw*, ei feddwl yw, i fod Duw wedi ordeinio rheol neu gyfraith; ac na chai dynion fyw'n benrydd fal bleiddiaid y coed neu fwystfilod y maes; ac mae ordinhad Duw yw llywodraeth wladol: Ond o ran ei dull a'i threfn, *ordinhad ddynol* ydyw hi.

Ynghylch Degymmau, mae'n ddiammau mae hwn oedd y modd a arferid ymhlith yr Iddewon cyn dyfodiad ein Iechawdwr, ac ymysg y crist'nogion wedi ei enedigaeth; i dalu gweinidogion yr Efengyl: Canys yr oedd pobl yn y modd hyn, yn offrymmu i'r Arglwydd ac i'w wasanaeth, y ddegfed rann o'u hŷd a'u gwin, a chynnyrch eu defaid, a'u gwartheg, a'u hanifeiliaid.

Ond ychydig yn fyr am Esgobion; mae Clemens Romanus, yr hwn y mae St. Paul yn crybwyll am dano, *Phil.* iv. 3 yn henwi Esgobion neu olygwyr yr eglwys; a'r *Presbuteroi*, Henuriaid; a'r Diaconoi, neu'r Gweinidogion o râdd is na'r *Presbuteroi* felly y mae Ignatius hefyd; a Pholycarpus, Esgob *Smyrna*; a Irenœus; a Chlemens o Alexandria; a Thertulian, ac eraill. Yr hwn a chwenycho 'chwaneg o foddlondeb ynghylch y pethau hyn; darllened *Dr. Hickes' Christian Priesthood*, a *Dr. Prideaux on Tythes*.

Wyf eich Ewyllysiwr da,
Mewn pob daioni,
PERIS.

(THE EDITOR,

THE followers of *Tom Paine*; (one of whom is John Jones, Translator of the "Seren tan Gwmmwl" (A Star under a Cloud)) are utterly hostile to Kings, Bishops, Priests, Tithes, and established religion, (indeed, in my opinion, they hate, and oppose every kind of religion and Godliness; as *Tom Paine* has clearly set out in his book called the "*Age of Reason*";) they are also idiotic and impudent enough to insist that kings have been the cause of all present and past wars on the face of the earth; but if they understood the Holy Scripture or knew their own hearts and were aware of the corruption of their nature, they would see the Root and source of all wickedness and sin: "From whence come wars, and fightings (or contentions)

Pan el dyn, (yr hwn, hwyrach, y parheir ei alw yn rhaglaw, yn dywysog, yn Frenhin, neu'n Ymerawdr,) yn drahaus, yn anfad, yn orthrymmwr, ac yn sychedig am waed; nid yw mwyach, yr hyn a elwir gan yr apostol, yn "ddynol ordinhad;" nac ydyw; eithr dynol ofid, ffieiddiad, a dygasedd ydyw; distryw'r gyfraith ac adfeiliad Rhinwedd: A phan newidir ymddygiad y dyn, neu'r swyddog ein dyledswydd ninnau sy'n newid; ac y mae yn awr gymmaint o rwymau arnom i ffieiddio'r dyn, ag oedd o'r blaen arnom i'w anrhydeddu ef. Yn enw rheswm a gwirionedd, bydded i ni gofio, bob amser, nad yw yr ysgrythyr yn gorchymmyn i ni anrhydeddu neb, ond y rhai y mae anrhydedd yn *ddyledus* iddynt. Nid yw Duw yn gorchymmyn ini, ac nis *gall* 'chwaith, yn gysson ag ef ei hun, geisio gennym, wneud un peth ag sydd ynddo ei hun yn ammhosibl, neu yn afresymmol; a'i fod, nid yn unig yn beth afresymmol, ond yn waith hollol ammhosibl i ni anrhydeddu dyn anllad afradlon, meddw, trahaus, gormesol a gwaedlyd, sy'n ddiamheuol; ac afreidiol yw ceisio ei brofi. – Duw a roddo i FRYDAIN bob amser Swyddogion *teilwng* o barch ac anrhydedd; ac a wnelo'r *Brython* yn ufudd yn ostyngedig, ac yn ffyddlon iddynt!

Y GORUWCHWILWYR.

among you? (says the Apostle James) come they not hence, even of your lusts that war in your members?"[109] We read that "Abel killed his brother [*sic*], out of envy,"[110] and that "every imagination of the thoughts of his [man's] heart was only evil continually;"[111] and this before there was either king or priest on the earth: There must be some master over everyone, if there is not, there will be no order or governance. In antiquity, in the age of the Patriarchs or the forefathers of the church, God saw fit to rule the faithful without any king; but after a long time, they grumbled against him; and craved an earthly king to govern them, (like the unbelieving nations) instead of the Lord their God: as we can see more amply in the Explanation of the *Rev. Peter Williams* on the viii *Chapter* of 1 *Sam.* "Israel took the opportunity, as a result of the wickedness of the sons of Samuel, to seek a king, but they did not do well; it would have been better to wait patiently for the eternal king to arrange better judges for them:" But seeking a king was not sinful; for God makes kings (as we read in the Prophecy of Isaiah xlix. 23) as foster fathers to his church; and God did not forbid setting a king over them; but commanded through *Moses*; if they *placed* one over them, to choose him from among their brothers; and one of virtuous disposition. But their sin was to seek him *according to the customs of the nations*, and not according to the authority of the scripture. They also sought to change the order of Government; but they did not take care to reform the morals of the state. When God granted the placing of a king over Israel, according to their wishes, he also prophesied the hardship that they would bring on themselves through this; thus we see that God suffers some things with which he is not content and that men by following their own will bring harm upon themselves: Therefore, in every thing, God's ordination is best. Our Blessed Lord himself testifies that there will be wars and talk of wars before the end of the world. "And when ye shall hear of wars and rumours of wars (he says): see that ye be not troubled: for all these things *must* come to pass:"[112] – We see here that it is necessary for wars and conflicts to happen in the world: not as desirable events, we may think; but as the consequences of our sins, and the corruption of our nature.

I believe that the word of God will endure until the end of the world: Every thing that is written in it pertains to us as much as to our ancestors; and to the people to whom the epistles were addressed. *St Peter* commands us to fear God, and honour the king: And if the Apostle had foreseen that every king's head would be cut off before the end of the world; he would not have given us such a *command. I hope that my fellow-countrymen,

* Looking closely at the construction or the connection of *Peter's* words (*Peter* ii. 13, 14, 17) and comparing them with that which *Paul* said (*Romans* xiii. 1, 2, 3, 4, 5, 6, 7), it

the Welsh, will be more willing to listen to the Apostle of God than to *Tom Paine* or any one of his riotous unruly followers.

Regarding Tithes, there is no doubt that this was the method practised among the Jews before the coming of our Saviour, and amongst the Christians after his birth, to pay the ministers of the Gospel: For in this way, the people offered up to the Lord and to his servants the tenth part of their corn and their wine, and the produce of their sheep, and their cows, and their animals.

But briefly a little about Bishops; Clemens Romanus, who is mentioned by St. Paul, *Phil.* iv. 3, names Bishops or church overseers; and the *Presbuteroi*, Elders; and the Deacons, or the Ministers of a lower order than the *Presbuteroi*, so too do Ignatius; and Polycarpus, Bishop of *Smyrna*; and Irenæus: and Clement of Alexandria; and Tertullian, and others. Whoever desires more satisfaction regarding these things; let him read *Dr. Hickes' Christian Priesthood*, and *Dr. Prideaux on Tythes*.

I am your well wisher,
In all goodness,
PERIS.)

may clearly be seen that he does not command us to honour any state officials, except those to whom honour and respect are due; namely those *who are sent by him for vengeance on the evil-doers* (*i.e.* who fulfil, or set the law in force against every kind of immorality and disorder;) *and for the praise of those who do good* (*i.e.* for the support and safety of the obedient and virtuous). When Paul asserts that *the powers that be are ordained of God*, and that *whosoever therefore resisteth the power, resisteth the ordinance of God*, his meaning is that God has ordained rule or law; and that men may not live unrestrained like the wolves of the forest or the beasts of the field; and that God's ordination is civil government: But as regards its manner and order, it is a *human ordinance.*

When a man, (who, perhaps, continues to be called a lieutenant, a prince, a King, or an Emperor) becomes oppressive, wicked, a despot, and bloodthirsty; then he is no longer that which is called by the apostle of "human ordinance;" no, this is human affliction, abomination, and hatefulness; the desolation of the law and the ruin of Virtue: And when the conduct of the man, or the officer, changes, then our duty changes too; and we are now as much bound to despise the man as we had been to honour him before. In the name of reason and truth let us always remember that the scripture does not command us to honour anyone, except those to whom honour is due. God does not command us, nor can he, being consistent with himself, require us to do any thing which would be impossible in itself, or unreasonable; and that it is, not only an unreasonable thing, but worse, utterly impossible for us to honour a wanton, prodigal, drunken, oppressive, despotic and bloody man, is undoubted; and it is unnecessary to try to prove it. – May God always give Britain Officers who are worthy of respect and honour; and make the Briton obedient, humble, and faithful to them!

THE EDITORS.)

## *9.7 An address in praise of the periodical*

*Y Geirgrawn: Neu Drysorfa Gwybodaeth.* Am Gorphenaf, 1796. Rhif. VI (The Magazine: Or Treasury of Knowledge. For July, 1796. No.VI), 185–6.

AT GYHOEDDWR Y GEIRGRAWN

DDINESYDD

OS byddwch yn gweled yr hanes canlynol yn deilwng o le yn eich *Trysorfa*, wele, y mae at eich gwasanaeth.

Yn ddeweddar y'nghymdeithias y *Cymreigyddion* (yr hon a gynhelir yn gyfagos i Bont Lundain) ar noswaith cyfarfod, i ddadlau ar byngciau gosodedig, y cododd *J. Jones, Glanygors*, ar ei draed, ac a ddymunodd gael cennad i siarad ar achos neullduol. – wedi iddo gael cennad gan y *Cadeiriwr* a'r Gymdeithias yn gyffredin, dechreuodd areithu – Cymmerais rai o'r pethau mwya' hynod yn yr araith i lawer, sef fal y canlyn.

"HYNAWS GAREDIG GYDWLADWYR,"

Mae'n hyspys i chwi gymmaint o ddaioni, o oleuni, ac o wybodaeth, y mae'r gelfyddyd o Argraphu llyfrau wedi roddi i'r Byd. Er bod gwyr da, cywrain, doniol, a dysgedig yn y byd, yn yr hên oesoedd aethant heibio; etto, nid oes ond ychydig o'u scrifénadau wedi cyrrhaedd i'n dwylaw ni; ac y mae y rhan fwyaf o'r rheini sydd, yn anhawdd i'w cael, ac yn anhawsach i'w darllen, – Wrth feddwl am hyn ni fedraf lai nag ochneidio, a thristau, pan fyfyriwyf fod cymmaint o hen weithredoedd ardderchog ein cyndeidiau wedi desgyn i lwch angof; a hynny o eisiau bod y gelfyddyd o Argraphu mewn bod yn eu hamser hwy. Ond Ow! mor resynus yw meddwl fod y gelfyddyd uchod, yn bresenol yn disgleirio fel yr haul, a'n cydwladwyr tlodion y'Ngymru heb gael goleuni na gwybodaeth oddiwrthi: Mae hefyd, lawer o gymry (os teilwng eu galw felly) wedi iddynt ddysgu trawsnaddu rhyw ychydig o Saesoneg, er mwyn porthi eu balchder uffernol, yn cymmeryd arnynt, eu bod wedi gollwng iaith eu mammau yn angof; ond daliwch chwi sylw ar y *tyrchod* coeg-feilchion, y rhai sydd haws ganddynt roddi darn o aur, am roi llwch yn eu gwalltau (i fod megis yn arwydd weledig oddiallan nad oes dim synwyr oddifewn) nag y rhônt un ddimmau i wneuthur daioni i'w cydwladwyr, nac i neb arall a f'o ag eisiau arnynt. Pan fyddo dyn yn gwadu iaith ei fam ac yn ceisio gwadu ei wlad, mae hynny'n dystiolaeth, fod yn dda gan ei wlad gael ei wadu yntau, a'i fod e'n wradwydd i'w wlad pan oedd ynddi: – Cymmaint a hyn yma, *Mr. Llywydd*, am y Gwŷr Boneddigion sydd yn ceisio gwadu a gwradwyddo ei gwlad, eu hiaith, a'u cenedl. – Ond i ddyfod at y pwngc. Dyma *Eirgrawn*, neu Drysorfa gwybodaeth, yn gymraeg, wedi cael ei argraphu tan oruwchwiliaeth un *Dafydd Davies, o Dreffynnon, yn sir Flint*: Er nad ydwyf yn adnabod y Dyn, yr wyf yn meddwl ei fod yn ddyn cymmwys i gymmeryd y fath orchwyl buddiol mewn llaw; nid oes un ffordd fwy cymmwys i'w chymmeryd i oleuo ein cydwladwyr, na danfon llyfr o werth mor isel a phedair ceiniog i'w plith un waith yn y Mis; tan obeithio y byddant yn ei dderbyn yn galonog ac yn ddiolchgar. Mae'n enbyd meddwl bod y cymry yn cael eu diystyru gan gywion cenhedloedd tramor, o herwydd eu dallineb, a'u hanwybodaeth; a hynny yn eu hen wlad eu hunain: Gan hynny, Gyfeillion, gadewch i ni ddeffro yma yn *Llundain*, i fod yn golofnau tán yr hen Fam-iaith trwy gynnyg y *Geirgrawn* i bob cymro sydd yn caru ARFERION, AC IAITH EU GWLAD.* I ddiweddu, yr ydwyf yn deisyf cael cennad i yfed Iechyd Goruwchwiliwr y *Geirgrawn* yn gyhoeddus; gyd a diolch, llwyddiant, a rhwydd-deb iddo ef fyn'd y'mlaen a'r gwaith."

Yna'r yfwyd Iechyd y Goruwchwiliwr, yn gyhoeddus, ac addawodd amryw iawn o'r aelodau dderbyn y Geirgrawn yn *Fisol*; ac heb law hynny, y gwnaent yrru defnyddiau at y Cyhoeddwr.

*Llundain,* 1796. M. GLUSTFAIN.

(TO THE PUBLISHER OF THE GEIRGRAWN

CITIZEN

IF you consider the following account worthy of a place in your *Treasury*, here it is at your service.

Recently, in the *Cymreigyddion* society (which is held close to London Bridge) on a meeting night to debate set topics, *J. Jones, Glanygors*, rose to his feet and desired permission to speak on a particular cause. – Having had permission from the *Chairman* and the Society in general, he began to deliver an oration. – I took down some of the more noteworthy things in the speech, which are as follows.

* Motto, neu arwydd 'scrifen y *Gwyneddigion*.

"KIND AND GENIAL FELLOW-COUNTRYMEN,"

It is known to you how much benefit, enlightenment and knowledge the art of Printing books has given the World. Although there were good, skilful, witty, and learned men in the world in past ages gone by; yet, only a few of their writings have come down to us; and the majority of those that have are hard to come by, and harder still to read. – While I think of this, I can only sigh and grieve when I consider that so many of the excellent old works of our forefathers have fallen into the dust of oblivion; and that because the art of Printing was wanting in their time. But Oh! it is so deplorable to think that the aforesaid art presently shines like the sun, and our poor fellow-countrymen in Wales have had neither enlightenment nor knowledge by it: There are also many Welshmen (if they are worthy to be called such), after they have learned to rough-hew a little English, in order to feed their hellish pride, who affect to have forgotten their mothers' language; but observe the conceited *moles* who find it easier to give a piece of gold for putting powder in their hair (to be as a visible outer sign that there is no sense within) than to give one halfpenny to do good for their compatriots or for anyone else who is in need. When a man denies the language of his mother and tries to deny his country that is proof that his country is glad to deny him also, and that he was a disgrace to his country when he was in it: – So much, *Mr. President*, on those Gentlemen who attempt to deny and dishonour their country, their language, and their nation. – But to come to the point. Here is a *Geirgrawn* (Magazine), or a Treasury of knowledge in Welsh, published under the editorship of one *Dafydd Davies, of Holywell, in Flintshire*: Although I do not know the Man, I think that he is competent enough to take such a beneficial undertaking in hand; there is no better way to enlighten our countrymen than to send a book of as low a price as four pence into their midst once a Month; hoping that they will receive it heartily and thankfully. It is grievous to think that the Welsh are disrespected by fledgling foreign nations because of their blindness and their ignorance; and that in their own ancient country. Therefore, Friends, let us awaken here in *London* to be upholders of the old Mother-tongue by offering the *Geirgrawn* to all Welshmen who love the CUSTOMS AND LANGUAGE OF THEIR COUNTRY.* To finish, I desire to have permission to drink to the Health of the Editor of the *Geirgrawn* publicly; wishing him thanks, success and prosperity in carrying out his work."

* The Motto, or written sign of the *Gwyneddigion*.

The Health of the Editor was then drunk publicly, and many of the members promised to receive the Geirgrawn *Monthly*; and in addition that they would send materials to the Publisher.

*London*, 1796. M. EAVESDROP.)

### *9.8 A response by the author of* Seren tan Gwmmwl

*Y Geirgrawn: Neu Drysorfa Gwybodaeth*. Am Fedi, 1796. Rhif. VIII (The Magazine: Or Treasury of Knowledge. For September, 1796. No. VIII), 243–6.

LLYTHYR ODDIWRTH AWDWR Y *SEREN TAN GWMMWL*, AT ORUWCHWILWYR Y GEIRGRAWN.

HYNAWS GYMRY,

GWELAIS mewn amryw Rifynau o'r Geirgrawn ddadlu mawr, mewn perthynas i'r llyfr a elwir *Seren Tan Gwmmwl*; ac er nad ydyw'r llyfr hwnnw ond gwaith brys, wedi ei draws-naddu yn lled anghywrain; yr wyf yn mwynhau'r dedwyddwch a'r esmwythdra cydwybod o fod yr Awdwr o hono. – Nid eisiau budd na pharch, nac anrhydedd, na molach gan y cyffredin; na henwau drwg a rhuthriad y Bonedd, a'm cynhyrfodd i 'scrifénu'r fath lyfr; nac er enllib na malais i un dyn, nac i unrhyw râdd o ddynion, ond ar fedr gwneuthur lleshad, i'r bobl gyffredin. Ni feddyliais ddim fod y llyfr cyn gystal ac ydyw, tan y clywais fod cnafiaid gorthrymmedig (y rhai sy'n byw yn esmwyth wrth anrheithio eu cydgreaduried) yn codi, fel llewod rheibus yn chwilio am ysglyfaeth, yn fy erbyn i a'r llyfr: – yr hyn sy'n tystio fy mod wedi taro rhai gwŷr coegfeilchion ar eu dolur; ac, yn wir, y maent wedi cyfaddef hynny wrth geisio gwingo tan wyniau'r ddyrnod. – Darfu iddynt (yn ddiachos) roddi i mi a'r llyfr bob enwau drwg a fedrai eu cynddeiriogrwydd hwy feddwl am danynt: – Heblaw hynny dywedasant fy mod mewn carchar yn Llundain am fod mor rhyfygus, ac ysgrifénu'r GWIR, a hynny sy'n peri i gydwybodau rhai pobl waeddi allan yn eu gwynebau – euog! – euog! – euog!

Pan ddaeth y Rhifyn cyntaf o'r Geirgrawn allan, dyma ryw ddyn tan enw *Antagonist*, yn ei feddwl ei hun yn ddigon nerthol i roi dyrnod marwol i'r llyfr, gan feddwl hefyd y gwnai gamenwi'r Awdwr, roi gorchudd ar y gwirionedd ag oedd ynddo. – Gwedi hyn dyma ryw ddyn arall tan enw *Tudur* (yn meddwl y medrai ef daflu carreg i lêd y blewyn a'i law chwith) yn rhoi fflangell ysgorpionog[113] i *Antagonist*; ac yn rhoi i mi a'r llyfr fwy o wâg-ogoniant nag ydwyf deilwng o hono: Ac yn y trydydd Rhifyn, mae *Antagonist*, wedi ail-ymarfogi yn erbyn y gwirionedd, a chwedi scrifénu rhyw hulldod mewn ffordd newydd, (medd' ef) sef "dechreu yn niwedd yr ymadrodd yn lle'r dechreu"![114] – Ond rhag i *Antagonist* na *Thudur* golli dim ychwaneg a'r eu hamser efo'r llyfr, dylent wybod (ac os na wyddant, mae'n elusen dywedyd iddynt) mai'r peth cyntaf sydd i sylwi arno mewn perthynas i'r "*Seren*" yw, a ydyw Llywodraeth Lloegr yn bresénol fel ag y dylai fod; ac a ydyw pob dyn ag sy'n byw dan y Llywodraeth yn cael cyfiawnder, a Rhyddid, ac uniondeb, cyn belled ac y mae modd i'r naill ddyn ymddwyn yn weddus, ac yn uniawn tu ag at y llall? – Os medr *Antagonist* neu ryw wrthwynebwr arall ddangos fod llywodraeth Lloegr yn bresénol yn ei lle, (neu yn gysson a'i Sefydliad yn y Cyfnewidiad) yna byddant yn ddangos ar yr un pryd fod "*Seren*" o'i lle. Nid buddaru ei hunain efo'm fi, trwy chwilio a ydwyf yn ddysgedig a doniol, neu'n annysgedig ac heb ddim doniau ydyw'r peth sydd i sylwi arno; oblegid dichon dyn dysgedig a doniol 'scrifénu'r rhyw gau-athrawiaeth, ac anwiredd yn llefn a hardd, er mwyn cadw'r cyffredin mewn tywyllwch, rhag iddynt weled mai ar eu llafur hwy mae ef yn byw: dichon hefyd ddyn annysgedig, ac heb ond ychydig o ddoniau, lefaru neu scrifenu'r GWIR, er daioni i'w gydwladwyr; er ei fod yn ddyffygiol o ddysg neu o ddawn i addurno'r gwir a gwychder Iaith i dywynnu yn ddisglaeriol yn ei belydr ei hun. Mae amryw bethau rhesymol a wna arwain y call a'r diduedd, i faddeu i'r Awdwr, os bydd ef yn gweled rhyw bethau annrhefnus yn y llyfr.

Yn *Gyntaf*, Yr ydwyf yn meddwl mai myfi yw'r *cyntaf* a scrifénodd yn Gymraeg ar y testyn o Lywodraeth yn unig er's amryw gantoedd o flynyddoedd. Yn *ail*, Ni ddarfu' mi scrifénu dim mewn Iaith rydd, ar fedr ei argraphu erioed o'r blaen: cerddi Cymraeg ar amryw destynau yw'r pethau mwya' diddanol gan i fyfyrio arnynt, pan fyddwyf yn cael hamdden oddiwrth orchwylion angenrheidiol. Yn *drydydd*, Ni ofynais farn un dyn am y llyfr, ac ni ail-scrifenais un llinell o honno: Ond dangosais y Copi i un cyfaill dysgedig, ac a ddymunais arno nodi allan ryw anwiredd, neu ryw beth anghyfreithlon i'w ddywedyd. – Dywedodd y gwr da nad oedd ef yn gweled dim ond y GWIR ynddo. – Pan glywais hynny, aethym yn galonog a'r gwir tan fy ngesail at yr *Argraphydd*.

Pe buasai *Antagonist* mor fwyn a dangos, yn amyneddgar i mi, fy mod wedi cyfeiliorni mewn rhyw bwngc, buaswn yn ddiolchgar iddo: yn lle hynny, y mae ef yn ceisio gwyrdroi ambell *air* a gyfarfu ef yn y llyfr; ac yn sôn am "ysgothdai," ac am "ddarllain pottiau mewn sïop Apoticari;" ac am "ddal caccwn a thriagl," ac am lawer o bethau eraill, nad ydyw'r llyfr na gwaeth na gwell erddynt, pe 'scrifenai fel y dechreuodd hyd ddydd y farn! Mae'r dyn wedi dywedyd yn nechreu'r eilfed bennod, ei fod ef yn ei feddwl ei hun yn "ddyn doeth iawn!" Gadewch i ni ddal ychydig sylw ar ei ddoethineb ef. Pan y mae yn atteb *Tudur*, medd' ef, "Wele Tudur druan, – ow Tudur bach, – a glywi di *Tudur*, – Wfft i chwi," &c. Yr ydwyf fi yn cyfaddef fy mod yn rhy annoeth i weled dim doethineb mewn ymadroddion disylwedd, gwrachiaidd o'r fath yma. Ond gan ei fod ef yn dywedyd ei fod ef "ddoeth iawn," caiff fod felly o'm rhan i. – Meddyliwn ei fod hyd yn [hyn] wedi cadw y rhan fwyaf o'i ddoethineb iddo ei hun: – Mae'n beth lled afresymol i ddyn "doeth *iawn*" [. . .] fyned i holi am wybodaeth at ddyn anneallus, ansynwyrol annysgedig, fel ag y mae ef yn dywedyd fy mod i. Ond wele y gwr doeth yma yn ymostwn[g] ynghanol ei ddoethineb i ofyn i mi yn bennodol, am atteb, ac eglurhad ar bethau na ŵyr ef ddim am danynt! – Mae arnaf ofn anurddo'r *Geirgrawn* os af i atteb ei holiadau; o herwydd hynny, ni chaf ddal sylw ond ar ddau o honynt. Ebr ef "pwy a roddodd gennad i chwi i eglurhau rhyw bethau o'r Bibl at eich meddyliau eich hunain." – Mae hwn yn annheilwng o un atteb arall, amgen na gofyn yn ôl iddo yntau, Pwy a roddodd iddo ef gennad i wyrdroi, ac eglurhau rhyw ychydig eiriau ar y sydd yn y "*Seren Tan Gwmmwl*" at ei feddwl ei hun? – Ond gan nad yw'r dyn "doeth iawn" ddim yn foddlon [i] ni i gael ein meddyliau ein hunain am y Bibl, dylasai ddywedyd, meddyliau *Pwy* a ydym ni i gael? – pa un a'i meddyliau *Thomas Paine*, a'i meddyliau *Dr. Watson* Esgob Llandâf? – A pha un a'i credo St. *Athanasius* a'i credo *Voltaire* sydd fwya rhesymol, a thebygca o fod yn wir? – Mewn lle arall, mae ar y dyn doeth eisiau cael gwybod, A pha Enaint y byddis yn eneinio brenhin wrth ei goroni? Rhyfedd fod un dyn yn ei alw ei hun yn *ddoeth iawn*, ac yn ceisio ymddiffyn brenhinoedd ac heb wybod dim am y gallu ag sydd yn llaw brenhin; ac am y Seremoniau plentynaidd, a'r Enaint dieffaith, a'r tyngu, a llawer o bethau eraill, ag sydd yn cael eu harfer wrth wneuthur dŷn yn frenhin. Mae'r holiad uchod yn ymddangos yn fwy hynod erbyn i ni gofio mae'r dyn a ddadguddiodd fod "*Phosphorus* yn dangos pethau bychain yn fawrion, a'r pethau pell yn agos," sydd yn holi. Mae lle i feddwl hefyd, wrth ei weled yn sôn am bottiau cyffeiriau, ei fod ef yn lled gydnabyddus mewn sïop apoticari, lle gallasai ef gael gwybodaeth am amryw fath o Enaint. – Ond nid af i flino'r darllenydd yn hwy efo'r pwngc ireiddlyd yma: eithr os na fedr y dyn "doeth iawn" fod yn esmwyth heb gael llawn wybodaeth o hono *Arch-Esgob Caer-Gaint* Mrs. F–tz– –r– –rt, neu Mrs. J–rd–n[115] sydd debyca i wybod y ffordd y byddis yn eneinio cyrph brenhinol.

Yr ydwyf yn ddiolchgar i *Antagonist* a *Tudur* am gymmeryd cymmaint trafferth efo'r *Seren*; ac y mae'n dda gennyf fy mod wedi ei 'scrifénu, er mwyn iddynt gael cyfleusdra i ddangos eu cywreinrwydd i'r byd. Yr wyf yn credu hefyd fod eu dadleuaeth er addysg i'r Cymry. Addewais yn niwedd y *Seren*, "scrifenu llyfr arall, tan enw TORRIAD Y DYDD. Pe gwyddwn yn siccr, y byddai'r fath lyfr yn dderbyniol gan y rhan fwya' dysgedig a diduedd o'r cymry, awn ymlaen efo'r gwaith, a hynny yn ddiofn y'ngwyneb yr holl fygythion a gefais am 'scrifénu'r *Seren*. A bydded hyspys i'r gwyr croesion ag sy'n son am fy rhoi mewn carchar, fod yn well gan i gael yr anrhydedd o *farw* yn ddyn RHYDD, na chael yr anglod o *fyw* yn ddistaw, yn gaethwas tan rwymau gorthrymder, mewn gwlad lle mae cwyno yn amyneddgar am Ryddid a chyfiawnder yn cael ei gyfrif yn drosedd.

Wyf, eich Carwr;

Cyn belled ag yr ydych yn caru'r Gwirionedd,

J. JONES, *Glanygors*.

## (LETTER FROM THE AUTHOR OF *SEREN TAN GWMMWL* (A STAR UNDER A CLOUD), TO THE EDITORS OF THE GEIRGRAWN.

GENIAL WELSHMEN,

I have seen great debates in various Numbers of the Geirgrawn concerning the book called *Seren Tan Gwmmwl*; and although that book was but a hasty work, rough-hewn rather unskilfully; I enjoy the happiness and ease of conscience of being its Author. – It was not want of profit or respect, nor honour or praise from the common people; nor was it bad names and attacks from the Nobles that moved me to write such a book; nor for slander or out of malice to any man or to any class of men, but in order to benefit the common people. I did not think that the book was as good as it is until I heard that oppressive knaves (who live comfortably by plundering their fellow-creatures) were rising, like rapacious lions looking for prey, against me and the book: – this proves that I have hit the sore point of some conceited men; and, indeed, they have admitted that as they have flinched from the smarts of the blow. – They have (without cause) given me and the book every bad name their rage could think of: – In addition, they said that I was in prison in London for being so daring as to write the TRUTH, and this makes the conscience of some people cry out in their faces – guilty! – guilty! – guilty!

When the first Number of the Geirgrawn came out, some man under the name of *Antagonist* thought himself strong enough to deliver a fatal blow to the book, thinking also that abusing the Author would put a cover on the truth that was in it. – After this came some other man under the name of *Tudur* (thinking that he could throw a stone to a hair's breadth with his left hand) giving *Antagonist* a scorpion lash;[113] and awarding me and the book more vainglory than I deserve. And in the third number

*Antagonist* has rearmed against the truth and has written some nonsense in a new kind of way (he says), that is "starting at the end of the expression instead of the beginning"![114] – But lest *Antagonist* and *Tudur* lose any more of their time with the book, they should know (and if they do not know, it is charitable to tell them) that the first thing to be noted concerning the "*Seren*" is, whether the English Government is presently as it should be; and does every man who lives under the Government receive justice, and Liberty, and fair play, as far as it is possible for one man to behave properly and justly to the other? – If *Antagonist* or some other opponent can show that the English government is presently correct (or consistent with its Establishment in the Revolution) then they will at the same time show that the "*Seren*" is incorrect. They need not weary themselves about me by searching to see whether I am learned and talented or ignorant and without talent; for a learned and talented man may write some false teaching and untruth smoothly and beautifully in order to keep the common people in darkness, lest they see that he lives off their labour: it is also possible for an unlearned man with but a few talents to speak or write the TRUTH, for the good of his compatriots; though he lacks the learning or the talent to adorn the truth with the splendour of Language to shine radiantly in its own beam. There are various reasons which will lead the sensible and the unbiased to forgive the Author some confused things he may encounter in the book.

*Firstly*, I think that I am the *first* to write solely on the subject of Government in Welsh for several hundred years. *Secondly*, I have never before written anything in prose with the intention of publishing it: Welsh poems on various subjects are the things most congenial to me upon which to meditate when I have leisure from necessary duties. *Thirdly*, I did not ask the opinion of any man about the book, and I did not rewrite one line of it: But I showed the Copy to one learned friend, and I desired him to point out any untruths or anything that it was unlawful to say. – The good man said that he saw nothing but the TRUTH in it. – When I heard that, I went in good heart to the *Printer*, with the truth under my arm.

If *Antagonist* were so kind as to show me patiently that I have gone astray in some passage, I would be grateful to him: instead of that, he tries to distort the occasional *word* he encounters in the book; and mentions "toilets," and "reading pots in an Apothecary's shop;" and "catching wasps with treacle," and many other things by which the book is neither better or worse even if he wrote on as he began till the Day of Judgement! At the beginning of the second chapter the man said that he considered himself a "very wise man!" Let us pay a little attention to his wisdom. When he answers *Tudur*, he says, "See poor Tudur, – Oh, poor Tudur, – do you hear *Tudur*, – Fie on you," &c. I confess that I am too ignorant to see any wisdom in unfounded, old-womanish expressions of this sort. But as he says that he is "very wise", he may be so as far as I am concerned. – I think that he has kept most of his wisdom to himself up to now: – It is a pretty unreasonable thing for a "*very* wise" man [. . .] to go to ask for knowledge from an ignorant, foolish, unlearned man, as he says that I am. But behold, this wise man stoops in the midst of his wisdom to ask me in particular for an answer and enlightenment about things of which he knows nothing! – I am afraid of disgracing the *Geirgrawn* if I answer his questions; therefore, I shall just give attention to two of them. He said "who gave you permission to explain some things from the Bible according to your own mind." – This is unworthy of any answer other than to ask him back, Who gave him permission to distort and explain some words in the "*Seren Tan Gwmmwl*" according to his own mind? – But as the "very wise" man is not willing for us to have our own thoughts about the Bible, he ought to have said *Whose* thoughts we are to have – *Thomas Paine*'s thoughts, or the thoughts of *Dr. Watson*, Bishop of Llandaff? And is it the credo of St. *Athanasius* or the credo of *Voltaire* that is the most reasonable and most likely to be true? – In another place the wise man wishes to know With what Ointment is the king anointed when he is crowned? It is strange that a man calls himself *very wise*, and attempts to defend kings without knowing anything of the power that is in a king's hand; and about the childish Ceremonies, and the ineffectual Anointment and the oaths and many other things which are practised when making a man a king. The above question appears even more remarkable when we remember that it is the man who revealed that "*Phosphorus* makes little things appear big and far things near," who is asking. There is reason to think also, observing him mentioning medicine jars, that he is reasonably familiar with an apothecary's shop, where he could get information about various sorts of Ointment. – But I will not tire the reader longer with this oily subject: but if that "very wise" man cannot rest without having a full knowledge of it, the *Archbishop of Canterbury*, Mrs. F–tz– –r– –rt, or Mrs. J–rd–n[115] are most likely to know the ways that royal bodies are anointed.

I am grateful to *Antagonist* and *Tudur* for taking so much trouble with the *Seren*; and I am glad that I wrote it in order for them to have the opportunity to show their ingenuity to the world. I also believe that their debate is educational for the Welsh. I promised at the end of the *Seren* "to write another book, under the name TORRIAD Y DYDD (THE BREAK OF DAY). If I knew for sure that such a book would be acceptable to the most learned and unbiased section of the Welsh, I would go ahead with the task and that fearlessly in the face of all the threats I received for writing the *Seren*. And let it be known to the ill-tempered men who talk of putting me in prison that I would rather have the honour of *dying* a FREE man, than to have the ignominy of *living* quietly, as a slave under the shackles of oppression, in a country where calling patiently for Liberty and justice is counted a crime.

I am, your Friend,
As long as you love the Truth,
J. JONES, *Glanygors*.)

### *9.9 An anti-war poem*

*Y Geirgrawn: Neu Drysorfa Gwybodaeth*. Am Hydref, 1796. Rhif. IX (The Magazine: Or Treasury of Knowledge. For October, 1796. No. IX), 286–7.

CYHOEDDWR, *Llanbedr, Hydr.* 7, 1796.

OS ewyllysiwch ddodrefn o'm naddiad i, i'w gosod yn eich *Trysorfa*, wele hyn i'ch dewisiad yn bresènol: Bydd fy ngell etto yn agored. Byddwch wych,

Wyf Eich Ewyllysiwr da,
DAFYDD SAUNDERS.

GOLWG AR YR RHYFEL PRESENOL; AC AR FYNEDIAD DYNION I *AMERICA*, YNGHYD A'R FANTAIS O FYNED YNO.

Ar diroedd a moroedd,
Rhyw filain ryfeloedd
A mawr iawn gwyn hir-faith,
Yn nawr ymgynhyrfodd:
Pwy goll, 'n enw'r Gallu,
Sy'n tynnu'r *Brytaniaid*,
Rai fu Duw'n eu llwyddo,
Nawr fyned yn lleiddiaid?
A ddaeth yspryd celwyddog,
Fel llidiog hyll Hediad,
At *Sïor* a'i Gynghorwyr,
Trwy sarrug anghariad;
Gan wneud pob rhyw ffwdan
I hudo'r prophwydi:
Attebwch, y dynion,
Beth dybiwch am dani?

Pwy'r ŵan all ddangos
Yr achos goruchel
O'r cynnwrf, yn rhywfodd,
Amcanodd y rhyfel?
A oedd rhai yn dyfod
O'r *Frangcod* i'n difa,
Er braw in' bryd hynny,
O'r bron, yn *Brytania*?
A ddaethant i'r golwg,
Er amlwg wir ymladd;
Ag wyneb hiraethlon,
Am gynnyg i Borthladd?
Neu ynte, mewn trefn,
Mi fentraf i ofyn,
A fu rhyw fygwthiad,
Pan fwrwyd mor gethin?

Pe sylw'em ni beunydd,
Pa sawl un ddibènwyd,
'R hyn sy olwg erchyllaf,
A sawl un archollwyd;
Ebrwydd y tystiem,
Gan brudded y testun,
Mae enbyd i feddwl
Yw bod yn y fyddin:
Heb ddim ond creulondeb
Fyth yn cael ei wrando,
Yr hyn sy'n hyll ofyd,
A'r einioes yn llifo;
A lluoedd yn digwydd
Fod yn lladdedigion,
I'w troedio'n gelanedd,
Rhwng traed eu gelynion!

Ni glywn etto'n fynych, –
"Mae'r *Gilotîn* finiog,
Mewn purion awenydd,
Yn para'n newynog.
Pwy sydd yma draetha,
O'r sawl fu draw weithiau,

Am hon trwy ddibènion,
Faint dorrodd hi o bènau!
Er syndod, ac arswyd,
Mae'r Sandir yn gorsog
(Och! on'd yw'n erchyll?)
Gan waedach tywarchog!"
Pa fodd 'r w'i'n dymuno,
Clywch etto, rhowch atteb,
Na chlywn i, wrth wrando,
Pa le'r aeth *Tiriondeb*?

'Rwy fi'n barnu'n fynych,
O'm rhan i fy hunan,
Wrth ganfod y drefn,
I hwn fyn'd i ryw fàn,
'R hyd wyneb y dyfn-for:
'R ydwyf fi'n ofnus,
Ei fyn'd ymhell enbyd
'R hyd llwybr *Columbus*,
At *Washington* anwyl,
'R hwn sy, on' tê, 'n hynod
I 'mddiffyn *Tiriondeb*,
A'i hoffi trwy Undod?
O mor hoff yw'r elw,
Ymrown i ffarwèlo –
Mwy, wyr da, tan ganu,
Mordwywn tu ag yno!

(I'w orphen yn y nesaf.)

(PUBLISHER, *Lampeter, Oct.* 7, 1796.

IF you wish to furnish your *Treasury* with items I have carved, behold the following for your selection. My repository will be open again. Farewell,

I am Your Well-wisher,

DAFYDD SAUNDERS.

## A LOOK AT THE PRESENT WAR; AND AT THE EMIGRATION OF MEN TO *AMERICA*, TOGETHER WITH THE ADVANTAGE OF GOING THERE.

On land and on sea,
such savage wars
and a very great grievous wrath
were bestirring:
what insanity motivates the *Britons*,
whom God used to bless,
to now turn into slayers
in the name of the Almighty?
Did a lying spirit,
like a fierce, hideous creature,
fly to *George* and his Councillors,
with scowling hatred;
making all effort
to beguile the prophets:
answer, you men,
what think you of this?

Who can now explain
the higher cause
of the discord, which somehow
the war brought about?
Did some of the *French*,
to our alarm at that time,
come to destroy us
in *Britannia* altogether?
Did they come into view
in order to fight openly for real;
with lustful faces,
making for a Harbour?
Or rather, I venture to ask
in the circumstance,
was there really any threat
when one struck out so hard?

If we observed daily
how many were killed,
it is the most terrible sight,
and how many were wounded;
we would immediately testify,
so grave is the subject
that it fills us with fear to imagine
being in the army:
with naught but cruelty
ever to be heard,
which means dreadful sorrow,
while life ebbs away;
and armies being routed
and slaughtered,
to be trampled as corpses
under the feet of their enemies!

Again we often hear that, –
"The sharp *Guillotine*,
in fine fettle,
remains hungry.
Of those who've been over there,
who is here to recount
how many heads it cut off
by design!
To our horror and dread,
the Sands are sodden
(Oh! is this not terrible?)
with blood-soaked clods!"
How I desire,
listen, give an answer,
I do not hear, listening out,
where *Humanity* went?

I often judge,
on my own part,
in beholding the order,
that it went somewhere,
over the face of the ocean:
I am fearful
that it went awfully far
on the path of *Columbus*,
to dear *Washington*,
he who is remarkable, is he not,
defending *Humanity*
and celebrating it through Unity?
Oh, so marvellous is the gain,
let us say farewell –
now, good men, while singing,
let's voyage over yonder!

(To be finished in the next number.))

## *Notes*

1 Adam Phillipe, Comte de Custine (1740–93), a career soldier, rallied to the Third Estate in June 1789 and returned to the army in 1791. He was general-in-chief of the revolutionary Army of the Vosges and, in autumn 1792, he took the main Palatinate towns of Speyer, Worms, Mainz and Frankfurt, where he levied heavy taxes on nobility and clergy and circulated revolutionary propaganda. A coalition of Austrian, British and Prussian forces, to which this poem refers, forced him to fall back beyond the Rhine in the winter of 1792–3. Convicted of conspiring with the enemies of the Republic, he was condemned to death and guillotined on 28 August 1793. See *LCFR*, p. 336.

2 Both were admirals of the British fleet who had taken part in the Seven Years' War and the American War of Independence. Admiral Samuel Hood, first Viscount Hood (1722–1816), was commander-in-chief of the Mediterranean Sea from May 1793 to October 1794, during which time he took possession of Toulon. Admiral Richard Howe, first Earl Howe (1726–99), was the commander of the British fleet on the 'Glorious First of June' 1794. See endnote 30.

3 The Duke of York and Albany, Prince Frederick Augustus (1763–1827), was the second son of George III of the United Kingdom and Charlotte of Mecklenburg-Strelitz. He commanded the British troops within the alliance which attempted to invade France via Flanders in 1793–4. After initial victories, his army was forced to retreat, which led to the rise of the satirical song 'The Grand Old Duke of York'. He redeemed himself as commander-in-chief during the Napoleonic wars.

4 'Edward Jones, the Miner', is an otherwise unknown poet. The linguistic forms used in his poem indicate that he was from south Wales.

5 Jehu, *c.*842–815 BC, became king of Israel by slaying King Ahab and his wife, the notorious Queen Jezebel, as well as their son Prince Jehoram, thus avenging Naboth, whose vineyard Ahab had coveted and acquired using the device of a day of public fast (suggested by the power-hungry Jezebel). Jehu is notorious for the subsequent slaughter of over a hundred of the nobles of Israel.

6 Ahab, a king of Israel, *c.*869–850 BC, was forcefully deposed by Jehu's revolt in 842 BC. His reign receives unfavourable comments in the Bible for his worship of Baal, his disobedience of prophetic warnings and his murder of Naboth.

7 Sennacherib (*c.*704–681 BC) was a king of the Assyrian Empire whose siege of Jerusalem was thwarted by a God-sent angel who wiped out his 185,000 soldiers overnight. At his return to Nineveh, Sennacherib was murdered by his own sons, Adrammelech and Sharezer (2 Kings 19: 35–7).

8 Louis XVI, the deposed king of France, was sentenced to death and executed as 'Citizen Louis Capet', possibly to draw attention to the fact that the Bourbons, a cadet branch of the Capet dynasty, had usurped the throne illegitimately.

9 Dafydd Risiart (or Richard) was a late eighteenth-century preacher and poet at Waun-lwyd, Cross Inn, Llandybïe, who was suspected of harbouring sympathies with the French Revolution. See Gomer M. Roberts, *Hanes Plwyf Llandybïe*

(Caerdydd, 1939), p. 101. Text and translation of his more loyalist 'Cerdd newydd ar yr amser' (A new song on the present time), published in Harris's almanac a year earlier, may be found in Cathryn Charnell-White, *Welsh Poetry of the French Revolution 1789–1805* (Cardiff, forthcoming).

10 This is Newcastle Emlyn in south-west Wales.

11 The meeting had been summoned by the influential Baptist preacher William Williams (1732–99), who took a public part in the religious controversies in rural west Wales at the end of the eighteenth century and also contributed to *Cylch-grawn Cynmraeg*. Despite being a Dissenter, he was a Justice of the Peace. See *DWB*. His public writings earned him an anonymous accusation of subscribing to the 'doctrines of Equality and the RIGHTS of Man', *Shrewsbury Chronicle*, 3 January 1794.

12 George Talbot (1765–1852) had become third baron Dynevor in 1793. The seat of this old Welsh family was at Dinefwr, Llandeilo, Carmarthenshire.

13 George Hardinge (1743–1816), well known for his solemn addresses at court, was senior judge for the counties of Breconshire, Glamorganshire and Radnorshire from 1787 until his death. He was also a writer and antiquary interested in Welsh antiquities. See *ODNB*. The sentences he pronounced here and in DOCUMENT 2.16 are lenient compared to the two years in prison to which he sentenced the Unitarian minister Tomos Glyn Cothi (see p. 29 above) and the death sentences meted out to the Merthyr Tydfil rioters in 1801 (see pp. 25–6 above and DOCUMENT 3.21).

14 Stingo is a strong traditional ale.

15 The source has not been identified and the couplet may well have been composed by 'Bard of Rhaiadr', i.e. Thomas Jones (Rhaiadr) (see pp. 13–14 above), in order to draw attention to the participation of miners in these celebrations.

16 On 2 May 1792, the *Shrewsbury Chronicle* reported a change in tactics by the 'Combined Forces', who now attempted to 'penetrate into the very heart of the enemy's country'. It also contained several gazettes of small naval victories.

17 The modern Welsh spelling for this phrase is 'a'm cipio'.

18 Mathrafal, near Meifod, was the main residence of the royal Welsh house of Powys until the thirteenth century.

19 Dafydd Ddu Eryri later sent a version of this poem to *Y Geirgrawn*, where it was published as 'Dymuniad am Heddwch cyffredinol' (Wish for a general Peace) in the June issue. See *Y Geirgrawn*, no. V (1796), 160. An extended five-stanza version appeared in the second edition of his anthology *Corph y Gaingc* (The Main Refrain of the Song) (Caernarfon, 1834), pp. 159–60, and will be discussed in Charnell-White, *Welsh Poetry of the French Revolution*.

20 This is Penllyn, the picturesque area around Bala in north-east Merionethshire.

21 The same core text, but addressed to 'the Freeholders and Inhabitants of Carmarthenshire, who assembled on the third instant, at the shire-hall, as convened by the High Sheriff of that county', opened by a paragraph which claimed that 'several branches of my family owned considerable property' there, and signed 'William de Common Church, Derllys, Jan. 20, 1798', had already been published in the

*Oracle*, 29 January 1798. The author had thus ensured that it came to the attention of the Welsh in the metropolis and at home. I am grateful to John Barrell for bringing this reference to my attention.

[22] The source has not been identified.

[23] Given the geographical location of Haverfordwest, they were most probably refugees from County Wexford, where the United Irishmen temporarily enjoyed great success before being defeated at the battle of Vinegar Hill on 21 June 1798, and where a particularly high number of atrocities appear to have been committed.

[24] On 15 June 1800, King George III survived an assassination attempt at Drury Lane theatre when former soldier James Hadfield shot him, but missed. This otherwise unknown poet is probably from Llangurig (here 'Llangerrig'), mid Wales.

[25] In the days following the attempted landing of a French force at Fishguard, five Dissenters were arrested, of whom two, the Baptist preacher Thomas John and the Presbyterian Samuel Griffiths, were held in prison until they were brought to trial for high treason in September 1797.

[26] The 'combustibles' refer to the 'Breeches Plot' of 9 May 1792, when a pair of smouldering breeches were found in a closet in the House of Commons. In the days which followed, satirical connections between Thomas Paine and 'smouldering breeches' began to be made in papers such as *St James's Chronicle* and *The Star.* I am indebted to John Barrell for this information.

[27] Note especially Sir Watkin Williams Wynn, fifth baronet, the greatest landowner and William Wilkinson, the most influential industrialist in the area. For the previous political career of the chairman William Shipley, see Anthony Page, 'The Dean of St Asaph's Trial: Libel and Politics in the 1780s', *Journal for Eighteenth-Century Studies*, 32, no. I (2009), 21–35.

[28] Iolo Morganwg here chose to sign Edward Williams. A longer version of this poem with a paratext of copious politically resonant footnotes had already been published in his *Poems Lyric and Pastoral* (2 vols., London, 1794), II, pp. 160–8, which had appeared at the beginning of the year. The version reproduced here misses the original stanza five and varies slightly in vocabulary. In stanza one 'dreadful' replaces 'deceitful', in stanza three 'friends' replaces 'fiends' (which may be a misprint), in stanza five 'trade' replaces 'skill', and in stanza six 'eagle-pinions' replaces 'eagle's pinions'. Also missing are the introductory remarks and the final bardic motto of the original.

[29] A footnote in the version contained in *Poems Lyric and Pastoral* confirms that this is, indeed, a reference to the soldier and statesman John Churchill, first duke of Malborough (1630–1722), whom Iolo Morganwg calls 'a most execrable character'. See *Poems Lyric and Pastoral*, II, p. 165.

[30] This was the victory Admiral Lord Howe and his British Channel Fleet won over the French Atlantic Fleet on 1 June 1794, a day which became known as the 'Glorious First of June'.

[31] A public day of fast in support of the war effort was proclaimed for 9 March 1796.

[32] This is probably a reference to the attack on the coach of George III on his return from the theatre, which was reported in the *Chester Chronicle*, 12 February 1796. The astonishing sum of £1,000 was promised for information leading to the arrest of the perpetrators.

[33] Charles Howard (1746–1815), eleventh duke of Norfolk, was a celebrated and influential Whig politician.

[34] Owain Glyndŵr (*c*.1354–*c*.1416) is a Welsh national hero. He was proclaimed Prince of Wales on 16 September 1400 and led a Welsh war of independence against English oppression between 1400 and 1413, when he disappeared. See *NCLW*.

[35] The poem was republished in the *Sporting Magazine* in the same year and again in the *Chester Chronicle* in 1802. Until 2010, this earliest version was unknown. See Marion Löffler, 'Cerddi newydd gan John Jones "Jac Glan-y-Gors"', *Llên Cymru*, 33 (2010), 143–50.

[36] This is the 'Gazette' which appeared in all of the border papers and is here reproduced in DOCUMENT 4.3.

[37] This refers to the window tax, first introduced in 1696, according to which every house with more than seven windows (from 1766) was obliged to pay a variable (this from 1778) rate of tax.

[38] Llywelyn ap Gruffudd (*c*.1225–82), who is known in Wales as 'Y Llyw Olaf' (The Last Prince), led a Welsh rebellion against English and Anglo-Norman rule from 1255 and was declared Prince of Wales in 1258. In 1267, King Henry III confirmed him and his heirs in this title. However, King Edward I pursued more aggressive policies, as a result of which Llywelyn ap Gruffudd was killed by English troops in an ambush at Cilmeri in 1282. See *NCLW*.

[39] The first two lines are taken from Shakespeare, *Macbeth*, Act IV, Scene i, though the second line has been changed from 'or where conspirers are' to 'who conspirers are'. The third line has been added in order to politicize the verse.

[40] This is a reference to a Welsh folk tale, according to which the young warriors who were in the retinue of the legendary King Arthur are asleep in a cave on the slopes of the Lliwedd mountain in Snowdonia, awaiting his second coming to regain the Crown of Britain. The 'it' in the line of poetry refers to this crown. The author of the line is unknown and only referred to as 'hen air gwir' (an old true word) in later descriptions. See 'Plwyf Bedd Gelert', *Y Brython*, IV, no. 36 (1861), 371.

[41] This is probably a reference to the efforts, in March 1798, of establishing a 'sister republic' to France in Switzerland.

[42] Virgil, *Aeneid* ii: 65–6.

[43] This passage attempts to reproduce Shakespeare, *Hamlet*, Act I, Scene v, though some minor changes in spelling and vocabulary have occurred, e.g. 'porpentine' has become 'porcupine'. A significant change has occurred in the last line, where the 'father' of the original has been replaced by 'country', thus making the verse strongly patriotic.

[44] Shakespeare, *Hamlet*, Act I, Scene v. In the original, the last line reads 'Adieu! Adieu Hamlet, remember me.'

[45] David Samwell (Dafydd Ddu Feddyg) died on 23 November 1798.

[46] Helen Maria Williams (1761–1827) was a controversial British novelist, poet and translator, whose letters from France, where she lived for long periods during the 1790s, and poems were reprinted in the provincial papers close to the Welsh border. Count Alvise Zenobio (1762–1816) was a Venetian nobleman in exile, mainly in London, a member of the Society for Promoting Constitutional Information and a correspondent of John Horne Tooke and William Godwin.

[47] Edward Jones (Bardd y Brenin [The King's Poet]; 1752–1824), a native of Merionethshire, was harpist to the Prince of Wales, later George IV. He was an important member of the circle of London Welshmen who succeeded in gathering and publishing the literary and historical treasures of their country. See *NCLW*; *DWB*.

[48] 'Monensis' is Paul Panton, junior (1758–1822), of Plas Gwyn, Anglesey. Following in the footsteps of his father, he was an ardent collector of Welsh manuscripts as well as patron and friend to Welsh poets and antiquaries, such as Dafydd Ddu Eryri. The first volume of the *Myvyrian Archaiology* is dedicated to him. Politically, he was a staunch loyalist. See *DWB*.

[49] Romans 9: 17.

[50] Matthew 24: 2.

[51] This seems to be a combination of 1 Peter 2: 13–15, Romans 13: 7, and Luke 20: 25 or Mark 12: 17.

[52] Note that Welsh political terms which were either new or presumed to be unfamiliar to the reader were often followed by their English equivalents in brackets and italics or explained in footnotes. In this volume's English version, these translations are not separately explained or repeated.

[53] Stephen Báthory (1533–86), a nobleman of Hungarian origin, became king of Poland by marrying Ann of Jagellonia at the invitation of the Polish nobility. His reign, 1576–86, was destabilized by the threat of counter-reformation emanating from the Habsburg monarchy. Welsh radical sources in the 1790s showed much interest in and sympathy with the ill treatment of Poland in recent history.

[54] The tale of Prince Madog ab Owain Gwynedd, who, following internecine strife, left Wales in AD 1170, first mentioned in Welsh poetry at the end of the fifteenth century and described fully by Humphrey Llwyd in his *Chronica Wallia* (1559), bears striking similarities to the story of the historically attested Norwegian Erik the Red (*c*.950–*c*.1003) who was forced to leave his native Norway and later Iceland to escape revenge. In search of refuge, he and his followers discovered and settled Greenland around AD 985. See also p. 39 above.

[55] Psalms 46: 10; Exodus 14: 13.

[56] This is a reference to the feet of the statue which Nebuchadnezzar saw in a dream that was interpreted to him by Daniel. The image of clay and iron alludes to the brittleness of the political alliance against France and the proximity of the everlasting heavenly kingdom. See Daniel 2: 22, 44.

[57] Galatians 6: 7.

58 The meaning of this clause and the missing word have not been identified fully.

59 Charles François Dumourier (originally Dumouriez, 1739–1823) was foreign minister when France declared war on Austria in 1792, but resumed his military career after his dismissal from this post. He commanded the Northern Army in 1792–3. Following defeat at Brussels in spring 1793 and fearful of a hostile reception in Paris, he deserted on 5 April 1793. See *LCFR*, pp. 342–3. His subsequent high life in London attracted the attention of press, poets and artists alike. Robert Burns wrote an 'Impromptu On General Dumourier's Desertion from the French Republican Army' and James Gilray created a series of cartoons in spring and early summer 1793. In Wales, David Davis (Castellhywel) composed an epitaph on the traitor for *Cylch-grawn Cynmraeg*. See DOCUMENT 7.10.

60 See endnote 1.

61 See endnote 3.

62 Armand Louis de Gontaut, duc de Biron (1747–93), was a French aristocrat who served against England in the American War of Independence. As lieutenant general, he commanded the Army of the North, the Army of the Rhine, and the new Army of Italy for the French Republican government. However, like many of the old military men of noble descent, he was arrested and tried for conspiring with the enemy in 1793. He was guillotined on 31 December 1793. See *LCFR*, p. 322.

63 In this case 'Brython' (Briton) means an inhabitant of Brittany, speaking Breton, the Celtic language closely related to Welsh.

64 Isaiah 2: 4.

65 This interesting *englyn* was probably not composed by Morgan John Rhys, the author of this text. The reference to clouds veiling liberty suggests that it may be the work of Jac Glan-y-gors, the author of the radical pamphlet *Seren tan Gwmmwl* (A Star under a Cloud). See Introduction, pp. 12–13.

66 This is the Welsh Quaker John Griffith (1713–76) who spent long periods of his life in America winning new members for his denomination and who published several volumes of writings. *DWB*.

67 This is the motto on which Iolo Morganwg settled for his Gorsedd of the Bards of the Isle of Britain around the same time.

68 This may be a reference to Brutus or Britto, the legendary forefather of the Britons, after whom the island of Britain was named. According to Geoffrey of Monmouth, Brutus of Troy, a great-grandson of Aeneas, led part of his people from Greek bondage to freedom on the shores of the British Isles.

69 *Brut y Brenhinedd* (The Book of Kings) refers to the various translations made of Geoffrey of Monmouth's *Historia Regum Britanniæ* between the thirteenth and fifteenth centuries (see endnote 75). Late eighteenth-century Welsh scholars (following the lead of Iolo Morganwg) erroneously believed that a version of this chronicle, allegedly composed by the seventh-century saint Tysilio, was Geoffrey's source. See *NCLW*, s.v. Brut y Brenhinedd, s.n. Tysilio.

70 The contents and language of this address, especially its postscript, suggest Iolo Morganwg as its author. Iolo had apparently promised Morgan John Rhys

contributions for the first and the second number. See G. J. Williams (ed.), 'Original Documents: 4. Letters of Morgan John Rhys to William Owen [-Pughe]', *NLWJ*, II, nos. 3&4 (1942), 132, 134.

71 Triads are mnemonic devices attested in early and medieval Welsh, and to a lesser extent Irish, literature. They enabled poets and historians to remember major events, people and axioms of life by grouping them in threes. See Rachel Bromwich, *Trioedd Ynys Prydein: The Triads of the Island of Britain* (3rd edn., Cardiff, 2006).

72 This refers to Lewis Morris's 'Celtic Remains', which remained unpublished, but exerted an enormous influence on antiquaries like Iolo Morganwg.

73 Robert Fychan (Robert Vaughan; *c*.1592–1667) from Hengwrt was one of the most important antiquaries and collectors of Welsh manuscripts in seventeenth-century Wales. His collection, known as the Peniarth manuscripts, is at NLW.

74 *Eulogium Brittaniæ* is the title of a prologue to the *Historia Brittonum* which occurs in MS Corpus Christi Cambridge 139 and which attributes the *Historia* to Nennius. See endnote 76.

75 Geoffrey of Monmouth (d. 1155) was one of the most influential authors of the High Middle Ages. His pseudo-historical account of the British kings from Brutus down to Cadwaladr at the end of the seventh century AD, known as *Historia Regum Britanniæ*, which he claimed to have translated from ancient Welsh sources, was widely accepted as historically true until the beginning of the nineteenth century. *NCLW*.

76 Nennius was credited with the authorship of the ninth-century *Historia Brittonum*, a history of the British Isles down to the seventh century AD. *NCLW*.

77 William Baxter (1650–1723) was a grammarian and scholar, whose grammar and translations from Latin were widely used in eighteenth-century British learning. In 1719 he published the *Glossarium Antiquitatum Britannicarum* which is attacked here.

78 Camber was one of the sons of Brutus. He was credited with founding Cambria, i.e. Wales. See endnote 68.

79 Gomer was one of the sons of Japheth and a grandson of Noah. He is said to have led his people to Europe, where, in a more Christian foundation myth than that of Brutus and Camber, he became ancestor to the Welsh. The Welsh language, 'y Gymraeg', was therefore often referred to as 'y Gomeraeg' in the nineteenth century.

80 Matthew 3: 12.

81 The first part of this text is a direct and acknowledged translation of the chapter on Kentucky in Gilbert Imlay, *A Topographical Description of the Western Territory of North America* (London, 1792). The following are the core advantages of the American way of life ascribed to a preacher in London and attached to the Imlay text.

82 This is Thomas Paine, *Letter Addressed to the Addressers on the Late Proclamation* (London, 1792), in which he responded to the harsh critique of the second part of his *Rights of Man* and the charge of sedition.

[83] Charlotte Corday (1668–1793) assassinated Jean-Paul Marat on 13 July 1793 because she believed that King Louis XVI should not have been executed and to avert civil war. She was executed by guillotine on 17 July 1793.

[84] Charles-Bertin-Gaston Chapuis de Tourville (1740–1809) became divisional general in the Girondist army in March 1793 and repeatedly beat the Republican troops in Brittany.

[85] Georges-Félix Wimpfen (also Wimpffen; 1744–1814) was appointed commander of the Army of the Coasts of Cherbourg in 1792, but changed allegiance when he was appointed general of the troops of the Federation of Departments in June 1793. Following their defeat he went into hiding for the remainder of the 1790s. See *LCFR*, p. 400.

[86] This refers to the insurrection against the king on 10 August 1792.

[87] This poem on the traitor General Dumourier refers back to the news item in DOCUMENT 7.5. See also endnote 58. Though unsigned, its author is known to be David Davis, Castellhywel. See 'Dumourier, Cadpen y Ffrancod, yr hwn a drows yn eu herbyn' (Dumourier, General of the French, who turned against them) in *Telyn Dewi; Sef Gwaith Prydyddawl y Parch. David Davis o Gastell-Hywel, Ceredigion* (Dewi's Harp; Which is the Poetic Works of the Revd David Davis of Castellhywel) (Llundain, 1824), p. 128.

[88] Edward Charles (Siamas Wynedd; 1757–1828), originally from Denbighshire, was a leading member of the London Gwyneddigion society. His contributions to the Welsh radical press were entertaining and highly controversial. His diatribe against Methodist preachers had been published as 'Y Pregethwr Bol-clawdd a'r Teiliwr Bongleraidd' (The Hedgerow Preacher and the Bungling Tailor) in *Cylch-grawn Cynmraeg*, no. IV (1793), 198–201. For his contributions to the debate of the radical pamphlet *Seren tan Gwmmwl* (A Star under a Cloud) in *Y Geirgrawn*, see DOCUMENT 9. 2. See *DWB*; *NCLW*; J. Hubert Morgan, 'Edward Charles (Siamas Wynedd)', *Y Llenor*, X (1931), 25–34.

[89] Japheth and Gomer, son and grandson of Noah, are among the mythical ancestors of the Welsh. See also endnote 79.

[90] The religious credo of the scientist and philosopher Emmanuel Swedenborg (1688–1772) excited considerable interest in Wales (as in England) in the second half of the eighteenth century. According to his teachings the Divine Trinity existed only in the form of the Lord Jesus Christ; and salvation was possible by a combination of faith and charity.

[91] This is the poet and translator of Welsh poetry Evan Evans (Ieuan Brydydd Hir; 1731–88) who received patronage from Paul Panton, senior. The poem referred to here is probably 'Teifi, neu Hiraeth y Bardd am ei Wlad' ([the river] Teifi or the Poet's Longing for his Country), which he wrote when he was a curate in Kent.

[92] In 1870 the Methodist cleric Peter Williams (1723–96) brought out the first edition of the Welsh bible which was printed in Wales itself. A great success, it was reprinted several times and became known as 'Peter Williams's bible'. However, Williams's annotations led to accusations of Sabellianism and to his bitter

exclusion from the Methodist denomination in 1791. See Eryn Mant-White, 'Peter Williams a'r Beibl Cymraeg', *THSC* (2008), 58–72.

93 The English text on which this Welsh prayer is based was published in *Politics for the People*, II, no. V (1794), 4–6. Since Tomos Glyn Cothi attempted a close translation, the original text has been utilized widely for the English version in this anthology.

94 The English text on which this Welsh adaptation is based was published in *Politics for the People*, II, no. IV (1794), 3–5.

95 1 Corinthians 3: 11.

96 This was Major General Anthony Wayne (1745–96), after whom Wayne County, USA, is named.

97 Revelation 8: 13.

98 Matthew 4: 16.

99 From autumn 1794 until winter 1797–8, George Turner (1759–1843), who had been born in England and had previously pursued a military career, was the territorial judge of what is now Illinois.

100 These are the settlements of Cahokia and Kaskaskia, Illinois. See also Gwyn A. Williams, 'John Evans's Mission to the Madogwys, 1792–1799', *BBCS*, XXVII, part IV (1978), 588–9.

101 Luke 18: 8.

102 In his *Seren tan Gwmmwl* (A Star under a Cloud) Jac Glan-y-gors mentioned Sir Watkin Williams Wynn, fourth baronet, who died in 1789, as an example of a good MP and a 'good old Welshman' ('hên Gymro cyfiawn'). The relationship between Dafydd ap Gwilym, the most famous Welsh poet of the Middle Ages (whose poems had been published by the Gwyneddigion society in 1789), and his beloved Morfudd served as an example of a love untrammelled by financial stringencies of the kind war-time London suffered and which forced women, for instance, to marry once their 'apron strings' got too short, i.e., when they fell pregnant. See John Jones Glan-y-Gors, *Seren Tan Gwmmwl. Toriad y Dydd* (Liverpool, 1923), pp. 32, 42–3.

103 Thomas Edwards (Twm o'r Nant; 1739–1810) was a well-known folk poet and the most important author of satirical Welsh plays (*anterliwtiau*) in the eighteenth century. See *NCLW*.

104 'Bol Haul' (Pointy Belly) was the derisory nickname for William David, a solicitor from Caergybi. See *CIM*, I, p. 244.

105 'Hanes y Trwstan' (A History of the Unfortunate) was the title of at least three poems in the eighteenth century.

106 The Austrian Johann Peter Beaulieu de Marconnay (1725–1819) successfully fought against the First French Republic, but was beaten by the young Napoleon in 1796 and retired from active service.

107 Several key lines in the poem indicate that Gwilym utilized the partial English translation of the 'Marseillaise' which had appeared as 'The Marseilles March' in *Pig's Meat*, I (1793), 67–8, for his Welsh version. In addition, he translated the rather seditious fourth verse of the original, which directly threatens tyrants,

and its last verse, which was, apparently, sung by children. Neither had been reproduced in *Pig's Meat*. Verse four from the *Pig's Meat* version was not included and the remaining verses were freely adapted.

[108] Exactly the same reference to the window tax, also italicized, appeared in the translation printed in *Pig's Meat*. On the window tax, see endnote 37.

[109] James 4: 1.

[110] Based on Genesis 4: 8.

[111] Based on Genesis 6: 5.

[112] Matthew 24: 6.

[113] The anti-Methodist pamphlet, *Epistolau Cymraeg at y Cymry* (Welsh Epistles addressed to the Welsh People) (London, 1797) by 'Antagonist', alias Siamas Wynedd (Edward Charles), was advertised as 'Fflangell yscorpionog i'r Methodist-iaid' (A scorpion's Lash to the Methodists) in the *Chester Chronicle*, 1 September 1797. Jac Glan-y-gors and Siamas Wynedd, both leading members of the Gwyneddigion society, were close friends, though political adversaries, and may have discussed their work with each other.

[114] See Antagonist, 'Atteb i Dudur' (An Answer to Tudur), *Y Geirgrawn*, no. III (1796), 90–4.

[115] Maria Anna Fitzherbert (1756–1837) had been the mistress of the future George IV since 1784. The actress Dorothea Bland (Mrs Jordan; 1761–1816) had lived with the third son of George III, William (1764–1837), later to succeed George IV to the throne, since 1791.

# Select Bibliography


Aspinall, A., 'The Circulation of Newspapers in the Early Nineteenth Century', *The Review of English Studies,* XXII, no. 85 (1946), 29–43.

Balderston, Katharine C. (ed.), *Thraliana: The Diary of Mrs. Hester Lynch Thrale (Later Mrs. Piozzi) 1776–1809* (2nd edn., 2 vols., Oxford, 1951).

Ballinger, John, *The Bible in Wales* (London, 1906).

Barker, Hannah, *Newspapers, Politics, and Public Opinion in Late Eighteenth-Century England* (Oxford, 1998).

—— 'England 1760–1815', in *eadem* and Burrows (eds.), *Press, Politics and the Public Sphere*, pp. 93–112.

—— and Simon Burrows (eds.), *Press, Politics and the Public Sphere in Europe and North America* (Cambridge, 2002).

Barrell, John, *The Spirit of Despotism: Invasions of Privacy in the 1790s* (Oxford, 2006).

Bowen, Geraint, and Zonia Bowen, *Hanes Gorsedd y Beirdd* (Abertawe, 1991).

Braithwaite, Helen, 'From the See of St Davids to St Paul's Churchyard: Joseph Johnson's Cross-Border Connections', in Davies and Pratt (eds.), *Wales and the Romantic Imagination*, pp. 43–64.

Bromwich, Rachel (ed.), *Trioedd Ynys Prydein: The Triads of the Island of Britain* (3rd edn., Cardiff, 2006).

Brown, Richard, *Church and State in Modern Britain 1700–1850* (London, 1991).

Capp, Bernard, *Astrology and the Popular Press: English Almanacs 1500–1800* (London, 1979).

Carr, Glenda, *William Owen Pughe* (Caerdydd, 1983).

—— 'The London Welsh', in Jones and Rees (eds.), *A Nation and its Books*, pp. 147–57.

—— 'An Uneasy Relationship: Iolo Morganwg and William Owen Pughe', in Jenkins (ed.), *A Rattleskull Genius*, pp. 443–60.

—— 'William Owen Pughe and the London Societies', in Jarvis (ed.), *A Guide to Welsh Literature* c.*1700–1800*, pp. 168–86.

Carradice, Phil, *The Last Invasion: The Story of the French Landing in Wales* (Pontypool, 1992).

Carter, Harold, *The Towns of Wales* (Cardiff, 1965).

Charles, B. G., 'Letters of Hester Lynch Piozzi', *NLWJ*, II, no. 2 (1941), 49–58.

Charnell-White, Cathryn A., *Barbarism and Bardism: North Wales versus South Wales in the Bardic Vision of Iolo Morganwg* (Aberystwyth, 2004).
—— *Bardic Circles: National, Regional and Personal Identity in the Bardic Vision of Iolo Morganwg* (Cardiff, 2007).
Clark, Simone, 'Visions of Community: Elizabeth Baker and late 18th Century Merioneth', in Michael Roberts and *eadem* (eds.), *Women and Gender in Early Modern Wales* (Cardiff, 2000), pp. 334–58.
Cohler, Anne M., Basia Caroline Miller and Harold Samuel Stone (eds.), *Montesquieu: The Spirit of the Laws* (Cambridge, 1989).
Colley, Linda, *Britons: Forging the Nation 1707–1837* (New Haven, 1992).
Constantine, Mary-Ann, 'Beauty Spot, Blind Spot: Romantic Wales', *Literature Compass*, 5, no. 3 (2008), 577–90.
—— 'Welsh Literary History and the Making of "The Myvyrian Archaiology of Wales"', in Dirk Van Hulle and Joep Leerssen (eds.), *Editing the Nation's Memory: Textual Scholarship and Nation-Building in Nineteenth-Century Europe* (Amsterdam, 2008), pp. 109–28.
—— and Elizabeth Edwards, 'Bard of Liberty: Iolo Morganwg, Wales and Radical Song', in Kirk, Noble and Brown (eds.), *Political Poetry and Song. Volume 1.*
Dafis, D. Jacob (ed.), *Crefydd a Gweriniaeth yn Hanes Hen Dŷ Cwrdd Aberdâr* (Llandysul, 1951).
Davies, Andrew, '"Redirecting the Attention of History": Antiquarian and Historical Fictions of Wales from the Romantic Period', in Davies and Pratt (eds.), *Wales and the Romantic Imagination*, pp. 104–21.
Davies, D. Elwyn J., *'They Thought for Themselves': A Brief Look at the History of Unitarianism in Wales and the Tradition of Liberal Religion* (Llandysul, 1982).
Davies, Damian Walford, '"Sweet Sylvan Routes" and Grave Methodists: Wales in De Quincey's Confessions of an English Opium-Eater', in *idem* and Pratt (eds.), *Wales and the Romantic Imagination*, pp. 199–227.
—— and Linda Pratt (eds.), *Wales and the Romantic Imagination* (Cardiff, 2007).
Davies, David, *The Influence of the French Revolution on Welsh Life and Literature* (Carmarthen, 1926).
Davies, Hywel M., '"Transatlantic Brethren": A Study of English, Welsh and American Baptists with Particular Reference to Morgan John Rhys (1760–1804) and his Friends' (unpublished University of Wales PhD thesis, 1984).
—— 'Loyalism in Wales, 1792–1793', *WHR*, 20, no. 4 (2001), 687–716.
—— 'Morgan John Rhys and James Bicheno: Anti-Christ and the French Revolution in England and Wales', *BBCS*, XXIX, part I (1980), 111–27.
—— 'Wales in English Travel Writing 1791–8: The Welsh Critique of Theophilus Jones', *WHR*, 23, no. 3 (2007), 65–93.
Davies, John H. (ed.), *The Letters of Lewis, Richard, William and John Morris, of Anglesey (Morrisiaid Mon) 1728–1765* (Aberystwyth, 1909).

Davies, R. R., and Geraint H. Jenkins (eds.), *From Medieval to Modern Wales: Historical Essays in Honour of Kenneth O. Morgan and Ralph A. Griffiths* (Cardiff, 2004).

Davies, William Ll., 'David Samwell (1751–1798): Surgeon of the "Discovery", London-Welshman, and Poet', *THSC* (1928), 70–133.

—— (= Davies, W. Ll.) 'David Samwell's Poem – "The Padouca Hunt"', *NLWJ*, II, nos. 3 and 4 (1942), 142–52.

Dickinson, H. T. (ed.), *Britain and the French Revolution 1789–1815* (Basingstoke, 1989).

—— (ed.), *British Radicalism and the French Revolution 1789–1815* (Oxford, 1985).

—— (ed.), *A Companion to Eighteenth-Century Britain* (Oxford, 2002).

Doyle, William, *The Oxford History of the French Revolution* (Oxford, 1989).

Eagleton, Terry, *The Function of Criticism: From The Spectator to Post-Structuralism* (London, 1984).

Edwards, J. B., 'John Jones (Jac Glan-y-Gors): Tom Paine's Denbighshire Henchman?', *Denbighshire Historical Society Transactions*, 51 (2002), 95–112.

Evans, John James, *Cymry Enwog y Ddeunawfed Ganrif* (Aberystwyth, 1937).

—— *Dylanwad y Chwyldro Ffrengig ar Lenyddiaeth Cymru* (Lerpwl, 1928).

—— 'Y Cylchgronau Cymraeg Cynharaf', *Yr Ymofynnydd*, XLII, no. 12 (1942), 162–4.

Evans, R. J. W., 'Was there a Welsh Enlightenment?', in Davies and Jenkins (eds.), *From Medieval to Modern Wales*, pp. 142–59.

Evans, Thomas, *The Background to Modern Welsh Politics 1789–1846* (Cardiff, 1936).

Fitzpatrick, Martin, 'The "Cultivated Understanding" and Chaotic Genius of David Samwell', in Jenkins (ed.), *A Rattleskull Genius*, pp. 343–402.

—— 'Enlightenment', in McCalman (ed.), *An Oxford Companion to the Romantic Age*, pp. 299–311.

——, Peter Jones, Christa Knellwolf and Iain McCalman (eds.), *The Enlightenment World* (London and New York, 2004).

——, Nicholas Thomas and Jennifer Newell (eds.), *The Death of Captain Cook and Other Writings by David Samwell* (Cardiff, 2006).

Franklin, Caroline, 'The Welsh American Dream: Iolo Morganwg, Robert Southey and the Madog Legend', in Gerard Carruthers and Alan Rawes (eds.), *English Romanticism and the Celtic World* (Cambridge, 2003), pp. 69–84.

Glenn, T. A., *The Family of Griffith of Garn and Plasnewydd in the County of Denbigh* (London, 1934).

Grenby, M. O., 'Writing Revolution: British Literature and the French Revolution Crisis, a Review of Recent Scholarship', *Literature Compass*, 3, no. 6 (2006), 1351–85.

Griffith, John T., *Rev. Morgan John Rhys: The Welsh Baptist Hero of Civil and Religious Liberty of the Eighteenth Century* (Carmarthen, 1910).

Habermas, Jürgen, *The Structural Transformation of the Public Sphere: An Inquiry into a Category of Bourgeois Society* (London, 1989).
Harris, Bob, *The Scottish People and the French Revolution* (London, 2008).
Hechter, Michael, *Internal Colonialism: The Celtic Fringe in British National Development, 1536–1966* (London, 1975).
Herbert, Trevor, and Gareth Elwyn Jones (eds.), *The Remaking of Wales in the Eighteenth Century* (Cardiff, 1988).
Higgins, Padhraig, 'Bonfires, Illuminations, and Joy: Celebratory Street Politics and Uses of "the Nation" during the Volunteer Movement', *Éire-Ireland*, 42, nos. 3 and 4 (2007), 173–206.
Hole, Robert, *Pulpits, Politics and Public Order in England, 1760–1832* (Cambridge, 1989).
Howard, Sharon, 'Riotous Community: Crowds, Politics and Society in Wales, *c.*1700–1840', *WHR*, 20, no. 4 (2001), 656–86.
James, E. Wyn, '"Seren Wib Olau": Gweledigaeth a Chenhadaeth Morgan John Rhys (1760–1804)', *Trafodion Cymdeithas Hanes y Bedyddwyr* (2007), 5–37.
Jarvis, Branwen (ed.), *A Guide to Welsh Literature* c.*1700–1800* (Cardiff, 2000).
Jenkins, Geraint H., *The Foundations of Modern Wales 1642–1780* (Cardiff, 1987).
—— *Thomas Jones yr Almanaciwr 1648–1713* (Caerdydd, 1980).
—— 'Clio and Wales: Welsh Remembrancers and Historical Writing, 1751–2001', *THSC* (2002), 119–36.
—— 'The Eighteenth Century', in Jones and Rees (eds.), *A Nation and its Books*, pp. 103–22.
—— 'An Uneasy Relationship: Gwallter Mechain and Iolo Morganwg', *The Montgomeryshire Collections*, 97 (2009), 73–99.
—— '"A Very Horrid Affair": Sedition and Unitarianism in the Age of Revolutions', in Davies and *idem* (eds.), *From Medieval to Modern Wales*, pp. 175–96.
—— (ed.), *A Rattleskull Genius: The Many Faces of Iolo Morganwg* (Cardiff, 2005).
——, Ffion Mair Jones and David Ceri Jones (eds.), *The Correspondence of Iolo Morganwg* (3 vols., Cardiff, 2007).
Jenkins, Philip, 'Wales', in Peter Clark (ed.), *The Cambridge Urban History of Britain. Volume II: 1540–1840* (Cambridge, 2000), pp. 133–49.
Jenkins, R. T., *Hanes Cymru yn y Bedwaredd Ganrif ar Bymtheg: Y Gyfrol Gyntaf (1789–1843)* (Caerdydd, 1933).
—— *Hanes Cymru yn y Ddeunawfed Ganrif* (Caerdydd, 1928).
—— 'Political Propaganda in West Wales in 1793', *BBCS*, VI, part III (1932), 276.
—— 'William Richards o Lynn', *Trafodion Cymdeithas Hanes y Bedyddwyr* (1930), 17–68.
—— and Helen M. Ramage, *A History of the Honourable Society of Cymmrodorion and of the Gwyneddigion and Cymreigyddion Societies (1751–1951)* (London, 1951).

Jewson, C. B., *The Jacobin City: A Portrait of Norwich in its Reaction to the French Revolution 1788–1802* (Glasgow, 1975).

Johnson, Nancy E., 'Fashioning the Legal Subject: Narratives from the London Treason Trials of 1794', *Eighteenth-Century Fiction*, 21, no. 3 (2009), 413–43.

Johnston, Kenneth R., 'Whose History? My Place or Yours? Republican Assumptions and Romantic Traditions', in Damian Walford Davies (ed.), *Romanticism, History, Historicism: Essays on an Orthodoxy* (London, 2009), pp. 79–102.

Jolliffe, M. F., 'The Druidical Society of Anglesey, 1772–1844', *THSC* (1941), 189–99.

Jones, Aled, 'The Newspaper Press in Wales, 1804–1945', in Jones and Rees (eds.), *A Nation and its Books*, pp. 209–19.

Jones, Colin, *The Longman Companion to the French Revolution* (London, 1990).

Jones, David J. V., *Before Rebecca: Popular Protests in Wales 1793–1835* (London, 1973).

—— (= Jones, D. J. V.) 'The Corn Riots in Wales, 1793–1801', *WHR*, 2, no. 4 (1965), 323–50.

Jones, E. D., 'Hugh Maurice (?1775–1825), a Forgotten Scribe', *NLWJ*, I, no. 4 (1940), 230–2.

Jones, Frank Price, 'Y Cylchgrawn Cynmraeg', *JWBS*, VIII, no. 2 (1955), 101–2.

Jones, James Ifano, *A History of Printing and Printers in Wales to 1810, and of Successive and Related Printers to 1923: Also, A History of Printing and Printers in Monmouthshire to 1923* (Cardiff, 1925).

Jones, Middleton Pennant, 'John Jones of Glan-y-Gors', *THSC* (1911), 60–94.

Jones, Philip Henry, and Eiluned Rees (eds.), *A Nation and its Books: A History of the Book in Wales* (Aberystwyth, 1998).

Jones, R. W., *Bywyd Cymdeithasol Cymru yn y Ddeunawfed Ganrif* (Llundain, 1931).

Kidd, Colin, 'Wales, the Enlightenment and the New British History', *WHR*, 25, no. 2 (2010), 209–30.

Kirk, John, Andrew Noble and Michael Brown (eds.), *Political Poetry and Song in the Age of Revolution. Volume 1: United Islands? The Languages of Resistance* (London, forthcoming).

——, Michael Brown and Andrew Noble (eds.), *Political Poetry and Song in the Age of Revolution. Volume 2: The Cultures of Radicalism in Britain and Ireland* (London, forthcoming).

Leathart, William Davies, *The Origin and Progress of the Gwyneddigion Society of London Instituted M.DCC.LXX* (London, 1831).

Löffler, Marion, *Englisch und Kymrisch in Wales: Geschichte der Sprachsituation und Sprachpolitik* (Hamburg, 1997).

—— *The Literary and Historical Legacy of Iolo Morganwg, 1826–1926* (Cardiff, 2007).

—— 'Cerddi Newydd gan John Jones, "Jac Glan-y-Gors"', *Llên Cymru*, 33 (2010), 143–50.

—— 'Serial Literature and Radical Poetry in Wales at the End of the Eighteenth Century', in Kirk, Brown and Noble, *Political Poetry and Song. Volume 2.*

McCalman, Iain (ed.), *An Oxford Companion to the Romantic Age: British Culture, 1776–1832* (Oxford, 1999).

McKenna, Catherine, 'Aspects of Tradition Formation in Eighteenth-Century Wales', in Joseph Falaky Nagy (ed.), *Memory and the Modern in Celtic Literatures, CSANA Yearbook 5* (Dublin, 2006), pp. 37–60.

Magnuson, Paul, *Reading Public Romanticism* (Princeton, New Jersey, 1998).

Matthews, E. Gwynn, 'Holywell and the Marseillaise', *Flintshire Historical Society Journal*, 38 (2010), 117–31.

Mee, Jon, 'Language', in McCalman (ed.), *An Oxford Companion to the Romantic Age*, pp. 369–78.

Millward, E. G. (ed.), *Cerddi Jac Glan-y-gors* (Barddas, 2003).

Miskell, Louise, *Intelligent Town: An Urban History of Swansea, 1780–1855* (Cardiff, 2006).

Morgan, F. C., 'Herefordshire Printers and Booksellers', *Transactions of the Woolhope Naturalists' Fieldclub* (1941), 106–27.

Morgan, Gerald, 'The Morris Brothers', in Jarvis (ed.), *A Guide to Welsh Literature c.1700–1800*, pp. 64–80.

Morgan, J. Hubert, 'Edward Charles (Siamas Wynedd)', *Y Llenor*, X (1931), 25–34.

Navickas, Katrina, *Loyalism and Radicalism in Lancashire, 1798–1815* (Oxford, 2009).

Nida, Eugene, 'Principles of Correspondence', in Lawrence Venuti (ed.), *The Translation Studies Reader* (2nd edn., New York, 2004), pp. 153–67.

Nuttall, D., 'A History of Printing in Chester', *Journal of the Chester Archaeological Society*, 54 (1967), 37–95.

Ó Ciosáin, Niall, *Print and Popular Culture in Ireland, 1750–1850* (London, 1997).

O'Gorman, Frank, 'The Paine Burnings of 1792–1793', *Past & Present*, 193 (2006), 111–55.

Owen, Geraint Dyfnallt, *Thomas Evans (Tomos Glyn Cothi): Trem ar ei Fywyd* (n.p., 1963).

Owen, Hugh (ed.), *Additional Letters of the Morrises of Anglesey (1735–1786)* (2 vols., London, 1947, 1949).

Owen, J. Dyfnallt, 'Morgan John Rhys yn ei Gysylltiad a Threfecca', *Cylchgrawn Hanes y Methodistiaid*, VII, no. 1 (1922), 14–20.

Page, Anthony, 'The Dean of St Asaph's Trial: Libel and Politics in the 1780s', *Journal for Eighteenth-Century Studies*, 32, no. I (2009), 21–35.

Palmer, Alfred Neobald, 'John Wilkinson and the Old Bersham Iron Works', *THSC* (1899), 23–64.

Parry, Thomas, *A History of Welsh Literature*, trans. H. Idris Bell (Oxford, 1962).

Phillips, D. Rhys, 'The "Eurgrawn Cymraeg" of 1770', *JWBS*, V, no. 1 (1937), 49–57.

Phillips, T., 'Y Parch. Morgan John Rhys a'i Ddydd-Lyfr', *Seren Cymru*, 17 Mai 1867.

Philp, Mark (ed.), *The French Revolution and British Popular Politics* (Cambridge, 1991).

—— (ed.), *Thomas Paine: Rights of Man, Common Sense, and Other Political Writings* (Oxford, 1995).

Pratt, Lynda, 'Southey in Wales: Inscriptions, Monuments and Romantic Posterity', in Davies and *eadem* (eds.), *Wales and the Romantic Imagination*, pp. 86–103.

Quinault, Roland, 'The French Invasion of Pembrokeshire in 1797: A Bicentennial Assessment', *WHR*, 19, no. 4 (1999), 618–42.

Rees, Eiluned, *The Welsh Book-Trade before 1820* (Aberystwyth, 1988).

—— 'An Introductory Survey of 18th Century Welsh Libraries', *JWBS*, X, no. 4 (1971), 197–259.

—— and G. Walters, 'Swansea Libraries in the Nineteenth Century', *JWBS*, X, no. 1 (1966), 43–51.

Schleiermacher, Friedrich, 'On the Different Methods of Translating (1813)', in Douglas Robinson (ed.), *Western Translation Theory from Herodotus to Nietzsche* (Manchester, 1997), pp. 225–38.

Scrivener, Michael, *Poetry and Reform: Periodical Verse from the English Democratic Press 1792–1824* (Detroit, 1992).

Shankland, Thomas, 'Hanes Dechreuad "Gorsedd Beirdd Ynys Prydain"', *Y Llenor*, III (1924), 94–102.

Simpson, David, *The Politics of American English, 1776–1850* (New York, 1962).

Simes, Douglas, 'Ireland 1760–1820', in Barker and Burrows (eds.), *Press, Politics and the Public Sphere*, pp. 113–39.

Stansfield, D., 'Agweddau ar Fywyd a Gwaith Dafydd Saunders', *Trafodion Cymdeithas Hanes y Bedyddwyr* (2008), 35–51.

Tague, Ingrid H., 'Eighteenth-Century English Debates on a Dog Tax', *The Historical Journal*, 51, no. 4 (2008), 901–20.

Thomas, Ben Bowen, *The Old Order: Based on the Diary of Elizabeth Baker (Dolgelley 1778–1786)* (Cardiff, 1945).

Thuente, Mary Helen, *The Harp Re-strung: The United Irishmen and the Rise of Irish Literary Nationalism* (Syracuse, 1994).

Walters, Huw, *A Bibliography of Welsh Periodicals 1735–1850* (Aberystwyth, 1993).

Whelan, Kevin, *The Tree of Liberty: Radicalism, Catholicism and the Construction of Irish Identity 1760–1830* (Cork, 1996).

White, Eryn M., 'Popular Schooling and the Welsh Language 1650–1800', in Geraint H. Jenkins (ed.), *The Welsh Language before the Industrial Revolution* (Cardiff, 1997), pp. 317–41.

Williams, David, *A History of Modern Wales* (2nd edn., Cardiff, 1977).

Williams, G. J., *Iolo Morganwg – Y Gyfrol Gyntaf* (Caerdydd, 1956).
—— 'Eisteddfodau'r Gwyneddigion', *Y Llenor*, XIV (1935), 11–22.
—— 'Hanes Cyhoeddi'r "Myvyrian Archaiology"', *JWBS*, X, no. I (1966), 2–12.
—— (ed.), 'Original Documents: 4. Letters of Morgan John Rhys to William Owen [-Pughe]', *NLWJ*, II, nos. 3 and 4 (1942), 131–41.
Williams, Gwyn A., *Artisans and Sans-Culottes: Popular Movements in France and Britain during the French Revolution* (2nd edn., London, 1989).
—— *Madoc: The Making of a Myth* (Oxford, 1987).
—— *The Search for Beulah Land: The Welsh and the Atlantic Revolution* (New York, 1980).
—— *When was Wales?* (Harmondsworth, 1985).
—— 'The Beginnings of Radicalism', in Herbert and Jones (eds.), *The Remaking of Wales in the Eighteenth Century*, pp. 101–47.
—— 'John Evans's Mission to the Madogwys, 1792–1799', *BBCS*, XXVII, part IV (1978), 569–601.
—— 'Morgan John Rhys and his Beulah', *WHR*, 3, no. 4 (1967), 441–72.
—— 'Morgan John Rhys and Volney's *Ruins of Empires*', *BBCS*, XX, part I (1962), 58–73.
Williams, John, *Digest of Welsh Historical Statistics* (2 vols., Aberystwyth, 1985).
Williams, T. Oswald, *Undodiaeth a Rhyddid Meddwl* (Llandysul, 1962).

# *Regular Bardic Names of Welsh Poets and Authors*

| | |
|---|---|
| Dafydd Ddu Eryri | Thomas, Dafydd or David (1759–1822) |
| Dafydd Ddu Feddyg | Samwell, David (1751–98) |
| Gwallter Mechain | Davies, Walter (1761–1849) |
| Ieuan Fardd Ddu | Evans, Thomas (1734–1814) |
| Iolo Morganwg | Williams, Edward (1747–1826) |
| Jac Glan-y-gors | Jones, John (1766–1821) |
| Llwyd / Bard of Snowdon | Llwyd, Richard (1752–1835) |
| Monensis | Panton, junior, Paul (1758–1822) |
| Owain Myfyr | Jones, Owen (1741–1814) |
| Peris | Williams, Peter Bailey (1763–1836) |
| Rhaiadr | Jones, Thomas (*fl.* 1789–1810) |
| Siamas Wynedd | Charles, Edward (1757–1828) |
| Siôn Dafydd y Crydd | Davies, John (1722–99) |
| Tomos Glyn Cothi | Evans, Thomas (1764–1833) |
| Welsh Freeholder | Jones, David (1765–1816) |

# *Index*

Headwords are in English with Welsh equivalents following in brackets, as for instance in 'Wales (Cymru)'. All Welsh words and cross-references are cited in their unmutated form, so that what in the main text of the volume may appear as 'Gymru' is given as 'Cymru'. Page numbers which contain Welsh text only are italicized.